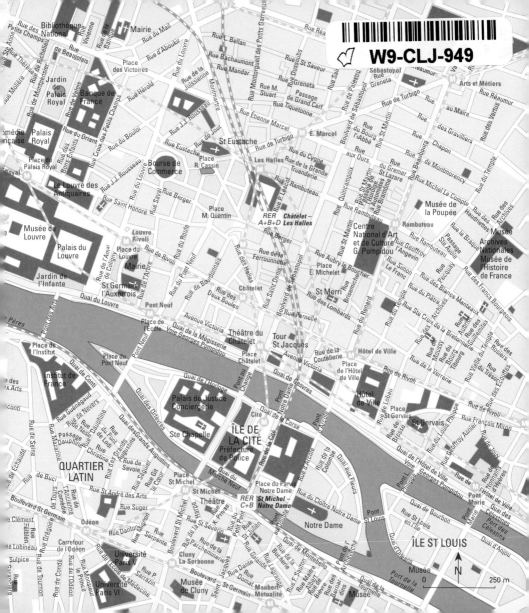

THE LOUVRE

ART & ARCHITECTURE

THE LOUVRE

Gabriele Bartz • Eberhard König

KÖNEMANN

Frontispiece:
*Barthélemy d'Eyck, The Louvre from the Seine, ca. 1450,
picture for October from the Très Riches Heures (Detail)*

Highlights of the Collection

© 2000 Könemann Verlagsgesellschaft mbH
Bonner Strasse 126, D-50968 Cologne

Publishing and Art Direction: Peter Feierabend
Layout: Bärbel Messmann
Picture Research: Stefanie Huber, Fenja Wittneven
Lithography: C.D.N. Pressing, Caselle di Sommacampagna VR, Italy

Original Title: *Kunst & Architektur Louvre*

© 2001 for this English edition:
Könemann Verlagsgesellschaft mbH

Translation from German: Mo Croasdale, Richard Elliott, Sandra Harper and Judith Phillips
in association with First Edition Translations Ltd.
Editing: David Price in association with First Edition Translations Ltd.
Typesetting: The Write Idea in association with First Edition Translations Ltd.
Project Management: Mine Ali for First Edition Translations Ltd, Cambridge, UK
Project Coordination: Tammi Reichel
Production: Petra Grimm
Printing and Binding: Neue Stalling, Oldenburg
Printed in Germany

ISBN 3-8290-2647-1

10 9 8 7 6 5 4 3 2

Table of Contents

Guillaume Larrue,
Before the Great Sphinx

Hubert Robert, *Imaginary View of the Grande Galerie*

Hubert Robert, *Drawing of the Furnishings of the Grande Galerie*

École Française, *The Galerie d'Apollon*, 19th century

Hubert Robert, *The Grande Galerie as a Museum*

Basement

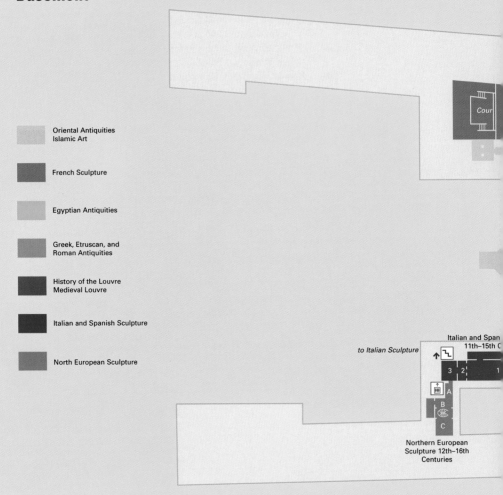

Oriental Antiquities
Islamic Art

French Sculpture

Egyptian Antiquities

Greek, Etruscan, and
Roman Antiquities

History of the Louvre
Medieval Louvre

Italian and Spanish Sculpture

North European Sculpture

Cour

to Italian Sculpture

Italian and Span
11th–15th C

3 2 1

A
B
C

Northern European
Sculpture 12th–16th
Centuries

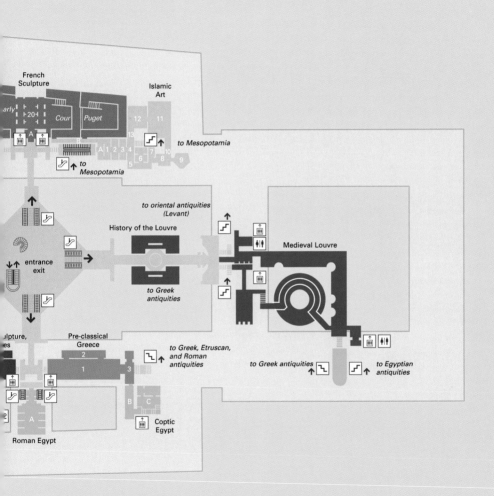

French
Sculpture

Islamic
Art

arly
20

Cour

Puget

12

11

13

A

B

A 1 2 3 4

6 7

5

10

8 9

to Mesopotamia

to
Mesopotamia

to oriental antiquities
(Levant)

History of the Louvre

Medieval Louvre

entrance
exit

to Greek
antiquities

Pre-classical
Greece

2

1

3

to Greek, Etruscan,
and Roman
antiquities

to Greek antiquities

to Egyptian
antiquities

culpture,
es

B

C

A

Coptic
Egypt

Roman Egypt

First Floor

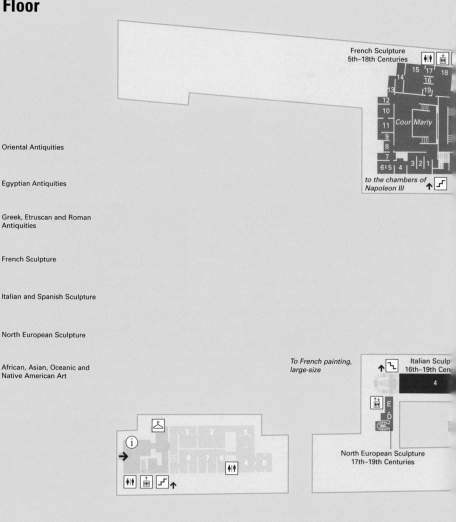

Oriental Antiquities

Egyptian Antiquities

Greek, Etruscan and Roman Antiquities

French Sculpture

Italian and Spanish Sculpture

North European Sculpture

African, Asian, Oceanic and Native American Art

French Sculpture
5th–18th Centuries

15 17 18
14 16
13 19
12
10
11 Cour Marly
9
8
7
6 5 4 3 2 1

to the chambers of
Napoleon III

To French painting,
large-size

Italian Sculp
16th–19th Cen
4

E
D

North European Sculpture
17th–19th Centuries

1 2 3
8 7 6 4 5

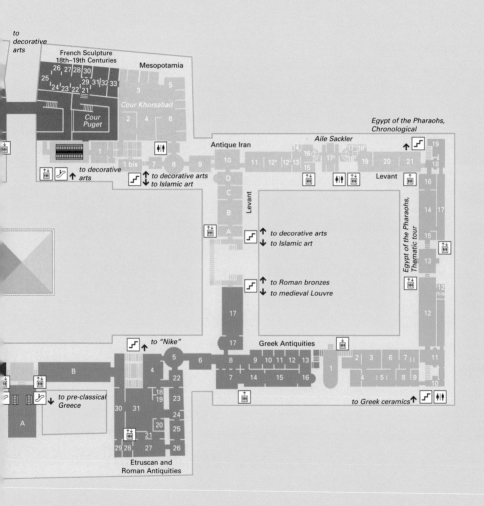

to
decorative
arts

French Sculpture
18th–19th Centuries

26 27 28 30
25 29 31 32 33
24 23 22 21

Mesopotamia

Cour Khorsaud

3 5

Cour
Puget

2 4 6

1

1 bis

to decorative
arts

to decorative arts
to Islamic art

Antique Iran

Aile Sackler

Egypt of the Pharaohs,
Chronological

8 9

10

11 12" 12"13

17" 18"
16
15

17" 18"
19 20 21

19

18

D

C

Levant

Levant

16

B

to decorative arts
to Islamic art

14 17

A

16

Egypt of the Pharaohs,
Thematic tour

13

to Roman bronzes
to medieval Louvre

12
bis

17

12

17

to "Nike"

Greek Antiquities

5 6

8 9 10 11 12 13

2 3 6 7

11

B

4

22

7 14 15 16

1

4 5 8 9

10

18
19

23

to pre-classical
Greece

24

30 31

25

A

20

21

to Greek ceramics

29 28

27

26

Etruscan and
Roman Antiquities

Second Floor

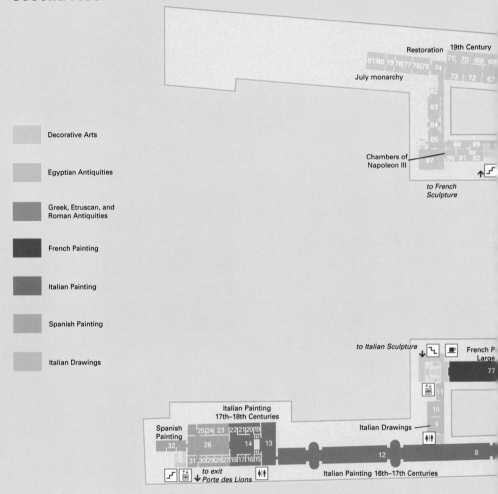

Decorative Arts

Egyptian Antiquities

Greek, Etruscan, and
Roman Antiquities

French Painting

Italian Painting

Spanish Painting

Italian Drawings

Restoration

19th Century

July monarchy

81 80 79 78 77 76 75 74

71 70 69 68

73 72 67

82

83

84

85

86

88 89

Chambers of
Napoleon III

87

90 91 92

*to French
Sculpture*

to Italian Sculpture

French P
Large

77

11

10

9

Italian Drawings

Italian Painting
17th–18th Centuries

Spanish
Painting

25 24 23

22 21 20 19

32

26

14

13

31 30 29 28 27 18 17 16 15

to exit
↓ *Porte des Lions*

Italian Painting 16th–17th Centuries

12

8

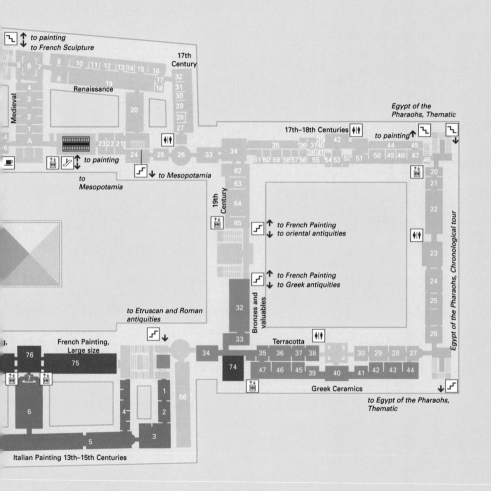

to painting
to French Sculpture

17th
Century

5   6   7   9   10   11   12   13 14 15   16

8   19   17
                                18

Renaissance   32
                                31
                                30
20   29
                                28
                                27

Medieval

4
3
2
1
A

23 22 21

24   25   26   33   34

to painting

to Mesopotamia

to Mesopotamia

17th–18th Centuries

Egypt of the
Pharaohs, Thematic

to painting

35   36 37 40   42   44   45
             39
             38 41   50 49 48 47
61 60 59 58 57 56   55 54 53 52 51   46

20
21
22
23
24
25
26

62
63
64
65

19th Century

to French Painting
to oriental antiquities

to French Painting
to Greek antiquities

Egypt of the Pharaohs, Chronological tour

to Etruscan and Roman
antiquities

Bronzes and valuables

32

33

Terracotta

French Painting,
Large size

76

75

6

5

74

34   35 36 37 38   30 29 28 27

47   46 45 39 40   41 42 43 44

Greek Ceramics

to Egypt of the Pharaohs,
Thematic

1
2
66
3

4

Italian Painting 13th–15th Centuries

Third Floor

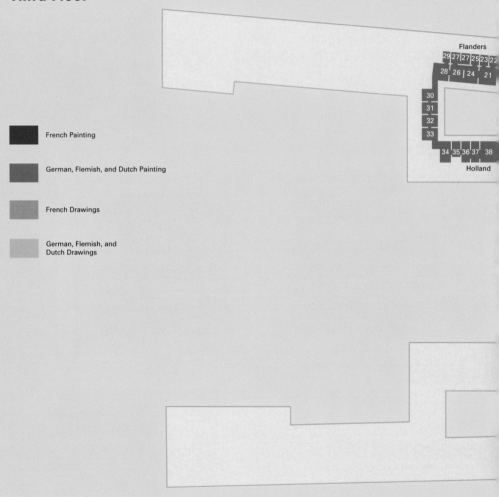

French Painting

German, Flemish, and Dutch Painting

French Drawings

German, Flemish, and
Dutch Drawings

Flanders

29 27 27 25 23 22
28 26 24 21
30
31
32
33
34 35 36 37 38

Holland

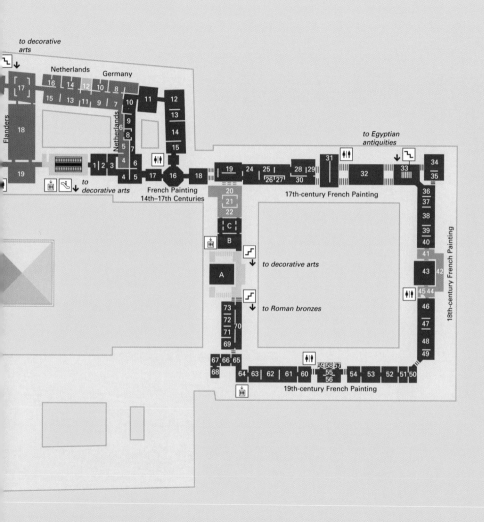

to decorative arts

Netherlands Germany

Flanders

17

16 14 12 10 8

15 13 11 9 7

Netherlands

18

10 11 12

9 13

8 14

6 15

1 2 3 5 7

4 6

4 5 17 16 18

to decorative arts

French Painting
14th–17th Centuries

19 24 25 28 29 31

26 27 30

32

20

21

22

C

B

A

73

72 70

71

69

to decorative arts

to Roman bronzes

to Egyptian
antiquities

33 34

35

36

37

38

39

40

41

43 42

45 44

46

47

48

49

18th-century French Painting

17th-century French Painting

67 66 65

68 64 63 62 61 60 59 58 57 54 53 52 51 50

55

56

19th-century French Painting

From Wolf Enclosure to the Greatest Museum in the World

In 1793, the same year as Louis XVI and his wife Marie Antoinette were taken to the guillotine, the government of the Revolution opened a museum in the old royal palace of the Louvre which today can hardly be matched by any collection in the world. The Louvre was to be a museum for the people, with free admission.

Not only is the sheer number of works of art which had previously been stored in the treasure-chambers of the Louvre immense; also unique is the number of outstanding individual works of art, among them some of the most famous works created by the most important artists in the world. Hardly any major European master is absent here; almost all are represented by at least one of their main works. In addition you are offered an enthralling look at the old cultures of the Mediterranean lands and the Middle East, which laid the foundations of Europe. Ideally situated in the city center, the old palace in which the French kings resided from time to time until 1682 provides more than 19 hectares of rooms, over three and in some places four stories. There are similar treasures in London of course, but they are distributed between many more buildings and institutions. Since the

Aerial view of the Louvre and the Tuileries looking west

French kings left the palace at an early date and the building was nevertheless preserved, the capital of France was presented with an opportunity unrivaled anywhere else in the world, which the great Revolution recognized in 1793.

What the Tower was to London, the Louvre was to medieval Paris: a fortified tower on the river on that side of the town which points toward the sea and was most likely to encounter the enemy. A fortress such as this was initially, and for a long time afterward, used exclusively as dungeons and arsenal. The Louvre forms the old west end of the city outside the city walls. The Bastille was its opposite number in the east; it was there that the areas heavily populated by the poorer people were concentrated, so that those areas and not the Louvre were targeted by the Revolution of July 14, 1789. On the east side of the Louvre, Paris provided a great spectacle which was so expertly captured in the paintings of Claude Monet (see p. 422 f.). The medieval church of Saint-Germain-l'Auxerrois nestles against a little 18th-century lane; next to it on the left stands the Neo-Gothic facade, dating from the Romantic period, of the 1st arrondissement's town hall with its clock tower, so that today the church and the city are in front of the palace. Yet, up until the Revolution, Paris only had a

How the Louvre appeared at the end of the reigns of the monarchs who made the most significant alterations to the buildings:

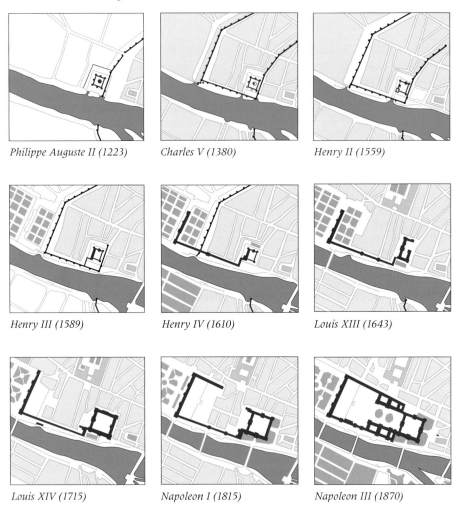

Philippe Auguste II (1223)

Charles V (1380)

Henry II (1559)

Henry III (1589)

Henry IV (1610)

Louis XIII (1643)

Louis XIV (1715)

Napoleon I (1815)

Napoleon III (1870)

town hall where the Hôtel de Ville stands today, a few hundred meters away, which cannot be seen from the Louvre.

Anyone wanting to understand the grand plan of the Louvre does best to enter it from the town, that is from the east. Over the moat, which was dug out again in 1993, a bridge leads into a huge square courtyard, the Cour Carrée. At the southwest corner there was once the Louvre Tower, begun by Philippe Auguste (1165–1223) after 1190 and extended by Charles V (1338–1380) by 1380. In 1527, Francis I (1494–1547) took an interest in the Louvre, remodeling it for the visit of Emperor Charles V (1500–1558) in 1540.

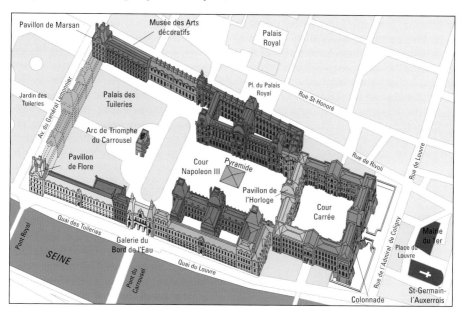

Architectural history of the Louvre

Francis I, 1515–1547, and Henry II, 1547-1559

Catherine of Medici 1560–1563
Facade under Napoleon III

Henry IV, 1589–1610, rebuilt under Napoleon III

Louis XIII, 1610–1643

Louis XIV, 1643–1715

Napoleon, 1804–1814/15

Napoleon III, 1852–1870

François Mitterrand, 1981–1995

A Palace in the French Classical Style

In 1546, the architect Pierre Lescot (1510–1578) took over the supervision of the Louvre, and with his work the building as seen today from the outside was begun. Lescot replaced the old hall of the castle running from north to south by a royal palace, a so-called *corps-de-logis* with a symmetrical facade that has only survived on the east side. The original plan, which had nine axes, today forms the southern half of the west wing. On the inside, with the Caryatid Room, it has remained fairly faithful to Lescot's main hall (see page 184 f.). At first sight, the three-story wall structure suggests elements of the French Renaissance from the middle of the 16th century – continuous cornices and a sudden change in

Lescot's facade of 1546 and Lemercier's 1639 clock tower today

the window axes produce a break in the rhythm. Pillars set into the wall are so subordinated to the sequence of stories that they hardly extend higher than the windows. The intricate design of the detail is given a rhythm by the axes which protrude slightly as risalits. The doors with round windows above them would provide quite a large number of possible entrances if the museum today did not require just one central access point.

Lescot erected his new building on the west side of the medieval square, whose total measurements, along with the ground plan of the circular central tower, are today indicated on the pavement. Henry IV (1553–1610) had already wanted to make the court of the Louvre four times as large in his *grand dessein des Bourbon*, but this plan was not realized until the reign of his successor, Louis XIII (1610–1643). To achieve this, the late-Gothic wings to the north and east were pulled down and the foundation stone for a clock tower with its gateway facing west was laid initially at the northwest corner. On the north side a facade was added on the basis of Lescot's plan and identical facades continued around the empty square of the now enormous Cour Carrée, in such a way that the 16th-century elevation is now repeated eight times. One can best appreciate the time it took to achieve the massive size of the courtyard through the figurative reliefs in the architectural decoration, where the Mannerism of Jean Goujon (see p. 35) gives way to later variations in style.

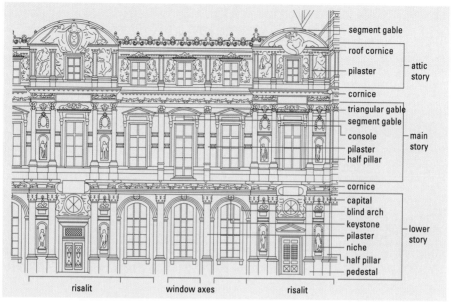

Labels on the drawing (top to bottom, right side):

- segment gable
- roof cornice
- pilaster — attic story
- cornice
- triangular gable
- segment gable
- console
- pilaster — main story
- half pillar
- cornice
- capital
- blind arch
- keystone
- pilaster — lower story
- niche
- half pillar
- pedestal

Labels along the bottom: risalit · window axes · risalit

Pierre Lescot (1510–1578), facade of the Cour Carrée, 1546 (modern drawing), which adjoins Jacques Lemercier's clock tower on the right, as can be seen from the photograph on the opposite page

In 1624, Jacques Lemercier (1585–1654) began work on the clock tower, the Pavillon de l'Horloge, which clearly needs the present-day size of the Cour Carrée. The Chapel of Notre-Dame-de-la-Paix, planned by the architect in 1639, is situated in the tower, although it has been desecrated in the meantime and is now unrecognizable.

The clock tower, as the highest structure, not only crowns the central facade named after Maximilien de Béthune, the Duc de Sully (1560–1641), but the whole of the Louvre. The central pavilions on the south and north sides of the Cour Carrée play a subordinate role to it. To the west, Lemercier's building provides the way through to the Cour Napoleon which opens out onto the Tuileries. Here there are two copies of the clock tower built in the 1850s under Napoleon III in order to provide a central point for the side wings added at that time. The left wing, by the Seine, is named after Dominique-Vivant Denon (1747–1825), appointed director of the Louvre by Napoleon, and the other is named after Cardinal Richelieu (1585–1642).

The Colonnade of the Louvre
and the Battle between Baroque and Classicism

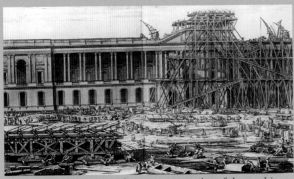

The colonnade in construction: a representation of the machines with which the stones over the former main entrance were moved, engraving 1677, Bibliothèque Nationale de Paris

Some architecture is seen and then immediately forgotten. For many people this is the case with the facade of double pillars on a flat base which was once such a pioneering design at the Louvre. There are all too many buildings in the world – palaces for governments, law courts, banks, and museums – which have a similar luxurious appearance. Admittedly, the fresh stone color after the last clean improved the once gloomy impression, but it is regrettable that nothing more noble or more exciting was created here. This was partly because of a desire, in making additions, to preserve French culture in the face of Italian influences. There was bitter dispute during the building period about the facade that was facing the town. In the 1660s, Louis Le Vau

(1612–1670), as the royal architect, opted for the idea of turning the unfinished Louvre into a breathtaking palace for the Sun King. Considerable progress had already been made at the east end when, in 1694, the building work was interrupted because the king first wanted Le Vau's design for the facade examined by French architects. No proposal from Paris found favor; so they turned to architects from Italy: the famous painter Pietro da Cortona (1596–1669; see p. 174), and the even more famous sculptor Gianlorenzo Bernini (1598–1680; see p. 269), produced, among other things, plans that are some of the most beautiful ideas for palaces known today.

Ridicule was naturally not long coming: for French critics, Bernini's first plan contained more mistakes than the stones needed to build the whole of the Louvre. Diplomatic complications with the papal court in Rome were the result. In 1665, the artist himself was invited to Paris like a statesman in order to put forward a new plan. As a sculptor he created a delightful bust of the Sun King and worked on a less successful equestrian statue, which has stood in a modern casting near the pyramid to the left of the museum entrance since 1993.

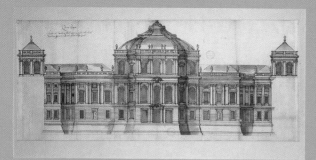

Pietro Berretini, called Pietro da Cortona (1596–1669), design for the east facade of the Louvre, 1664. Pen, wash, on paper, 49.8 x 118.5 cm. Recueil du Louvre, Vol. 1 fol. 14

Gianlorenzo Bernini (1598–1680), design for the east facade of the Louvre, 1664/1666. Pen, wash, on paper, 53.1 x 76 cm, Recueil du Louvre, Vol. 1, fol. 3

Out of this battle an argument developed about the "French" and "Italian" elements in art. At first the Roman *cavaliere* Bernini was successful; the Sun King in person laid the foundation stone on June 17, 1665, but as early as 1667 the plan was dropped as a result of count-less mistakes. The high colonnade was executed as the perfect example of French Classicism, according to plans by Claude Perrault (1613–1688). Perrault was a doctor and mathematician who received his first architectural commission with the east facade of the Louvre. The responsibility for building supervision lay with Le Vau and François d'Orbay, so credit is not due simply to the self-taught Perrault.

So now, rising up above a deep moat, there is a plain first-floor story with uniform windows ending in segment arches. Twenty-eight pairs of pillars are spread out over the wide area which is framed by corner risalits and dominated by a central risalit. The wide triangular gable is intended to be in complete accordance with classical tradition, as are the pillars. But where in Greece or Rome would double columns have been lined up so prosaically, so academically, beneath a plain entablature?

Philippe-Marie Chaperon (1823–1907), Cour Napoleon (detail), 1854, washed chalk, 45 x 174.5 cm

A Palace for Museum, State, and Emperor

Irregular in its effect but completely symmetrical, the Cour Napoleon opens out onto the west side with two extremely large wings. The nineteenth-century outside architecture stems from the time of Napoleon III (1808–1873).

What the Revolution of 1848 had defined as a people's palace turned into a large state and museum building, which from 1861 was called the Cité Impériale. Already

Nicolas Gosse (1787–1878), Napoleon III inspecting the building site of the Pavillon de Flore, the architect Lefuel with the plans next to him, and the old Western facade of Lemercier's clock tower and Lescot's Louvre, in front of that is the Carrousel Triumphal Arch, 1854, oil on canvas, 34 x 23 cm, Musée du Louvre

in the years of the Second Republic, which preceded the installation of Napoleon III as emperor in 1852, the remodeling had begun with the demolition of the perimeter buildings to the north. In the present-day area of the Louvre the architects Louis Visconti (1791–1853) and Hector Lefuel (1810–1880) began the clearing up of the old town which, under the town planner Georges Eugène Haussmann (1809–1891), allowed the modern-day Paris to develop in the 1850s and 1860s. At the Louvre itself there was some brutal treatment of its historical make-up: by the Seine there had previously only been the narrow building of the Grande Galerie with a facade dating from Henry IV's day; its western half was demolished along with the corner pavilion, and Napoleon had all the facades of the courtyard rebuilt in the same style.

Edouard Baldus (1813–1889), view of the Tuileries over the site of the demolished western part of the Grande Galerie, 1865

Contemporary photographs show the open view from the river to the Tuileries Palace, which has also disappeared in the meantime. During reconstruction all the facades facing the river and the town were renovated. In the courtyard, wide buildings with large interior courtyards were added. Toward the Seine around the central Denon pavilion new rooms for the State and for the museum were built: the State Room the (Salle des Etats), positioned diagonally, formed the center; today it contains Leonardo's *Mona Lisa*. In the north wing opposite, Napoleon III furnished a state suite. From its terraces he could look over the courtyard; in its center, surrounded by walkways, is the small triumphal arch, the so-called Carrousel Arch, which commemorates the victory over the Holy Roman Empire in 1806.

Since the second half of the 16th century the Tuileries Palace, built for Catherine de' Medici (1519–1589), had cut off the view to the west. A squat section of the building, which had a kind of cupola, dominated the wide main body of the building. Napoleon III liked to live there and so this building was regarded as the seat of the emperor. It was against the Tuileries, which had already experienced the famous "storm" in 1792, that the people's anger turned again in the Revolution which followed the French defeat by Prussia at Sedan in 1870, and which ended in 1871 with the Commune. Fire destroyed the palace. During this time, if the guards, supported by government troops, had not protected the museum, the whole of the Louvre and not just the Richelieu pavilion would have been completely destroyed.

A Triumphal Style of Architecture

Since the ruins of the Tuileries Palace were torn down in the 1880s, the Tuileries Gardens have been directly adjacent to the wings of the Louvre. Through the colorful Carrousel Arch one can see, behind the Tuileries Gardens, the obelisk of the place de la Concorde. Behind it the Champs-Elysées with Napoleon's great Arc de Triomphe on the star-shaped Place de l'Etoile, today named after Charles de Gaulle. While the monumental triumphal arch at the western end of the city used previously to dominate the horizon, now the new high-rise buildings of La Défense tower up far behind it. In 1989, in order to give new meaning to this perspective, the Grande Arche was built on a hill, just visible from the Louvre, affording a rectangular view which is the eye's final resting point. Ieoh Ming Pei (born 1917) developed the con-

The Carrousel Triumphal Arch, 1806

cept in collaboration with the former President François Mitterrand (1916–1996); the Grande Arche had been designed in 1982 by the Danish architect, Johan Otto von Spreckelsen.

The Tuileries and the Cité Impérial of the Louvre (detail), ca. 1860, Charles Rivière, lithograph

The Glass Pyramid of the Modern Pharaoh

The Louvre Pyramid at night; sketch by the architect Ieoh Ming Pei

Pierre Corneille (1606–1684), in his 1636 tragedy *Le Cid* I, 3, wrote, "On doit de respect au pouvoir absolu, de n'examiner rien, quand un roi l'a voulu." This justification of "absolute power, which out of respect for itself demands no examination of anything that a king has willed" just happens to introduce, in the most expensive book about the architects of the Louvre (Jean-Claude Dufresne, *Louvre & Tuileries*, Liège 1993), a chapter about the man who built the last great pyramid in the history of mankind, even if it was half buried in the Paris earth: Ieoh Ming Pei. In 1983 the architect, who had impressed

previously with the extension of the National Gallery in Washington, put forward his plan for the Louvre. After President François Mitterrand had freed the north wing on the rue de Rivoli, occupied for generations by the Ministry of Finance, the possibility arose for what has since been called "Le Grand Louvre," or the Great Louvre. A central entrance for the museum through the development of previously unused space under the massive Cour Napoleon was to be created. The purpose of this entrance is above all to make it possible for the hordes of visitors to cross between the Richelieu wing in the north, now also used by the museum, and the old Denon wing in the south, without having to negotiate the Cour Carré and the many hundreds of meters to the Sully wing. Since an underground area was also dug out to the west, a cross-shaped ground plan was necessary from which the only possible exit was in the center of the Cour Napoleon.

In choosing the architect, the president had dismissed both national and Western narrow-mindedness. Pei was not allowed to touch the buildings themselves and so his only choice was to go underground. This restriction led not only to the one realistic solution, but at the same time to an unexpectedly attractive discovery. In the course of the work so many traces of the medieval Louvre were discovered that these could be presented not only to visitors with a special interest in them but also for the general public. The underground Louvre was thus not only usable as a gallery of shops but offered a monumental visual effect from past ages, so that a mall there promised to be one of the most meaningful entrances to the building complex – though only one of them, because they wanted to give people the choice of entrances in order

French President Mitterand and Ieoh Ming Pei at the opening of the Pyramid in 1993

to distribute the large number of visitors around the building.

Anyone who is familiar with the unsightly tall constructions designed for subway stations throughout the world, which are destroying historical sites in many big cities, must be fascinated by this bold, and at the time, strongly disputed solution by the architect and the French president. Neoclassical forms in stone would have been seen as a poor imitation of the existing structure of the majority of the Louvre. A simple flight of steps down into the depths would not have done justice to the main entrance to such a complex. This is shown by the stairs used only by a few people that also lead into the depths of the new Louvre alongside the small triumphal arch.

The aim was greatness, but at the same time the preservation of the old. In all the disputes the architect could rely on a strong ally: the president. Mitterrand, for his part, had at least learned from his predecessor Georges Pompidou (1911–1974). The latter's bold, conspicuous Pompidou Center, also a museum, guaranteed lasting fame. In addition, a matter of dispute that whips up feelings during the building period only serves to imprint itself all the more markedly on the memory.

The modern Pharaoh decorates his pyramid builder: Conferment of the Legion of Honor on Ieoh Ming Pei, presented by the French President Mitterand, Paris, 18th November 1993

The Pyramid forms a central entrance to all wings of the Louvre.

Although democratically elected and coming from the Socialist Party, in this matter the president became like an autocrat obsessed with building. This was not only the case with the Grand Louvre – after all, none of his democratic predecessors in office had dared to make such far-reaching changes to Paris as he did.

With his intrusion into the structure of the Louvre and the perspective from the Cour Napoleon onto La Défense, the president took a risk which until then had only been taken by monarchs like Francis I, Henry IV, and the Sun King. Not even the great Napoleon had risked anything like this, but his imitator Napoleon III did, when he gave the whole of Paris its present-day appearance through architects like Lefuel and Haussmann.

In the Grand Louvre of François Mitterrand and Ieoh Ming Pei, the modern age triumphs in the materials: they chose an airy construction of glass and metal, but at the same time giving large sections of the interior the bright color of the sandstone common in Paris from the Seine valley and the Côte d'Or.

The basic idea of the pyramid provides a link with the real quintessence of the autocrat, the Egyptian pharaoh. Pei, with his sharp-edged building set deep into the ground, is placing the president himself in a role which goes far beyond the opening citation from Corneille and links him simultaneously with one of the oldest and most famous collections of the museum. Nowhere apart from in the land of its origin, Egypt, is there so much visual material on offer from the age of the great pyramids as in the Louvre. Alongside an idea like this, Bernini's unsuccessful statue of the Sun King on his horse, which stands near the entrance to the pyramid in a modern lead casting, creates a rather miserable impression.

The Louvre after the Modern Excavations

In the Sully wing at the western end, the magnificent foundations of the bastion which Louis Le Vau (1612–1670) laid out for the young Louis XIV (1638–1715) are still preserved. The entrance to the clock tower was in those days defended like a fortress in the same way as the moat to the east. Behind it a surprising view of the medieval Louvre opens up underground. The new finds confirm the impression given by the October picture from the Duc de Berry's *Très Riches Heures*. Looking out from the Germanus Fields, whose name reminds us of the present-day Saint-Germain-des-Prés, the area of the city beyond the Seine, Barthélemy d'Eyck shows first

and foremost the city wall across the river. Behind this rises the very compact, four-wing building with the round corner towers and twin towers around the central entrances as they have appeared since the death of Charles V in 1380.

The bases of two moats have been excavated with the result that the lower parts of the north and east facades can be seen. In the few areas that have been damaged, the splendid masonry reveals that an outer skin, made of large hewn stone blocks, was laid over badly constructed masonry in order to firmly strengthen the building against shelling. The en-trance into the inner moat, which is dominated by the mighty round main tower, is quite sensational.

A medieval hall has been preserved, today named after the king and saint, Louis IX (1226–1270). Even in the late 19th century there was a creepy descent from this area into the remains of medieval vaults. A hint of the medieval romantic is still preserved in the new lighting; the faces contained in the building's decoration also provide a lively impression.

Barthélemy d'Eyck, The Louvre seen from the Seine, ca. 1450, October picture from the duc de Berry's Très Riches Heures, illumination on parchment, 29 x 21 cm, Musée Condé, Chantilly

Salle Basse, the so-called Room of St. Louis, ca. 1200

From Wolf's Walk to Louis

The Capitoline she-wolf with the twins Romulus and Remus, Roman copy of the statue at the Ficus Ruminalis, 296 B.C., bronze, 75 x 114 cm, Musei Capitoloni, Rome

One can play with the name of this place in various ways: what in Latin is *lupara* or *lupera*, is *lovre* or *louvre* in French. In the Germanic language of the Saxons *lower* means simply "fortress." You should disregard this and other explanations that try to see a home for lepers in the word or assume that an "r" at the beginning of the word has become an "l" to come up with "*rouvre*," the French word for "oak," or the color red for the river sand. The most likely explanation is that the word *loup* is hidden in the name Louvre; this word, meaning "wolf," is pronounced in French without sounding the final letter, simply as "Lu," and is contained in the name held by eighteen French kings: Louis.

It is also possible that the name Louvre makes reference to a *luperia*, a pack of wolves kept for the hunting expeditions of the king and court, which may have been situated outside of the city walls, if only in almost mythical past times.

Because of this the Louvre has a strange link with Rome: however much the dog-like animal was despised in the Middle Ages, the ancient world had a certain admiration for the wolf. In the founding myth of Rome a she-wolf reared the infants Romulus and Remus with her own milk after they had been left abandoned in the wilderness. Thus they survived, and, much later, as adults founded the Eternal City. The "Capitoline She-wolf" has been the embodiment of Rome right up to its grotesque treatment in Fellini's film *Roma* (1972), whose advertising poster showed a beautiful woman on all fours with the breasts of a she-wolf. Even today on the Capitoline Hill there is a pack of wolves.

Anyone who has a name derived from a word meaning "wolf" assumes something of the strength of this savage, predatory beast, together with its wily nature. Those named Louis, or Aloysius – a name originating in Italy, or from the Jesuit St. Aloysius Gonzaga – would be interested to learn that their more descriptive name would be "step of the wolf." They may remember the origin of their name, like tourists from all over the world, as they approach the Louvre.

Jean Goujon (ca. 1510–1564), Caritas Romana (detail), 1547/1562, stone 269.5 x 133 x 40 cm

Not just because of the wolves did people constantly refer to Ancient Rome when building and furnishing the Louvre; on the south facade of the Cour Carrée, for example, they strengthened the reliefs now taken inside with examples of virtue from Ancient Rome. The Manneristic figures appear grotesque. The motifs, too, are disturbing, as in this one showing Pero feeding her imprisoned father with her own milk.

In the Louvre of the Kings

Everywhere in the Louvre you find the remains of a palace used only temporarily as a residence by royalty. There is no evidence at all of the splendor of Charles V before 1380. Under Francis I there was no time for furnishing new rooms between the start of building in 1546 and the death of the king in 1547. Particularly sumptuous traces, however, have been preserved from the building activities of King Henry II (1519–1559). His Caryatid Room was both a

Georges Braque (1882–1963), Birds, 1952, after a 1938 drawing, oil on canvas, 347 x 501 cm. Picture on ceiling in the Salle Henri II with its 19th-century restored paneling

banqueting hall and court (see p. 184 f.) because, contrary to the plans, the stairwell was moved out of the central axis toward the north where the later clock tower is now directly adjacent to it. The reliefs on the flat arches of the staircase display the Paris Mannerism in the style of Jean Goujon (ca. 1510–1564). This stairwell connects the two stories of a typical Renaissance corps-de-logis: on the upper story, which at that time in France was still more important than the first floor, is an equally large room which, uncompleted in its time, is today used as the bronze room

Pierre Lescot (1510–1578), Caryatid Room with its 17th-century vaults; gallery seen from the position of the court

for antique objets d'art. It leads into the Salle Henri II where the ceiling, restored in the early 19th century in the Renaissance style, has paintings by Georges Braque (1882–1963) completed in 1952, but actually designed in 1938 and then painted in the Louvre itself. There are hardly any traces of Henry IV and his son Louis XIII inside. On the other hand, some magnificent rooms have been preserved fairly well from the years after 1652, when Anne of Austria (1601–1666) and her son Louis XIV furnished the Louvre. Among these are the Small Gallery with the Summer Apartment (see p. 174 f.) and the Galerie d'Apollon (see p. 554 f.) as well as the Salon Carré built after the fire of 1661 by Louis Lé Vau (see p. 264 ff.).

In the Louvre of the Revolution, Empire, and Republic

In 1793 the Revolution turned the Louvre into a museum, but there was neither time nor money for large-scale building alterations. Even the extensive alterations carried out to the Louvre under Emperor

Auguste Couder (1789–1873), Percier and Fontaine showing Napoleon's museum plans in 1809 in the stairwell replaced today by the Nike staircase. Oil on canvas, Musée du Louvre

Napoleon (1769–1821) hardly make any impact on the visitor. There is no trace of the alteration of the Salon Carré into a

chapel for Napoleon's wedding to Marie-Louise of Austria in 1810. To accommodate the art treasures brought to Paris by Napoleon, Pierre Fontaine redesigned the winter apartments of the regent, Queen Anne of Austria (who occupied the wing parallel to the Seine built under Charles IX in the 16th century) so radically that apart from its summer apartments nothing else remains to be seen from the High Baroque period. A sober classicism took over, which covers the smooth walls with surfaces of colored stone, which favors the arch and, whose bareness accords with the classical works of art displayed here since that time. Yet old pictures also show how extensively most of these rooms have changed in appearance in the intervening years.

The remains of an abandoned stairwell which used to lead up to an old entrance in the Cour Napoleon, leading southward to the Salon Carré, is the best testimony to the high quality of the works of the Empire in the Louvre. Only two through rooms are preserved, but these, with their colorful marble, reveal some of the best interior decoration remaining in the Louvre. They were built by Charles Percier (1764–1838) and Pierre Fontaine (1762–1853), who, of all the architects of the building held that post for the longest time, from the years 1801 to 1848.

The kings of the Restoration could still only reside in individual wings of the Louvre. Charles X (1757–1836) invested a lot of energy there after he had succeeded Louis XVIII to the throne in 1824. He spread himself out with cold and glittering splendor in the state rooms north of the clock tower. A museum named after him situated on the south side of the Cour Carrée does Charles X more honor, while Louis XIV's Grand Cabinet du Roi (see picture below, Musée du Louvre) was turned into a mere museum room.

There are definite traces of Napoleon III in the building itself. His handsome apartment with the heavily ornate ceiling is part of the museum today. Thus in the very place where the last French emperor once strode to the State Apartment in Neo-Baroque pomp, Antonio Canova's *Cupid* bends over Psyche (see p. 211 f.), Michelangelo's *Slaves* rattle their chains nearby, and the emperor's stable now bears Donatello's name (Galerie Donatello, see p. 196 ff.). The sumptuous staircase, however, through which Napoleon III destroyed what was built by Napoleon the Great, has lost the stucco and mosaics of that great period of Salon painting. In the frosty splendor of the 1930s, styles from Napoleon the Great's time are revived. Of course France in 1940 became a victim of the German invasion. However in this stairwell one feels just how highly Paris prized a greatness beyond that of human beings. The museum is here turned into a monument to a victory, expressed by the classical goddess of the island of Samothrace (see p. 166 f.).

Joseph Auguste, Louis XIV's Grand Cabinet du Roi as Salle des Bijoux, with entrance to the Musée Charles X, ca. 1835, oil on canvas

Life in the Louvre

Only a few kings have lived in the Louvre. As a fortress the building fulfilled a purely military function until Charles V. After the death of Charles V in 1380, the kings once again abandoned the Louvre as a place of residence. Francis I only got round to renovating the palace in a makeshift way in order to hold State receptions here, such as for the Habsburg Charles V. This did not last long, since under Henry II the Caryatid Room served as a court and a ballroom.

Yet kings resided here from time to time, and under Henry's successor, Charles IX, the Louvre, with the Tuileries, became the starting point for an unforgettable night of terror. Spurred on by the queen mother, Catherine de'Medici, the St. Bartholomew's Day Massacre originated here. The marriage of the future King Henry IV to Margaret of Valois was arranged for that apostle's feast; because of this the entire high nobility – Catholics as well as Protestants – were assembled in Paris, in spite of the conflict sparked off by the Reformation. In the night leading up to August 24, 1572 the queen had the respected leader of the Protestants, Admiral Coligny, killed; around 2,000 Protestant noblemen then died in a succession of frenzied murders. The same mania carried off around 30,000 Protestants in the following weeks, much to the joy of Spain as well as of the Roman Catholic Church. Decades of stagnation that were filled with various wars and tensions followed.

Henry IV, with whom peace was restored again in the 1590s, never lived in the Louvre. After the short period when Anne of Austria occupied the first floor of the Louvre from 1652, and the Apollo Gallery was redesigned for her son Louis XIV after 1661, the latter gave his whole attention to

Hubert Robert who lived in the Louvre, in order to change it into a museum, in a portrait by Elisabeth-Louise Vigée-Lebrun (1755–1842), 1788. Oil on wood, 105 x 84 cm, Musée du Louvre

the construction of his new palace at Versailles. Immediately all the efforts to complete the Louvre Palace for the use of the king ceased.

In the years that followed, the building served as a home for academies and artists, and for a while was reputed to be a brothel, while for decades the north wing of the Cour Carrée was partly without a roof. In 1754, the citizens of Paris insisted on putting an end to the confusion. Ideas for its use changed: thus the Grande Galerie under Louis XVI was designated a museum for exhibiting collections of art. Hubert Robert (1733–1808), the king's loyal artist, was engaged in altering the Grande Galerie into a museum (see p. 264 f.) during the king's reign, and still played a part in its fate after the king's head had fallen under the guillotine during the revolution, after he was freed from imprisonment.

Only in 1806 did Napoleon make sure that the last artists, and the different artistic and scientific institutions had left the Louvre. Yet his plans to live here came to nothing. His successors furnished the State rooms; Napoleon III had the apartment in the Richelieu wing at his disposal which is preserved almost intact today in museum-like splendor. He hardly lived there, however, because, like his greater predecessor, he had the more familiar rooms of the Tuileries behind the small Carrousel Triumphal Arch available to him, and these proved much more to his taste.

After the Republic was restored, France's wealth was embodied by the Louvre for over a hundred years, in two ways. The Ministry of Finance was housed here in the north wing of the Cour Napoléon, while the art treasures claimed the rest of the

Anne of Austria's summer apartment as a museum of antiquities: the Salle des Saisons before the First World War.

enormous palace for themselves. Then in 1993 art finally drove the State out of this unique realm once and for all.

The Grande Galerie as it was shortly after the Second World World War

The Largest Museum in the World

The opportunity offered to the people of France by the Louvre has only recently been fully utilized: since 1993, the Musée National du Grand Louvre has broken all records as one single colossal building with its exhibits. Assuming that a day could be found on which all the rooms were open, then one would find it difficult simply to cope with the route which leads from the beginning of documented human activity right up to the middle of the 19th century. To allow even a single glance at every work in such a tour would hardly be possible.

The Melpomene room with the "Borghese Fencer" as originally displayed

In addition, not everything which once belonged to the museum for a shorter or longer spell of time is concentrated in the old royal palace.

Thus the Louvre today offers only a part of the whole world. The rooms opened in the spring of 2000 for "African, Asian, Oceanic, and Native American Art" constitute an alien element. The museum's perspective continues to be governed by France and Western Europe, with the Mediterranean as its central point. India is absent, as is Indochina, once occupied by France, and to which the Musée Cernuschi is devoted. Some wonderful East Asian exhibits have been removed from the collection in order to create the independent Musée Guimet.

The former Games Hall in the Tuileries: as the Jeu de Paume, the treasure house for the Impressionists from 1947 to 1986

America, it seems, has barely been discovered in the Musée du Louvre. The art of the primitive people in Paris continues to be mainly represented in the Musée de l'Homme at the Palais de Chaillot. Only objects that originate from the Mediterranean area, from Egypt, North Africa, and the Middle East indicate France's role as a leading colonial power from Napoleon's Egyptian campaign in 1798 to Algerian independence in 1962.

A formative criterion for the creation of the collection of exhibits in the Louvre is the emergence of a written culture in the countries assembled here. Early prehistoric exhibits, even of the homeland Gaul, have been banished to the National Museum at Saint-Germain-en-Laye outside the city gates of Paris. As a result the oldest objects come from the Nile Valley in Egypt, Mesopotamia, and Persia, in other words those regions of the world which invented writing; and only a few objects from the period before writing come from Egypt and the Middle East. The French were world leaders in the founding of the relevant departments in the Louvre: the Egyptian department was opened as early as 1826; even more surprising, but of profound importance, was the founding of an Assyrian museum in 1847.

Alongside membership of a written culture a second criterion must be fulfilled for a place in the Louvre. The museum still does not devote itself to everyday things, but sees itself as a treasure house of arts and crafts, even if it does exhibit a few objects from the everyday life of submerged cultures alongside those that were created specifically as art, or are regarded today as works of art.

Ever since it was founded at the height of Classicism in 1793, the museum has been undergoing a steady change in accordance with the changing art of the time. Western art that was created up to 1793 has, theoretically since then, held a rightful place in the Louvre. Yet it was difficult for the very modern works of their time, as standards were constantly changing; for generations the museum also fought a battle with the established institutions against the avant-garde. As elsewhere in the world private sponsors broke the resistance of both the general public and the custodians of art toward many new kinds of art. Around 1900, for example, the museum received so many paintings by the little-appreciated Camille Corot (1796–1875) and his contemporaries from the Barbizon School, that their work was given a firm place here once and for all and ranks alongside the most important exhibits.

After periods of blunt refusal, works by Edouard Manet (1832–1881) as well as many major works by the Impressionists found their place in the Louvre. Then in 1947, directly after World War II, with the exception of a few paintings belonging to private foundations, they were given their own building in the Jeu de Paume situated in the nearby Tuileries Gardens. Finally, in 1986, all French painting after 1848 was moved so that Gustave Courbet (1819–1877) along with the Impressionists and all art that blossomed up to the outbreak of the First World War is now to be found in an old station building on the opposite bank of the Seine. With this redesignation of an abandoned railway building, examples of which are also to be found in other towns, the Musée d'Orsay found its home; indeed, this was the first large museum project of the former French president, François Mitterrand, who held office from 1981 until 1995.

The Musée d'Orsay: a former luxury railway station now houses art of the period 1848–1914.

The Origin of the Collections

National museums such as the Louvre draw from countless sources. As the state institution of a republic that has emerged from kingdom and empire, such a collection has at its disposal old crown estate and treasures of the long-forgotten monarchs. The French kings since Charles VIII (1483–1498) had been traveling to Italy, returning with art treasures. Napoleon (1769–1821, emperor 1804–1815) conquered most of Europe and for some years made his Louvre into the treasure house of the best works of art of all time. In 1815, most of the works of art, though by no means all, returned to their places of origin.

As a treasure house of cultural possessions the Louvre reached world-class levels for the first time in the 1370s, since at that time it housed the library of King Charles V (1338–1380), known as "the Wise." After his death, however, the amazing holdings were scattered to the winds. In the footsteps of this great patron of the arts came first of all the rulers of the Renaissance, who were now also very eagerly collecting sculpture and painting. Francis I (1494–1547) set the standard in France. He already owned Leonardo da Vinci's *Mona Lisa* (see p. 304 f.), and the Medici pope, Leo X, gave him Raphael's *Michael* (see p. 324). Without royal patronage the school of Fontainebleau would be unimaginable as the most vital contribution of France to international Mannerism, as also would be the beginnings of the royal collection of antiquities.

The religious wars which overshadowed France for almost two generations also limited the role of the kings as patrons. Only with Henry IV, the former king of Navarre, did peace gradually return; the Louvre's famous Medici Galerie (see p. 488 ff.), which was planned for the Palais de Luxembourg on the left bank of the Seine, reminds one of the ruler murdered in 1610. Peter Paul Rubens (1547–1640) stylized Henry's widow Marie de Médicis as a glorious princess in his huge paintings.

The Kingdom of France, made strong again by Louis XIII, was able to acquire complete princely collections from several countries; Cardinals Richelieu and Mazarin also played a decisive role in this: the transportation of the pictures of the Gonzaga from Mantua in 1630 led to strong protests. After the execution of the English King Charles I in 1649, his art collection went to Paris, and also a vast amount remained in Paris from the treasures of the unfortunate Catholic Queen Christina of Sweden, who abdicated in 1654.

From 1682 onward Versailles occupied the Sun King's whole attention, but his collections and those of his successors grew without the Louvre having been their primary destination. Diderot, who in his encyclopedia demanded a museum for the whole of France, had already recognized just how suitable the powerful palace by the Seine was as the central gallery of France. Louis XVI, who was beheaded in 1793 in the year the museum opened, had commissioned the artist Hubert Robert to

From left to right: Charles V, Francis I, Henry IV, Maria de' Medici, Richelieu, Louis XIV, Louis XVI, Napoleon

concentrate the royal art collections in the Grande Galerie.

A state administration of national art treasures has had its office in the Louvre under various names since then. It monitors the export of works of art appearing on the international art market, and even today still oversees an exchange between the provincial museums and the institutions in the capital. Movements in the art market are followed with a keen eye; again and again, even in times of stringent state economy measures, there are some amazing new acquisitions by which the Louvre actively supplements its stock.

Napoleon's Art Thefts

Art theft is as old as art itself. Even three thousand years ago, important monuments were carried off as trophies from Mesopotamia to the Susa mountains in Persia (see p. 58). Works of art have always been part of the precious spoils of warring hordes. They wanted to secure not only precious objects but also ritualistic objects of value and of historical tradition belonging to those people whom they had conquered and often enslaved. In so doing, the gods mingled with the heroes and rulers so that every army leader who triumphantly took the treasures from distant lands with him appeared to both himself and his people as a second Alexander or Caesar. It was not this basic notion but the vast scope of his activities that distinguished Bonaparte, the later Emperor Napoleon, from those before and after him. The graduate of the military school at Brienne, born in Ajaccio on the island of Corsica on August 15, 1769, who at the outbreak of the Revolution in 1789 was a lieutenant-colonel in Grenoble, went back to Corsica to fight for the freedom of the island until 1792. Back in Paris he fought on the side of the French and freed Toulon for them in 1793. After the confusion of that same year, when he was taken into custody and released from the army, he was eventually, in February 1796, appointed as commander-in-chief of the Italian army.

Now began Napoleon's rise, which at the same time brought countless art treasures to Paris from all over the world: from Nice, Bonaparte led his army to Italy and made his first great series of art raids, after he had forced the pope to sue for peace and dealt with the Republic of Venice. With the exception of the Uffizi in

Gold-painted vase manufactured by Sèvres, Musée de la Céramique, Sèvres. The transportation of large antique marble statues from the Vatican to the Louvre

Florence, the French army plundered all the great collections of Italy. They brought classical sculptures and paintings of the Renaissance to Paris where the most wonderful works of art were suddenly placed side by side.

In 1798, Bonaparte set out on his Egyptian expedition and at the pyramids of Giza he defeated the Mamelukes, lost his fleet, but managed to reach Acre overland in 1799. At any rate, by this time Napoleon could not only feel like a second Hannibal, who had crossed over the Alps to Italy, but also like Alexander the Great. Elevated to first consul in 1799, he then crowned himself emperor of the French in Paris in December 1804 (see p. 252 f., 424) and in the following year also accepted the iron crown of the Langobards.

In a very short time he conquered large parts of Europe, destroyed the Holy Roman Empire, and together with that also the old structures which offered a permanent home to the art possessions of the nobility and Church. Only after he had advanced to Moscow, and in particular during his retreat in the winter of 1812, when he had to accept heavy losses, did his luck turn. In 1813, defeated at the Battle of Leipzig, he returned to France, and abdicated in 1814. Exiled at first to the island of Elba and later to St. Helena, the emperor died on May 5 1821. Napoleon had ransacked Europe with his armies to such an extent that almost all the traditional structures were disrupted. Art as an imperial means of representation had always fascinated him. In Paris he proudly showed his guests the main works which he had brought back from Italy. After his abdication France naturally had to give back most of what he had plundered – or as people still say today in France, trivializing the issue, "transferred to Paris." However, only those regions whose newly strengthened rulers were influential at the Congress of Vienna profited. Egypt, for instance, received nothing back. Moreover, the origin of many works was covered up. The Borghese family in Rome, who had been related to Bonaparte by marriage, suffered permanent damage. Much of what they

On the carriages which are magnificently decorated, we can recognize from left to right the Laocoon Group, a seated woman, the Aphrodite of Knidos, and the "Belvedere Apollo."

handed over to Paris in 1808 was lost to them forever. Some of the most glorious works of art which even today go to make the Louvre famous were associated with the name Borghese. For example, the *Borghese Fencer* (see p. 168 f.) or the vase from Caesar's gardens which, after his murder in 44 B.C., had belonged to the Roman historiographer Sallust (86–34/35 B.C.).

Napoleon himself and his destiny have set standards for manic imperialism, as well as for the legitimate settling of accounts with a ruler, since after his abdication the spoils of war found in Paris gave rise to a new way of regarding such objects. This was the degree to which people identified with the works of art demanded back from the defeated French.

One discipline has profited permanently from the frenzy for art in Paris that was made possible by Napoleon's art thefts: the subject of art history, still equally committed to Antiquity and to the

Napoleon presents the "Apollo Belvedere." Anonymous etching, ca. 1800, Bibl. Nat., Paris

Hubert Robert (1733–1808), La Salle des Saisons in the Louvre, 1802/03, oil on canvas, 38 x 46 cm, Musée du Louvre

post-Classical period. Where so many objects were on view alongside each other, it was necessary to rethink the method of display, especially as the Louvre director Dominique-Vivant Denon (1747–1825), who was appointed by Napoleon, insisted on setting up the works chronologically as far as possible. In this way Napoleon gave a boost to scholarship through his art thefts.

The Louvre in a Nutshell

As of spring 2000

The Grand Louvre

The Louvre is not only one of the most important museums in the world, but also a modern cultural theme park in the center of the metropolis of Paris. The glazed pyramid in the inner courtyard marks the dividing line between the hectic activity of the outside world and the amazing art treasures inside the Louvre.

Contents

- 55,000 sq m of exhibition area, to be extended to 60,000 sq m by 2001
- 30,000 exhibits in seven collections
- the permanent exhibition contains five percent of the total museum exhibits, the main part of which is stored in the strongrooms
- more than 90 temporary exhibitions since 1989
- a section on the history of the Louvre

Visitors

- more than 50 million visitors since 1993
- with around 5 million visitors annually, one of the most visited exhibition sites in the world
- museum tours in six languages for the international public

Louvre Auditorium

- multimedia usable lecture room for concerts, readings, films and theater

- since opening in 1989, over 1000 conferences and colloquia
- at time of writing, around 700,000 visitors so far

Behind the Scenes

- 1800 employees
- 40 different professions, including administrative staff, academic staff, museum education officers, security staff and others
- annual running costs come to 652 million francs. A third of the sum is raised by the museum itself, the rest is financed by taxes
- workshops for restoration and conservation in the Louvre itself and studios in Versailles, coordinated by the "Centre de Recherche et de Restauration des Musées de France"

École du Louvre

- higher teaching institution of the Ministry of Culture and Communication
- founded in 1882, situated today in the Louvre's Flore wing
- around 2000 students
- seminars on art history, archeology, history of civilization, and museology
- variety of day and evening courses, conferences, and lectures for the general public

Entrances
- main entrance through the Pyramid
- secondary entrances:
  – through the shopping precinct at the Carrousel du Louvre, entrance by the Jardins des Tuileries or by 99 rue de Rivoli
  – through the Richelieu arcade between the rue de Rivoli and Cour Napoleon (only for groups, so-called "friends of the Louvre," and those holding pre-purchased tickets)
  – Porte des Lions, Pavillon de Flore, from the banks of the Seine

Transport
- metro: Palais Royal/Musée du Louvre
- (Lines 1, 7)
- bus: 21, 27, 39, 48, 68, 69, 72, 81, 95
- underground car park: entrance from the avenue du Général-Lemonnier, daily 7am–11pm

Opening Times
- open daily except Tuesdays
- closed on January 1, May 1, November 11, December 25, occasionally on other holidays
- permanent exhibition 9am–6pm, Mondays in one smaller part of the museum until 9.45pm, Wednesdays whole museum until 9.45pm. Carrousel du Louvre shopping mall daily 9am–9pm
- ticket sales until 5.15pm, for the small guided tour until 9.15pm
- closure of the galleries begins at 5.20pm or 9.30pm
- temporary exhibitions 9am–6pm, Wednesdays until 9.45pm

Admission Charges
- permanent exhibition: FF 45 until 3pm, FF 20 after 3pm and Sundays all day
- temporary exhibitions in the Salle Napoleon FF 30
- combined museum and exhibition ticket: FF 60 until 3pm, FF 40 after 3pm and Sundays all day. Tickets are valid for the whole day and allow repeated entry.

Advance Ticket Sales
- in France: Minitel (3615 Louvre)
- FNAC +33 – 08 03 80 88 03
- Internet: www.louvre.fr; www.fnac.fr
- advance purchase is recommended in order to avoid long lines at the cash desks

Telephone Information
- info louvre: +33 – 01 40 20 53 17
- answering machine in five languages: +33 – 01 40 20 51 51
- info Louvre – Auditorium: +33 – 01 40 20 51 86
- answering machine in five languages: +33 – 01 40 20 67 89
- Internet: www.louvre.fr; www.paris.com

The room plans in this book and the details on the location of the exhibits may be subject to alteration. Among other things the opening of new rooms for English painting is being planned. In May 2000 the African, Asian, Oceanic, and Native American Art section was opened, but unfortunately could not be dealt with in this book for technical reasons of production.

Antiquities

One of the main regions where advanced human civilization emerged was the Land of the Two Rivers, formed by the Tigris and the Euphrates. Over a period spanning several thousands of years, people at prayer stare at us through large eyes. The effect is immediate; yet anyone who stands before these pictures from early cultures, facing their smile and their trust in a god as signified by their apparent deference and humility, should not forget: these men may appear almost childlike to us but they were the rulers of their time. Admittedly large areas of ancient oriental history and topography still remain unknown. Of course we know the names and empires of many figures through inscriptions; yet in the case of Prince Ginak of Edin-E, for example, we know neither when he lived nor in which town.

When they became settled tribes, the people cultivated the fertile land on the plains brought to life by the rivers so that they could create riches for themselves around their temples. But the nomads from Persia and Kurdistan always presented a threat. The story of Cain and Abel symbolizes the battle of the farmer who slaughters the shepherd and hunter and in this way experiences the superior power of his god.

Previous pages: Guillaume Larrue (1851–1935), Before the Great Sphinx (detail), oil on canvas, 69 x 88 cm. Musée du Louvre

The Departure of King Assurbanipal's Hunt (detail), Nineveh, ca. 650 B.C., alabaster with plaster, first floor, room 6

Ginak, Prince of Edin-E. Sumerian, Northern Mesopotamia, 3rd millennium B.C., limestone, height 26 cm, first floor, room 1

The conflict between these two brothers from the Bible basically marks the start of the history of Mesopotamia until the present day: chained to their native soil, the Sumerians repeatedly had to learn that the armies invading their land were superior; in the Louvre, the stele of the Akkadian King Naram-Sim (see p.64 f.), who admittedly managed to repel mountain people from the plain, provides eloquent testimony to such battles.

The basic conflict between farmers and the intruders led to alternate periods of independent nationhood. These were based at Lagash, with its capital Girsu, or Babylon, interrupted by the rule of foreign mountain people who, like the Assyrians, mostly settled on the plain themselves. Plundering led to the most important Sumerian and Babylonian antiquities not being found in the Land of the Two Rivers but in Susa in Elam; the conquerors, for example, carried off the steles of Naram-Sin and Hammurabi into one of the capital cities of the later Great Kingdom of Persia.

The Louvre collection, like that of the British Museum in London or the Pergamon Museum in Berlin, is dependent on finds in individually selected places: in Susa, Persia, in Tello, ancient Girsu, in the desert town of Mari, and in Chorsabad in Assyria, the French brought to light some sensational treasures which have ended up in Paris. The smaller the objects, the more they have remained intact. Therefore an immense treasure house of often very small objects awaits visitors to the Ancient

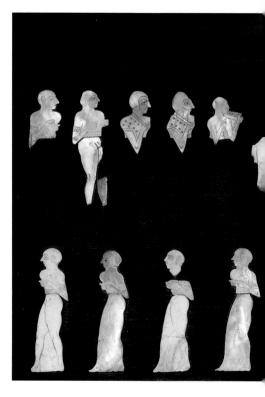

Oriental section. Anyone examining patiently the cylindrical seals and the spectacular pictures of animals and men, tools, and script is given an informative picture of life in the Land of the Two Rivers. Some of the oldest examples of pottery in the world are to be found here as well as monumental bronze nails with which they authenticated the laying of foundation stones. The cuneiform script – the earliest known form

Standards from Mari, 3rd millennium B.C., reconstructed, height of figures 3.3 cm, first floor, room 1

of writing that has been deciphered – was primarily used for financial transactions but also for reporting on historical events. Its significance lies in it being the oldest method of conveying myths.

The Land of the Two Rivers was familiar in biblical subjects and from the Sumerian "Epic of Gilgamesh." In the Old Testament, Ur of the Chaldees retains its significance like Babylon, where a tower was built that led to humanity being punished with a profusion of languages, according to the Book of Genesis. The diversity of races in the Land of the Two Rivers makes it difficult to document a continuous history. The selection in the Louvre does not try to do this either; therefore the exhibits are not arranged chronologically here.

Oriental antiquities

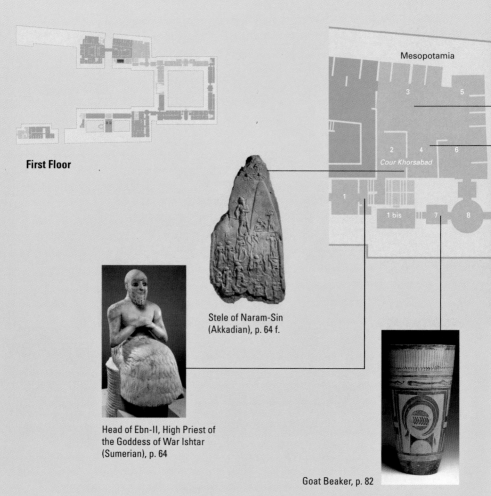

First Floor

Mesopotamia

Cour Khorsabad

Stele of Naram-Sin
(Akkadian), p. 64 f.

Head of Ebn-II, High Priest of
the Goddess of War Ishtar
(Sumerian), p. 64

Goat Beaker, p. 82

Stele with King Hammurabi's

Winged Bull with
Human Head, p. 72 f.

Female Nude
Statuette, p. 88 f.

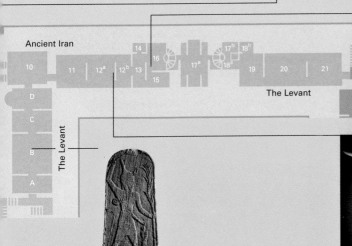

Ancient Iran

10   11   12^a 12^b 13   14   15   16   17^a 17^b 18^a 18^b 19   20   21

D
C
B
A

The Levant

The Levant

Stele of Baal as God of
Lightning, p.90

Capital with Two Bulls' Heads from the
Palace of the Persian King Darius I,
p. 85

Sumeria and Akkad in the 3rd Millennium

Stele of the Vulture King, Eannatum of Lagash,
Sumerian, Tello, formerly Girsu,
ca. 2450–2425 B.C.
Limestone, height 180 cm

This section begins with a large and monumental work which effectively blocks the way; framed by a huge wall piece apparently created for the visitors, it forms the spiritual gateway to the Ancient Orient. At first sight there is not much to interpret: on the fragments of an upright rounded solid stele a strong man, small in stature with a long beard, can be seen in the foreground. In his left hand he is holding an eagle and also a net full of captured people. Through the eagle and the lions' heads decorating the net, Ningirsu the tutelary god of the Sumerian state of Lagash can be seen. King Eannatum, whose deeds the stele describes, can also be seen bearing the attributes of his god.

On this stele is inscribed one of the very first texts to describe a historical event.

According to this text a king of Umma must swear never to violate the borders of Ningirsu again and not to harm the irrigation canals or the images of the gods. In contrast to the attack from Umma, which cost Eannatum's father Akurgal his kingdom and his life, the victor makes his appearance in the picture on the back of the stele. On the largest and most beautifully preserved fragment he is walking in a kaunakes, a rough skirt, protected by a coat, in front of his spear bearers who are shown together in a block. Yet the victory has already been won; for on the right, only recognizable on a few small fragments, lie the bodies of the defeated enemy, whose heads and limbs the vultures are carrying off. Sadly, only a small part of the subsequent triumphal procession has been preserved for us today.

Stele of Ur-Nanshe, Sumerian, Tello, formerly Girsu, ca. 2500 B.C.
Limestone, height 40 cm

Two generations of the first dynasty of Lagash precede Eannatum. The founder as well as builder of Ur-Nanshe is to be found on steles in surrounding showcases; the largest of these works, which like others has a hole bored in the center, perhaps because it was attached to the wall with a nail, is particularly notable. In two rows of people, one on top of the other, is the king, without decoration, and only distinguishable from the others by his size. He is surrounded by dignitaries and family members with their names. In each case, the bare-headed king is half-naked, only clothed with the kaunakes made of shaggy strands of wool. In the upper row he is carrying, as a ritual, a rush basket holding clay bricks for building the temple and in the lower one he is eating. The inscription on the stele celebrates the construction of shrines for the two chief gods of Lagash, Ningirsu and Nanshe, and tells of the transportation of wood by ship from what is now the Persian Gulf.

Ebih-II, High Priest of the Goddess of War, Ishtar, Sumerian, Mari, ca. 2400 B.C.
Alabaster, lapis lazuli, steatite, and shell, height 52.5 cm

Among the richest of French finds in the Middle East are the palace and temple of Mari in the central Euphrates region on the border between Syria and Iraq. Around the

middle of the third millennium B.C. a particularly significant culture flourished here; a library and numerous objects made by the most differing techniques. Among them, bronze lions and wall paintings were discovered (two rooms further on in the Louvre). Unquestionably the most significant sculpture is the almost perfectly preserved statue of the high priest Ebih-II, who sits on a round woven chair with his hands clasped together in prayer, the right hand clenched around the left hand. Translucent alabaster lends the figure a strange liveliness, which is further emphasized by the large eyes surrounded by steatite with their eyeballs made of shell, and their irises of lapis lazuli. Only the eyebrows and the feet, which were attached from below (the holes for these can still be seen), are missing.

Stele of Naram-Sin (2255–2220 B.C.), Akkadian, found in Susa
Reddish sandstone with yellow patches (signs of having being burnt?), 200 x 105 cm

It was only the Akkadians, whose city has still neither been found nor identified, who managed to occasionally subjugate the diversity of states in Sumeria within a greater kingdom. The great King Sargon is a man of myth. In his legend, which he recorded himself, there are themes which are familiar from Judeo-Christian tradition: born without a father to a chaste priestess, the later ruler was abandoned in a rush basket on the river, like Moses. As a

gardener, he became the lover of the goddess Ishtar. Portrayals of King Sargon himself are only preserved as crude fragments. However this stele in the Louvre shows his grandson Naram-Sin elevated to a god in heroic pose under three, formerly possibly as much as seven, radiating stars. The ordinary people, portrayed on a reduced scale, are following him. Naram-Sin's soldiers all dressed in short loincloths, with axes, bows, and standards, are driving the Lullibis mountain dwellers from the east, wearing spotted tunics, into the abyss.

The Louvre is in possession of this unique early monument for a very special reason: there is a second inscription that relates that in the 12th century B.C. an – unnamed – king of Elam seized it in the Land of the Two Rivers and took it with him as booty into his native Susa. In this capital city of the later Persian Empire, the French brought the work to the world's notice before 1900, along with other treasures.

Gudea of Lagash and the Monumental Mesopotamian Sculptures

The kingdom of Akkad did not last long because around 2150 B.C., the Gutians from the Iranian mountains invaded and devastated Sumeria. From Lagash, the inhabitants of the plain gained the upper hand again so that a period of prosperity known today as the New Sumerian period could be established. This new beginning finds splendid expression in the reign of Gudea (2141–2122 B.C.). The statues of this king, which were excavated in Tello from 1877, have revolutionized the view of the culture of the land between the Euphrates and Tigris. Until then it was thought that there were no monumental sculptures in existence until Assyrian times, in other words only after the beginning of the first millennium B.C.

Small Seated Gudea,
Tello, early Girsu, 2141–2122 B.C.
Diorite, height 45 cm

Gudea is shown in an ankle-length and flared gown probably made of linen and not the wool of the kaunakes of older times, and is distinguished by the princely head decoration of a broad-brimmed woollen or fur cap. Most of the statues are made from diorite, a very hard granular stone; their inscriptions describe rituals regarding the reconstruction and the renovation of the Ningirsu temple.

All the copies found by official excavators had lost their heads in Antiquity. Indeed, in 1877 they found just the well-preserved head of the seated image of the king; not until 1903 did they discover the body, also in near-perfect condition. As a result it is the only complete statue today belonging without doubt among the early finds brought to light by French excavations.

**Standing Gudea, with
Overflowing Vessel,
Tello, formerly Girsu,
2141–2122 B.C.**
Calcite or dolerite, height 62 cm

Whenever statues of Gudea came to light the Louvre took great pains to acquire them. Complete copies with heads appeared on the scene in 1953, 1967, and 1987 through the art market; they appear in Christopher Wright's – admittedly sensationally presented – *The Art of Forgers*, published in 1984. This statue from extremely granular stone is one of them, and is dedicated to the goddess Geshtinanna. Gudea is holding an overflowing container as part of a fertility rite.

Law, Script, and Picture: The Hammurabi Codex

From 1792 to 1750 B.C. the most famous king of Babylon, the sixth in the line of kings, was on the throne. Hammurabi, who is possibly portrayed by a head from Susa and a praying statue, became famous through his body of laws, several copies of which have been preserved. The "Hammurabi Codex" is the name given to the text as well as to the copies that were made, although books were still not known at the time. The laws have been recorded on steles completely covered in cuneiform script. The colossal stele in the Louvre is the most beautiful example of these; it offers a complete, authentic, version of Babylonian laws through which the king, Hammurabi, began the history of humanity. The basalt is irregularly rounded off, as in the case of other Ancient Oriental steles in the Louvre, covered in cuneiform script, and crowned by a picture. The bas-relief does not portray the king on his throne, but a god, Marduk, the principal Babylonian god, or perhaps it is Shamash, the sun-god of Sippar. Whichever theory is chosen determines whether

the stele comes from the capital city or from the shrine of Sippar. The king of Babylon is presenting himself to the god in reduced form as a mark of respect. Hammurabi steps forward reverently as he raises his right hand to his mouth. Anyone examining the image closely is rewarded with a

Stele with King Hammurabi's laws (detail)

masterpiece very characteristic of Babylonian sculpture. Its language and type of script also mark this monument as an example of Babylonian culture at its height.

The Babylonian king occupies an outstanding position in the history of law-making for a number of reasons: before Hammurabi there is no known equivalent attempt to organize a legal system and to put it down in writing. Admittedly, famous legislators such as Draco and Solon of Athens followed him in classical Antiquity, but only their names have remained by which to remember them. No text or even part of a comprehensive body of laws has survived prior to the late Roman Emperor Justinian (ca. 500 A.D.).

The fact that Hammurabi does not present any systematic legislation, but a collection of sayings, is symptomatic of all initial attempts to construct a legal system. Older customs must have gone into those sayings; an essential achievement, however, is the fact that the cases which the king judges are arranged very systematically according to different areas of life. The Hammurabi Codex consequently describes Babylonian society as it was almost 4000 years ago. The stele also throws light upon the lawmaker himself. In a poetic prolog it praises Hammurabi's reign from his ascent to the throne under divine protection; after that it comments on the defeated towns whose prosperity and temple cult Hammurabi secured after they had been conquered by his armies.

Stele with King Hammurabi's laws, found in Susa, Babylon, or Sippar, ca. 1750 B.C., basalt, height 225 cm, width 55 cm, first floor, room 3

The Praying Man of Larsa: Sculpture of (?) King Hammurabi, found in Larsa, Babylon, 1792/1750 B.C., bronze and gold, height 19.6 cm, first floor, room 3

essentially it settles questions of possession and money, after first of all dealing with penalties for false witness (1–5). It deals with offences of theft (6–25) and very quickly moves on to the administration of the royal estates (26–41). After that come questions of agricultural economy (42–65), the increase and the upkeep of residential space (66–76), trade, interest, and the use of capital (88–111), as well as deposits and securities (112–126). Marriage, divorce, children, adoption, and inheritance occupy the greater part (127–214). Professional codes are laid down for doctors (215–223), veterinary surgeons (224/225), barbers (226/227), architects (228–233), and shipbuilders (234–240). After that it comments on agricultural workers (241–260), shepherds (261–267, 274), slavery, (275/76) as well as on debt disposal and prisoners of war (278-282).

Along with all this there are also lists of penalties for bodily harm; we can conclude that it was quite a peaceable society from the fact that capital crimes like murder are not awarded their own section. The verdict of the king differs according to whether a notable person, a member of the lower classes, or a slave has commit-

Individual cases set out in 282 paragraphs form the main part of the Codex. First a legal or social question is raised with an "if" clause, which is then followed by an appropriate penalty clause. Admittedly it is a penal code; but

ted the offense. But we should not be surprised about such differences stemming from the structure of society, but rather about the extent to which Hammurabi also concerns himself with the protection of the weak against the strong. Finally, it is also notable that although his stele has him appearing with these laws before the deity, the king dissociates his administration of justice from the religious context.

At the end the king is praised as the protector of the poor. He claims to have kept the language extremely simple so that in disputes everyone can go to the stele and have the paragraphs read out to him: "thus run the just verdicts which the wise king Hammurabi has decreed so that in his country discipline and order shall reign." The Hammurabi Codex concludes with a prayer for the god's blessing, advice to his successors to heed the guidelines, and finally, with curses against any possible desecrators of the monument.

Head of a king – possibly Hammurabi, found in Susa, Babylon, 1792/1750 B.C., diorite, height 15 cm, first floor, room 3

The Assyrians

Winged Bull with Human Head, Chorsabad, ca. 706 B.C.
Alabaster with plaster, height 440 cm

As a result of French finds in the old city of Sargon in 1843, (Chorsabad or Dur-Sharukin) the world has been made aware that the Assyrians, who are familiar to us from the Bible, created some monumental sculptures. An Assyrian museum was opened in Paris in 1847, the first institute in Europe devoted to a culture in existence prior to the Greeks. There was a sudden fashion for Assyria which the artist Gustave Courbet explored through self-portraits (e.g. *The Painter's Studio*, Musée d'Orsay) in 1855, portraying himself in profile with a beard in imitation of representations by the Assyrians. The rooms were imagined to be somber and as richly colored as in Delacroix's depiction of *The Death of Sardanapalus* which was painted in 1827 (see p. 440).

The mighty stones from the residence of the Assyrian King Sargon II still create some of the most powerful impressions in the Louvre. Creatures with human heads on winged bodies of bulls were obviously made both for protection and as a deterrent. Looked at diagonally they have five legs. From the front they place their hooves parallel, but in profile they are walking and therefore putting one leg behind the other. Not all of the pieces that were recovered at the site reached Paris, because their transport was attacked by Bedouins, and ships with irreplaceable loads were sunk in the Euphrates. To augment the display, reconstructions made of plaster complement the originals. The light well was opened in 1993, and this made it possible to view the main pieces almost as the excavators must have seem them, especially on bright days.

The Sumerian King Ur-Nanshe of Lagash, whose foundation stone from ca. 2500 B.C. is featured on page 63, comments on this stone and similar monuments and on the efforts needed to bring tree trunks by river into a treeless land. In the Sargon Palace in Assyria it is clearly shown how the cedar wood was transported by ships and rafts:

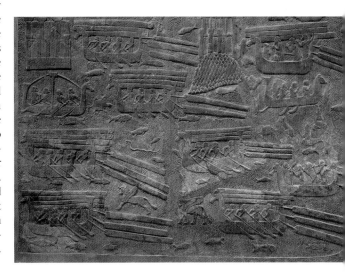

The Transportation of Wood from the Lebanon, Chorsabad, ca. 706 B.C.
Alabaster with plaster, height 308 cm

In the Land of the Two Rivers the people used clay to build walls, but for doors and roofs they needed suitable timber, which posed a major problem due to its scarcity. snakes and fish, winged bulls, and creatures which were half bull and half man appear in the waves between the flat boats with four oarsmen, which move upstream laden with wood as well as towing nets full of tree trunks.

King Sargon with a Dignitary, possibly the Crown Prince Sennacherib, facade, Chorsabad, ca. 706 B.C.
Alabaster with plaster, height 330 cm

Only the place where this was found, as well as the inscription, reveal that it is Sargon II (721–705 B.C.) portrayed on this relief. The king is wearing a three-tiered crown and the person he is talking to is adorned with a diadem. King Sargon is talking with the heir to the throne, Sennacherib (704–681 B.C.), whom we know from the Bible for his campaign against the Pharaoh Taharka. The army of Sennacherib was defeated outside the gates of Jerusalem (2 Kings, 19) by God's Angel of Death; therefore he is also often depicted in Christian paintings.

Lion-tamer, Chorsabad, ca. 706 B.C.
Alabaster with plaster, height 552 cm

The giant who is taming a lion as if he were dealing with a mere cat may be a portrayal of Gilgamesh. The legend attached to him anticipates elements from other Mediterranean cultures of a later age in which there is the story of the Flood, and one man pleasing to God in whose ark the human race survives. In the tests to which the hero himself is subjected, the labors of Hercules (who receives immortality, purified in a similar way to Gilgamesh) are already suggested (see p. 160 f.).

The Demon Pazuzu, Assyrian, 9th/7th century B.C.

Bronze, height 15 cm

"I am Pazuzu, son of Hampa, the king of the evil wind spirits, who rushes wildly down from the mountains in order to start a storm." These words are to be found inscribed on this enchanting little fellow. He is given a double pair of wings because he is an evil wind spirit. His body is composed of both human and animal elements. He has claws, fur on his lower legs, and a humanized animal face. His whole form can only be read anthropomorphically; the snout and nose, however, are very reminiscent of a beast of prey. Western images of the devil also feed off ancient Oriental pictures of demons such as this. Statues of this kind were used for warding off evil spirits and in invocations. Pazuzu is a splendid example of the bronze culture of Assyria, which is also exhibited in the Louvre by means of long friezes of ornamental door mountings.

Anatolia

**Stele of the Scribe Tarhunpija, Marash,
end of 8th century B.C.**
Basalt, height 74.5 cm

The Louvre has in its possession rather
few exhibits that come from Anatolia.
Admittedly, there are some works here
typical of the Hittites, yet the French
hardly had any involvement in the
great burial sites located in the highlands of Turkey. The most conspicuous
piece comes from one of the countless
minor kingdoms of the Neo-Hittite
period. The basalt did not allow any
detailed execution; there was obviously
a stylistic intention behind it which
valued a compact, easily read, large-
sized format. The Aramaic inscription
informs us that a scribe by the name of
Tarhunpija was the author of the stone.
As he could write, he was naturally
one of the most important and presti-
gious members of his society. Yet you
might think that you were looking at a
playful image of a mother and child:
Tarhunpija is standing on his mother's
lap like a child, and is holding a writing
instrument and a bird in his hand. The
childlike impression is not created
purely because he is standing on her
lap, but because Hittite art in general is
inclined to represent heads as too large,
thus creating childlike proportions.

The Ancient Orient – Cradle of Civilization

by Joachim Willelmer

Two cultural landscapes are considered to be the cradle of human civilization, the Nile Valley with its narrow fertile strip, and Mesopotamia, literally "The Land between the Two Rivers," between the Euphrates and the Tigris in present-day Iraq. The current, but inexact translation as "Land of the Two Rivers" shows that this is regarded as including the whole area around the two rivers together with their tributaries: an approximately crescent-shaped cultural landscape, the so-called "Fertile Crescent." This forms a massive semicircle around the desert and semidesert areas north of the Arabian peninsula and is limited in part to the north by the fringes of the southeast Anatolian Taurus Mountains and the northwest Zagros Mountains in Iran. The western "horn" of this crescent also covers some edges of the eastern Mediterranean along the then still densely wooded mountains of the Lebanon and anti-Lebanon – in its southern extension – the Hermon Mountains, and the Jordan basin. Here in Jericho, lies possibly one of the oldest towns of humanity, Ugarit the cradle of alphabet writing. It is now known that in the areas where the rivers flood, and on the slopes of the adjacent hills, cereal cultivation and animal domestication originated, for here the amount of precipitation was probably sufficient to enable the fields to be cultivated by rainfall.

Research in the last decade has modified this picture a little. We know that about 12,000 years ago, at the end of the last Ice Age, when a large part of the oceans' water was trapped in frozen form in the polar caps, the sea level was so low that what is today the Persian Gulf, lay dry. After their confluence, the Euphrates and Tigris rivers flowed out into the Shatt-al-Arab, and thus directly into the Indian Ocean. It was the melting of the polar ice caps that caused the present-day sea basin to gradually fill up. Until about 5000 years ago the climate and the coastline became firmly established and from that time have not changed much. Possibly the stories of the Great Flood reflect this change in the climate, because a raising of the sea level by only 1 cm caused a land loss of several kilometers in the very flat basin between the Arabian peninsula and the Asiatic continent. This might explain the origins of the Sumerians, the first archeologically identifiable population of southern Mesopotamia. It is certain that the Sumerians were not the original people in the area, because linguistic studies show that they took over the place names, for example, Ur, Uruk, Eridu, Kish, or Lagash, from even earlier settlers. Possibly they were forced by the slowly advancing masses of water to move away to the north where they seem to have displaced the proto-Sumerians.

The Sumerians are credited with the invention of cuneiform script on clay tablets, which developed toward the end of the 4th millennium B.C., as economic texts from Uruk demonstrate. But admittedly we cannot discount the possibility that Elam (with its capital Susa) in present-day western Iran is where cuneiform originated. Whatever the case, its invention took place more or less simultaneously with that of Egyptian hieroglyphs, the oldest version of which has recently come to light in Abydos. Although Egypt and the Middle East probably did not have a mutual influence on each other in the development of the script, there must nevertheless have been contacts. The ivory knife-handle from the Egyptian Gebel el-Araq, preserved today in the Louvre, shows motifs, for example, which otherwise only appear on Mesopotamian cylindrical seals. How, and in which ways these early relationships developed is still disputed today in its essential points.

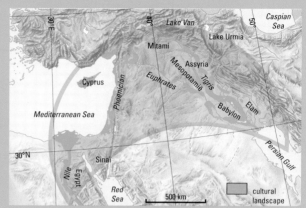

The term "Fertile Crescent" is used to describe the cultural landscape which stretches from the Nile in a curve over the Land of the Two Rivers to the Persian Gulf.

It was not art, however, but economic interests which first fostered these mutually desired contacts. Thus in the Sumerian cuneiform texts we already find the three areas Dilmun, Magan, and Meluhha. Meluhha embraced the region from the west bank of the Persian Gulf to the culture of the Indus Valley; Dilmun was situated on the opposite side of the Gulf and had its two centers on the island of Failaksa by the Bay of Kuwait and on the Island of Bahrain; Magan, which was very important to the people of Mesopotamia mainly as a producer of copper, has been located by experts to be in present-day Oman.

The Sumerians lived in urban states which from time to time cooperated peacefully with each other, but also settled their conflicts by force. Although there was no overriding central power the "early dynastic period," as the Sumerian epoch is called by archeologists, spread far upstream: the best-known example of this is the town of Mari on the central Euphrates from where there are many finds in the Louvre. But also in the upper reaches of the Chabur, the most important tributary of the Euphrates, there existed similar settlements. Further north, too, at the point at which the Euphrates is closest to the Mediterranean, a whole series of early dynastic settlements like Habuba Kabira have been excavated. Around 2300 B.C. Semites, who probably had also moved into Mesopotamia at an earlier date, suddenly seized power: King Sargon of Akkad subjugated the Sumerian city states and founded the first Great Empire of the Middle East, which also embraced parts of Syria and Asia Minor as well as Elam. Even later, for most of the time, the power center of the Middle East remained in Mesopotamia where Babylon and, further north, Assyria alternated as the dominating power.

The old Assyrian Empire established trade centers in present-day Keyseri around 1800 B.C., deep in central Anatolia. Shortly before this, the Hittites had immigrated there, and soon afterward founded their own large empire with the capital at Hattusa, which quickly expanded, and around 1530 B.C. also overcame the old Babylonian Empire. Only during weak periods in Assyria and Babylon were other powers able to establish themselves: for example around 1500 B.C. the Hurritic Empire of Mitanni in northern Mesopotamia, and in southern Mesopotamia the Kassites, who came from the mountain country in Iran.

In the Syrian-Palestinian area – a bone of contention in the 13th century B.C. between the Hittites and the Egyptians – there arose in the following period along the Mediterranean coast the Phoenician city states, separated from each other by river valleys which flowed from the mountain slopes of Lebanon into the Mediterranean. From here developed trading centers throughout the whole Mediterranean area, among them Carthage in 814 B.C., until the Assyrians also took control of this area.

The original people from Arta in western Anatolia, and those in present-day Armenia suffered a similar fate. Between around 835 and 714 B.C. they were able to defend themselves

against the Assyrians; after that they had to accept defeat. Their territory finally fell to the empire of the Iranian Medes who, in alliance with the Babylonians, succeeded in annihilating

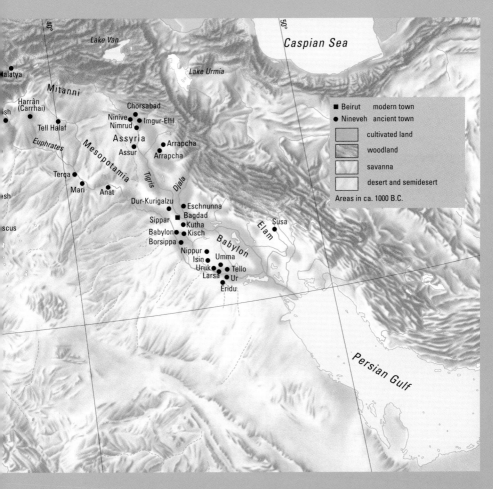

Assyria. The Achaemenian Persians, on the other hand, as vassals of the Medes were able to rise up successfully against their former overlords around 550 B.C. They were the last major Oriental power to subjugate the whole Middle East, until they in their turn were then defeated by Alexander.

Ancient Iran

Time and again in the Louvre you come across finds from Susa, the capital city of the Elamites, which the Persian king Darius the Great made his place of residence. Into this fertile area on the slopes of the Persian highlands Elamite kings had earlier hauled treasures from the Land of the Two Rivers. The French excavations there have given the Louvre a unique view of the art and history of Mesopotamia since the times of Naram-Sin and Gudea. But they also, of course, allow the independent culture of Elam and of its capital Susa to be traced back for thousands of years. In so doing, the regional division of the Ancient Orient leads here, as it also does in later eras, to a sudden step backward into the depths of human history. With its Persian antiquities the Louvre goes back to thousands of years before the arrival of the first decipherable script.

Goat Beaker, Susa, ca. 4200–3800 B.C.
Painted, fired clay, height 29 cm

One of the most amazing pieces, sure to make a lasting impression on even the most hurried visitor, is the tall clay beaker with a fascinatingly stylized form showing the geometrically shaped body of a goat which accentuates the curve of the horns to unrealistic proportions. Above that is a narrow border with cowering animals. The shapes are more monumental than in the much later geometric ceramics from Greece. Framed by thick lines the picture area looks modern to today's eyes, with the result that the featured beaker prompts us to view the earthenware treasures of the showcase with the same fascination as contemporary art.

Statue of the Goddess Narundi, Susa, ca. 2100 B.C.

Limestone, height 109 cm

One king of Elam who distinguished himself by his particularly enthusiastic patronage of the arts was called Puzur-Inshushinak. He lived only a short time after the great King Gudea of Lagash, who initiated the golden age of the Neo-Sumerian Epoch from 2141 to 2122 B.C. (see p. 66 f.). In front of the windows, and facing the Cour Napoleon, there are statues which Puzur-Inshushinak had erected in Susa. The main figure is of the goddess Narundi, whose face looks distorted, as it was fashioned with deep inset metal eyes above a crude limestone block. The fertility goddess, comparable to the Sumerian Innana or to the Babylonian Ishtar, or to Astarte in the Greek world, is veritable proof of the link between Elam and the Land of the Two Rivers: the attitude, together with the dress, the typical kaunakes, look Sumerian (see the male figures p. 64 ff.).

Sit-shamshi or Ceremony of the Sunrise, Susa, 12th century B.C.
Bronze, surface area 60 x 40 cm

A model on which two completely naked priests crouch opposite each other provides us with a particularly lively insight into Ancient Persian sun worship. One of them is pouring water over the other's hands. The ceremony takes place in a sacred grove among pools and steles set in front of a construction of several layers, possibly an altar. This bronze offers the only three-dimensional representation of such a ritual anywhere. In the generous setting only made possible in 1990 by the American couple, the Sacklers, a genuine ritual instrument can be seen: a huge bronze table with snakes, which was possibly used for animal sacrifice, comes from the time of King Untash-Napirsha (ca. 1340–1300 B.C.). In addition to this, there are objects on display both for everyday use and for rituals, including outstanding bronzes from Luristan, located in Persia, from an ax to a statuette.

The Great Kings of Persia

**Capital of Pillar with Two Bulls' Heads
from the Palace of the Persian King Darius I,
Susa, ca. 500 B.C.**
Limestone, height 760 cm

Persia swept into the world of the Greeks
with Darius the Great. He conquered the
Ionian coastline, which was at that time
occupied by the Greeks, destroyed cities
such as Milet, and made the first attempt to
advance to Athens, the great capital, only
to fail at Marathon in 490 B.C. He made
Susa into a capital city and built an enormous palace there, whose reception hall
was given colossal pillars around 21 meters
high. In the Louvre the leaves constructed
in the Egyptian tradition which finish off
the pillars are missing. Only one enormous
capital reached Paris. This capital shows
two bulls' heads over scrolls that look
almost Ionic.

Frieze of Darius' Archers (detail),
Susa, ca. 500 B.C.
Colored, glazed ceramic, total height 475 cm

Archeological sections are often huge: they are at their most beautiful when they succeed in giving the visitor the impression that he or she is actually entering a palace or a temple. In the Louvre, Darius' archers create just such an impression. They come from Susa and were not hewn from stone but made from loam and clay. People created lasting decoration with fired bricks; early examples such as the older wall from Susa with inscriptions of King Shilhak-Inshushunak (12th century B.C.; room 11) are only glazed. Later on, similar wall coverings were produced in color, but Darius' archers were treated with a form of enamel. The Babylonians had developed the color technique used here for their 7th-century showpiece street, which can be seen in the Pergamon Museum, Berlin; in an exchange with Berlin, the Louvre was given a part of this and Berlin received an archer. But Paris' claim to fame is that it possesses the colored archers from the palace of Darius. At the court ceremonial they surrounded the living with their brightly colored throng. They represent either the 10,000 immortals that are mentioned by Herodotus, or alternatively, may be the Persian people themselves to whose strength Darius is referring in his inscriptions. The men with the black beards are wearing earrings and other jewelry.

Vase Handle in the Shape of a Winged Goat,
Susa, ca. 500 B.C.
Silver and gold, height 27 cm

Faced with the king's palace in Susa, Herodotus expresses some doubt as to whether Zeus possessed similar magnificence. This delicate fragment of a splendid vase suggests what he saw there. The satyr's head looks Greek; but the motif and stylization are still reminiscent of the goat beaker from around 4200–3800 B.C. (see p. 82).

Empire and its capital Byzantium, later Constantinople. This extremely stylized bronze with its fashionable design provides the most lively impression of the Sassanids: on this evidence, it would seem that they wore curled moustaches as in the late 19th century and put their beards through rings. Heavy decoration on the neck and a breast-plate which is now broken off were similarly a part of the ornamentation, as is a winged crown which at first glance resembles deers' antlers.

Babylon and the Levant

Female Nude Statuette, Babylonian, ca. (?)300 B.C.
Alabaster, ruby, gold, height 25 cm

Statuettes of nude goddesses like this one can illustrate for us what pious Jews and early Christians were afraid of when, in the Bible, they conveyed a negative and derogatory picture of life in the Middle East: the rites and festivals relating to fertility goddesses in particular are physical embodiments of sex.

In this sensitive figure made of the most precious materials the "great goddess" appears nude, in all her feminine voluptuousness, elegant and seductive. In contrast to ideas found in Greek and Roman mythology she combines two incompatible things: the body of the lascivious Venus and the crescent of Diana, the chaste goddess of hunting.

The Sassanids

Bust of a Sassanid King, Iranian, 6/7th century A.D.
Bronze, height 33 cm

Only a few monuments present us with a picture of the important kings of Persia. They are mostly rock reliefs because no sculptures of the rulers have survived. All the more remarkable for this, are the small representations of nameless Sassanids who ruled Persia from 224 and were an increasing threat to the eastern part of the Roman

**Goddess Feeding Goats, Minet el Beida,
Port of Ugarit, end of 2nd century B.C.**
Ivory, height 11.5 cm

Fertility and care of the flocks are combined in this work from Ugarit in Phoenicia, which in dress and headgear suggests quite close links with Minoan Crete. There, women with bare breasts performed religious rites on bulls. But here a fertility goddess is feeding two goats with three ears of corn in her hand. Many works made of hippopotamus ivory were fashioned in Ugarit, but the most valuable pieces were made of elephants' tusks. Both resulted from trade with Egypt. Cedar wood was the most important material from the Levant that was used in the Nile Delta – not least for the coffins of mummies. Between these two cultures there developed the Jewish culture, which was determined not to tolerate either goddesses with bare breasts or the influence of the pharaoh in their Promised Land.

Stele of Baal as God of Lightning, Ugarit, (?) 2nd millennium B.C.
Limestone, height 142 cm

This bas-relief which, in its two-layered effect, admittedly shows certain features that are common with other works from the Middle East, is extremely stylized, but has an independent graphic simplicity. It comes from Ras-Shamra or Ugarit in Syria, in other words from the region of the Levant to which Palestine also belongs. The god, Baal, whose worship in the Old Testament is persecuted with a special rigor, and who as Beelzebub remained the quintessence of evil right up until our own times, is shown on an altar. His head covering reminds us of both the Akkadian king Naram-Sin and one of the two Egyptian crowns. The club in his hand with which he is drawing back his arm is a sign of his status as a weather god presiding over good or bad harvests, but who comes close to the Greek god Zeus in his power. The town from which this monument comes was inhabited by the Phoenicians. A highly developed written script was in existence there and the later history of the Mediterranean is unthinkable without the Phoenicians who, for example, set out from the Levant to found Carthage in North Africa.

**Paten with Hunting Scene,
Ugarit, end of 1st millennium B.C.**
Gold, diameter 18.8 cm

Finally from the riches of the Phoenicians we have works in gold which compensated the treasure seekers among the excavators for their efforts. The problem of inscribing the strip running from left to right into a circular area, and depicting an animal hunt is marvellously resolved here: as if he does not need reins, a prince stands alone on a carriage pulled by several horses, and aims his bow at the stag in front of him, which is preceded by three huge charging bulls.

Arabia

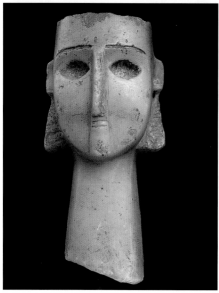

**Stylized Head, Southern Arabia,
(?) 1st century B.C. alabaster, height 22.5 cm**
Alabaster, height 22.5 cm

There are some parts of the section dealing with treasures of the Middle East in the Musée du Louvre, which are still under construction. Palestine, because of the Jewish religion's hostility to images, has few visual items to offer. On the other hand the distant world of southern Arabia, present-day Yemen, presents us with stylized alabaster heads of great aesthetic and historic charm. They come from that culture referred to in the Bible when the Queen of Sheba visits wise King Solomon bringing with her the immense treasures of Arabia.

This rather peaceful section is the newest in the sequence; it was put together only after the expansion of the Grand Louvre, from collections that were previously scattered around. The royal collections as well as that of the Benedictine Abbey of St. Denis (see p. 526) already possessed some very important works of Islamic art. Because these old treasures are now included, the new department is one of the most important collections of Islamic art in the West. Individual centers are shown in chronological order – the arc stretching from North Africa toward the Caucasus and to India.

Anyone not familiar with the religion of Islam will be amazed by the lack of sculpture and painting. The Koran forbids the representation of people and animals in sacred contexts; Mohammed perceived artistic illustration as an intrusion into the creative power of Allah. Valuable materials such as gold and silver were equally undesirable. Therefore Islamic artists confine themselves, along with architecture and illumination, primarily to works executed in ceramic, wood, glass, bronze, and ivory. Although the Islamic East was famous for its wealth, only a little of it has survived, like, for example, the Fatimite gold jewelry of the Louvre, since such works were often melted down into coins.

Not only did art have other purposes in the Islamic world, but the calculation of the years and division of months also followed their own rules. The reckoning of time for the Muslims begins with the Hidjra or Hedshra on the 16 July 622 A.D., when Mohammed set out from Mecca, his place of birth, to Jathrib (the present-day Medina) to preach about his visions. The Islamic calendar of the caliph Omar I was standardized in 639. As a result, the year 622 A.D. is understood as the year 1 a.h. *(anno hegirae)*. The year is divided into lunar months, whose differing lengths make it difficult to convert into the Gregorian calendar now used worldwide. The ninth month of the year is Ramadan, the sacred month of fasting.

Because of the sensitivity to light of the textiles and book illuminations the lighting in the rooms is subdued. At the same time there are not so many famous individual pieces, but instead superior examples from rich resources. The few codices from Egypt, Persia, Turkey, and India, which are always changing in the exhibition, are testimony to the calligraphic skill and the multifaceted illustration of literary works.

The textile exhibits are also rotated on a regular basis. Materials such as silks from Chorasan often bear the name of the caliph who controlled their production in the workshops, known as tiras. Anatolian carpets, particularly those made in Ushak in the west of Turkey, made their way to the West at an early date.

Tiles glazed with floral pattern, Iznik,
16th century, basement, room A

Islamic Art

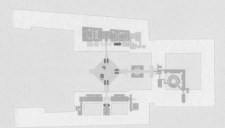

Basement

"Carpet of Mantes", p. 98 f.

Other Works:

Celestial Globe, 1145, room 5, p. 97

Pyxis bearing the name
al-Mughira, p. 96

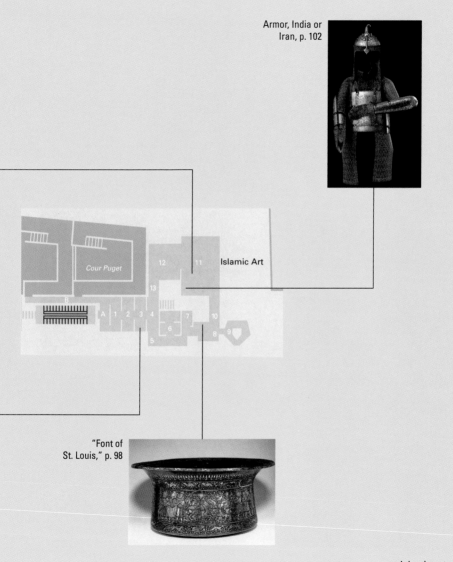

Armor, India or
Iran, p. 102

Cour Puget

12   11   Islamic Art

13

B

A 1 2 3 4   7   10
         5   6   8 9

"Font of
St. Louis," p. 98

**Pyxis bearing the name
al-Mughira,
Spain, Medina al-Zahara, 968**
Ivory, height 15 cm, diameter 8 cm

Islamic vessels are described
in accordance with concepts
developed by archeologists
when dealing with Greek
finds. As a result of this, a
link between classical works
of art and Muslim art is also
established. The pyxis here
names, on the rim of the
domed lid, a son of the Omayyad caliph Abd ar-Rah-
man III (889–961). Carved
from one piece, it conceals
in its medallion shapes with
a free pattern, many different individual motifs. All
these motifs tend toward a
symmetry. Four large med-
allions function as divisions
for the decoration. The
theme of the decoration
comes from the world of
princes: falcons and lions
are shown to be tearing at
gazelles, there is drinking to
the music of a lute, and
cheetahs are shown under a
palm tree. The individual

elements have been carved deep into the
ivory and are also accentuated by bore-
holes. It is a masterpiece from the ivory
workshops in Andalusian Córdoba, where

one of the most important centers of
Mediterranean culture arose during the
caliphate of Abd ar-Rahman III, at the end
of the first millennium.

Celestial Globe,
(?)Baghdad, 1145

Cast brass with inlaid silver,
diameter 16.5 cm

On the globe hanging from a bronze meridian, the small silver points mark the fixed stars whose names are written alongside them in Kufic characters. The images of the stars are engraved in the same way as the star signs. In the model, which is a representation of the sky, the earth is the intended central point. The theory of astronomy that is employed here comes from the writings of the Greek, Ptolemy (ca. 100–160 AD) in the *Almagest* (Arabic: al-Majisti), which has been preserved through its translation into Arabic. Of the 48 images of stars described, we still know 47 today. In the 9th and 10th centuries new lists of stars and tables along with the movement of planets were drawn up. The celestial sphere bears the inscription, "This globe contains all the constellations in the Almagest corresponding to the distance in time between the calculations of Ptolemy and the year 540..." Thus the calculation goes beyond the globe's date of origin by 17 years because the Muslim calendar begins in 622 A.D. This is the oldest Arabian globe that has survived intact. Such a work was much in demand in the West, too, in the Middle Ages, by scholars and noblemen, both as a prized possession and as a scientific instrument.

Mohammed ibn Zayn,
the "Font of St. Louis," Syria or Egypt,
end of 13th or beginning 14th century
Beaten brass, encrusted with silver and gold,
height 23 cm, diameter 50.5 cm

was used as the font of St. Louis (1226–1270), but this has no historical foundation, although evidence suggests that it probably was used for the baptism of Louis XIII (1610–1643).

The "Carpet of Mantes,"
Northwest Iran,
end of 16th century
wool, 783 x 379 cm

In the central section, the battle of the phoenix with the dragon is shown, along with four depictions of a panther attacking an antelope. The areas around the large medallion contain a decoration mirrored in two axes. The battle between the dragon and the phoenix also provides the link with the

Monumental figures on the basin in room 8 form the decoration of the outer curved surface in which four medallions with knights appear at the centers. Strips showing animals run along the top and bottom: leopards, dogs, elephants, camels, and even unicorns. On the inside, hunting scenes alternate with battle scenes; the bottom is decorated with fish and sea creatures. We are familiar with another work by the same artist: a basin bearing the name ibn Zayn in the same room. It comes from the treasures of the Ste-Chapelle in the castle of Vincennes outside the gates of Paris. Its name indicates a desire to believe that the basin

border around the edge. Under the Safawid dynasty (1501–1732), whose capital was Isfahan, carpet craft in Iran with hunting and garden motifs reached a high standard. Contemporary book illumination provided inspiration for the patterns. The Duchesse de Berry presented the carpet to the collegiate church of Mantes where it was used to decorate the choir for important weddings. Luxurious carpets of this kind came to France via Iranian embassies. Silk carpets on the other hand were produced specially for the European market and commanded high prices.

Islamic Ceramics

In its diversity of production, Islamic pottery continues age-old traditions which, like the Abbassidish ceramics (8th–10th century) in the shape of vessels and in the figureless decoration, ultimately derive from local traditions from the Ancient Orient.

Many techniques from the Middle East spread throughout the whole Islamic world and even reached Christian areas. Among these, there is luster painting in ceramics, in which the already glazed material is fired again in order to give a shimmering and metallic gleam to the colors. Yellow, green, brown, and dark red predominate. Other ceramics testify to the contact of the Muslims with the Far East: for porcelain from China inspired the thin Persian faience vases from the Seljukian period (11th-13th century). Openwork patterns and the application of shapes from the animal world predominate. In Iznik, pots had already been made before the founding of the Ottoman Empire; under the rule of Suleiman the Great (1494–1566) production was started which flourished until around 1700. This can be seen in the

Plate with inscribed decorations, Chorasan, 10th century, fired clay with transparent glaze, diameter 22 cm, basement, room 12

decoration principally in cobalt blue and turquoise, then also later in violet and red on a white ground with transparent glaze.

Plate with peacock decoration from Iznik, mid-16th century, fired clay with transparent glaze, diameter 22 cm, basement, room 12

The decoration found on mosaic tiles from Kashan from the time of the Mongol invasion is extraordinarily fine. The enthusiastic inventiveness of the potters produces the most varied of patterns in which depictions of people and animals are also found. Their unusually good condition is just as remarkable as that of the vessels and plates themselves.

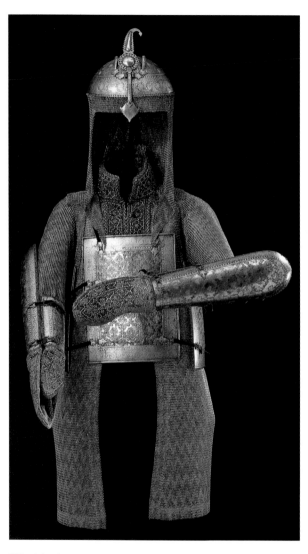

Armor, India or Iran, 17th–18th century

Helmet: steel, silver foil, partially gilded, height 50 cm
Coat of mail: steel, copper, brass, velvet, brass nails, height 86 cm
Brassards: steel, silver foil, velvet
Armored plates: steel, silver foil, height 29.9 cm

In order to be able to attack quickly on horseback, the armor in India, Persia, and Turkey was very light. The finely patterned chain shirt is strengthened by rectangular plates which protrude wider on the breast and back than on the sides of the body. From the helmet there are more chains, and these hang down like a curtain in order to protect the neck. This magnificent armor is impressive in its completeness as well as in the richly engraved decoration, which is pleasing even to pacifists. European rulers highly valued such showpieces. This type of armor often reached the West as presents from princes of the Orient, and may never have been worn.

**Portrait of Fath Ali Shah,
Iran, ca. 1805**
Oil on canvas, height 189 cm

The influence of Western European art on painting under the Kadshars (1796–1925) is shown by this life-size portrait of a shah, that is highly unusual in an Islamic art hostile to pictures. The strange work is amazing in its monumental greatness. It offers a rather unsuccessful synthesis of traditional ornamentation and Western imitation of nature: space is indicated, but, just like the volume of the body, is very curiously played down. The picture, like the works of 18th-century Polish silk weavers, who imitated silk scarves imported from Persia in shorter and in stylized forms, is evidence of the vibrant trade between East and West. At the same time it represents Persian culture. The contrast between the rulers that were Western-oriented, and rigidly orthodox clergy lives on down to our own time.

The Egyptian section is different from the rest of the Louvre in some respects. Split into three, its division follows contradictory ideas throughout. Instead of only being confronted with works of art, rooms arranged for educational purposes start and end the tour in the same way as in the Ethnology section. The first rooms familiarize you with the basic lifestyle in the Nile valley, with the economy, writing, luxury, and ritual as well as with the nature of burials; the latter introduce you to late forms of death rituals.

Certainly the exhibits of the Louvre are so unbelievably rich and magnificent that in most cases, with the exception of those exclusively showing grain and fruits, they also involve the most precious objets d'art. Since the high culture of Egypt apparently changed little over almost 3,000 years in this area, temporal development plays no great part, and objects from different times are found next to each other. Everything that was considered to be artistically outstanding was separated from the educationally displayed showpieces of the first floor. The presentation is chronological, and takes visitors from the prehistoric eras by way of the Old, Middle, and New Kingdoms down to the times of Persian domination and the Ptolemys.

The different areas are divided up to good effect: we encounter lifestyles illustrated by

Ducks over a clump of papyruses (detail), grave of Neferhetep, Thebes, middle of the 18th dynasty (Ca. 1450–1400 B.C.), first floor, room 5

pictures and maps in the first floor with its modern setting and in the other areas below ground level, but we encounter art in luxurious rooms on the second floor, the *piano nobile*. The most important items of Egyptian art partly occupy those rooms which King Charles X opened in 1827 after basic restructuring, and which had already been intended for the land of the Nile. So we look upward from the cases to impressive ceiling paintings with romantic visions of Ancient Egypt.

The stream of visitors is evidence of the success of this still quite new idea, which does not devote the whole area to art: visitors definitely do not gather around the art sections so much as around the cases containing items of everyday use. Objects which are thousands of years old, and models of ships and houses, peasants and servants, scribes and gods fascinate both the young and old. Interest wanes for many people on the second floor, possibly also because of the length of the route, which begins in room 20 with the oldest items of Egyptian culture and only ends in room 30 in Cleopatra's times.

The Egyptian department has two further tours geographically far apart that are devoted to burial customs in Roman times and the practices of early Christian monasticism in the Nile valley.

Since the educational parts can also be understood without reading the French notices, and this is a guide to art, we shall only include works that are artistically outstanding from the beginning of the route.

Egyptian Antiquities I

First Floor

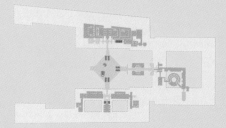

Basement

The Crypt of the Sphinx, page 110 f.

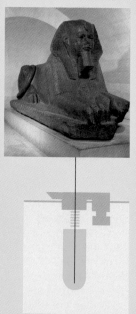

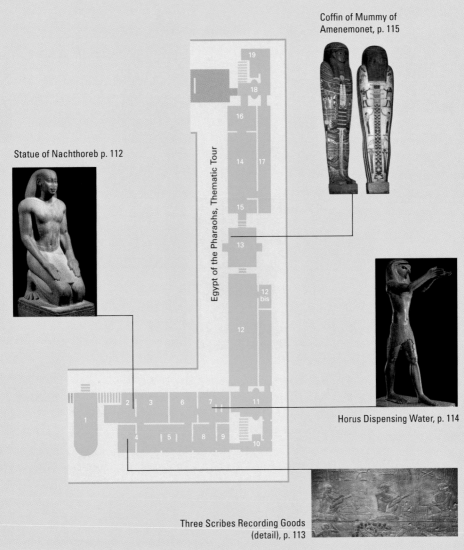

Coffin of Mummy of
Amenemonet, p. 115

Statue of Nachthoreb p. 112

Egypt of the Pharaohs, Thematic Tour

Horus Dispensing Water, p. 114

Three Scribes Recording Goods
(detail), p. 113

Second Floor

Pharaoh Djedefre, p. 124

The Triad of the Pharaoh Osorkon II, p. 136 f.

The Goddess Hathor and Pharaoh Seti I, p. 135

Other works:

1 Sepa and Nesa, 3rd dynasty, room 22, p. 122 f.

2 Funeral dance, end 18th dynasty, room 26, p. 135

Head of a Man, the "Salt-head," p. 132

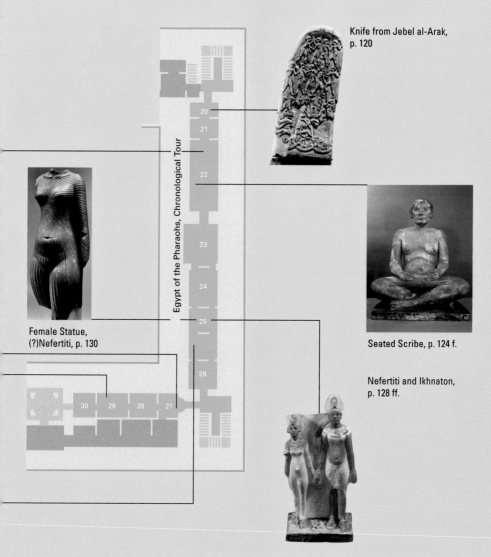

Knife from Jebel al-Arak,
p. 120

Egypt of the Pharaohs, Chronological Tour

20
21
22
23
24
25
26

30 29 28 27

Female Statue,
(?)Nefertiti, p. 130

Seated Scribe, p. 124 f.

Nefertiti and Ikhnaton,
p. 128 ff.

The Crypt of the Sphinx

No department in the Louvre has such an impressive entrance as the Egyptian one. From the excavations of the medieval royal palace, the path leads along the former moat toward a bend in which a rose-colored granite sphinx, far larger than life-size, sits on a block. Part man and part beast, it evokes the whole mystery of the Egyptian religion, yet the sphinx was already known as a mysterious creature in Greek myths.

Sphinx bearing the name of the King Amenemhet II, from Tanis in the Nile Delta, 12th dynasty (1898–1866 B.C.), but possibly from the reign of King Snefru (2620–2590 B.C.: beginning of 4th dynasty)
Rose granite, 183 x 154 x 480 cm

The Louvre possesses the largest perfectly preserved example of a monolith, that is an image of the sphinx carved out of a single block of stone. What was originally conceived as an enormous guardian to be placed before a shrine is today presented as an object of veneration. The lion's body lies in his barrel vault with a mysteriously illuminated apse, like a chapel, in such a way that no visitor can walk around him.

A sphinx is a creature that combines the head of a pharaoh with the body of a lion. Such monuments are usually marked with the name of a king, which can be seen on the tall rectangular curved surround; there is one just like this on the breast of the monument. For a long time people attached significance to the oldest decipherable king's name and thus linked the Louvre sphinx with Amenemhet II from the Middle Kingdom (1898–1866 B.C.). His name, in front of the right hind paw, was almost completely erased by later pharaohs who claimed the work for themselves: the names Apepi (ca. 1550 B.C.; a "Hykos" of the 15th Dynasty), Merneptah (1213–1203 B.C.) and Sheshonq I (945–924 B.C.) can be seen.

Since it is possible that the original name may have completely disappeared, many in the meantime have ascribed the Louvre sphinx to Snefru (2620–2590 B.C.). He was the first king of the 4th dynasty, which built the largest pyramid under Cheops (Khufu) (2590–2581 B.C.) and under Chephren (Khafre) (2558–2533 B.C.) produced the "Great Sphinx" of Giza. Reliefs on the walls which show Ramesses II (1279–1213 B.C.) in prayer before the "Great Sphinx" of Giza, and which Napoleon found between its paws demonstrate the great mystery that sphinxes had already represented for the Ancient Egyptians. While for the great pharaoh of the 19th Dynasty, a "Horus of the horizon" was apparent in the old image, and while the possibly even older Louvre sphinx had been newly inscribed over millennia, the entrance to the Egyptian section clearly shows how for Egyptians time and eternity were held in balance.

Life on the Nile

Statue of Nachthoreb,
from the Reign of Psamtik II,
26th Dynasty (595–589 B.C.)
Limestone, 148 x 46.5 x 70 cm

The image of a man keeling in prayer clothed only in a loincloth, follows the elevation of the pharaoh to a sphinx. It stems from the late period, shortly before foreign influences were also noticeable in Egypt. As a result of the constancy of type, form, and appearance of Egyptian statues it is neither stylistic criticism, nor expertise which determine the date but the inscription. Hieroglyphs run all around the base and tell us that this life-size work does not originate in the Old Kingdom, in spite of its quite archaic appearance. In accordance with older principles, the prince-priest Nachthoreb is depicted in prayer. For visitors he is a symbol of the eternal validity of Egyptian form and religion.

**Three Scribes Recording Goods (detail)
in the Mastaba Chapel of Achethetep,
Saqqara, 5th Dynasty (ca. 2400 B.C.)**
Painted limestone, height 35 cm

Because of the Egyptians' desire to take
their own life circumstances with them to
the grave and into the afterlife, we have a
wealth of knowledge about Ancient Egyptian life. In the burial chambers with their
false doors, in front of which sacrificial gifts
of the living were placed, the wall paintings
largely remained untouched in spite of
thefts from the tombs. The most important
occupations, from agriculture, animal hus-
bandry, hippo hunting, and navigation to
the trading of goods, are displayed on the
walls. Series of pictures such as this offer a
dominant canon rather than an individual
selection. The portrayal unfolds in several
rows one above the other. The scribes are
awarded special significance: three are
recording the goods, which are set up
behind them. Thus the dead are not only
taking the products and the pursuit of
them into the grave with them, but the
bureaucratic administration of them too.
Anyone familiar with the story of Joseph in
the Old Testament will understand just
how important good stock keeping was in
a country like Egypt. Incidentally, in a case
opposite the entrance, a small procession
of servant girls who are bringing goods to
the Mastaba's false door, as no doubt they
did in real life, is in keeping with the
museum's educational aims.

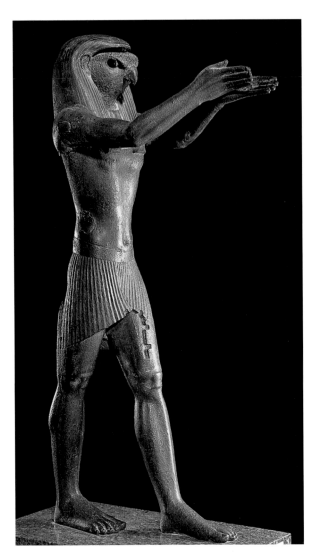

Gods and Death Rituals

**Horus Dispensing Water,
3rd intermediate period
(1069–664 B.C.)**
Bronze, height 99.5 cm

This statue of the god Horus with a falcon's head is the main exhibit in the exceptionally interesting section about the various materials and techniques. With both hands he is administering water to a pharaoh whom we have to imagine is illustrated beneath him. This dark bronze conjures up an almost uncanny idea of Egypt, which is deceptive in several ways: we have to think of the metal as being encrusted with colors and decorated with glass and gold; instead of the terribly empty eyes we see today we have to imagine the colors which brought out the dark magic from the sculpture. This magnanimous gesture calls to mind water as being a giver of life and purifying agent with which we are familiar later in the Christian rite of baptism.

Coffin of the Mummy of Amenemonet, 3rd intermediate period (1069–664 B.C.)
Cloth dipped in stucco, painted
187 x 48 cm

The legend of the dreadful murder of the god Osiris, whose sister-wife Isis reassembled his body, is part of the death ritual. Shrines in Abydos and Busiris expressed the memory of the god's body in various symbols which – as objects and pictures – were familiar to them: the Djed pillar (in Egyptian, "stability"), for example, a kind of tree stump in which the god's backbone could be seen. Accordingly, a cult object in Abydos has been interpreted as the head of Osiris. On coffins of mummies such as Amenemonet's, famous for its perfect condition, this symbol appears on the front, the pillar of Djed behind. Imitations of the objects painted on the cover have also been made as small souvenirs. Examples of these can be seen alongside the coffin.

With Napoleon in Egypt

by Matthias Seidel

Only seldom have the origins of an academic field of inquiry been so dependent on armed conflict over so long a period of time, as is the case with Egyptology. For without Napoleon's Egyptian campaign the famous "Rosetta stone," which provided the key for Jean-François Champollion (1790–1832) to decipher hieroglyphs, would probably never have been found. Alongside his military preparations, Bonaparte had also decided to attach an elite unit to his troops. This so-called Commission of Arts and Sciences of the Oriental Army consisted of 65 members from many different fields and with a wide diversity of qualifications. At first, for reasons of secrecy, the aim of the expedition was not explained to them. Napoleon was such a highly reputed figure that many of the scientists asked agreed to the adventure without giving it a second thought. After their arrival in Egypt and the speedy capture of Alexandria, the Corsican set off for Cairo with his army at a quick march. On July 25, 1798 in the so-called Battle of the Pyramids he was able to deal a crushing blow to the much larger army of the Mamelukes; and a

"Temple site on the island of Philae" from Description de l'Égypte, Paris, 1809–1828

little while later, on August 19, he founded the Egyptian Institute with its seat in Cairo. Its members immediately began some intensive work, which at first was not primarily devoted to the country's archeological remains. Yet, systematic research into the monuments of the pharaohs was to become the main task of the scientists of the Oriental Army. A painter and engraver who was also a talented travel writer took charge: he was Dominique-Vivant Denon (1747–1825).

In the autumn of 1798, Denon left Cairo for nine months to study the old monuments under quite difficult conditions in Upper Egypt. Back in Cairo, at an audience with Napoleon, he was able to interest him in his mission to such an extent that he immediately sent two groups from the Institute to Upper Egypt to study the antiquities. The extensive yield of plans, drawings, and sketches later formed the basis of the multi-volumed monumental work *Description de l'Égypte* with imperial format plates (108 x 70 cm). The publication was to take up almost 20 years (1809–1828) of his life.

Before Bonaparte left the land of the Nile on the frigate La Muiron in August 1799 he ordered the Julien Fort to be built to protect the town of Rosetta from the English and Turkish armed forces which had landed at Abukir. When digging trenches they accidentally came across an engraved basalt disc, the "Rosetta Stone." This extremely important object is today kept in the British Museum in London and not, as one might presume, in the Louvre. For in spite of many successful battles, the French could not in the end maintain their position in Egypt since they were cut off from their ammunition and

Léon Cogniet, Jean-François Champollion, 1831, oil on canvas, 73.5 x 60 cm, Musée du Louvre

catering supplies by the supremacy of the British fleet. In the capitulation of Alexandria (September 1801) the English army not only demanded the handing over of all the antiquities the French had amassed, but also all the documents of the Scientific Commission. But ambassadors from the Commission announced to General Hutchinson that they would rebel and throw the manuscripts and collections into the sea if he insisted on their handing over all the material. The Scientific Commission's protest was successful and the French were as a result able to keep all the drawings for the *Description*. However the works of art became British spoils of war.

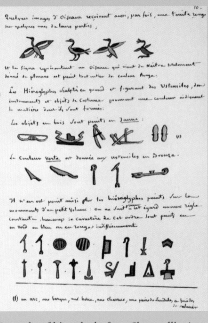

Examples of hieroglyphs from Champollion's "Grammaire égyptienne," 1836, about 18x27 cm

summer of 1809, at the age of 18, he was appointed assistant professor of history at the newly founded University of Grenoble. For political reasons he had to leave both the town and his post, and moved to Paris in 1821. With superhuman commitment he now directed his genius toward his life's work, namely unravelling the mystery of hieroglyphs. This he managed in September 1822. In his famous "Letter to M. Dacier," which could be described as Egyptology's birth certificate, Champollion published the basic system of hieroglyphs. He followed this two years later with more detailed proof in "Summary of the Hieroglyphic Script System."

The last decade of the scholar's life brought him further successes in his research into Ancient Egyptian culture, which showed him to be more than just a philologist and grammarian. Two trips to view the Italian collections and the great Egyptian journey of 1828/29 as a member of a French-Italian expedition gave Champollion ample opportunity to study the monuments, and allowed him to confirm that his deciphering was correct. In 1831, just a year before his death, the first chair of Egyptology at the Collège de France was instituted for him.

The scientific results of the Egyptian campaign, which also included copies of the Rosetta Stone, were to play an important role in a great achievement in the humanities during the 19th century. By this, we mean the deciphering of the pharaonic script, hieroglyphs, by Jean-François Champollion in 1822. He had already begun to study Oriental languages as a schoolboy, and his main interest lay in Coptic, the final phase of the Egyptian language. In the

The Rosetta Stone, Ptolemaic, 96 B.C., Granodiorite, 118 x 77 x 30 cm, British Museum, London

Knife from Jebel al-Arak, later pre-dynastic age (ca. 3150 B.C.)

Flint blade with hippopotamus ivory, handle: height 25.5 cm, width 4.2 cm

This stone knife with a magnificently carved handle stems from the pre-dynastic period. The side with the knob shows a lion-tamer, the other side two rows of warriors with ships beneath them, also in two rows and, between them in the water, dead bodies. There is no king portrayed and nothing can be deciphered from the writing. The figures are admittedly lined up in rows, but the clarity that is characteristic of the age of the pharaohs is missing in the confusion.

Stele of the Serpent King Wadj (Djet), Abydos, Thinitic period, 1st dynasty (ca. 2950 B.C.)

Limestone, 143 x 65 cm

The serpent is shown to be above a palace, and above that, in a much larger format, is the falcon of Horus. The very natural images of animals indicate like hieroglyphs the name Djet or Wadj, and also his office as pharaoh, in the symbol of the falcon. Monuments such as this document Egypt's history. According to the lists of pharaohs that have survived, the serpent king would have ruled between 2952 and 2939 B.C.

The Age of the Pyramids

Sepa and Nesa, Saqqara,
3rd Dynasty (ca. 2700–2620 B.C.)
Limestone, height 165 and 152 cm

The stylization which was to exist in later epochs was already true of these early kinds of monumental statues. The surface remains solid and block-like; the sculptor places a staff of office close to the body. But there is a liveliness about the facial features which paves the way for more individual portraits in the not too distant future.

Stele of Nefertiabet,
Giza, 4th dynasty (2620–2500 B.C.)
Painted limestone, 39 x 58 cm

This small valuable tablet in relief comes from the burial chambers under the great pyramids. Its theme was to be repeated for thousands of years: for in almost every Egyptian tomb there is a representation of the dead at table. But Nefertiabet, as the daughter or sister of King Cheops (Khufu), stands on the threshold of this development. The relief preserved in color is one of the few works to have survived from the period when the greatest pyramid was being built.

Seated Scribe, Saqqara,
4th dynasty (2620–2500 B.C.)
Limestone, rock crystal, magnesite, copper, height 53.7 cm

One of the most beautiful
works in the Louvre is this
seated scribe, who presents
us with a wonderful mix-
ture that hovers between a
faithful example of a for-
mulaic picture and an individual expression. The inset
blue eyes, which have lent
the man a lively expression
over so many thousands of
years, are made of copper,
rock crystal, and magnesite.
Distinctive facial features ensure that the
face remains unforgettable. The "scribe"
has only recently been dated as originating
from the time of the great pyramids, after
people had for a long time placed him in
the 5th dynasty and the rise of government
officials within the Old Kingdom at that
time. This statue is the most impressive of
the many figures from Ancient Egypt who
bring home just what an outstanding ability a knowledge of writing was in this early
culture. The ability to write qualified a person for high office because it was the main
means of administration and dealing with
the economy, and also played an important
role in religious life and rituals of the dead.
This scribe determined how people were
portrayed in Ancient Egypt for generations.

Pharaoh Djedefre, Abu Roash,
4th dynasty (2620–2500 B.C.)
Silicified sandstone, height 26.5 cm

Sometimes just one single representation is
enough to keep alive the memory of a king
about whom nothing else is known. This is
the case with Djedefre, the successor to
Cheops, whose father has been immortalized in the pyramid and to whose brother
and successor the Great Sphinx and countless other sculptures testify. From Djedefre's reign of almost ten years only this
head remains from an uncompleted temple
of the dead in Abu Roash. It is one of the
most subtle works of the early portrait
sculptures, whose sandstone appears hard
and shiny due to carbonization.

Middle and New Kingdom

Statue of the Pharaoh Senusret III (detail),
Medamud, 12th dynasty (1872–1853/52 B.C.)
Diorite, height 120 cm

Sculptures of the Ancient Egyptian kings were mostly not designed for them individually, but rather they embody their office without any indication of their age. But Senusret III had portraits erected in the temple of Month at Medamud which show the pharaoh in many different ways, sometimes, as in the example here, determined, youthful, and full of tension; sometimes also old and tired, with wrinkles; and finally as a lion with immeasurable strength.

Statue of the Toury,
18th dynasty (1550–1292 B.C.)
Red ebony on a karite base, 33 x 7 x 17 cm

Round curved shapes of uncommonly fine elegance are the particular distinguishing features of art under the reign of the Pharaoh Amenhotep III (1388–1351/50 B.C.). The statue carved in red ebony of a supervisor of the god Min's harem is an enchanting piece which already heralds the sensitivity of art under Ikhnaton. The detailed inscription on the base which at the same time contains prayers to Isis and Osiris also provides us with her name, so that here, too, the relationship to burial becomes clear through the deities of death.

Nefertiti and Ikhnaton

ascended the throne the worship of the sun god Amun-Ra dominated religious and political life. The successor to the throne bore the name of the god in his own name; he performed the religious ceremonies in Karnak near Thebes. In the fifth year of his reign, however, Amenhotep IV broke with the worship of the ancient sun god, and moved the royal residence further down river to Achet-Aton, a town founded by him which he then dedicated to the new sun god Aton. At the same time the Pharaoh adopted his name and from then on was known as Ikhnaton.

Under the name Tell el-Amarna in modern times the place became one of the most wonderful sites for Egyptian art finds. What had possibly begun as a court intrigue against the priesthood of the traditional god Amun-Ra developed an amazing dynamism in the history of spirituality. There is a hymn to the sun origi-

Head of a princess, possibly Bakhet-Aton, Amarna, 1351–1334 B.C., painted limestone, height 15.4 cm, 2nd floor, room 25

The most exciting chapter in Egyptian art is concentrated on the royal couple Ikhnaton and Nefertiti. Ikhnaton, later known as Amenhotep IV (1351–1334 B.C.), inherited the throne from his father Amenhotep III (1388–1351/50 B.C.) toward the end of the 18th dynasty. When he

Cosmetic spoon in the shape of a duck, 18th dynasty, length 32.5 cm, wood and ivory, 2nd floor, room 25

nating with Ikhnaton, the fundamental ideas of which are repeated in Psalm 104 in the Bible. An echo of this can still be felt in St. Francis of Assisi's hymn to the sun more than 2500 years later. From observing the sun and from the experience of its life-giving power all these texts find an inner enthusiastic vision of God which, in the case of Ikhnaton, begin with the words: "You look so beautiful in the light of heaven, O living sun, who first began to live."

Certainly only the pharaoh and the people closest to him approached the god Aton so directly; but a brief and far-reaching change in art was visible: artists who worked for the pharaoh made a complete break with the old conventions of viewing. The bodies of Ikhnaton and his wife Nefertiti no longer fit into the schematic

Nefertiti and Ikhnaton,
Amarna, 1351–1346 B.C.,
painted sandstone, height
22.2 cm, 2nd floor, room 25

conventional outlines: the gossamer-thin gown allows the buttocks and protruding stomach to stick out above spindly legs. Emaciated heads rise up very expressively on scrawny necks; and similarly spindly arms reach up to the sun, personifying Aton. Aton's rays have hands which reach down to the praying people in order to give them the keys of the Nile, the hieroglyphs for life.

This worship of the sun, in the center of which sit the pharaoh and his wife with their naked daughters, is conscious of the body. Even the faces change as if the new rites were exhausting them. Earlier, when Ikhnaton was still living near the Amun temple at Karnak, he was portrayed with a strangely gaunt face and deep lines around his nostrils. But the change is pleasingly complimentary to the women. The small torso in the Louvre that portrays the queen Nefertiti herself or one of her daughters is unforgettable. It makes an

Female statue, (?)Queen Nefertiti , Amarna, 1351–1334 B.C., dark- red silicified sandstone, height 29.5 cm, 2nd floor, room 25

archaic and at the same time avant-garde impression with its emphasis on fertility and the bold stylization of the material over the swelling body. Only the faces are ascetic in the Amarna period which was brutally ended shortly after Ikhnaton's death, during the reign of the unfortunate Tutankhamun by General Haremhab (see p. 134 f.) and the priest Eje. Luxury goods of the finest style, which are some of the most refined designs in the history of humanity, are the legacy of the rule of a strange pharaoh who raised his eyes to the sun and was given a completely new view of body and nature.

Bust of the Pharaoh Amenhotep IV, the later Ikhnaton, East Karnak, 1351–1346 B.C., sandstone, height 137 cm, 2nd floor, room 25

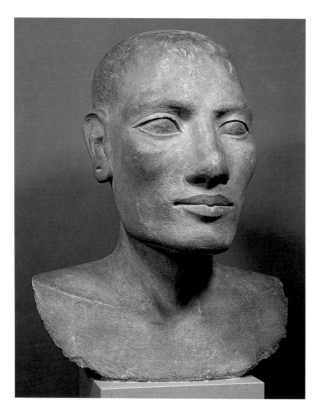

holds its own against many impressions. The fine asymmetries all lend the head, devoid of any indications of rank, an inimitable majesty. If indeed it is an Egyptian work at all then its creation would only have been possible after that turning toward nature which greatly inspired Ikhnaton and his artists and followers.

Amenemonet and his Wife Taka, Saqqara, end 18th dynasty (1337–1295 B.C.)
Painted sandstone, 56 x 66 cm

Toward the end of the 18th dynasty the capital was not moved to Thebes but to Memphis in Lower Egypt. With this, the old necropolis at Saqqara, which is still crowned today by the step pyramid dedicated to the 3rd dynasty pharaoh Djoser acquired a new significance. One of the finds from there is this painted sandstone relief that portrays Amenemonet and his wife Taka. In their gentle features the memory of Amarnan art is kept alive, even if conventional forms had been readopted, with their customary high reliefs, as a result of the return to worship of the old sun god Amun-Ra.

Head of a Man, the "Salt-head,"
(?)end 18th dynasty (1337–1295 B.C.)
Limestone with traces of color, height 34 cm

This nameless work, which previously one always had to search for, depending on the museum's director, was either exhibited in the pyramid age of the Old Kingdom or, as today, at the end of the 18th dynasty, and

Funeral Dance from the Tomb of General Haremhab, Saqqara, end of 18th dynasty (ca. 1330 B.C.)
Limestone, whole tablet: height 75 cm

The religious revolutions which were brought about by Tutankhamun's early death in 1323 B.C., as well as the threat from the Hittites, led to a strengthening of the army. Eje, a priest, was the first successor to the royal throne after the pharaoh's untimely death; Haremhab, who even under Tutankhamun had asserted himself as the most powerful man, inherited it in 1319 B.C. As the leader of the royal army he had already had a magnificent grave made for himself in Saqqara.

The Goddess Hathor and Pharaoh Seti I, Thebes, 19th dynasty (1290–1279/78 B.C.)
Painted limestone, 226.5 x 105 cm

Ramesses I and Seti I founded the 19th dynasty. It was at its height in the reign of Ramesses II, who is often associated with Moses, as if Moses had been rescued under Seti I. This relief tablet comes from his tomb in the Valley of the Kings near Thebes and shows him with Hathor. The goddess, ruler of the west and therefore of the dead, is offering the pharaoh her necklace. The exceptionally fine technique has led to a stylistic trend in Egyptian art named after Seti I.

The Late Age of the Pharaohs

Karomama, presumably from Karnak, 22nd dynasty (ca. 870 B.C.)
Bronze with gold and silver damascene, height 59 cm

Jean-François Champollion (1790–1832), the founder of Egyptology, regarded this statuette acquired in 1829 as the most beautiful of the Egyptian bronzes that portrayed the wife of Pharaoh Takelot II of the 22nd dynasty. In more recent times she has been presumed to be a daughter of Osorkon I (925/24 – ca. 890 B.C.) and thus one of those priestesses like the king's unfortunate daughter Aïda in Verdi's opera; the priestesses were kept chaste all their lives, possessed great wealth, and had an amazing influence on spiritual and political life. In the dedicatory inscription, the priest of Amun and guardian of the royal treasure, Iahentefnacht, is requesting that his mistress, Karomama, an admirer of Amun-Ra, and

the guardian of the crowns, should stay young and full of life. The bronze is covered with a filigreed inlay of silver and gold in a technique that is still referred to today as damascene.

The Triad of the Pharaoh Osorkon II, Tanis, 22nd dynasty (874–850 B.C.)
Gold, lapis lazuli, glass, 9 x 6 cm

Tomb robbers used to look in particular for items of value, which is why most objects of gold and silver, apart from the treasures of Tutankhamun, fell victim to them. One of the few excellently preserved pieces of Egyptian gold work is this trio of figures: Osiris, crouching on a pillar bearing the name of King Osorkon II, takes up the central position; the figures at the side, his son Horus and his wife Isis, are protecting the god. This very fine work which is in miniature, can quite easily stand comparison with all the magnificent works of monumental art that we have.

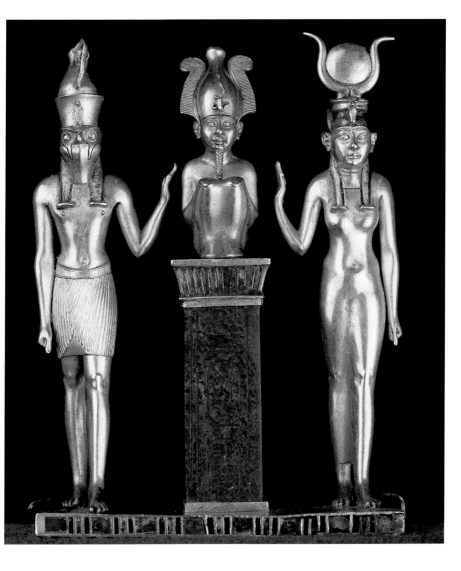

Egyptian Antiquities II

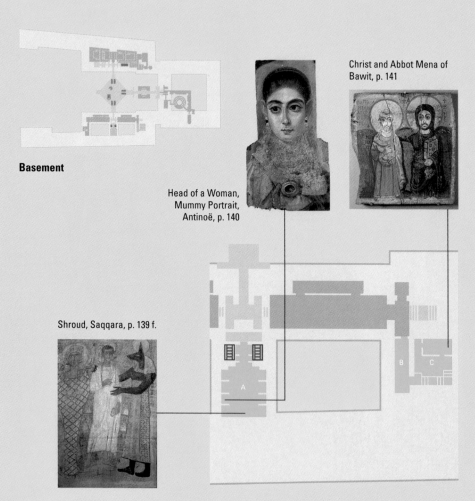

Christ and Abbot Mena of Bawit, p. 141

Basement

Head of a Woman, Mummy Portrait, Antinoë, p. 140

Shroud, Saqqara, p. 139 f.

Egypt under Roman Rule and in Early Christian Times

The Louvre takes us back to the Nile Valley in two places: anyone taking the entrance straight ahead in the Denon Wing in the basement is confronted with the burial rites of the Late Age in a small windowless section (next to the Denon café). After the integration of the kingdom of the pharaohs into the world of the Romans the worship of Isis and Osiris also found its way to Rome, while in Egypt itself foreign religions took root. The temporary domination by the Persians had already made some great kings of Asia into pharaohs. The Ptolemys, who ruled the country after the defeat by Alexander the Great, let go of their Greek tradition in a wise political move by combining the sun god Amun with the Olympian Zeus, in order to be accepted as pharaohs.

Under the Ptolemys the Egyptians maintained the burial rites for people and animals, but came to rely less and less on the effectiveness of embalming. Instead of the stylized faces on the great coffins of the mummified dead, which showed little individuality, they did paintings in wax, a technique known as encaustic. This created lively faces with a bright sparkle to the eyes, emphasized by the effects of light on the gold of the jewelry and their gowns.

In the Egyptian section of the Late Age in the Louvre there are also some exhibits of real mummies, sometimes only heads from

Shroud, Saqqara, end 1st century A.D.
(see following page)

Roman times that have been separated from the body. These have rather disturbingly found their way into the showcases unclothed, as the museum wants to show how a human head was covered with gold after it had turned black. This way of presentation is meant to be educational because the objects are not to be perceived as works of art but rather as documentary evidence of rituals and religious beliefs of the past.

**Shroud, Saqqara,
end 1st century A.D.**
Linen, painted
(see previous page)

The dead person, clothed in
a white robe that is reminiscent of the Roman toga (if it
is not one officially), appears
between the god of death,
Osiris, who looks like the
mummy of a king from a
past age, and Anubis, the
black-skinned, dog-headed
god of death. Anubis is em-
bracing the youthful man in
order to prepare him for life
after death.

**Head of a Woman,
Mummy Portrait, Antinoë,
2nd/3rd century A.D.**
Encaustic painting on wood,
42 x 24 x 1.2 cm

Only Greeks lived in the
town founded in 130 A.D.
which Emperor Hadrian
dedicated to his beloved
Antinous, who drowned in
the river Nile. The Greeks
of this town adopted mum-
mification. Their mummy
portraits testify to a new
sense of individuality and to
great artistic talent.

Christ and Abbot Mena of Bawit, 6th–7th century
Painting on wood, height 57 cm

The reconstruction here is suggestive of the church at the Bawit monastery. On the altar wall hangs one of the oldest representations of Christ, which shows Him accompanied by an abbot. To see this work, when at the *Torso of Miletus* (see p. 158), turn toward the Seine. In the basement of the Denon wing, walking past wonderful textiles and tiny objects fashioned out of ivory and wood, you come across a spacious architectural museum which incorporates fragments from Coptic monasteries in the Nile valley. Anyone finding their way here becomes immersed in a past which was of great worldwide significance: Upper Egypt in fact became the cradle of Christian monasticism, one of the oldest monasteries of which we still have the sculptural representation illustrated here.

Postclassical European culture has always, and almost everywhere, been conscious of its classical roots. People were acquainted with many more ruins from the past than are still visible today, particularly in the areas conquered by the Roman Empire. France is one of these areas – after all, to a large extent one can equate the region with the Gaul which the prolific Julius Caesar (100 – 44 B.C.) conquered before he rose to dictator. Paris was the Roman Lutetia and still possesses clearly visible ruins such as the Roman theater, the "Arènes de Lutèce," on the rue Monge, and the mighty vault of the thermal baths which today forms part of the National Museum of the Middle Ages in the Musée de Cluny.

The history on show in the Louvre itself does not stretch back to the time of the Roman occupation, but very early on the princely collections placed great value on classical works of art. After the Revolution, with the summer rooms of Queen Anne of Austria, with windows facing southeast, they chose a particularly beautiful and above all an extremely sunny area for the Roman and Greek sculptures, which today still contains items at least from the time of the emperors.

From its very beginnings the European art market has dealt particularly in classical sculptures, which were soon reconstructed so that figures deprived of noses and limbs were sometimes reworked by prominent

Venus de Milo (detail), ca 120 B.C.,
marble, height 202 cm, see p. 168

postclassical sculptors. To serious archeologists today these reworkings are intensely annoying. And so whole collections such as the classical sculptures in Munich and Kassel have been "purified," even though it was the Danish sculptor, Bertel Thorvaldsen (1768 –1844), who made the arms and legs in his workshop. In the Louvre, however, there is no capacity for such work since there are too many exhibits and the cost would be too great to remove all postclassical elements from its sculptures.

In the Roman Empire countless marble copies of Greek originals were relatively easy to obtain as art possessions. Innumerable copies of the works of Polyclitus (sculpting around 450 – 420 B.C.) or Praxiteles (4th century B.C.) were made in Rome; reproductions of this kind were used particularly for decorating the palaces of Roman nobles during the Renaissance. Marble copies formed the basic stock of all older collections of classical art; in possessing them the Louvre can offer a whole phalanx of reproductions of the same design and can prompt one to consider how the famous Athena sculpted by Phidias (working around 460 – 430 B.C.) may really have looked on the Acropolis in Athens.

In contrast to the royal collections of the Baroque age, as they are found in many smaller museums – one thinks of Dresden or Kassel – the Louvre possesses, along with the British Museum in London and the Berlin museums, the most extensive collection of original works (apart from those in the countries of origin) that came

to the galleries directly from the excavation sites and not through the art market. Huge and significant discoveries in the Mediterranean area have been made as the result of wars from Napoleon's time, the activities of diplomats interested in finding art treasures, and finally by state excavations by archeologists. Uncertain political relations in the 19th century assisted an exodus of important holdings that is deeply regretted today in the countries of origin.

The Louvre holds some extremely valuable finds such as silver from a villa in Boscoreale which was hidden under the lava after the eruption of Vesuvius in 69 A.D. In addition, there are some spectacular finds from the home country, Gaul. Only a very few places in the world can provide visitors with such a complete view of the culture of Ancient Greece and Rome as the Louvre. Some individual monumental statues are famous the world over, such as the *Borghese Fencer*, for instance, the *Nike of Samothrace*, and above all the *Venus de Milo*. Many works like the *Diana of Versailles* or the *Torso of Miletus* have their place in post-classical culture. They have either become familiar to educated people through reproductions, or they have been incorporated in literature and have thus acquired an active role in the development of human consciousness in general.

Torso of a kouros from Actium, Corinth or Naxos, ca. 570 B.C., marble, height 100 cm, basement, room 1

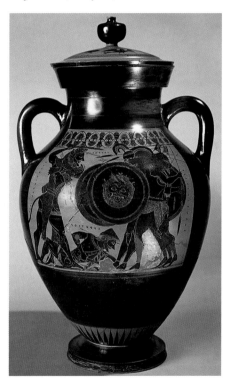

Exekias, amphora with black figures, showing the victory of Herakles over Eurystos from Oichalia, Athens, ca. 550–540 B.C., terracotta, height 46 cm, 2nd floor, room 42

Greek, Etruscan, and Roman Antiquities

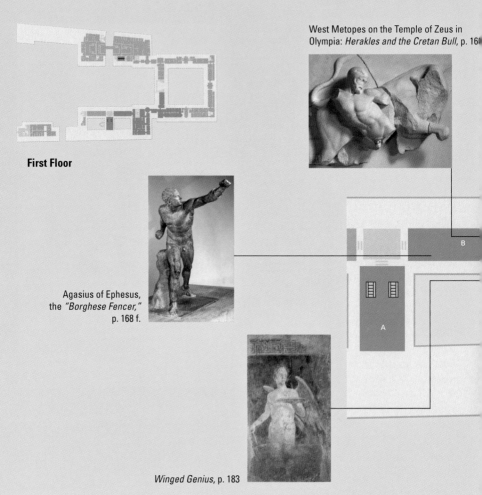

First Floor

West Metopes on the Temple of Zeus in Olympia: *Herakles and the Cretan Bull*, p. 16

Agasius of Ephesus, the *"Borghese Fencer,"* p. 168 f.

Winged Genius, p. 183

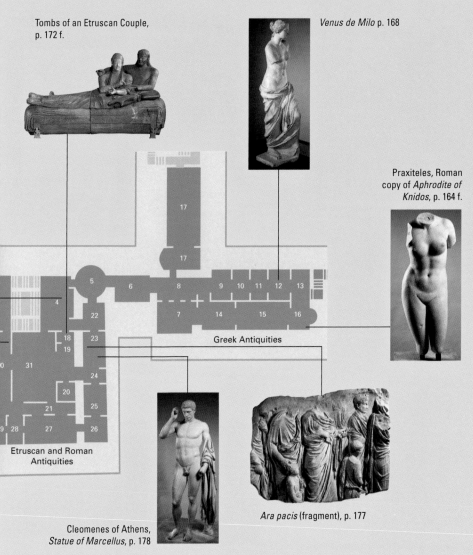

Tombs of an Etruscan Couple, p. 172 f.

Venus de Milo p. 168

Praxiteles, Roman copy of *Aphrodite of Knidos*, p. 164 f.

17

17

5

6

8

9   10   11   12   13

4

22

7   14   15   16

18
19

23

Greek Antiquities

31

24

20

21

25

9   28

27

26

Etruscan and Roman Antiquities

Cleomenes of Athens, *Statue of Marcellus*, p. 178

Ara pacis (fragment), p. 177

Torso of Miletus p. 158 f.

Basement

Euphronius, red- figure calyx krater, p. 155

Female statue, the "_Dame d'Auxerre,_" p. 150 f.

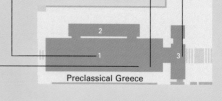

2

1

3

Preclassical Greece

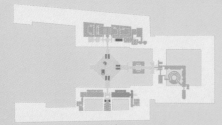

Bust of a Horseman, known as the "_Rampin Head,_" p. 156 f.

Other Works:

Head of a female statue, 2700–2300 B.C., room 1, p. 150

Other Works:

1   *Apollo*, 2nd century A.D., room 32, p. 188

2   *Medallion with Portrait of Constantine*, 1st quarter 4th century A.D., room 32, p. 187

Second Floor

Painter of the Niobids, *Herakles and the Argonauts*, p. 189

Nike of Samothrace, p. 166 f.

32

33

34

35   36   37   38

47   46   45   39   40   41   42   43   44

Greek Ceramics

Goblets with Skeletons from Boscoreale, p. 186

Beginnings of Greek Art

Head of a Female Statue,
Cyclades (Island of Keros),
2700–2300 B.C.
Marble, height 27 cm

In myth, art begins with Daedalus who builds the labyrinth on the island of Crete for King Minos. This was preceded by some extremely stylized works from the Cycla-

des. The basic convention and variations on it are clearly visible in the Louvre. The imposing marble head, suggestive of a lyre, comes close to modern formal ideas with its lack of any representation of the eyes. Only the nose is emphasized as a long, drawn-out trapezoid. The side view shows how sharply the shape projects from the surface and the position given to the ears. This head was part of the statue of a woman with her arms crossed over her breasts. The legs, whose feet are turned outward, are joined together. The whole sculpture, around 150 cm high, is one of the best-known works from the Cyclades.

Female Statue, the "*Dame d'Auxerre*,"
(?)Crete, ca. 640–630 B.C.
Limestone, height 75 cm

A puzzling work of art stands at the beginning of a row of sculptures of girls (known as the Kores) who are draped in gowns. The frontally displayed figure can only be traced back to Auxerre, a town in the west of Burgundy. In 1909, the Louvre made an exchange with the museum there for this work. There is no explanation as to how it had reached the Yonne from Crete. Thick strands of hair falling down over strong round shoulders frame the face with its broad shallow brow. While the left arm lies closely against the body, the right rests between the small breasts. From the pronounced and narrow waist a smooth skirt spreads out over the hips and legs down to

the ground, where sturdy feet are visible. Originally there would have been color in the engraved patterns on the skirt, this detail being revealed by the traces of red on the bust.

Hera of the Cheramys, Samos, ca. 570–560 B.C.
Marble, height 192 cm

Around the years 570–560 B.C. the Greeks had erected the "Heraion" on the island of Samos in the Ionian Sea as the first colossal temple. All votive sculptures for Hera, the consort of Zeus, that were used for ritual purposes had their heads removed during a period of iconoclasm. The women are wearing coats and veils over the tight chitons according to a strict pattern. Most of them hold a bird close to their body as a dedicatory gift. The monumental figures often name their donor in inscriptions; here, vertically and in large letters, it says, "Cheramys has presented me to Hera as a votive offering."

The Fragments of Archeology

Ceramics make up the largest part of the many remarkable examples of handicrafts. As a kind of index fossil, the fragments of simple vessels help to date archeological strata, because broken pieces reveal composition, shape, and decoration with some reliability – we only have to think of the contribution of fragments found in the course of the most recent excavations in the medieval Louvre. But from some periods we recover fragments of artworks of an amazing quality. This is true of Iranian vessels from pre-historic times (see p. 82), but the Greeks, as producers of pictures suitable for portraying myths as well as everyday life with vivid figures, were the first to discover ceramics. For centuries, therefore, not only have undecorated ceramics for everyday use been analysed, but also, and above all, that magnificent clay vessel, the vase, has served as a textbook for our knowledge of classical life and thought.

We can argue about the purpose of these richly decorated pots; presumably undecorated

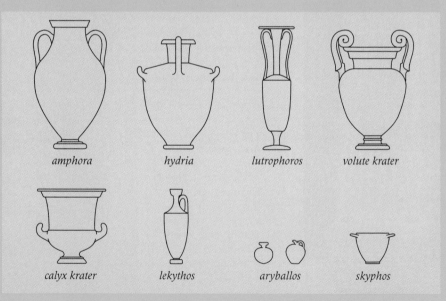

amphora   hydria   lutrophoros   volute krater

calyx krater   lekythos   aryballos   skyphos

earthenware was used for everyday life. Important pieces such as those found in the Adriatic port of Spina, for example, indicate the importance of such works for export. In Greece itself, the richest finds of artistically shaped vases come from tombs. These are not only typical of vessels obviously made explicitly for death rituals, but also ones used in everyday life.

Out of the large number of different shapes a few have survived into more modern times even if only in the endless flirting with classical Antiquity. The names which have taken root in postclassical times do not always tally with the original names. Neither do the shape and purpose always agree.

In classical Antiquity they called the water jug with two horizontal handles on the shoulder and a vertical handle on the back a hydria. Large vessels with no handle on the back, but with two handles on the shoulder which mostly sit vertically on the neck, but might also sit horizontally under it, were called amphoras; among other things, they were used for ceremonial oil for festivals and competitions. The mixed jugs with wide openings and a wide variety of shapes, perhaps for water and wine, are known as 'kraters'; their horizontal handles may be attached near the base or directly under the protruding lips. The definitions of smaller vessels that were used for scooping and drinking, the terms (stamnos, skyphos etc.) have already become somewhat confused.

Vessels such as the lutrophoros, that is a hydria with two or three handles, originally intended for the bridal bath, were used for rituals. In the classical age, love and death had quite a different relationship with each other than in Christian times; thus the idea of purification for marriage was connected with the preparation

Analatos, proto-Attic lutruphorus, Athens, ca. 690 B.C. fired clay, height 80cm

Vases from the Musée du Louvre, Galerie Campana; *1. Red-figure amphora, signed by the potter Andokides, fired clay, ca. 530–520 B.C., height 58 cm*

2. Red-figure skyphos, ascribed to the artist of Amasis, fired clay, ca. 540 B.C., height 11.5 cm
3. Column krater, Corinth, fired clay, ca. 600 B.C., height 46 cm

of the dead, and so the lutrophoros is also connected with the cult of the dead for both the married and the unmarried dead. Works in marble, probably made exclusively for the tomb, follow the early examples in the classical age. Uses for the lekythos and the aryballos, all-purpose vessels for oil in various sizes, can also fall between everyday use and tomb rituals. Painted with a white ground they were used above all in Attic burial rites.

Greek vases soon carried an important development in the history of surfaces for art – the individual picture area, which was not yet known in designs on walls. Areas for the depiction of figures on decorative surfaces were previously kept separate. In the early days, when the separation of decoration and picture was still fluid, artists preferred to portray specific rites. Thus the proto-Attic lutrophoros, a huge container used to scoop up water for marriage

or death ceremonies, shows a procession with a team of horses. But soon they were illustrating scenes of mythological events. Epic and later also dramatic poetry vessels dating from the 6th–4th centuries B.C. depict countless varieties of myths for which there is not always a text that has been preserved.

Many painters of vases took a decisive step toward what we today call art by signing their works. In no other area of Greek art were there any definite examples of works which could be placed in a definite timescale. There would be no really discernible oeuvre from an artist living before 500 B.C. if works of the masters, like the *Antaeus krater* in the Louvre by the Athenian, Euphronius, had not been signed beneath the main scene. At least between 520 and the beginnings of Athenian democracy, which began with the end of the dictatorship in 510, the work of this painter can be followed.

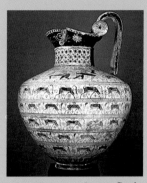

4. Black-figure hydria, Etruscan, fired clay, ca. 549–530 B.C., height 40.5 cm; **5**. *Calyx krater, signed by the artist Euphronius, fired clay, ca. 510 B.C., height 46 cm, basement, room 1*

6. *The "Oenochoe Levy," eastern Greece, fired clay, ca. 650 B.C., height 39.5 cm*

Even with the lutrophoros, made shortly after 700, it is thought possible to ascribe it to a known master, the Athenian Analatos. Geometric art still lives on in the dark-colored figures on a light ground. The figures are formed out of a few stylized shapes. But in the 6th century B.C., there develops an accurate reproduction of the body and attitude, which portrays objects and clothing in a way that no other medium was able to do in such a three-dimensional portrayal of life. At first, dark figures were put on a red ground as in the case of Exekias; from 530, however, they changed the colors so as to be able to portray the figures not as black shadows, but more realistically with a brown skin. Euphronius depicts Herakles in his battle with the giant Antalos as red figures set against a dark ground. In making the krater, the artist was faced with a problem of size which was to continue to affect surface painting from then on. He

had to portray his hero raising his opponent from the ground from which his mother Gaia is able to give him further strength. But there is only a flat square available as the picture area. It is worth looking more closely at the master's solution, then we can understand how archeologists reassemble worlds from fragments and remains of the past.

Archaic Art

**Bust of a Horseman,
known as the "*Rampin Head,*"
Athens, ca. 550 B.C.**
Marble, height 29 cm

The head, which is slightly inclined forward, is attached to a rather slim upper body; no lines are visible on the eyelids. The head is encircled by a crown of interwoven leaves, either oak, ivy, or celeriac. The thick curls wind around on the forehead; the beard adorns the chin like delicate pearls. The mouth is characterized by a smile that is familiar from the statues of the Archaic period, which lasted up until the Persian Wars of 490 and 480. The head was found on the Acropolis in Athens. Parts of the horse and body came to light later so that Paris and Athens were able to exchange casts.

A hole in the skull shows that there had been a disk placed above the head to protect it from birds. Therefore the statue of the rider was exposed to the elements, possibly together with a second one which has not survived. These might have been intended to depict the two Dioscuri, Castor and Pollux, or the sons of the Athenian tyrant Peisistratos, whose names, Hippias and Hipparchus, already link them with the horse (Greek: *hippos*).

**Funeral Stele with Floral Offerings,
Pharsalus, ca. 470–460 B.C.**
Marble, 60 x 67 cm

This powerfully poetic relief from Pharsalus in Thessaly has inspired the imagination and sculpture, particularly of the Art Nouveau period, since its discovery in 1863. Two women incline their heads toward each other to offer flowers; one of them also holds a little bag of seeds. This work comes from an outlying area, which probably accounts for its more stylized design. But the shapes of the peplos, the classical garments worn by the women whose folds swirl over the breasts, are nevertheless very delicately designed. Great care and attention have been given to the hair ornaments with the points in front of

Torso of Miletus, before 490 or probably ca. 480– 70 B.C. marble, height 132 cm, basement, room 3

On Viewing the Headless Body – Rilke's Sonnet
The Archaic Torso of Apollo

the ears.

For archeologists, the *Torso of Miletus* was a milestone in the development of Greek sculpture. Traces of burns supposedly proved that it was made before the Persian attack which reached the shores of Asia Minor in 490 B.C. In this case the mighty torso would be the first datable evidence of possibly the most revolutionary change in sculpture in the whole of humanity. We would be standing in front of the first work which made frequent use of the pose known as the contrapposto. With the artistic trick of moving the body's stance onto one leg while the other is free to move around, the forced repose of the statue is transmuted into a highly fluid drive toward motion that has stimulated European art since classical Greece. In the Louvre itself, a glance back to the torso of a kouros from Actium (see p. 144 f.) may illustrate just how much the portrayal of man has advanced with this pose.

The archeologists, admittedly, have undermined this nice certainty which attributes such a key role to the *Torso of Miletus*; all we really know is that the statue was already damaged in classical Antiquity and restored, finally to end up on the main façade, the *scena frons*, of the theater in Miletus. It is not even considered to be indisputably a Greek original. Yet looking at it from another angle the torso fills us with strong emotion. Rainer Maria Rilke (1875–1926), secretary to the French sculptor Auguste Rodin

(1840–1917), wrote this sonnet in 1908:

We never knew his legendary head
in which the eyeballs slowly ripened. Yet
his torso shines out like a street-lamp, set
in which his seeing gaze, compressed instead

maintains its steady gleam. Or else the breast's
sharp bow would never be so blinding
nor in the twist of loins a smile go winding
toward that point where generation rests.

Or else this stone, defaced, would never shine
under the shoulders' transparent decline
and would not glisten like a wild beast's skin;

and would not burst from all its faces, giving
light like a star: for there's no place therein
which fails to see you. Change your way of living.

At the center of every contemplation of art there is a reversal of the relationship: the work itself is observing the person looking at it. The headless giant retained in his body a countenance which cannot only smile, but out of the depths of time can call on the observer alienated from any religion to change his ways.

Classical Art

West Metopes on the Temple of Zeus in Olympia: *Athena and the Birds of Lake Stymphalus* and *Herakles and the Cretan Bull*, Olympia, ca. 460 B.C.
Parian marble, total surface originally around 160 x 150 cm

The sanctuary of Zeus and Hera is situated in Elis in the west of the Peloponnesus; from 776 B.C. the Olympic Games were held there every four years. From the 5th century B.C., figures of marble decorated the exterior of the building of the Temple of Zeus, which later collapsed in an earthquake. In 1829 the French made the first finds there; from 1875 to 1881 German archeologists successfully reconstructed the gables and also some metopes on the spot. They were greatly assisted by the detailed description of the classical author Pausanius, who wrote in the 2nd century B.C.

The Louvre possesses some important fragments from the six metopes on the front of the building. The metopes of Olympia depicted the twelve labors of Herakles, the son of the god Zeus and his mortal mother Alkmene, which he had to perform for his cousin Eurystheus. Different dimensions were to be incorporated into one picture format, which determined the form of the hero and excluded the far distance as well as the landscape. The battle with the Cretan bull which was devastating Poseidon's island can be understood in this way, because the struggle of the man with the strong animal fills the picture area in a thrilling way.

The killing of the birds of the Stymphalus Swamp, on the other hand, would have made a miserable impression; for Herakles chased these creatures, whose wings were equipped with feathers that functioned like arrows, out of the marshes with a rattle in order to shoot them later with a bow. The metope of Olympia depicts the peace after the fight: on a rock Athena receives the shot birds from the hero's hands as a token of thanks for her help. To portray a heroic deed in this way is a step in the direction of truly classical art.

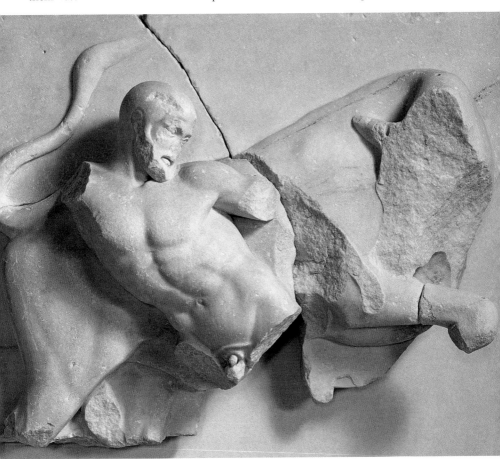

The Ergastins, Fragment of the Parthenon Frieze, Athens, 447–438 B.C.
Marble, 96 x 207 cm

The Parthenon's great sanctuary of Athena on the Acropolis was constructed in the period of peace between 447 and 438. A disjointed frieze of figures depicting the celebratory procession of the Athenians with sacrificial animals on the day of the Great Panathenaea encircled the huge temple. The figures move on foot and on horseback toward an assembly of the gods, which shows the Olympians on the same plane as the people. Of the 110 tablets, most of which are in London today, the Louvre possesses only one, unfortunately without a head, but nevertheless highly significant: the high point of the rite, celebrated every four years, was the handing over of a garment, a peplos, to the goddess Athena, by the Ergastins, the most noble virgins. They appear on the relief held in Paris, which was positioned directly alongside the main scene: from the right a woman walks in after hastily adjusting her peplos; she turns toward a companion who is on the adjacent tablet in London. She is holding a scented offering. Alongside this, two temple officials are receiving sacrificial gifts.

Nike from the West Gable of the Parthenon, known as the "*Laborde Head*," Athens, 440–432 B.C.
Marble, larger than life-size

The Louvre also possesses a very valuable fragment which comes from the west gable of the Parthenon; it has been so extensively reworked that merely by comparing it with the tablet from the Parthenon frieze on the opposite page we can see how much is lost when modern sculptors get their hands on such works. On this head, named after the noble Laborde family, which has produced some great scholars among its members, the nose, lips, and chin betray the intervention of a modern hand.

On Classical Nudity in the Museum

Ernest Hemingway (1899–1961) wrote a wonderful book about Paris, *A Movable Feast*, which only appeared posthumously in 1964. In it he tells us that he took Scott Fitzgerald to the Louvre simply because of Fitzgerald's doubts about whether his manhood was sufficiently well-endowed. He had examined the statues there – and continued to have doubts. It is hard to imagine today what a provocative, even stimulating impression a gallery full of classical statues must have made in a sanctimonious environment hostile to the body.

We can still feel something of this when looking at the *Venus de Milo,* which has justifiably become one of the magnets to attract the public. In accordance with its rank it stands in isolation, so that many people who have never been photographed with a nude woman in their life pose proudly in front of it. Not infrequently, one can observe young couples from those parts of the world where stricter moral codes hold sway basking in the magic of the classical goddess, as if publicly displayed nudity were the most natural thing in the world. It has not always been the case that nudity causes no offence. For centuries it did: the postclassical world destroyed such sculptures all too often out of moral indignation. They were an embodiment of pagan immorality in the eyes of the Church, but from a humanist point of view they showed the innocent purity of the human form that people thought was nearer to the Golden Age than was the present. The tradition about *Aphrodite of Knidos* illustrates that both views are not in accordance with classical

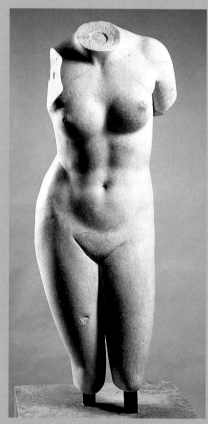

Aphrodite of Knidos, Roman copy after Praxiteles, 4th century B.C., marble, height 103 cm, 1st floor, room 16

sensibility. According to legend, her creator, the great Praxiteles (working ca. 370–ca. 320 B.C.), offered the residents of the island of Kos two statues of the goddess, one clothed and one naked. Faced with such a choice in Kos they preferred the demure version and let Knidos have the other, not suspecting that Knidos was to gain everlasting fame through the nude Aphrodite. Neither of the original statues have survived; the nude goddess has particularly been immortalized through copies. This demonstrates that nudity was not as natural to the Greeks as later generations thought when they saw Antiquity as an age of blissful or classical nudity. Ennobled by works of art, nudity was also able to remind the inhibited moralists either of an original state, from which they have irreversibly removed themselves both spiritually and in real life, or of the very center of their being, which is primarily physical. Hemingway's friend only uses the statues for a comparison with his own manhood; in so doing he does not feel the vital strength emanating from the bodies of powerful nude figures, even if they have faded or been robbed of beauty, and even if it were only a memory of better times.

Yet nudity also creates problems for archeologists, because it strips the figures of easily recognizable and datable signs, such as clothing styles. Thus they considered the baffling statue of Apollo, taken from the sea near Piombino (south of Pisa), to be one of the rare examples of Archaic kouros of the 6th century B.C. (cf. the *Torso of Actium*, see p. 144). But then they came across a similar work in Pompeii which was buried in 79 A.D. Since then people have credited early restorers, claiming to have read on a lead plate found with the statue the names of artists from Rhodes who were active during the 1st century B.C.

Apollo of Piombino, in the style of an archaic kouros, 1st century B.C., bronze, height 115 cm, 2nd floor, room 1

Nike of Samothrace (with detail),
Samothrace, ca. 190 B.C.
Gray Lartos marble for the ship,
light Parian marble for the statue,
height 328 cm (incl. wings)

In 1863, an enormous statue was discovered in thousands of pieces, on Samothrace, a little-known island in the north of the Aegean. It turned out to be purely a non-functional work of art overlooking the sea, and not a fountain figure as had been expected. On a ship's bow in dark stone the goddess Nike with her mighty wings rises up in gleaming marble. In her hands, whose fragments can be seen in a showcase, she held a trumpet; with this she was proclaiming a victory, but exactly which one is disputed. The work was linked with coins showing Demetrius Polyorketes, the besieger of cities (d. 283 B.C.), who conquered Athens in 307 and won a naval battle the following year near Salamis. Yet its style suggests that the figure dates from the age of the great Pergamon frieze that is known to have been made around 180–160 B.C. (now in Berlin). That would link this monument with the naval victory at Side in 190 in which Rhodes, allied with Pergamon, asserted itself against Antiochus III, the ruler of Syria.

Under Napoleon III (1808–1873) the architect of the Louvre at that time, Hector Lefuel, linked the historic wing of the Galerie d'Apollon and the Salon Carré with the new rooms built parallel to the Grande Galerie that today house the large 19th-century French paintings. In 1870, at the outbreak of the Franco-Prussian War, the site was still not finished. In 1883 the wing was completed and the *Nike* was finally given a fitting place in keeping with its importance. In 1934, however, the mosaic decoration in the wing, that had been applied during that period was removed, so that the ensemble now displays the international style which was so admired by Mussolini and the German National Socialists at that time.

Venus de Milo,
Melos, ca. 120 B.C.
Marble, height 202 cm

Ever since this life-size figure of an Aphrodite was found on the Greek Island of Melos in 1820, the assessment of Greek originals in comparison with Roman copies has changed radically. The extraordinarily delicate surface, and the characteristic harmony of form and expression, made the figure world-famous as the *Venus de Milo*. It comes from a Hellenistic workshop whose style can still be detected in other works displayed around it: the head known as *Aphrodite Kauffmann* has much in common. The relationship to a sculpture of King Mithridates VI, which must have been made around 100 B.C., proves to be more historically informative. The goddess of love is not completely naked, but her body emerges from the folds of her rich gown. In other words, not even in the case of Aphrodite did the Greeks consider the nude to be natural. The sculpture from Melos is the only well-preserved Greek statue of the goddess of love, and continues to enchant Paris and the world.

Agasias of Ephesus, Nude Fighter, known as the "Borghese Fencer," Antium, (?)ca. 100 B.C.
Pentelikon marble, height 157 cm

This most conspicuous sculpture, which appears to be guarding the room in which it stands, was restored at considerable expense in 1977. If tense composure was part of the classical ideal of a *Torso of Miletus*, then this figure is powerfully striving toward direct

expression. The work is famous as being on the borderline of aesthetic change. Its unclassical emotion was ennobled even for the stern critics because it originated in Antiquity. Found in the villa of Emperor Nero, in Anzio outside of Rome, the statue bears the signature of Agasius of Ephesus on the base, the son of Dositheus, and what is more it is made from the kind of marble used in Athens. Generations of artists used it as a yardstick: in the Louvre itself there are countless variants dating from the Baroque era up until the 19th century, in which the figure is lunging forward in a similarly dramatic way.

From 1611 this statue belonged to the papal Borghese family in Rome; in 1808 it ended up in Paris with other important works of the Borghese family, where it remained after 1815. The signature marks it as an original, yet Agasias himself very closely imitated a Hellenistic work from around 300 B.C.

Living Antiquities – or How a Fisherman Turned into a Philosopher

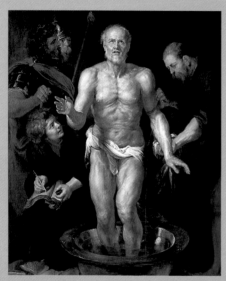

Peter Paul Rubens (1577–1640), Death of Seneca, 1608/9, oil on wood, 185 x 154.7 cm, Alte Pinakothek, Munich

Works of art without titles demand interpretations, occasionally acquiring greater significance than their creators had ever imagined. There is a general reluctance to believe that costly materials and artistic skill are ever employed in the service of an unworthy subject. In such cases, the art of interpretation helps create something unique from the banal, although the attempt to turn something banal

into a great work of art may in fact have been the source of that uniqueness.

It should not be forgotten, however, that there have been periods during which trivia had no place in art, and in which only weighty cultural or historical themes were considered suitable subjects for paintings. The humanist view of Antiquity, in particular, had difficulty comprehending the playful approach to reality that was widespread in the late art of the Greeks. In the period known as Hellenistic, art was able to abandon divine and historical images and give serious consideration to genre painting. Ernest Hemingway's novel *The Old Man and the Sea* (1952) was not the first example of an anonymous old fisherman becoming the subject of a work of art. In Roman times, a life-size copy of a Hellenistic original was executed in precious black marble and alabaster. An old man stands erect, gazing into the distance, his eyes opened wide as though he has seen something terrible. The figure was conceived as that of a fisherman, standing up from his work to look out over the water; for practical reasons he is unclothed apart from his loincloth.

The figure was found as a fragment, without feet, but otherwise with the man's naked expression of horror astonishingly well preserved. It has recently been displayed as it was mounted for the Roman Borghese: on a sumptuous vase of purple veined stone, the old man rises from the impressive basin with powerful thighs. According to this 17th-century interpretation, the subject is Seneca (4–65 A.D.), the philosopher who, as tutor to the emperor Nero, criticized his government and was forced by imperial order to commit suicide. He was obliged to open his veins himself, and climbed into a tub of warm water to do so, as this early 17th-century montage shows – albeit in a remote corner of the vestibule in the Denon wing, which for many generations housed the museum's cash tills and is now a graceless passageway.

Thus it was that a restorer, no doubt at the instigation of scholars in the entourage of Cardinal Scipione Borghese, created an image of the philosopher that was to endure for centuries, his composure intact despite the horror in his eyes. Confronting his own mortality, he collapses in such a way that he will bleed to death in the tub. This was excellent material for a period in which a lively interest in ancient history was still being expressed. Peter Paul Rubens (1577–1640), who visited Rome shortly after the discovery, took up the theme and painted a picture in which the figure of the Hellenistic fisherman, representing the philosopher, is surrounded by pupils who are unable to achieve the stoical composure of the more experienced man.

Fisherman in a montage portraying the dying Seneca, date of origin uncertain, restored in Rome shortly after 1594, in black marble and alabaster with a ram's-head vase of purple marbled stone, first floor, room A

Etruscan Art

**Tombs of an Etruscan Couple,
Cerveteri, ca. 530–510 B.C.**
Fired clay with traces of color, painted wood,
obsidian or molten glass, 111 x 194 x 69.5 cm

Alongside the Olympian metopes stands
the most magnificent example of Etruscan
sculpture; this is an ideal starting point
from which to approach the genuine Italian world through Roman art, which did
not confine itself to copying the Greeks.
This is the most imposing example outside
Italy of the culture of the Etruscan people,
who, from their native Tuscany, helped
shape the destiny of Italy before Rome
became a world power. This work probably
dates from the end of the regal period in
Rome, which was superseded by the
Republic, following the killing of Tar-
quinius Superbus by Brutus in the year 510
B.C. However, this gigantic clay sculpture,
which has only recently been restored, is
not of Roman origin. The memorial group
is distinctly different from the now distorted ideal of classical marble sculptures,
which were painted in bright colors and
adorned with decorative accessories when
they were first created. The fashion of the
times is reproduced with enormous care in
this work, all the details of which are of
interest to folklore and classical enthusi-
asts. The ensemble is composed of several
parts, with the ears and hands clearly
added. The brown-skinned man and his

paler wife were intended to appear as lifelike as possible, so the figures have eyes in
which the irises and pupils are made from
painted wood with obsidian or molten
glass. Tombs with sculptures like these
have never been found anywhere outside
Etruria; nevertheless, as far as scholarly
archeologists are concerned, such a unique
work would be unimaginable without the
influence of the Greeks. These images are
therefore thought to be inspired by works
from the coast of distant Ionia.

The Queen's Summer Residence as an Archeological Museum

One wing of the palace lies at an angle to the Seine, comprising a series of rooms with ornate ceilings decorated with paintings and stucco. The windows open onto an area of grass, left in an unkempt state by more than a decade of constant building work, which divides the section of the building around the Cour Carrée from the road along the river bank. Nevertheless, there is a wonderful view over the Pont des Arts and the Ile de la Cité, including the Pont Neuf, which dates from the time of Henry IV. These rooms are spared the fiercest heat of the day, since the bright sunlight falls on them from the southeast; as a result of this, it is very easy to dream of the Mediterranean in this particularly pleasant atmosphere.

Anne of Austria (1601–1666), the wife of Louis XIII and mother of the Sun King, once resided here, and it was for her that the decorations, which are no longer completely intact, were created. The rooms were designed in 1655–1658 by the architect Le Vau, who worked in conjunction with the sculptor Michel Anguier and the painter Romanelli. The latter artist worked alongside the most famous Roman Baroque painter at that time, Pietro da Cortona (see p. 22 f.), on his picture of the triumph of Rome. As a result the decorative, Roman style of these ceilings, which survive in their entirety, were known to be impressive throughout Europe before Versailles was built. The subjects of the colorful ceiling paintings are taken from Antiquity, resulting in a harmonious relationship with the sculptures, even though this was hardly the original intention. It was, in fact, only as a consequence of the Revolution that the queen's summer residence became a museum for antiquities. In various stages of the transformation the wall decorations disap-

Madeleine Gobbot, Salle des Saisons in the summer apartments, with pillars seized by Napoleon in Aachen, late 19th century, oil on canvas, 38 x 55 cm, Musée du Louvre

peared, and the Salon de la Paix in the center was enlarged by replacing walls with antique granite pillars, brought from Ravenna to Aachen by Charles the Great, then by Napoleon from Aachen to Paris, where they have since remained. The final room, known as the Chambre de Parade or the crown prince's apartments, was extended on the south side between 1798 and 1800 by Jean-Arnaud Raymond, the architect responsible at that time, with the result that classical paintings by Philippe-Auguste Hennequin are juxtaposed with Romanelli's High Baroque ceiling paintings. The purpose of the extension was to engineer an appropriately grand opening to the right into the adjoining large room built by Louis Métezeaux in 1595, during the reign of Henry IV. Initially, this room was used to receive ambassadors, and was therefore called the Salle des Ambassadeurs, but it rapidly ceased to be used for this purpose and became instead a key element in what would later be the museum. In the mid-17th century, as the Salle des Antiques, it housed the royal collection of antiquities, which was considerable even then. After the Sun King's withdrawal to Versailles, it became a courtroom, still named with reference to Antiquity. The *Belvedere Apollo*, which Hubert Robert had imagined in the ruins of a future Louvre in 1796 (see p. 264 f.), was moved here after 1800. After the fall of Napoleon, however, the most important pieces returned to their usual places.

In 1865/1868 this room, which had for a short time housed the most famous Roman statuary, was named the Salle des Empereurs by Napoleon III, boldly drawing a parallel between his family, the Bonapartes, and the Roman

Giovanni Francesco Romanelli (1610/11–1662), Diana and Antaeus, 1656/57, fresco, first floor, room 23

emperors. The entire Parisian stock of imperial portraits from ancient Rome was assembled here until very recently. The 200 years that passed between the time of the queen's apartments and the final attempt to stake an imperial claim have barely left a mark. There is an impressive mixture of styles, with the ceiling in the Baroque section clearly showing the influence of Anne of Austria, while the walls, painted in Pompeii red provide a strong contrast. However, the assembled gods in the ceiling painting by Louis Matout did not give the last emperor their support for very long.

Roman Art

**Altar of Domitius Ahenobarbus,
Rome, ca. 100 B.C.**
Marble, 152 x 56.5 cm

This enormous ensemble, consisting of four slabs, three of which are now in the Glyptotek in Munich, belonged to Cardinal Fesch, Napoleon's uncle. It may possibly have once served as a plinth for a monumental statue such as Phidias' statue of Athena in the Acropolis. The scene depicts a procedure that was central to the republican constitution of ancient Rome, and that was abolished in the year 107 by Marius: the scribe on the left-hand side is making a note of the oaths sworn by individual citizens during the assessment of wealth on which the level of their contribution to military costs was based. There follows a cleansing ritual, in which animals to be sacrificed to Mars, the god of war, are led three times around the assembled Romans. Roman art frequently provides a much livelier insight into the life and customs of the times than that of the Greeks, laying the foundations for less elevated art forms in subsequent eras: this altar decoration constitutes a true genre scene as became familiar in much later works.

Ara pacis (fragment),
Rome, 13–9 B.C.
Marble, height 120 cm

A quite different aspect of Roman military life is captured by this monumental altar to peace, erected by the Senate for Augustus following his victorious return from Gaul; a reconstruction in Rome gives us an impression of the original. However, some fragments of outstanding quality were lost due to the trade in antiquities. By this means, the section showing the official celebratory procession arrived in Paris with the Campana collection in 1861. There are spontaneous allusions to works from the height of the classical Greek period, such as the Parthenon frieze, in the way the bodies are molded and in the delicate folds of the garments. The heads of the boys, in particular, identify its origins as being during the reign of the first emperor.

Cleomenes of Athens, *Statue of Marcellus*, signed, Rome, ca. 20 B.C.
Marble, height 180 cm

Greek artists were held in high esteem in Rome; they signed their works with pride, regardless of whether they were working in their homeland for the new masters of the Mediterranean world, or in Italy itself. An increasing tendency toward idealization crept into the rigid tradition of portraiture of republican Rome, in which age and ugliness were very ruthlessly captured; this is demonstrated by the sharply defined heads of Caesar, of which the Louvre has a fine example. The ultimate effect was to distance portraits from the real world, while at the same time portraying naked figures from the entourage of Augustus, especially after their death, in heroic pose. For example, Marcellus (ca. 43–23 B.C.), the prematurely deceased nephew of the emperor, was portrayed as the orator Hermes in a life-size nude study by an Athenian artist. Augustus himself kept alive the memory of the youth, promoting a kind of cult that grew up around him. The extent to which imperial Rome adopted Greek ideals is shown by the sheer number of examples. The otherwise obscure Cleomenes depicted the Roman youth in the style of the statue of Hermes that was erected by the city of Athens to honor the fallen after the defeat at Koroneia in the year 447 B.C. The sculpture, which was discovered in 1590 on the Esquiline hill in Rome, was initially in the possession of Pope Sixtus V.

Statue of Augustus,
Velletri, head ca. 20 B.C.,
body mid-2nd century A.D.
Marble, height 207.4 cm

Like Julius Caesar, we are familiar with Augustus Caesar (63 B.C.–14 A.D.) from his portraits. There is a certain similarity due to the hairstyle, which the first emperor no doubt deliberately emphasized with the full intention of appearing young and vigorous, and at the same time there is a clear family resemblance. This famous statue was found at Primaporta and now stands in the Vatican: the commander, blessed by the goddess Venus, is shown in shining armor. The head of the figure in the Louvre, which originates from Velletri, corresponds exactly with the example discovered at Primaporta. The exact reproduction of a specific physiognomy was obviously considered important. Now, however, Augustus is wearing a toga, which provides us with a clue when interpreting imperial portraits such as these. The figure, which at first glance appears intact, was in reality assembled at a much later stage. Close inspection of the stonemason's work reveals that a head of Augustus, probably from the period shortly after the death of the emperor, was incorporated a hundred years later. The new statue, probably fashioned during the reign of Hadrian (117–138), shows a figure in a toga with no armor.

Sarcophagus of Ariadne,
St.-Médard d'Eyrens, Gironde, from the city of Rome or the south of France, 220–240 A.D.
Marble, height 208 cm

Death and burial played an enormously important role in ancient Roman culture. Sarcophagi were decorated with extremely diverse subject matter, designed to make death appear more comforting, or to help overcome it. The muses, for instance, make the transition from life to death easier; as a

result they are frequently seen on such reliefs. Many myths promise that those who believe themselves lost are nevertheless saved; it is for this reason that Ariadne, the daughter of Minos, king of Crete, often appears on graves.

Abandoned on the island of Naxos by the ungrateful Athenian hero Theseus, she is set free by Dionysus, the god of wine. Like the king's daughter, who had helped the hero to find his way out of the labyrinth, the dead are assumed to be in a hopeless

situation. The image of Ariadne shown on the sarcophagi is linked to the dead person, buried under the stone, awaiting resurrection. There is no mourning or embarrassed silence here: on the contrary, the figures are extremely lively. Dionysus, who is to be seen standing on the right alongside the crouching centaur, and his wild, dancing entourage fill the air with noise, while Ariadne, who is awakened by them, appears to be almost a subsidiary figure in the overall design of the sarcophagus.

The *Sarcophagus of Ariadne* is one of the most beautiful works from the reign of the emperor Severus, distinguished by the fine handling of detail and the flowing movement, but above all by the expressive power of the heads. Discovered in 1805 near Bordeaux, this marble sarcophagus shows that there were antiquities of outstanding quality, in no way inferior to those from Rome, which either originated in France or which might have been imported into the province from Rome.

Salon des Empereurs

Hardly a trace of the glory of imperial Rome remains in the Salon des Empereurs today. It is one of a series of rooms that span the period of great triumphs and the period of decline in the 4th century. At the same time, it presents the transition to early Christianity in Rome: the Christian sarcophagus, center right, is an astonishing demonstration of the speed with which Christian imagery, dominated by the figure of Christ, was assimilated in the sarcophagus.

The covered inner courtyard that adjoins the Salon des Empereurs provides a suitable location for some huge floor mosaics. There is enough space here for monumental statues, and the frieze from the temple of Megara has been mounted on the walls. The west wing of the surrounding gallery then affords views of the paintings and mosaics as though they were decorations in an elegant Roman house. The subject matter is extremely varied; in addition to mythology, motifs taken from everyday life are increasingly regarded as worthy of representation. They provide a history of the origins of still-life painting, without yet having the status of autonomous works of art.

Winged Genius,
Wall Painting from the Villa of Fannius Synistor, Boscoreale, ca. 60–40 B.C.
height 126 cm

Very few examples of Greek painting, which is repeatedly extolled in the literature of antiquity, have survived. However, discoveries of paintings from Roman times provide glimpses of what it must have been like, since they are in some cases assumed to be extremely accurate reproductions of older paintings. The discoveries made in the vicinity of Vesuvius are particularly significant in this respect. The eruption of the volcano in the year 79 buried individual villas and entire cities such as Pompeii. Among the most astonishing finds were the treasures discovered in Boscoreale, including this painting of the *Winged Genius*, who appears against quite a neutral background beneath a rigidly defined meandering design. The figure appears to have been arrested by chance in mid-movement; the light falls from the left onto his naked body, so that his outstretched forearm and the shallow bowl, in particular, cast a striking shadow. Because of the lighting, the wings, which are in shadow, provide a wonderful illusion of freedom.

From Dancing and the Court to the Institut de France and Diana – the Room of the Caryatids

A king needs a palace for three reasons. In the poetically named Great Hall, the king ate, entertained his guests with dancing, and held court. Rooms like this were often completely renovated for banquets; today, the dance floors are barely distinguishable and the throne itself stood little chance of surviving several hundred years. However, the musicians' quarters and the architectural framework of the court, if built in royal style, were not so easily removed. We must visualize this in the hall of the old Louvre, which Pierre Lescot designed for Henry II between 1546 and 1549. Its name is derived from the Mannerist caryatids – female figures used as architectural supports – created in 1550 by Jean Goujon. He shows them without arms, as described by the Roman architect Vitruvius, writing in the first century B.C., for whom the famous caryatids of the Erechtheum in Athens were already a distant historical phenomenon.

No artist in ancient times would have produced caryatids for the purpose served by the

View from the throne of the ballroom, with caryatids and Cellini's Nymph, first floor, room 17

figures here. In the Louvre, they support a rostrum for the musicians, who played dance music. They appeared in public view in the hall in front of the *Nymph*, 1543/44, which Benvenuto Cellini (1500–1571) created for Fontainebleau. In 1849, this major Italian Mannerist work was replaced by a painted plaster cast by the animal sculptor Antoine-Louis Barye, because Hector Lefuel needed the original as a focal point for the staircase of the Pavillon Mollien; it can still be found there today, as a serendipitous, but nevertheless appropriate accompaniment to Italian sculpture. The hall was not used merely as a ballroom; opposite the caryatids is the royal tribune, featuring another basic motif of classical architecture, two timberwork sections supported by pillars, and spanned by an arch. It was not until the 16th century that Sebastiano Serlio (1475–1554) and Andrea Palladio (1508–1580) defined this form as "serliano," or the Palladian motif, adding a final touch of imposing grandeur to feasts and court sessions.

In 1639, Lescot's wooden roof was in danger of collapse; Jacques Lemercier had to replace it with broad arches. Once again, the newly restored hall could look forward to an era of great splendor: Molière (1622–1673) staged plays there for Louis XIV, such as *Le Médecin Amoureux* in 1658. In addition, sculptures that remained in Paris after Louis had moved to Versailles were assembled in this room. Another event of historical importance occurred in the Salle des Caryatides in 1795: the founding of the Institut de France, incorporating the French Academies as well as various important foundations. This national institution was based here until 1806, when it crossed over to the opposite bank of the

Diana of Versailles, Roman copy of a Hellenistic variant of an original by Leochares from the 4th century B.C., marble, height 200 cm, first floor, room 17

Seine. As the hall had been built by Henry II, one of the most famous statues in France, *Diana of Versailles*, had been placed in the center, a rather romantic reference to the king's lover, Diane de Poitiers. The statue of the goddess of hunting, who is clothed and casual in appearance, looking over her shoulder while leading a deer, has been subjected to extensive reworking in modern times. This work – which stood in the park at Versailles before it was moved to the Salle des Caryatides in the Louvre – has done more than most to shape the notion of the gods of Antiquity over the centuries.

Treasures of Antiquity

In order to reach the most precious items discovered at the villa in Boscoreale, it is necessary to climb the staircase on the left, passing the *Nike of Samothrace* on the way, then enter the Salle Henri II, the combined dressing room and antechamber of the king (1547–1559). The heavy wooden ceiling in the early 19th-century Renaissance style is resplendent, and adorned, surprisingly, with paintings of birds by the Cubist Georges Braque (1899–1963), which in 1938 replaced paintings by Merry-Josèphe Blondel (1781–1853) dating from 1821/22.

This transitional room, which served as a meeting room for the Academy of Sciences between 1699 and 1793 and for the Academy of Arts in 1795, now houses amazing antique treasures. There are glass wall cabinets containing bizarre montages, which are seldom illustrated, created by Luigi Valadier (1726–1785) in around 1780, and incorporating ancient gems carved from semi-precious stones. The really sensational items, however, are from around Vesuvius.

**Goblets with Skeletons,
Boscoreale, end of 1st century B.C.**
Silver

Archeologists uncovered more than 100 well-preserved silver implements in the ruins of a villa at Boscoreale, which also

contained works that were priceless from the point of view of the history of painting in Antiquity. The cache is distinguished by incredibly fine work of an amazing sculptural quality, which provides a unique glimpse of Augustan culture. The magnificence is accompanied by death, in the form of the macabre skeleton. Bronze and precious metal fill the spacious room, built by Lescot in 1551–1553 over the Salle des Caryatides on the first floor. This room, the central room in the original plans for the royal apartments, has long since been stripped of its original décor. Because of the many outstanding works of different sizes, a longer stay in this section is easily justified. The works on display range from sculptures such as the *Apollo of Piombino* (see p. 165) to discoveries made in France.

Medallion with Portrait of Constantine, first quarter of the 4th century A.D.
Gold, 9.2 cm in diameter

This piece provides evidence of the cult surrounding the emperors, even on the threshold of the Christian era. Around a golden coin bearing the image of Constantine the Great, struck in Sirmium near Belgrade in 321, is a perforated plate of pure gold in which six heads were originally mounted; one of these has been broken and is missing. Together with four other pendants, now scattered all over the world, this work forms a series that the emperor probably presented as a mark of recognition to some eminent dignitary. There is an artistic contrast between the low relief traditionally used in making medallions and the fully rounded miniature heads.

The Bronze Room

Apollo, Lillebonne near Rouen, 2nd century A.D.
Gilded bronze, height 190 cm

This slightly larger than life-size figure of a naked Apollo, which was found in 1823 in the theatre at Lillebonne, located at the lower reaches of the Seine near Rouen, testifies to the richness of Roman culture, even in the vicinity of Paris. It is the largest antique statue of a deity to have been found on French soil. Apollo, the god of health and prosperity, was originally shown with a lyre, an unmistakable link with the Greek classical period in the 4th century B.C.

The Museum of Charles X and the Campana Collection

Charles X established the museum that bears his name in the southern wing of the building surrounding the Cour Carrée. It was fitted out with cabinets that have largely survived, and as a result it still conveys an impression of those marvelous rooms crammed with treasures from various epochs, all kept behind glass. According to the Baroque tradition, the ceilings were decorated with paintings and stucco, in order to reflect adequately the greatness of the sovereign. Not long after its official

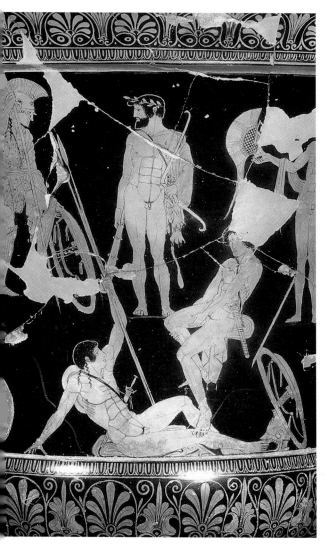

opening in 1827, however, came the July Revolution of 1830, after which personal references to the hapless King Charles X were largely expunged. As a result, the romantic notion of the role of France in the world of art, captured in a few paintings, is all that is left today. The best ceiling painting, Ingres' *Apotheosis of Homer*, has now been replaced by a copy, so that the original can be hung on the wall among the large-scale 19th-century paintings, contrary to the original intention of the painter. Terra cotta from Tanagra and the almost incredible number of vases in the Campana collection today occupy a space alongside Egyptian art. There must be few places in the world today where it is possible to gain such a magnificent overview of excavated painted vases.

Painter of the Niobids, Herakles and the Argonauts or Herakles in Marathon (detail), Athens, from Volsinii (Orvieto?), ca. 460–450 B.C., painted fired clay, height 54 cm, second floor, room 43

Sculptures

Nowhere in the Louvre is the change from the original purpose of the rooms in the museum as apparent as in the two galleries housing Italian sculpture. The utilitarian architecture of the basement indicates that it was destined for a quite different purpose from that of the magnificent first floor. The gallery now devoted to Donatello was once a stable; the horses negotiated the different levels by means of shallow, wide steps in the courtyard.

Above is the magnificent Pavillon Mollien, built by Héctor Lefuel from 1857 onward and named after one of the ministers of Emperor Napoleon I. Its first floor incorporates the Michelangelo gallery, from which an imposing staircase leads up to the French monumental paintings. The very great expenditure involved was justified on political grounds, for both the gallery and the staircase served during the reign of Napoleon III as an entrance to the Salle des Etats. The original of Cellini's gigantic bronze relief of the *Nymph of Fontainebleau* (1543/44) has an even more commanding presence here than does the plaster cast above the musicians' gallery in the Salle des Caryatides, where the original once stood (see p. 184 f.).

Previous pages: Hubert Robert (1733–1808), Imaginary View of the Grande Galerie des Louvre (detail), oil on canvas, 65 x 81 cm, Musée du Louvre

Michelangelo Buonarroti (1475–1564), The Dying Slave for the tomb of Julius II (detail), ca. 1513, marble, height 229 cm, see text on p. 205

The section begins with the monumental Armenian stone cross from the 12th or 13th century, a reminder both of early Christian art and its use of religious symbols as ornamental devices. After walking past a few medieval sculptures from Italy, one swiftly enters the Renaissance. In this section, the sensitive style of Donatello (ca. 1383–1466) is given expression in a particularly beautiful way in the various bas-reliefs, while Michelangelo (1475–1564) and his *Maniera* are celebrated in the gallery above. The Louvre has a large number of works of great interest for both the materials used and their state of preservation: the Renaissance style is by no means exclusively interesting to lovers of marble or bronze. The use of color gives the effect of alienation, as does heavily veined stone; papier-mâché is used in imitation of marble. A great virtuoso effect is produced by many of the works, while the variety of subjects is impressive. In the works of the Louvre, less emphasis has been given to the Madonna as the essential subject for sculptors, though major works by Donatello and Jacopo Sansovino (1486–1570) are indeed devoted to her. Portraits are prominent; some of these clearly owe much to ancient Roman tradition, of which there was increasing awareness among intellectuals due to the influence of humanism. Sculptors of bronze and stone then turned to the subject matter of Antiquity, such as the story that inspired Canova's work, *Cupid and Psyche*, and to Christianity. However, only Michelangelo was able to unite the physical and the spiritual.

European Sculpture since the Middle Ages

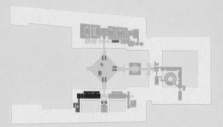

Basement

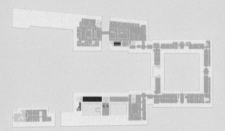

First Floor

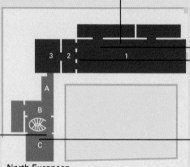

Jacopo della Quercia,
Madonna and Child, p. 199

North European
Sculpture
12th–16th
Centuries

Gregor Erhart,
St. Mary Magdalene, p. 213

Other works:

1	Nino Pisano, *Mary*, mid-14th century, room 1, p. 198
2	Dietrich Schro, *Count Palatine Ottheinrich*, ca. 1558, room C, p. 215

Donatello, *Tondo of the
Madonna*, p. 200 f.

Michelangelo Buonarroti,
The Rebelling Slave for
the tomb of Julius II,
p. 205

Jacopo Sansovino,
Madonna and Child,
p. 206

Unknown Florentine master,
Portrait of a Woman, p. 203

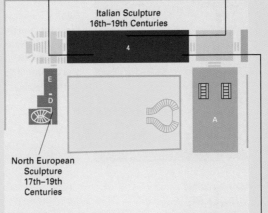

Italian Sculpture
16th–19th Centuries

4

E
D

North European
Sculpture
17th–19th
Centuries

A

Tilman Riemenschneider,
The Annunciation, p. 214

Antonio Canova,
Cupid and Psyche p. 211 f.

The Sculptures in Lefuel's Stable – From Late Antiquity to the Early Renaissance

Roman or Byzantine sculptor,
(?) *Empress Ariane*, ca. 500
Marble, 27.5 x 22.8 x 23 cm

During late Antiquity, the human image was largely suppressed in favor of the ornamental. This is demonstrated in the small number of monumental figures that are in existence, in which a great deal of effort was always expended on decoration: in this work the wide-open eyes, which originally had colored irises, stare out from the head of a woman. The tight-lipped mouth is drawn in at the corners, the expression conveying either an air of superiority over all onlookers or a marked concentration on a higher being, the Deity himself. This is undoubtedly a portrait, but identifying the subject remains problematic. Possible candidates, in addition to the Empress Ariane (464 – 515), also include Lecenia Eudoxia and Amalaswintha, daughter of Theoderic the Great, king of the Ostrogoths.

Central Italian sculptor, four figures from a
***Descent from the Cross*: Christ, St. John the**
Evangelist, Nicodemus, and Joseph of
Arimathea, Umbria or Lazio,
2nd quarter of the 13th century
Wood, dimensions of Christ: 183 x 123 x 43 cm

Like the French Romanesque period, the early Italian department in the Louvre is dominated by the monumental image of the Crucifixion. The relationship between the figures, on which the *Christus Courajod* from Burgundy is also based (see p. 222 f.), is easier to see here: two men are standing on the ground, preparing to lift down the body of Christ. They are joined by Saint John, his hands raised as if about to grasp the left hand of Christ; in order to do so, however, he would need to be higher and nearer to the cross, which has been lost. The message conveyed by the gestures of the Savior is curious: he appears to reach with outstretched arms toward those who are praying, in an expression of love and recognition.

Nino Pisano (ca. 1315 – before 1368),
Mary, **from an Annunciation group,**
Pisa, mid-14th century
Originally polychromatic wood, height 182 cm

Tuscan sculpture took a great leap forward
in the late 13th century, especially in Pisa,
where the artists acquired new modes of
expression as a result of their interest in
Antiquity and their contact with the French
Gothic style. These innovations preceded
subsequent upheavals within painting; the
painter Giotto (ca. 1266–1337), may have
been inspired by such art.

The Annunciation of the birth of Christ
to Mary is a subject that is well suited to the
talents of these sculptors. In the most subtle of variants, two examples of which can
be viewed consecutively in the Louvre, the
sequence of events can be interpreted: the
larger than life-size figure of Mary, which
was perhaps intended to have been accompanied by the figure of an angel that now
stands in the Cluny museum in Paris, conveys the impression of an astonishingly
silent, attentive listener, consenting with
some hesitation to God's plans for salva-
tion. All the original color has now been
leached away from the figure, making it
more attractive for purists; it is reminiscent
of one of the greatest works in Pisa, Nino's
Annunciation Group at the entrance to the
chancel in the Dominican church of Saint
Caterina. The effect of the elegant curve of
the slightly turned figure is Gothic, perhaps hinting at the art and sculpture of
French cathedrals.

Jacopo della Quercia (1374–1438),
***Madonna and Child*, Siena or Bologna, ca. 1425**
Polychromatic wood, height 178 cm

The step from Pisano's statue, which has only fairly recently lost its color, to della Quercia's *Madonna* may at first glance seem like a step backward, for this Madonna wears a white coat with a green lining, draped over her head and blond locks like a hood, over her scarlet dress. The plump child is standing, somewhat shakily, on her knees. The colored stripes in the white cloth in which he is wrapped are reminiscent of Jewish weaving.

The work is flat, like a relief, larger than life-size, and curiously soft. However, it has such enormous sculptural power, that after contemplating it for a while one realizes why no less an artist than Michelangelo admired this Sienese sculptor, 101 years his senior, more than practically any other of his forebears. The Florentine had become familiar with della Quercia's work on the doors of Bologna cathedral, where he executed monumental reliefs depicting scenes from Genesis.

Della Quercia, who despite his Sienese origins also became involved in the artistic life of Florence, persisted with the old forms, while Donatello, a Florentine who was 12 years his junior, was more aware of the upheavals of the early Renaissance. Donatello's feeling for form is more pronounced; however, the works by Donatello in the Louvre have a rather bizarre quality.

Donato di Niccolò Bardi, called Donatello (ca. 1386–1466), *Tondo of the Madonna***, ca. 1440**
Terra cotta with wax models behind glass, partly restored, 74 x 75 x 7 cm

The attribution to Donatello of several works in his style is a matter of contention, despite the fact that the artist lived a soli-

tary and eccentric life with no traditional studio. For this reason, there is no consensus that the tondo in the Louvre is exclusively his work, especially as it is a highly unconventional devotional picture: glass discs are assembled like window panes, and afford a view of a wax model with antique amphorae and heads of angels against a red background. Mary is seen to be in silent adoration of her child, which she has apparently laid to sleep on a couch in front of her. Although the head and body of the mother are swathed in quite a heavy fabric, she nevertheless has a powerful physical presence. There is in the tondo, a premonition of the Passion from the pain discernible beneath the lowered eyelashes, while at the same time there is an allusion to heaven in the figure of the Christ child, who is playing with the circlet and bird held in his hands.

Donato di Niccolò Bardi, called Donatello,
***Madonna of the Villa Vettori* in the Val d'Elsa, Florence, ca. 1440**
Terra cotta, gilded and painted,
102 x 74 x 12 cm

Following its recent restoration, the sumptuous golden brilliance of this relief depicting the *Madonna* by Donatello from the Villa Vettori comes as a surprise. Since by that time a pure gold background was no longer entirely acceptable on aesthetic grounds, the sculptor placed a curtain behind his figures, which he could decorate with a similar amount of gold. He placed the larger than life-size figure in profile and turned to the left, on a throne adorned with equally sumptuous gilding. The child is looking in the same direction, as if there had originally been a second relief showing worshippers that would have formed a diptych in conjunction with the existing one. However, it is perfectly possible that Donatello was merely concerned with the emphatic effect. Nakedness is alternated very skillfully with clothing.

**Mino di Giovanni, called Mino da Fiesole
(1431–1484), *Dietisalvi Neroni*, Florence, 1464**
Heavily veined marble, 57 x 52 x 34.6 cm

A number of younger contemporaries of
Donatello are worthy of mention. Along-
side the delicate figures by Desiderio da
Settignano (ca. 1430–1464) in the Louvre,
Mino's rather unkempt-looking portrait of

Dietisalvi Neroni (1406–1482) stands out.
This now largely forgotten humanist had at
first sided with the Medici faction, but was
then obliged to move to Rome. This bust,
which bears a detailed inscription, is one of
Mino's key works, meriting a reference in
Giorgio Vasari's *Lives of the Most Excellent
Italian Architects, Painters, and Sculptors*, a
work that was written between 1550 and
1568. Immediately on top of
the irregular plinth, as in an
antique bust, we first see
part of a cloak, tied at the
right shoulder. Pivoting, as
it were, on this knot, Dietisalvi turns to the left, gazing
out majestically from skillfully carved eyes. The un-
ruly locks that are falling
over the furrowed brow, the
bony jaw, and crooked face
are all really an invitation to
the sculptor to improve his
subject's appearance. However, Mino seems to have
been striving for a rugged
effect, even in his choice of
coarsely veined marble, an
approach which is quite in
keeping with the ideal of
fidelity to man that is fundamental to Florentine humanism; together with the
drapery and with the lively,
spirited expression, Mino's
work invests ugliness with a
certain dignity.

Benedetto da Maiano (1442–1497),
Filippo Strozzi, **Florence, 1476**
Marble, 51.8 x 56.7 x 30.3 cm

This noble bust, a portrait of Filippo Strozzi (1426–1491), cost 15 florins in 1476. The patriarch of a Florentine family is wearing a typically Burgundian costume, with his hair styled in the fashion of the Caesars. The sculptor was undoubtedly required to reproduce the features faithfully, but a hint of pretension may have crept in. This classical countenance with its flattened eyeballs is redolent of a new style of art with an orientation toward Roman portraits.

Unknown Florentine master,
Portrait of a Woman, **called "***La Belle Florentine***," second half of the 15th century**
Wood, painted and gilded, height 55 cm

Occasionally, even in the most striking works, there is no indication either of the artist or the subject. This applies in the case of this important wooden bust, the sumptuous colors of which are in stark contrast to the cool marble works of the early Renaissance, a reminder that color and a lifelike quality often played an ambivalent role in older art. This bust has been attributed both to Francesco di Giorgio Martini, a Sienese artist who worked in various media, and to Desiderio da Settignano.

The Galerie Mollien: from Michelangelo to Canova

Michelangelo Buonarroti (1475–1564),
***The Rebelling Slave* for the tomb of Julius II,**
ca. 1513
Marble, height 209 cm

The Galerie Mollien is today renowned for the forms of two men, larger than life-size, one of whom appears to be freeing himself from his bonds, while the other is reaching out with closed eyes, as if waking up, or making a final feeble stand against death. These statues are known as the *Rebelling Slave* and as the *Dying Slave* (see p. 192). Michelangelo created them for the tomb of Pope Julius II (1503–1513), which was originally intended to have 40 statues, but in the end had only five sculptures, including the *Moses*. In 1544, Michelangelo presented the unfinished slaves to Roberto Strozzi, a Florentine living in exile, who in turn gave them to King Francis I. The figures symbolize the soul freeing itself from the fetters of the body; one of them is still rebelling against his bondage, while the other has loosened the bonds still visible on his left arm. Neoplatonist thinking is thus combined with the Christian concept of death, in which the soul is released from the body – its earthly prison.

Old photograph of the Galerie Mollien

From Glass Eyes to Papier-mâché Marble –
The Materials of Sculpture

Jacopo Sansovino (1486–1570),
Madonna and Child, ca. 1500, painted
cartapesta, 143 x 106 cm, first floor, room 4

Followers of Alonso Cano, St. Francis in Death,
Seville, ca. 1650, walnut, glass eyes, bone teeth,
hemp cord, 87 x 26 x 25 cm, basement, room 3

Francis, who has a belt made from real hemp cord. The dead saint was portrayed in an immensely lifelike manner, supposedly as seen by Pope Nicholas V in the grave at Assisi in 1449. This frightening figure comes from Seville, where today life-size wooden sculptures, dressed like dolls, are still decorated and carried through the city in Holy Week. No other branch of art is so full of life and artifice as modeling and sculpture, which usually reflect something that does not exist in reality. The larger than life-size relief from Venice is as white as marble, and has been finely gilded. The large volume of printing carried out there

In no other branch of art are the materials used as varied as in sculptural works. The Louvre does not possess any of those holy pictures, thought to have miraculous powers, that have real hair, but it is frequently true that the more pious the purpose of the picture, the more curious the materials used. There are figures with glass eyes and teeth made of bone, such as St.

resulted in a great deal of waste paper, from which papier-mâché, or its precursor, cartapesta, was made. Printing waste was thus recycled as marble.

In their playful tactics, employing one material to masquerade as another and using reality to shock, Renaissance and Baroque sculptors were following an established tradition. We are

familiar with classical statues in shimmering white marble, apparently clothed in "noble simplicity and calm grandeur," the men and gods of antiquity gaze at us through eyes of stone.

Woman with Vessels, replica of a tanagra figure from the period around 320, 3rd century B.C., terra cotta, painted and gilded, height 32 cm, second floor, room 32

Rare attempts to add color, at least to the eyes, alarm us, as in the case of the Hellenistic fisherman who was metamorphosed by Rubens into Seneca (see p. 170 f.). Once, however, all these cold marble figures were just as colorful as is suggested by the terra cotta figures. Colorful effects were occasionally even achieved on bronze, to which paint did not adhere, and sometimes the figures were dressed in real clothes.

Polyclitus, Amazon, Roman copy in the manner of Sosikles of the lost bronze, ca. 440–430 B.C., only the head and torso antique (tunic substituted for short skirt for Cardinal Mazarin (1602–1662)), marble, slightly larger than life-size, first floor, room 14

Adriaen de Vries (1545/1560–1626),
***Mercury Robbing Psyche*, 1593**
Bronze, 215 x 92 x 72 cm

There have been few representations of Psyche being robbed by the god Mercury, even though this concerns the happier ancient myth of the attraction of Cupid, the god of love, to the beautiful Psyche. She is only allowed to touch Cupid in complete darkness, and must never look at him; however, she finds a lamp, loses her love, and only finds her way back to him after protracted wanderings. Dating from about the same time as the version in the Louvre, Adriaen de Vries created another sculpture based on this mythological subject that is now in Stockholm, in which Psyche is borne aloft by Cupid's followers. These are the oldest works by this artist, a native of The Hague. In Florence, the Dutchman had been taught by Giambologna (see p. 548); indeed, the latter's Mannerist style is evident in the serpentine, spiraling movement of the group, exhibiting the characteristics of what is termed the *figura serpentinata*.

The figures are considerably elongated; the eye glides over the smooth, polished bronze surfaces. In 1648 the group, created for the Prague court of the emperor Rudolf II, was one of the spoils of war seized by Protestant Sweden from Catholic Bohemia. However, thanks to Christina, the Catholic queen of Sweden, the bronze arrived in France soon after, in 1654, where it stood for a time in the royal parks of Sceaux, Marly (see p. 244 f.), and Saint-Cloud, before finding a place in the Louvre next to Michelangelo, whose style the Mannerists imitated.

Gianlorenzo Bernini (1598–1680),
Cardinal Richelieu, 1640
Marble, height 34 cm

The entrance to the glass pyramid of the Louvre is graced with the cast of a work by Bernini, who himself stayed in Paris in 1665 as a result of his failed quest to produce his own plans for the design of the palace, during which time he also produced portraits of Louis XIV. While still in Rome, during the time of Pope Urban VIII (1623–1644), Bernini made this striking bust of Cardinal Richelieu (1585–1642). The Flemish painter Philippe de Champaigne (1602–1674) had painted the powerful minister of Louis XIII (1610–1643), not only in the great state portrait in the Louvre (see p. 380), but also in a famous half-length portrait painted for the sculptor's use, showing the cardinal from three distinct sides (now in the National Gallery in

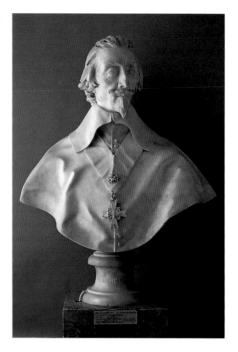

London). This painting was also used by Francesco Mocchi (1580–1654) for another bust, now in Niort. Bernini's virtuosity is evident in the expression on the face with its jaunty beard; the rendering of the Cross of the Order of the Holy Ghost (see p. 550 f.) is masterly. Bernini has left one of Richelieu's button undone, in keeping with the concept of faithful reproduction of life, also evident in his rendering of the hair, for which the sculptor used a deep boring technique borrowed from Antiquity.

Attributed to Antonio Corradini (1668–1752),
Veiled Woman – (?)Faith, **second quarter of 18th century**
Marble, height 138 cm

Faced with the famous centers of European art and the great names, we frequently overlook the unusual; this, however, is what is revealed in the Michelangelo gallery. The identity of the creator is unknown, as is the identity of the subject: a beautiful woman with her face veiled, and her hands the only exposed portion of her body, as she stands lost in thought. The sculptor appears to have put in a great deal of effort in order to unite antique, Renaissance, and Baroque elements in his art: the garment is a peplos, the ties of which are loosened, with the result that the breast and navel can be clearly seen instead of billowing folds. The debt to Michelangelo is evident in the folds around the legs. The virtuosity of a Bernini is apparent in the surface, into which the sculptor has carved deeply. One has only to think of the sombre veiled figure in the *Isle of the Dead* by Arnold Böcklin (1827–1901), produced nearly 200 years later, to be convinced that this is a study of death. However, this piece, acquired only recently, is usually interpreted as a personification of faith. In the context of the Enlightenment, the veiled countenance would have been almost subversive in its suggestion of the inability of the believer, and by logical association the Church, to look the world in the eye.

Antonio Canova (1757–1822),
Cupid and Psyche, **1793**
Marble, height 155 cm

When viewing the winged Cupid as he bends tenderly over the awakening Psyche to kiss her, one should discard everything one has learned from older sculptors. The artist penetrates the dark night, in which Psyche is forbidden to look at her lover, in order to reveal something invisible, sharply illuminating the paradoxical nature of art: indiscreetly, we see what is not meant for human eyes, and take pleasure in the play of light on the fine marble. The hard stone appears ethereal. This work has undoubtedly inspired a great deal of kitsch; but the prospect of the spirit, endowed with muscles, and love reaching out to it in a moment replete with tension, is irresistible. Canova's world was very different from the world in which Michelangelo found it necessary to use unusually tall men to portray the body as the prison of the soul.

The important collection of sculpture from the German-speaking countries is one of the most underexposed at the Louvre; for decades it was beautifully displayed, but was closed to the public owing to a shortage of attendants. Now it has been allocated new, well-lit rooms, but these are still somewhat remote and all too easy to miss. For this reason, the collection is again open only on an occasional basis – usually Sundays and holidays. However, in recent years France has rendered an outstanding service in acquiring new knowledge of such works.

Martin Hoffmann (active in Basle from 1507–1530/31),
***Madonna* from the Antonite Komturei at Isenheim in Alsace, Basle, ca. 1510**
Lime wood, 172 x 76 x 49.5 cm

This work is attributed to a sculptor who has only recently become known following an exhibition in the Louvre in 1997 that was devoted to this magnificent *Madonna* from Isenheim, and to the artist, Martin Hoffmann, his identity having been discovered from documents. The artist's legacy included no other comparable work; he was the best exponent of his art in the Basle area, although here, as in Strasbourg, the majority of works fell victim to the iconoclasm of the Reformation. The sculpture in Paris was originally from the famous Antonite knightly order, which possessed the most moving old German

painting, the great altar done by Matthias Grünewald (ca. 1460/1480–1528). Martin Hoffmann's *Madonna* in the Louvre casts light on the whirlwind that was sweeping through old German sculpture. Above the crescent moon that is largely hidden by the edge of her cloak stands the mother of God displaying her plump child, swathed in opulent drapes covering the base of the sculpture and lending grandeur and dignity to her appearance.

Gregor Erhart (ca. 1465/1470–1540),
***St. Mary Magdalene*, called "*La Belle Allemande*", Augsburg, ca. 1510**
Lime wood with old polychromy, 177 x 44 x 43 cm

The naked human body is extremely rare in old German sculpture. For this reason, this life-size statue of a woman, preserving her modesty with her long mane of hair, is quite sensational. The subject is St. Mary Magdalene, who did her penance far from civilization, on Mont Ventoux in Provence. German sculptors have often portrayed her, but none has succeeded in creating such an astonishing work as this, which even minus the feet, now restored, remains impressive. Art has often played the role of ambassador between countries, and Gregor Erhart's finest work, *St. Mary Magdalene*, is known and loved in France as the "beautiful German girl," *La Belle Allemande*.

Tilman Riemenschneider (1460–1531),
The Annunciation, from the
church of St. Peter in Erfurt,
ca. 1495
Alabaster, 53 x 40 x 19 cm

The key to a better understanding of the great artists who express feelings for their native land is often found in foreign collections. Tilman Riemenschneider, who from his native city of Würzburg helped to shape the Romantic tradition, and stood in opposition to his prince bishop in the Peasants' War, is now regarded as typically Franconian. Yet this master did not acquire his skills on the river Main, or in Nuremberg using lime wood, but in Thuringia, working in alabaster. This is illustrated by the delightful statuette of Mary, from an *Annunciation* scene in Petersberg, near Erfurt. A strong impression of the characteristic technique of the artist, and his delicate, late-Gothic ideal view of figures is conveyed very well by this early work.

Dietrich Schro (documented 1545–1568),
Count Palatine Ottheinrich, **ca. 1556**
Alabaster on colored marble, with inlaid
medallion dated 1556, 15.5 x 15.5 x 16 cm

Ottheinrich of the Palatinate (1502–1559)
enlarged the library at Heidelberg to such
an extent that it was coveted by the papacy

at the beginning of the Thirty Years' War.
The medallion and the material of the cube
below, as well as the fine alabaster work,
show how artists of the German Renaissance were able to become accustomed to
their patrons' quirks; their representations
of the latter were sympathetic, but uncom-
promising in their realistic portrayals.

No other department in the Louvre has been subject to such upheavals in recent times as the section housing French sculpture. In 1993/94, in the wing on the rue Richelieu, an enormous new space was built for sculpture: two covered illuminated courtyards, named the Cour Marly and the Cour Puget, now allow huge antique installations to be displayed in a manner that was previously impossible.

As well as the new acquisitions that have been made, a whole series of monuments has left Paris recently. As France's national museum, the Louvre has been obliged to return the small figures from the cloisters of Notre-Dame-en-Vaux in Châlons-sur-Marne in order to provide a new attraction in the cathedral crypt for visitors from all over the world to the Berry region. The magnificent fragments from the choir screen at Bourges have also found their way home.

From the Beginnings to the Romanesque Period

Provençal, South Portal of the Ste.-Cécile Priory Church, Estagel (St.-Gilles-du-Gard), mid-11th century
Stone, overall dimensions 442.5 x 365 cm; tympanum 81.5 x 161 cm; door lintel 52 x 202 x 26.5 cm

The reconstructed portal from the deanery at the St.-Gilles-du-Gard monastery, the main portal of which is itself decorated with world-famous sculptures, opens as if to admit the visitor into the late Middle Ages. Romanesque art in France originated on the pilgrims' route to Santiago de Compostela. From the monasteries that gave birth to the movement, there spread stylistic peculiarities as well as ideas for spiritual reform; as a result, the portal from Estagel

displays elements of the art of St.-Gilles. Although flanked by only one pillar on each side, it is a prime example of portal jambs. Everything that characterizes Provençal architecture is combined in the capitals, the relief on either side of the door lintel, and the tympanum: the acanthus shows antique influence, the interlacing was developed by Carolingian artists, while the birds in the branches are reminiscent of Oriental weaving. It is almost impossible to discern any symbolism.

Left page: The Madonna and Child of Lorraine (detail), first third of the 14th century, see p. 232 f.

French Sculpture

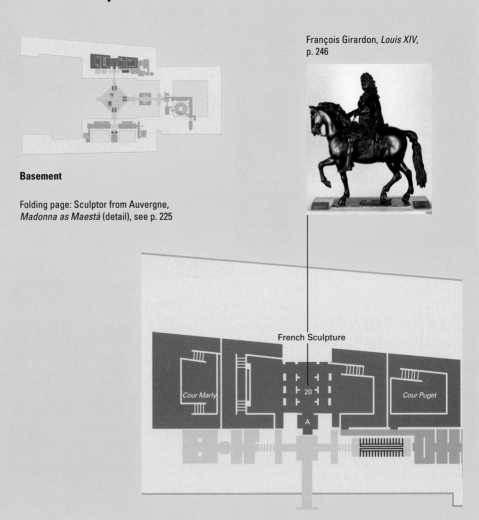

François Girardon, *Louis XIV*, p. 246

Basement

Folding page: Sculptor from Auvergne, *Madonna as Maestà* (detail), see p. 225

French Sculpture

Cour Marly

20

A

Cour Puget

Jean-Baptiste Pigalle, *Voltaire Naked*, p. 250

Jean-Antoine Houdon, *Voltaire*, p. 251

Pierre Puget, *Milo of Crotona Eaten by a Lion*, p. 248 f.

French Sculpture
18th–19th Centuries

26 27 28 30
25
24 23 22 21 29 31 32 33

Cour Puget

Madonna and Child of Lorraine, p. 232 f.

Other Works:

1 Martin the Monk, *Head of an Apostle* (Peter?), second third of the 12th century, room 2, p. 224 f.

2 Column Figures from Corbeil, second half of the 12th century, room 3, p. 226 f.

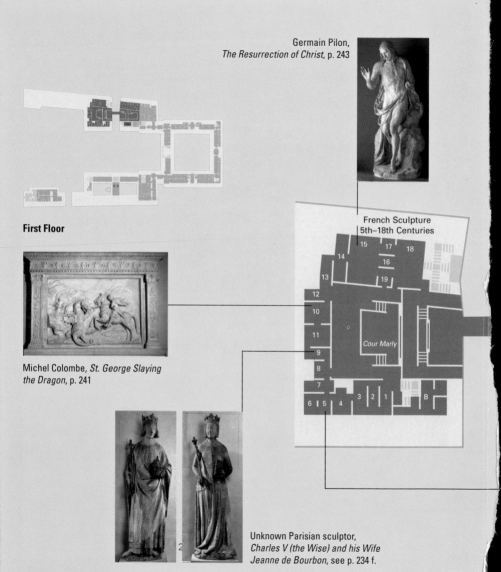

Germain Pilon,
The Resurrection of Christ, p. 243

First Floor

French Sculpture
5th–18th Centuries

Michel Colombe, *St. George Slaying
the Dragon*, p. 241

Cour Marly

15 17 18
14 16
13 19
12
10
11
9
8
7
6 5 4 3 2 1 B

Unknown Parisian sculptor,
*Charles V (the Wise) and his Wife
Jeanne de Bourbon*, see p. 234 f.

French, Chancel Front, known as the
***Tomb of the Leper*, from St. Denis,**
(?)8th/9th century
Marble, 98 x 202 x 15 cm

Burgundian Sculptor, ***Christus Courajod*, from**
a ***Descent from the Cross*, second quarter of**
the 12th century
Polychrome wood, 155 x 168 x 30 cm

Around a crucifix, flanked by two palms symbolizing martyrdom, is a vine, a reference to Communion wine. The origin of this relief has been a matter of considerable interest for a very long time; in the 12th century it was given an inscription in the monastery of St. Denis in Paris, because it was thought to be a rare relic; according to legend, Christ himself is said to have appeared to heal a leper on the occasion of the consecration of the priory church in 636. The stone has been revered as the grave of this leper. The relief may have been intended as the front of a chancel, and therefore served temporarily as the frontispiece of an altar.

This crucifix, bequeathed to the Louvre by the art historian Courajod in the 19th century, is the only surviving example of the numerous figures in a monumental *Descent from the Cross*, which resembles the Italian version dated somewhat later (see p. 196 f.): the surviving figure of Christ is approached by Mary and her companions, who are about to take down his body. Without the other figures, it looks as though Christ were reaching down from the Cross with his pierced right hand, as if entrusting himself to our care. Images such as this evoked a new spiritual empathy between the onlooker and the suffering Christ.

Monk from the Benedictine abbey at Cluny,
Eagle of St. John, **Cluny, 1115–1125**
Limestone, 63 x 46 x 23.5 cm

An extremely wide-ranging reform of the
monasteries began in the abbey at Cluny in
the 10th century. This fragment of an eagle
is from the great tympanum of the third
abbey church of Cluny, one of the wonders
of the world until the Revolution. The
attribute of St. John appears in the apoca-
lyptic vision of the throne to the right of
the figure of Christ.

Martin the Monk, *Head of an Apostle* **(?Peter)**
from the tomb of Lazarus in Autun cathedral,
second third of the 12th century
Limestone with lead inlay for the eyes,
21 x 14 x 19.5 cm

Burgundy is the focal point of a wonderful
revival of Romanesque sculpture; the finest
examples of the new image of man are to
be found in Autun, where the church of
Saint Lazare, a former Benedictine priory
of Cluny, has since been transformed into a
cathedral. Two masters can be identified by
name: they are Gislabertus in the period
around 1130, and Martin a generation

later. We owe to the latter the moving main piece of the former church decoration (most of which is now in the Musée Rolin in Autun): freestanding figures combine to form a scene from the burial of Lazarus, whom Christ was persuaded to awaken from the dead by St. Mary Magdalene, and who, according to legend, is supposed to have ended his days as a missionary in France. The smaller than life-size head of an Apostle in the Louvre is taken from this work.

Sculptor from Auvergne,
Madonna as Sedes Sapientiae,
second half of the 12th century
polychrome wood, 84 x 27 x 36 cm

The lifelike quality of the *Head of an Apostle* from Autun foreshadows a new direction in art, the noblest aim of which had previously consisted of the creation of religious symbols such as this *Madonna*. Statues like this often serve as reliquaries; the example in the Louvre has an opening for this purpose. The most frequent subject was the enthroned Virgin Mary. In France she is known as "majesté," since she presides over the saints; elsewhere the Latin term "sedes sapientiae," or seat of wisdom, is preferred: Mary's body is viewed as the throne of God made flesh, and thus becomes the embodiment of wisdom.

In accordance with the underlying theological concept, the images are rigidly symmetrical in construction, with the result that there is no tenderness in the relationship between mother and child. It is very probable that the major religious statues in Chartres and elsewhere, burnt during the Revolution, resembled this statuette.

Stonemason's yard at St.-Denis, Column Figures of a Queen and King (Queen of Sheba and Solomon?), from Corbeil, Essonne, second half of the 12th century
Limestone
queen: 235 x 44 x 38.5 cm
king: 244 x 45 x 41 cm

As the image located above the altar table progressively conquered new ground and became the object of new reverence, the monumental human form occupied the steps and walls of the portals in French churches. Figures with cylindrical cores were used as pillars. Two outstanding surviving examples, uprooted during the Revolution, were produced by the stonemasons of St.-Denis and are said originally to have stood in Corbeil. Both statues are characterized by rigidity of form, dictated by the dimensions of the pillars, and by an astonishing degree of detail; they bring to the Louvre a trace of the style that was to reach its apogee in the west portal of Chartres cathedral. There, too, we find King Solomon as the epitome of royal splendor; here he is seen alongside the Queen of Sheba, who visited him and is said to have honored him with precious gifts. Their meeting was viewed as a kind of precedent, a typological forebear, for the Adoration of the Kings and the Assumption of the Virgin Mary.

Parisian sculptor, *Christ with Angels*, transom from a portal in the cathedral of Notre-Dame in Paris, third quarter of the 12th century
Limestone, 35 x 86.5 x 41.5 cm

The identity of the specific portal that was originally adorned by these two fragments of transoms from High Gothic vaulted arches is a matter for debate, but it is nevertheless certain that they are from Notre-Dame. The style of the cathedral's west portals is evident in the rigid forms. The smooth, extremely finely worked faces of Christ and two angels from a vision stand already on the brink of the transition to a new style, in which the elongated proportions of the preceding generation must have appeared repugnant. Christ is the cornerstone here in more than one sense: the work originally supported the arch over which the judge of the world presided.

Iconoclasm Prior to the Revolution

The memory of the merciless battle against Christian images throughout France during the Revolutionary period lingers on. The Church had become so closely associated with secular power that its stone images incurred almost more hatred than its living dignitaries. Underlying fear of the power of idols drove the unenlightened to sacrifice these images in the name of the Enlightenment.

Works of art had already been destroyed as a result of Christian convictions, in two waves: the Albigenses, the powerful reform movement hostile to the Church in the period around 1200, had opposed works of art with equal vehemence as the Huguenots in the 16th century. Possessed by Calvin's reforming zeal, the latter were fundamentally hostile to images. In the ruthless wars, however, the destruction of works of art also constituted a reckoning with the detested official authority of the Church and the hostile monarchy. Movements such as these engender deliberate iconoclasm.

In France, however, there were quite different reasons why generations prior to the great Revolution treated medieval art with even less mercy than the so-called heretics or reformers. Clerical reform was one motive, for in many medieval buildings, cathedrals as well as collegiate churches, a stone barrier divided the community from the divine offices. These choir screens were destroyed from the 17th century onward, and with them disappeared many mag-

Sculptor from Chartres, Matthew with the Angel, Chartres, second quarter of the 13th century, limestone, 64.5 x 50 x 15 cm, ground floor, room 4

nificent reliefs. This was the case in the cathedral of Notre-Dame in Paris in 1627; the remaining fragments hint at the sensationally beautiful figures and moving depictions created there in around 1250. A century later, Rome demanded that all churches should be uniform, with the result that important works fell victim to the dismantling of internal walls in churches, a generation before the outbreak of the Revolution in

1789. Surviving fragments attest the virtuosity of skilled stonemasons, for example the young *Matthew*, probably from Chartres, where all the choir screens were torn down in 1763. Elsewhere, the reliefs featuring monumental figures in the Amiens choir screen, destroyed in 1755, were treated as building rubble.

The French monarchy also caused irreparable damage to medieval buildings. None of the kings of the *Ancien Régime* had experienced any difficulty, after being crowned in Rheims, in entering Notre-Dame in Paris in solemn procession via the center portal. However, in order to admit the final member of the Capetian dynasty, Louis XVI – who was later beheaded – into the cathedral in Paris, his head freshly anointed and held high beneath a magnificent canopy, the entrance was destroyed. In retrospect, this destruction of the main entrance to Notre-Dame seems like a premonition. Even the birth of this king had not passed without wanton damage to old ecclesiastical structures. Louis XV, in his desire to conceive an heir, an undertaking that was beset with medical problems, turned to one of the great local patron saints: He promised Saint Geneviève a new church. She is identified by the motif of a devil and an angel fighting to extinguish or relight her candle, a new church. Louis XVI was conceived and Geneviève's old collegiate church, high on a hill in the old Roman

Parisian sculptor, Geneviève and the Miracle of the Candle, from the central pillar of the main portal of the collegiate church of St. Geneviève, Paris, first quarter of the 13th century, limestone, 230 x 54.5 x 53.5 cm, height of figure: 154.8 cm, ground floor, room 4

Hubert Robert, The Desecration of the Royal Graves in the Basilica of St.-Denis, Paris, 1783,
oil on canvas, 54 x 64 cm, Musée Carnavalet, Paris

quarter of Paris, was forced to make way for the gigantic domed church that was never associated with the cult of the old saint, but instead was appropriated by the Revolution as the Pantheon. Although the figures that are in dispute over the candle have been damaged, the main figure of Geneviève has nevertheless survived in the central pillar of the door. The assembled major works of the 13th and 14th centuries in the Louvre, some of them brutally disfigured, remain a great reminder of the various phases of the destruction process. They originally included the choir screen from Bourges, which was returned later on.

Sculptor from Amiens, Fragment from Christ's Entry into Jerusalem, from the choir screen destroyed in 1755, ca. 1300, polychrome lime-stone, 103 x 65 x 33 cm, ground floor, room 4

tional works that seem to break free of any kind of prescribed framework in the most unlikely periods. A head such as the one illustrated, which was not acquired by the Louvre until 1981, sits uneasily alongside the fragile, almost transparent works made of marble and alabaster from the years around 1300. It is unusually rich and has been sculpted with genius, but traces of the sculptor's tools are apparent. The artist shies away from symmetry in the noble head, with the result that he achieves an incredibly lifelike expression. This lifelike quality is intensified to quite a remarkable degree in the floral motifs of the crown. These do, however, give rise to slight doubt as to whether the royal head is really an image of Christ.

From the workshop of Mussy-l'Evèque or the Master of the St. John the Baptist of Rouvres-en-Plaine, *Head of Christ from the Coronation of the Virgin Mary* on the portal of the Hôtel Dieu in Tonnerre, Burgundy, ca. 1295–1300
Polychrome limestone, 47.5 x 33 x 30 cm

Regardless of all the stylization, sculptors are ultimately obliged to return to a direct and intense confrontation with their own craftsmanship and vision. As a consequence, it is possible to encounter sensa-

***Madonna and Child of Lorraine,*
first third of the 14th century**
Limestone, polychrome with gilt, 44 x 34 x 20 cm

This *Madonna*, holding a book in her plump right hand while supporting the Christ child with her left, was acquired in 1995. The infant, dressed in stiff robes and holding a celestial globe and a bird in his hands, appears to want to climb onto her lap. Mother and child gaze at one another's faces, seemingly oblivious to the external world. The message conveyed by this rather robust work is one of human intimacy: the enthroned Queen of Heaven is shown here as a generously-proportioned mother with her child.

Unknown Parisian sculptor,
***Charles V (the Wise) and his Wife Jeanne de Bourbon*, Paris, ca. 1375**
Stone, height 195 cm

It would be interesting to know who created these impressive, slightly larger than life-size statues. Despite their disfigured hands, which have been replaced with the subjects' attributes, they convey, even in this weathered state, a vital image of the king who restored order to France in the confusion of the Hundred Years' War. He appears wise and humane, and so unmilitary-like and pious that it is difficult to imagine when viewing this statue that Charles V was able, with great military skill, to hold the English invaders in check. These honest portraits possibly stood on the great Louvre staircase, or on the portal of the Celestine monastery in Paris, which was destroyed during the Revolution.

André Beauneveu (employed by the Duc de Berry from 1397),
***Head of an Apostle from Mehun-sur-Yèvre*, Bourges, end of the 14th century**
Stone, height 31 cm

One of the great imponderables of history is the fact that the only well-known works of certain artists are works that are untypical of them. André Beauneveu was famous in his time as a sculptor, but is now known only for his authenticated illuminations of a book for the Duc de Berry; these are used to help identify some of his work in stone. The main candidate is this expressive, geometric head of an Apostle. The evidence of Beauneveu's authorship of this work relies on the fact that it originates from Berry's favorite castle, Mehun, where the sculptor worked for a time. Beauneveu epitomizes the blossoming of art under the four sons of the unfortunate King Jean II (the Good) (see p. 366), one of whom was the Duc de Berry. His brother Charles V (the Wise) commissioned three monuments for himself and his wife; one of the reclining figures in Beauneveu's style is in the Louvre.

The Cult of the Dead and the Beginnings of Portraiture

What defines man? Is it his status, his family, his office, or his face? These have always been important questions relating to the preservation of an image of a deceased person. Our museums are filled with attempts to preserve memories of the dead; art therefore either becomes death's accomplice, or conversely a force combating death and oblivion.

Nowhere other than in the Louvre is it possible to experience such a moving impression of a medieval funeral. Eight apparently life-size men with bowed heads stride forward, carrying on their shoulders the heavy slab bearing a man in full armor, gazing out of his visor and praying, accompanied by his dog. The bearers, portrayed as weeping mourners (*pleurants*), hide their faces under black hoods. They have already said prayers for the deceased in church, and are now carrying him to the grave. The scene is not very life-like: the corpse does not appear dead, but is praying with his

Jean d'Orléans, Last Respects and Funeral Rites, after 1404, manuscript, 27.9 x 19.9 cm, Bibliothèque Nationale, Paris

eyes open. As miniatures illustrate, eminent men such as this were not borne to their graves looking up to heaven, but were covered by a canopy. Neither the stone slab nor the heavy armor were, in actual fact, carried. Modesty required simply that the dead person be sewn into a shroud, and the stone erected over the sarcophagus when in place. However, the aspects taken from life are rendered as an abstract image. There is even something unnat-ural about the bearers, who convey all the movement: they are noticeably smaller than the figure of the deceased, and each carries one of the weapons depicted on the robes of the man lying in state, representing his domain, as if his own estate were affording him its last respects.

The face of Philippe Pot, the Grand Seneschal of Burgundy who died in 1493, is of little interest in a theatrical piece such as this. Even the dou-ble tomb commissioned by Catherine d'Alençon

(?)Antoine Le Moiturier, Monument for the Tomb of Philippe Pot (1428–1493), from Gîteaux, Dijon, (?)1493, polychrome limestone, 182 x 260 x 167 cm; bearers: height 134–144 cm, ground floor, room 10

Mino da Fiesole (1431–1484), Dietisalvi Neroni (detail), 1464, see p. 202

for herself and her husband Pierre d'Evreux-Navarre after her husband's death in around 1412/1415, demonstrates a more accurate representation of the deceased person's individuality and also a much closer attention to detail, although created 80 years before the tomb of Philippe Pot. At that time, detailed realism was dominant, and although it served to preserve the memory, it was deeply anchored in life, as if to console the widow. It was from such images on tombs that an interest in portraiture became widespread throughout Europe. This new approach had its fundamental roots in Italian humanism, and demanded ruthlessness. Mino da Fiesole's portrait of Dietisalvi Neroni of 1464, for instance, is brutal, or perhaps honest, even as regards the choice of stone (see p. 202).

Parisian sculptor, Monument for the Tomb of Catherine d'Alençon and Pierre d'Evreux-Navarre, Carthusian monastery in Paris, 1412/1415, white marble, life-size, ground floor, room 10

It was obviously essential that the Florentine humanist should appear as lifelike as possible; as a result, painters produced increasingly realistic interpretations of models who were frankly ugly. In a large painting from around 1450/1460, an unknown man lifts up his head from his food and drink to stare blankly at the onlooker. In *The Man with the Wine Glass*, portrait painting is combined with still-life painting for the first time. For a time it was supposed that this picture originated from Portugal, or France, more specifically from Anjou, where Mediterranean sculpture and Flemish painting were generating new ideas. The theory of French origin is favored on account of the imposing nature of the composition, which was first attempted in Italy in the time of Leonardo da Vinci (1452–1519). When hung on a wall, such a picture conveys the impression of someone who is gazing into the room through a window. French sculptors endeavored to produce such effects before painters; this technique results in an unsettling lifelike quality.

Unknown master, The Man with the Wine Glass, ca. 1450/1460, wood, 63 x 44 cm, second floor, room 6

The Renaissance

Guillaume Regnault (ca. 1465–1534), *Olivet Madonna,* **Loiret, ca. 1510/1520**
Alabaster, 183 x 60 x 41 cm

Like other sculptors of the French Renaissance, whose sculptures were largely destroyed during the Huguenot wars, little is known about Guillaume Regnault. Protestant iconoclasm in the 16th century focused particularly on images of the Madonna. In the Louvre, two marble statues attributed to Regnault stand side by side; both have heavy draperies and dispense with sophisticated poses. In one case, in lively contrast with the severity of her constricting robe, the head and torso appear to be elegant, even seductive. In the case of the other, however, which only reached the castle of Couasnon in Olivet from a church in Orléans in the 18th century, the eyes are downcast, suggesting that the artist had intended the onlooker to see in her only the handmaid of God.

Michel Colombe (?1430–1512/1515),
***St. George Slaying the Dragon*, from the Château**
Gaillon near Rouen, Tours, 1509
Marble, 175 x 272 cm; relief: height 134 cm

Georges d'Amboise (1460–1510), cardinal legate of the pope in France, chancellor to King Louis XII, and archbishop of Rouen (from 1494), was one of the most impressive patrons of the French Renaissance. A zealous comrade-in-arms of his king, he took part in the campaigns in Italy and fell as a prince of the Church at the battle of Pavia in 1510. He imported books from Italy, and

from there also introduced a new taste in art to which, later, the elderly sculptor Michel Colombe from Tours was to do justice.

Colombe's very fine technique of marble relief shows southern influences, as does the antique-inspired décor executed by the Tuscan sculptor Jérôme Pacherot (born 1463, at the court of Charles VIII from 1497, year of death unknown). The incongruous figure of the dragon appears all the more curious. This glorification of Saint George adorned the altar in the chapel of the castle at Gaillon, which was dedicated to the saint.

Unknown sculptor, *The Death of St. Innocent*, Paris, ca. 1530
Alabaster, height 120 cm

A renowned curiosity, this gruesome figure was once hanging from the tower of the church of Notre-Dame-du-Bois in the center of the Cemetery of the Innocent Children in Paris. Anatomical veracity does not play a major role; the terror aroused by the prospect of death, represented by the image that was widespread in France since the Middle Ages, is of greater importance. Death is portrayed not as a skeleton, but as a disemboweled corpse, in accordance with the then prevailing tradition of burying the entrails separately from the body.

In 1786, the cemetery in the heart of the French capital city was closed. The raised arm was restored after the Revolution; the work finally arrived at the Louvre by way of St.-Germain-des-Prés and Notre-Dame. The inscription on the shield tells us that death comes to all, and enjoins us to pray for the dead, while at the same time alluding to the very lifelike quality of the work: "Il n'est vivant tant soit plein art/ Ne de force pour résistance/ Que je ne frappe de mon dard/ pour bailler aux vers leur pitance/ Priez Dieu pour les trespassés."

Germain Pilon (1528–1590),
The Resurrection of Christ,
before 1572
Marble, 215 x 88.5 x 74 cm

Art that was able to portray death in all its horror was also able to give a compelling account of life in all its fullness. The risen Christ, whom Michelangelo had in the past portrayed in a figure of great physical beauty (Rome, S. Maria sopra Minerva), is symbolic of pulsating life. In the context of tombs, such an image of Christ promises ultimate triumph over death. Germain Pilon created this larger than life-size statue for the rotunda of the House of Valois in the royal tombs at St.-Denis, Paris. By contrast with many other royal monuments, this one was not destroyed during the Revolution, but fell victim to renovations in the early 18th century. The main figures, carved in shining marble, survive. The figure of Christ incorporates the astonishing muscular power of a statue by Michelangelo, combined with the graceful elegance that is characteristic of Mannerism. Pilon, the great French sculptor, attains almost classical stature as a result. The way in which the body and shroud emerge from the rugged crevice in the rock is particularly beautiful.

The Gardens of Marly

View of the horse troughs, surrounded by Coustou's horses, engraving by Jean Rigaud, ca. 1700

Following completion of the essential works at Versailles, Louis XIV (1638–1715) set about building a more intimate castle nearby. He had acquired Marly-le-Chatel, to the west of Paris, north of the forest of St.-Germain-en-Laye, in 1676. There, within a very short time, he had a "sun pavilion" constructed using insubstantial materials; symbolizing the "Sun King," it was surrounded by 12 other pavilions, one for each month. There is little evidence of these today.

Visitors to the park first encountered a trough from which horses could drink, surrounded by four sculptural groups, each carved from a block of marble, known as the "horses of Marly." The huge effort expended in this work is

described by Antoine Coysevox in an inscription below the figure of *Mercury*. Two groups extol the fame of the Sun King, showing Pegasus, the horse of the muses, ridden in one instance by fame itself and in the other by Mercury, messenger of the gods. To these were added horses ridden by knights, that were sculpted by Guillaume Coustou.

In 1794 the site was abandoned and the works of art impounded. The famous horses were placed at the entrance to the Champs-Elysées in Paris by the painter Jacques-Louis David (1748–1825). However, many sculptures were lost or were distributed among various institutions in Paris. In the Tuileries gardens, for instance, they deteriorated visibly when exhibited in the open air, so that the renovation of the Musée du Louvre following the departure of the Ministry of Finance in 1993 provided a welcome opportunity for one of the two huge inner courtyards, which were covered with glass, to house the sculptures. Consequently, pieces that were kept inside at an early stage and are in an excellent state of preservation now stand alongside statues that have suffered severe damage. Although incomplete, they nevertheless give an outstanding impression of the diverse nature of the royal project.

In addition, it is now possible to admire casts of the groups of horses in two open-air locations: in their original position, where the park at Marly is being reconstructed, and at the entrance to the Champs-Elysées.

The Cour Marly in the Louvre, where many of the sculptures from the gardens at Marly now stand

The Era of Louis XIV

François Girardon (1628–1715), *Louis XIV*, miniature version of the equestrian statue erected in 1699 in Paris, 1692
Bronze, height 102 cm

As well as Charles the Great, Louis XIV is the only ruler to be allocated key space by the Louvre in its most recent incarnation.

However, this principle does not apply to a heavy lead cast created in 1988, and placed directly adjacent to the pyramid as a reminder of Gianlorenzo Bernini's unsuccessful visit to France (see p. 22 f), particularly since the Sun King stands gazing out over the line of visitors in the direction of the Tuileries as if yearning for wide open spaces. However, once inside the Richelieu wing, the route leads past Girardon's highly polished and unusually delicate equestrian statue with its extraordinarily noble horse. The effect it has on the visitors is evident in the outstretched left foot of the king: although not worn away to the same extent as the feet of the apostle Peter in the famous statue in St. Peter's in Rome, it nevertheless shows signs of many a surreptitious touch. This has now been prevented by a Plexiglas screen.

The monumental work stood in a square near the Louvre known during the king's lifetime as Louis-le-Grand, now known as the Place Vendôme. The large bronze, like the statue in the group at the Place des Victoires, which was 14 years older and which Girardon was attempting to outdo, did not survive the Revolution.

Desjardins (Martin van der Bogaert) (1637–1694), *The Four Nations Bound in Chains by the Sun King*, from the Place des Victoires in Paris, models dated 1682, cast dedicated in 1685
Bronze, Spaniard: 220 x 200 x 170 cm; German: 185 x 120 x 180 cm; Brandenburger: 210 x 140 x 130 cm; Dutchman: 200 x 145 x 150 cm

Even France's Swedish allies were so incensed by this ensemble at the Place des Victoires that it was necessary to have it altered. Erected by a courtier of Louis XIV, already viewed with contempt by enlightened minds such as Voltaire, and rightly removed during the Revolution, the surviving remnants were for a long time regarded simply as a military memorial. Since 1993, the year that they arrived in the Louvre, the notion of these bronzes as a "glorious memorial to honor the memory of the great king in the middle of a square" has gradually been rehabilitated. François d'Aubusson, the *Maréchal de la Feuillade*, undoubtedly had the imperial Roman statues of Caesar in mind when he chained the grossly caricatured "barbarians" conquered by the Sun King to the equestrian statue of Louis XIV; nothing is gained by the monument in terms of humanity as a result. The Place des Victoires actually celebrates the forced surrender of Franche-Comté, Flanders, and Artois. The men in chains are an imperial German, a Spaniard, a Brandenburger, later Prussian, and a Dutchman; replicas are already on sale in the Louvre, with the price marked in euros.

Pierre Puget (1620–1694),
Milo of Crotona, eaten by a Lion **(with detail),**
1670–1682
Marble, height 270 cm

This major work by the extremely influential sculptor Puget had a place of honor at the top of the Allée Royale at Versailles; according to writers in ancient times, Milo is reputed to have been an athlete who triumphed on 13 occasions at Olympia and elsewhere. As an old man he tried with his bare hands to break the split in an oak tree, into which tree fellers had driven wedges. When these wedges fell out, one of his hands remained trapped. In this unfortunate position, Milo was eaten by wolves, for which Puget substituted a rather comical lion. With scant regard for the relative proportions of man and animal, he provides a very convincing illustration of Milo bracing both legs against the tree trunk in order to free himself. The sculptor was less successful in accommodating prudery, which required that the man's loins be covered by an item of clothing. However, the artist set new standards in

his depiction of pain, which is expertly shown in every detail. In room 25 we are given an inkling of the number of occasions on which the subject was repeated, while Eugène Deveria (1805–1865) even painted the presentation of the statue to the Sun King in his ceiling painting in room 43 of the Galeria Campana (1828–1832).

From the Enlightenment to the 19th Century

Jean-Baptiste Pigalle (1714–1785), *Voltaire Naked*, 1776
Marble, height 150 cm

Voltaire (1694–1778), writer and Enlightenment philosopher, is seated on a chair hidden from view. The portrait of an old man's lean body is a sober one, showing deep folds around the stomach as well as prominent veins and sinews. In contrast with the apparent signs of age on the body, the head radiates a fiery resolution. Modeled on Seneca (see p. 171), the champion of freedom of thought is portrayed as a naked hero. For a long time, because of the evident contradiction between heroism and realism, this sculpture was not appreciated. The sculpture was commissioned in 1770 by admirers of Voltaire, and money was collected in order that it be executed in marble.

**Jean-Antoine Houdon
(1741–1828),
Voltaire, 1778**
Marble, 63 cm

This bust of the Enlightenment writer shows him in contemporary garments and wig (*à la française*). Unlike the figure by Pigalle, which provides a naturalistic rendering of the body and then idealizes the head, Houdon's portrait is very realistic. The prominent chin, the large nose, the bags under tired-looking eyes, and the sarcastic expression all combine to form an image of an unerring satirist. Yet even Houdon was obliged to accommodate the wishes of his clients by stressing different aspects of a personality and thus varying the characterization, as is evident from the other portraits displayed in the room. The extent to which the artist was able to combine intensity of gaze and expression is also demonstrated in the bust of the four-year-old Sabine Houdon (1791), in the same room. This portrays the child naked in the antique style.

Claude Ramey (1754–1838),
Napoleon in Coronation Robes,
1813
Marble, 210 x 103 x 82.3 cm

This crowded section briefly attempts to recall imperial times. A larger than life-size Napoleon towers imperially, clad in his coronation robes, severe and impersonal, typifying his reign. D'Alembert (1717–1783), the philosopher of the Enlightenment, is seated opposite him, producing an unintentionally comic effect. An order for this statue of marble had already been placed in 1786 with Félix Lecomte (1737–1817), and it was later presented to the Institut by Napoleon. D'Alembert, also coeditor with Diderot of the *Encyclopédie*, is now looking up at the emperor like a prophet, full of concern, as if reluctant to take Napoleon's posturing seriously. Michel de Montaigne (1533–1592) is also sitting on the right hand of the emperor; this statue was created by Jean-Baptiste Stouf (1742–1826), who exhibited it at the 1800 Salon. Naked apart from a book, mirror, and cloth, the 16th-century philosopher leans backward: horrified, astonished, and yet with just a hint of hopeful anticipation, he stares up at the monumental statue as if not quite sure what to make of the impending coronation.

François Rude (1784–1855),
***Young Neapolitan Fisherman Playing with a Turtle*, from a plaster cast made in 1831 for the 1833 Salon**
Marble, height 82 cm

A naked youth, clad only in a Phrygian cap, is seated on a stone with his fishing nets. He is playing with a turtle, which he has tied up in a harness, to test its strength. Exhibited in the Salon in 1833, this sculpture soon became famous. The careful portrayal of the material is remarkable: the rugged stone, the fisherman's net, the adolescent skin, and the shell of the turtle are very accurately reproduced. However, the romantic feeling in this figure strikes us as alien today. Instead of the bygone era of classical Antiquity, genre sculptures such as this portray contemporary life on the shores of the Mediterranean. Rude executed the monumental sculptures at the Arc de Triomphe, and a wax model of the *Marseillaise* is on display in the glass cabinet.

Paris – a Synthesis of Artistic Forms

by Herbert Köhler

Epoch-making: L'Opéra de la Bastille – Notre-Dame – the Eiffel Tower

Nothing symbolizes unifying forces more than bridges. They symbolize understanding, inter-action, and love; in other words, communication on all levels. This becomes all the more impor-tant when the juxtaposition of opposites is involved, and Paris is a city of opposites: this is evident from the diversity in the buildings alone.

The most intimate aspects of this cohesion are still conveyed in the pictures – which he called his "children of Olympia" – taken by Eugène Atget (1857–1927), the photographer obsessed with Paris. However, the *Lovers of the*

Pont Neuf, the film sensitively shot in 1991 by Leo Carax, will surely not prove to be the last declaration of love for one of the city's cultural trouble spots. The oldest bridge in Paris, the Pont Neuf, which joins the left and right bank of the Seine via the Ile de la Cité, was completed in 1589 during the reign of Henry IV. In 1985 it was wrapped by Christo and his wife Jeanne-Claude in a spectacular performance, and lay like a gift in front of the Sainte-Chapelle. This bridge was not built solely for the purpose of transport, nor was it just intended to bring about a *rapprochement* between rival quarters and their inhabitants: much of the water supply for the city center was carried by integral pipes and pumping equipment. Nevertheless, the public health conditions in Paris at that time were disastrous, with countless sewage channels sharing a single destination — the stinking Seine. The underground sewage system which was later to become so famous was still a very distant prospect. Alain Corbin's book, *The Foul and the Fragrant: Odor and the Social Imagination,* deals comprehensively with the discovery of sanitation, without which the metropolis would probably not have survived. The great French Revolution, which began with the storming of the main prison in Paris, plans for which were largely hatched out in the public gardens of the Palais Royal, turned a new page in 1789. Daniel Burens' controversial marble pillars with their awning stripes, erected in 1986 in the ceremonial courtyard of the palace, today appear to hark back to the playful aspects of the *fêtes galantes* of a bygone era rather than to the outbreak of the Revolution. In 1789, however, a bourgeois parliament disposed of a bigoted aristocracy that had lost touch with the real needs of its subordinates. Fearing that the rabble could turn ugly, the ruling nobility withdrew to Versailles and to the Marais quarter.

The sublime ideals of liberty, equality, and fraternity, for which the bourgeois tricolor (devoid of awning stripes) ultimately stood, could not be realized immediately. During Robespierre's "Terror," around 60,000 people had lost their heads by 1795, himself included. Delacroix' enlightened view in the 1830 painting *Liberty Leading the People* created the revolutionary mythology that survives in a rather sterile form in the Louvre. Times, however, have changed.

Daniel Burens' sculptures, Palais Royal's inner courtyard, 1986

Under bourgeois rule, culture became public property, and this was crucial for the modern development of a city that had been obliged since the mid-19th century to submit to a major upheaval in its infrastructure. Postrevolutionary urban planning is synonymous with the name Haussmann, at whose instigation the great avenues were built; "imperial axis" and "star" were the magic words during that period.

Both are elements of the Grande Nation. The Champs-Elysées, starting from the Louvre, was intended as the point of departure for this magnificent axis; the concept of its perpetual extension in the form of an avenue resulted in other emblems of the city. Meanwhile, urban planning extended as far as Nanterre. What is now the Place Charles de Gaulle (formerly Place de l'Etoile), where twelve avenues converge in a star-shaped formation at a traffic junction, was given a focal point in 1836 in the shape of the Arc de Triomphe. This arch was intended to commemorate Napoleon's triumph at Austerlitz, while ignoring his defeat at Waterloo. Two important cultural events culminate there every year: the final stretch of the Tour de France cycle race and the celebrations on the anniversary of the Revolution. Both have broadened their appeal, rather than remaining exclusively sporting or military occasions.

By 1793, a year after the declaration of the Republic, the collections of the Louvre were already open to the public, although it is impossible to compare the circumstances and the inventory at that time with those of the Grand Louvre today. The museum's stock increased rapidly as a consequence of Napoleon's delusions of grandeur and his flexible attitude to the cultural property of other nations. However, the *Quadriga* stolen from San Marco in Venice had to be swiftly returned. Napoleon appointed the effervescent Baron Denon to be responsible for choosing the works of art and arranging their display in the Louvre, and a wing in the museum bears his name today. The glass pyramid likewise recalls a weakness of both Napoleon and Baron Denon, namely Egypt. Those wishing to combine this experience with the triumphal march from Verdi's *Aïda* can kill two birds with one stone and visit the Opéra de Paris in the

Quartier Marais, where all monuments are protected; the building by Carlos Ott, inaugurated in 1989 and conceived as the people's opera, stands on the former site of the Bastille. The CNIT conference and trade center, the first project in the long-term plan for La Défense, was

Henri de Miller's Listener in front of St.-Eustache

completed in 1958. By extending the imperial axis leading from the Louvre, along the Champs-Elysées, to the Arc de Triomphe, the intention was to create a gigantic, ultramodern city of offices to transform the field of view and skyline west of the Boulevard Périphérique and the

Seine. Concrete, steel, and glass are the dominant construction materials. Bold forms, new concepts for pedestrian areas, and a compact supply and distribution system make this city within a city practically self-sufficient. In this quarter, there is a heightened awareness of 40 years of architectural history. The big attraction of La Défense, however, is the Grande Arche at the end of the esplanade, designed by the Dane Johan Otto von Spreckeisen, and completed in 1989. It is intended to symbolize a kind of window onto the future. A century earlier, a certain Monsieur Eiffel had built a tower for the 1889 *Exposition Universelle*, soaring some 274 m (900 ft) into the sky. By contrast, the realist Spreckeisen, by means of his "view through a window" toward the east, initiates a kind of meditation on the old order and, with the view toward the west, on the new, on which the philosophers and genetic researchers of Nanterre are eagerly working. Paris, a melting pot for diverse concepts, has throughout history succeeded in juxtaposing the historical with the visionary and harnessing the resulting conflict as a source of constructive cohesive energy. In essence, this strategy has been

The Noble Axis: Musée du Louvre – Champs Elysées – Grande Arche

enthusiastically implemented, and for the most part, it has been implemented with a light touch, without ever taking itself so seriously that it omits to forge the decisive link with the rest of the world.

Paintings

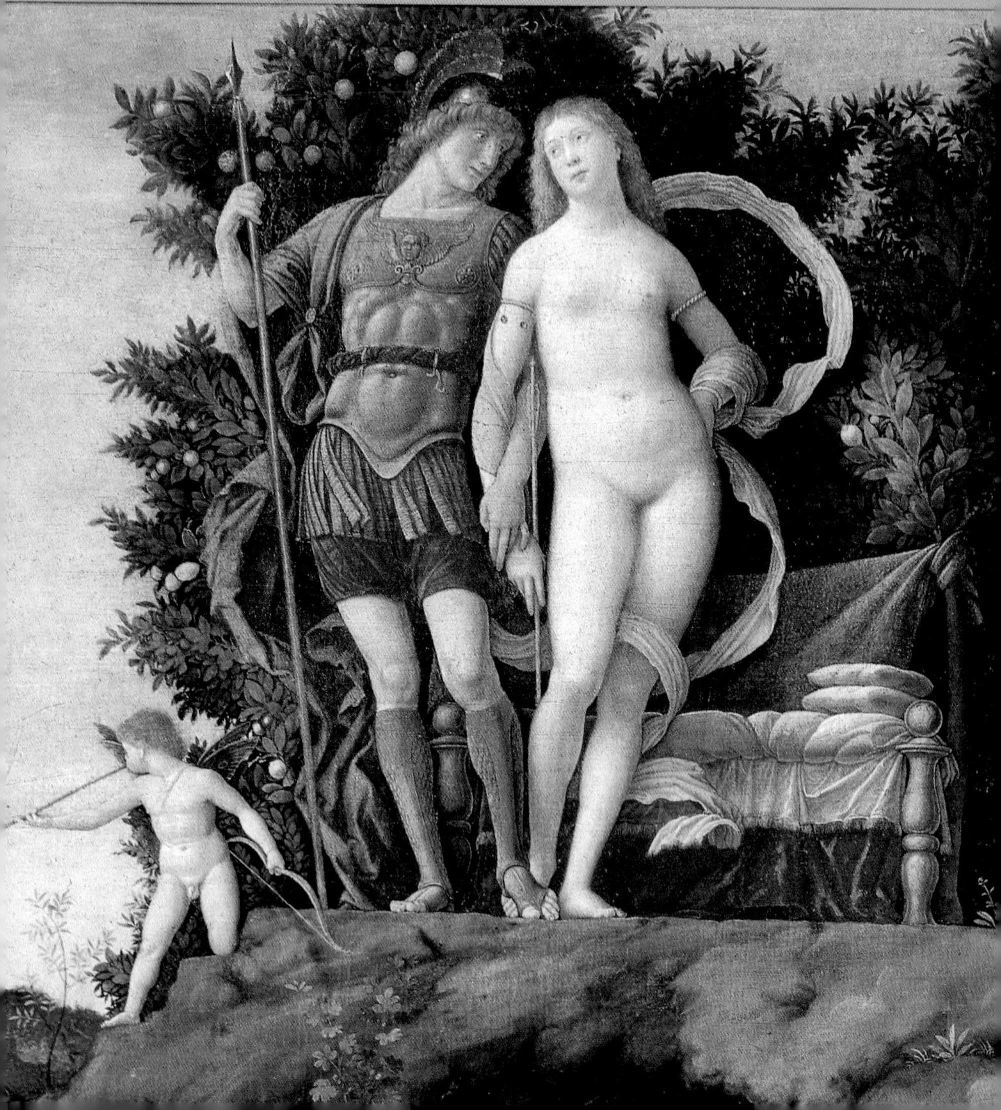

The French have focused their attention on Italy since they first began to collect art. Works of art were brought back across the Alps as a result of the military campaigns during the Renaissance, between the reigns of Charles VIII and Francis I. The latter king even summoned Leonardo da Vinci (1452–1519) to his court, although the old master could barely hold a brush by then; works such as the *Mona Lisa* have been in possession of the French rulers since that time. Also for King Francis I, Pope Leo X commissioned Raphael (1483–1520) to paint a great, monumental picture depicting Saint Michael, which found its way into the Louvre at a later date.

In the centuries that followed, French painters such as Nicolas Poussin (1594–1665) settled in Rome, resulting in a constant exchange of ideas with their Italian counterparts. Soon, major works from the Roman Baroque were arriving in Paris, including outstanding pictures by Caravaggio (ca. 1571–1610). The many large-scale paintings by Italian painters once greatly admired, such as Guido Reni (1575–1642), temporarily disappeared into storage, but now, thanks to the new structure of the

Perugino (Pietro di Cristoforo Vannucci; ca. 1450–1523), Apollo and Marsyas, 1495/1500(?), oil on wood, 59 x 29 cm, first floor, room 3

Previous pages: Hubert Robert (1733–1808), sketch for the refurbishment of the Grande Galerie in the Louvre (detail), 1796, oil on canvas, 112 x 143 cm, Musée du Louvre

Andrea Mantegna (1431–1506), Mars and Venus, known as "Parnassus" (detail), 1497, see p. 300

Grand Louvre, these too can once again be viewed by the public.

Nowhere else was Napoleon I (1769–1821) to seize as many works of art as he did in Italy, some of which remained in Paris. The Louvre offers a vast selection of great Italian painting, both in terms of quantity and quality, and it was here that the universal esteem enjoyed by these paintings originated. Leonardo da Vinci is particularly well represented, with his best

paintings grouped around the *Mona Lisa*. There is occasionally conflict in the Louvre occurring between the unique character of the palace and the chronological order, it being in some cases necessary to take major works out of their historical context. Frescos, which are wall paintings that have been executed on wet plaster, look incongruous alongside the framed panels and canvases in the gallery. For this reason, two works by Botticelli, and recently some frescos by Fra Angelico (ca. 1395–1455), have been separated from the other paintings. Unfortunately, there is always a high concentration of visitors passing in front of the them. When they are seen in peace and quiet, the joy that has emanated from Botticelli's delicate, cerebral figures since their discovery in 1873 in a Tornabuoni villa located near Florence becomes perceptible. They are the only surviving frescos of non-sacred subjects by the Florentine master of the early Renaissance, intended perhaps for a newly married couple to whom the graces and muses offer gifts. In the adjoining Salle Duchâtel, the ceiling of which has a painting of the *Fame of French Art*, executed by Charles Meynier between 1820 and 1828, more frescos have been mounted since 1999; these include the *Adoration of the Cross by St. Dominic* by Fra Angelico, who was a native of Fiesole. For the very first time in decades, it is now possible to view the impressive frescos from Greco Milanese in the style of Leonardo da Vinci, created in around 1520–1525 by Bernardo Luini (ca. 1485–1532).

Sandro Botticelli (1444–1510), Venus, offering Gifts to a Girl accompanied by Graces, ca. 1484–1486, fresco, transferred onto canvas, 211 x 284 cm, first floor, room 1

On the Origins of the Concepts of the "Gallery" and the "Salon"

Today, any large collection of paintings is often referred to as a gallery, regardless of the form of the building housing it. In the Renaissance, the term was not used to mean long, narrow rooms or corridors, in which paintings were hung, but denoted large spaces designed to accommodate both architecture and pictorial arts, as realized at Fontainebleau or in the Louvre in the Galerie d'Apollon (see p. 554 f.). In the Louvre, we gain an understanding, not so much of the origin of the modern concept, but rather of its application to the art collection itself: the Grande Galerie, today the major room containing Italian paintings, has its roots in the Renaissance. This magnificent room was initially just an immensely long corridor, a gallery in the technical sense. It was begun under Henry IV and built between 1595 and 1610 to connect the Louvre with the Tuileries palace, which no longer exists. The space was not required for paintings at that stage since the utilitarian building aroused very little contemporary interest, and it was therefore never decorated.

The suitability of long, narrow rooms for the purposes of exhibition was recognized during the reign of Louis XVI at the latest, who commissioned the painter Hubert Robert (1733–1808) to design the Grande Galerie of the Louvre as a prospective royal museum. After the Revolution, these plans metamorphosed into the design for the great Louvre museum, the major treasures of which were assembled in the Grande Galerie when the museum was opened in 1793. The

forward-looking character of the rooms in the Louvre had already been conceived by Hubert Robert in the era of the Directory. The painter, who lived in the Louvre from 1779 to 1806 – except for the time spent during his arrest under Robespierre in 1793 – initially acted as curator of the king's paintings, later fulfilling this same function for the museum.

The painter offered two alternative versions for the future of the Grande Galerie in 1796: an intact gallery, used by artists to make copies of the major works of older painters such as Raphael under lighting conditions that were unheard of at that time; and an even more astonishing scene, a destroyed Louvre, littered with statues in a manner resembling Roman ruins. The latter shows Michelangelo's *Slave* lying next to the antique *Apollo Belvedere*, which Napoleon only brought to Paris after the Italian campaign launched in 1796, but which was later returned to the Vatican. The relationship between the reality of war and the artist's viewpoint remains unclear; perhaps the famous antique had not reached France by the time that Hubert Robert painted the Louvre as a capriccio with ruins.

However, Hubert Robert was already thinking about overhead lighting, and under Napoleon work was carried out between 1805 and 1810 to improve lighting conditions. Héctor Lefuel finally introduced the skylights in 1856, during the reign of Napoleon III, a pioneering development that

Hubert Robert (1733–1808), Two Capriccios of the Grande Galerie; project to introduce overhead lighting; Idyll with Ruins, 1796, oil on canvas, 112.5 x 143 cm, 115 x 146 cm, second floor, room 5

pointed the way forward for many picture galleries all over the world. Not until alterations were begun in 1938 was today's rational solution adopted: in keeping with the revolutionary dreams of Hubert Robert, the barrel-shaped glass dome is divided into sections by means of simple encircling bands. Under Napoleon III, by contrast, a type of gallery filled with works by contemporary artists was still envisioned. The opulent bacchanalia, created by Carrier-Beleuse (1824–1887) in accordance with the tastes of Salon art, vanished.

From Salon art, we move on to the "Salon". The Louvre also leads us to the source of this term, since the sequence of Italian paintings begins in the Salon Carré, which gave birth to the concept. Built by Le Vau following the fire of 1861, this monumental room had housed the Royal Academy since 1693. Although exhibitions were only held here annually from 1725 to 1792, the annual show continued to be called the "Salon" when the Salon Carré had become part of the museum.

The Salon Carré had already witnessed some very diverse events: for instance, it served as a huge chapel for the ecclesiastical ceremony on the occasion of the marriage of Napoleon and Marie-Louise of Austria on April 2, 1810. This must have been a unique experience, for the room had already been equipped with skylights as early as 1789.

The term "Salon art" is today synonymous with obsolete trends in the art of the late 19th century. Following the rejection by Manet and the Impressionists in the 1860s and 1870s of the judgments of the Academy, which imposed constraints on painting, French art was divided. While one faction tried to accommodate subject matter and form within the established conventions, the avant-garde faction increasingly broke with tradition. An idea of how the Salon Carré looked at that time (see picture below, Musée du Louvre) is given by an outstanding Salon painter, who did not balk at the inclusion of a couple of Oriental scenes in this Second Empire drawing room. Whereas the extremely high-ceilinged Salon Carré is used today, not altogether successfully, to display Florentine painting from Cimabue to Botticelli in didactic chronological sequence, during the era of Napoleon III it was a treasure trove of major works: Lippi's work,

Giuseppe Castiglione (ca. 1810–1865), View of the Salon Carré, 1861, oil on canvas, 69 x 103 cm

Barbadori, was placed inexplicably above the door; Veronese was in conflict with Van Dyck, and so forth. Nowhere, as Paul Valéry castigated in his 1923 essay, *Le Problème des Musées*, were the problems of museums and the lack of circumspection when evaluating the old masters more evident than here. As far as the writer was concerned, the paintings were competing jealously for attention, and he remarked that the ear would not tolerate ten orchestras playing at once, and it was therefore unreasonable to assault the eyes in similar fashion.

In the 19th century, stately dignity was associated with the gallery and the Salon; under Napoleon III, between 1855 and 1857, Héctor Lefuel built the impressive Salle des Etats at right angles to the Grande Galerie, where between 1859 and 1870 – albeit with very different décor – the legislature held its sessions. The use of the room for matters of State was, however, a brief interlude, and it is here that Leonardo's *Mona Lisa* holds court, as it were. The Italians are thus in possession of the grandest rooms in the museum, comprising the actual picture gallery, having driven Salon art from the Salon Carré and the State from the Salle des Etats.

At least the overwhelming confusion has now been alleviated, even though the stream of visitors has not abated. Thomas Struth's photograph of the museum, taken in 1989, offers an almost idyllic view from the Salle des Etats of the changed conditions in the museum: it shows a ceiling painting by Veronese, which for practical reasons, despite the original intentions of the painter, has been hung on the wall alongside works by Titian and other Venetians. A group of schoolchildren is assembled beneath it, forming

Thomas Struth (b. 1954), Musée du Louvre II, Paris, 1989, color photograph, 218.5 x 180 cm

a living circle. From the perspective of the photograph, the overall shape formed by the group of schoolchildren seems to reflect the shape of Veronese's painting on the wall, playing on the reality of the paintings and the visitors to the museum. This important photograph marks a departure from the traditions of Salon photography in that it was intended not for an album, but for a photographic gallery, and is thus a work of art in its own right.

Cimabue to the Early Renaissance

Cimabue (evidence suggests 1272–1302),
***Maestà*, ca. 1280**
Wood, 427 x 280 cm

Mary is seen to be seated on an ornately carved throne, on which there rests a brilliant red cushion and some exquisite fabric. The Christ child is clad as a ruler, holding a scroll in his left hand. The tradition of Byzantine icons has merged with a typically Tuscan image of the majesty of Mary: the *Maestà*. Angels form a symmetrical frame around the throne; as the two angels beneath are turning their heads outward, the other angels are turning inward. The alternately blue and red wings of the angels lend vitality to the picture. The monumentality of the composition is matched by the size of the panel, representing both material value and esteem. This art genre blossomed under the influence of the young order of Franciscan monks. In his *Lives of the Most Excellent Italian Painters, Sculptors, and Architects*, 1550/1568, Vasari described this painting as the main altarpiece of the church of San Francesco in Pisa, the original frame of which survives along with 26 medallions bearing images of Christ, angels, prophets, and saints.

Giotto di Bondone (ca. 1266–1337),
The Stigmatization of St. Francis, ca. 1300
Wood, 313 x 163 cm

Francis of Assisi (1182–1226), founder of an order of mendicants, placed the suffering of Christ at the center of his meditations. He was stigmatized by the wounds of the Crucifixion in Alverna in 1224, the first in the history of Christianity to experience this. Giotto reproduces this extremely important event in the life of the saint in a clearly defined spatial composition. The kneeling saint is firmly ensconced in the landscape, with only the fingers of his left hand impinging upon the gold background, representing the domain of Christ. The eyes of the two figures are locked in an intense mutual gaze. Although the panel of the original frame is signed at the bottom (OPUS IOCTI FLORENTINI), some consider this a work from the painter's studio, since the figures do not appear very compact and only the best work is attributed to the master. The retable is from the Ughi chapel in the chancel of San Francesco in Pisa. The predella depicts three stages in the life of the saint.

Fra Angelico (Guido di Piero; ca. 1395–1455),
***Coronation of Mary*, ca. 1430–1432)**
Wood, center panel: 209 x 206 cm, predella:
29.5 x 210 cm

Mary is pictured kneeling humbly on the steps before the magnificent stone throne, in order to be crowned Queen of Heaven by her Son. Countless angels and saints are present at the ceremony. The weighty, earth-bound architecture is lightened by the bright colors of the stone and the pale-colored garments, resplendent with gold. The following scenes from the life of St. Dominic are depicted on the predella: *The Dream of Pope Innocent III, Vision of the Apostles Peter and Paul, Awakening of Napoleone Orsini, Resurrected Christ in the Tomb, Dispute of Dominic and the Miracle of the Books, Dominic and his Companions Fed by Angels*, and the *Death of Dominic*. The retable is from the S. Domenico monastery located in Fiesole, which the painter entered in 1420/1422.

Uccello (Paolo di Dono; 1397–1475),
***The Battle of San Romano with the Attack of Micheletto da Cotignola*, ca. 1435**
Wood, 182 x 317 cm (see p. 276 f.)

This curiously gloomy picture is full of mounted soldiers in armor. The bizarre aesthetic relies on the application of perspectival rules for the bodies of the horses and riders, as well as the weapons and stakes. However, the perspective contains puzzling elements, as if the composition in the Louvre was intended to be viewed obliquely. The battle of San Romano, 1432, in which Florence triumphed over Siena, is depicted in three surviving paintings in the Louvre, the National Gallery in London, and the Uffizi gallery in Florence. Uccello painted these pictures for Cosimo the Old, who had imposed his rule on the city of Florence in 1434. Additions were made to the picture, top right and below left, for it to be accommodated in the new Palazzo Medici in Florence in 1452.

Italian Painting

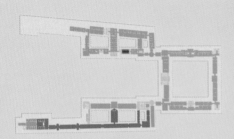

Giuseppe Arcimboldo,
Spring, p. 328

Second Floor

Folding page: Titian, *Concert
Champêtre* (detail), see p. 308

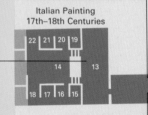

Italian Painting
17th–18th Centuries

22	21	20	19
14		13	
18	17	16	15

Salvatore Rosa, *The Ghost of
Samuel Appearing to Saul*,
p. 338 f.

Other Works:

1   Cimabue, *Maestà*, ca. 1280, room 3, p. 268

2   Uccello, *The Battle of San Romano*,
    room 3, p. 271, 276 f.

3   Master of San Francesco, *Christ
    Crucified*, ca. 1265–1270, room 4, p. 280 f.

Caravaggio,
The Fortune Teller, p. 330 f.

Andrea Mantegna,
Mars and Venus, p. 300 f.

Simone Martini, *Christ
Bearing the Cross*, p. 280

Giotto di Bondone,
*The Stigmatization of
St. Francis*, p. 269

Sandro Botticelli,
*Mary with Christ
Child and John
the Baptist*, p. 279

Domenico Ghirlandaio, *Old
Man with Grandson*, p. 286 f.

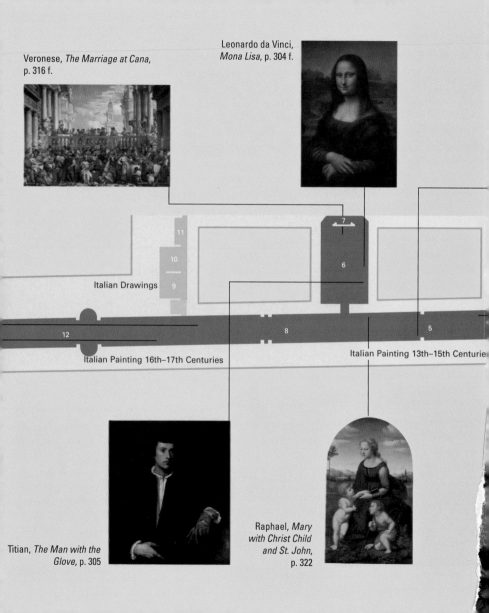

Veronese, *The Marriage at Cana*, p. 316 f.

Leonardo da Vinci, *Mona Lisa*, p. 304 f.

Italian Drawings

11

10

9

7

6

12

8

5

Italian Painting 16th–17th Centuries

Italian Painting 13th–15th Centuries

Titian, *The Man with the Glove*, p. 305

Raphael, *Mary with Christ Child and St. John*, p. 322

Filippo Lippi (1406–1469), *Mary with Child and Angels, with Sts. Frediano and Augustine*, known as *"Pala Barbadori,"* 1437
Wood, 208 x 244 cm

Against a backdrop of Renaissance architecture, heavy and thickset figures are crowded around Mary. The nearly naked Christ child is of an astonishingly monumental build. The predella in the Uffizi belongs to this altarpiece from S. Spirito in Florence. Commissioned by the captains of the *Parte guelfa*, the party sympathizing with the pope and with France, this work fulfilled the terms of the will of Gherardo Barbadori. Many people have identified a self-portrait in the monk on the left, behind the balustrade. Brought up as a Carmelite, Lippi later distanced himself from the rigid discipline of the order.

Sandro Botticelli (1444–1510), *Mary with Christ Child and John the Baptist***, ca. 1470–1475**
Wood, 91 x 67 cm

Art lovers on the threshold of the 20th century were especially fascinated by pictures such as this intense Madonna, framed by delicate foliage. The critical eyes of the experts have more recently focused on John the Baptist, with the result that this part of the painting has been attributed to an artist in the master's studio. The saint was profoundly revered in Florence at the time.

Alessio Baldovinetti (1425–1499),
*Mary with Christ Child***, ca. 1464**
Wood, 104 x 76 cm

The curious effect produced by some pictures can make them unforgettable. In this painting, thought at one time to be by Piero della Francesca (ca. 1425–1492), the baby Jesus is playfully holding the end of his umbilical bandage out to his mother, forming a line that is continued by the path in the background. Mary's face, with its serene, doll-like quality, defines the underlying mood.

The Salle des Sept-Mètres

Simone Martini (b. (?)1284, documented 1315–1344), *Christ Bearing the Cross*, ca. 1335
Poplar wood, 30 x 20.5 cm

Dense crowds of people are seen streaming through the city gates of Jerusalem. Christ, dressed in a dignified red robe decorated

with gold braid, is bearing his cross, aided by Simon of Cyrene. Mary pushes her way toward him, but is restrained by a soldier. Mary Magdalene is particularly impressive, as always in the work of Simone, with her long red hair and her arms raised in distress. Other panels for this altar, which was commissioned for a cardinal of the Orsini family, can be found in Berlin (*The Burial*), and in Antwerp (*The Crucifixion, The Descent from the Cross,* and *The Annunciation*). This polyptych executed by Simone Martini, one of the most important artists in Siena, was not necessarily painted in Italy, but possibly in Avignon, where the Cardinal Napoleone Orsini had died. On the back of the panel is a cardinal's coat of arms in the family colors. By 1400, these extremely precious panels were in the possession of the duke of Burgundy, Philip the Brave (1342–1404), and were therefore probably an influence on French painting.

Master of San Francesco (active in Umbria 1251–1275), *Christ Crucified*, ca. 1265–1270
Wood, 96.5 x 73 cm

This work, a typical *Croce dipinta*, shows Mary with a female saint to the left of the cross, with Saint John and another man to the right. The thin arms of Jesus are extended, and the body is arched. Blood is flowing from the side of the dead Christ and from the four wounds where he has been nailed to the cross. Painted crosses such as this often contained relics.

Master of the Fallen Angels,
St. Martin and the Descent into Hell,
1340–1345
Wood, transferred to canvas, each 64.2 x
29 cm, Dépôt des Musées de Bourges

This impressive panel from an unusual
altar is familiar only to connoisseurs.
At close quarters, appearing from behind the boldly foreshortened head of
a beggar, we see Saint Martin of Tours.
The reverse shows the fallen angels in
a vision that is grandiose, despite the
small figures. It is a possibility that the
Limburg brothers had become familiar
with this *Fall of the Angels* at the court
of Duc Jean de Berry (1346–1416).
They used it as a source for an important miniature, which influenced Jan
van Eyck and Petrus Christus.

Jacopo Bellini (1400–1470/71),
*Mary with Christ Child and a Member of
the Este Family*
Wood, 60 x 40 cm

Mary is seated in the open air. The tiny figure kneeling to pray is seen in profile. The
words that begin the prayer appear twice in
Mary's halo: "Ave mater regina mundi"
(Hail to the Mother, Queen of the World).

The light falls in such a way that the middle of the picture is in mysterious darkness,
and it is only the tops of the trees that are
illuminated. In the background, the light
falls from both sides, as if Mary were also a
source of light falling on the towns behind
her. The figure praying was originally identified as Lionello d'Este, duke of Ferrara,
but this is now known to be erroneous. It
is more likely to be one of his brothers, Ugo
or Meliaduse. A courtly style of painting
was introduced by Jacopo Bellini and by
Pisanello, a delicacy and eager attention to
detail which disappeared during the time
of the Renaissance.

Painters' Space –
from Gold Ground to Interiors and Landscape

Lorenzo Monaco (documented 1396 – before 1426),
The Banquet of Herod, ca. 1400, poplar wood, 34 x 68 cm

Painted figures cannot move. Therefore, painters are only able to tell a story if they show several phases in the narrative. These are best viewed alongside one another, rather than one after the other, and with the scenes preferably set in different spatial locations. For this reason, a change of location is indicative of the passing of time in many paintings. However, it was not until artists learned to paint interiors with some degree of conviction that such a concept could function at all.

Giotto (ca. 1266–1337) and his contemporaries in Florence and Siena succeeded in introducing movement into painting. Although painted on gold ground, which actually gives the picture an eternal quality, the narrative could now start to unfold. In this manner a Florentine monk in the entourage of Don Lorenzo Monaco depicted several stages in the story of the death of Saint John the Baptist, which can be read like a text from left to right. St. John has already been beheaded, since his decapitated body is lying at the prison gate on the left. Directly adjacent to this we can see the open banqueting hall where Herod's banquet occupies the center of the picture, and gives the painting the name by which it is known today. The blood-soaked head is brought to the table of the king, who is seated centrally. Princess Salome, who in this picture is just a bystander, has just danced for the king and been granted a wish. It was at her request that John the Baptist was killed, and Salome has received his head at the king's table in order to offer it to her mother, Herodias, seated on the right in a separate room, beneath an arch adjacent to the banqueting hall.

The gold ground is a substitute for the sky, and clearly demonstrates that the painter was not at pains to portray Herod's palace as a realistic, and unified structure comprising of the prison, banqueting hall, and queen's throne room. The figures are all easily identifiable if one knows something of the story. However, there is no question of artistic verisimilitude in this painting.

The fact that such paintings are still credible, despite what is portrayed, is due to the alienating effect of the gold ground, which distracts the onlooker from reality. Once the gold ground is substituted for the sky, our relationship to the subject matter changes, irrespective of whether or not the content of the picture is comprehensible. Andrea Mantegna, for instance, succeeds in his puzzling picture *Minerva* in giving its pictorial space a definite horizontal background, albeit of stagnant water. The architectural effect produced by the foliage leads on the left to a dark and uninviting place, but opens out in the center onto a landscape, simultaneously creating space and movement. Mountains tower up on the left into a sky that represents the infinite simultaneously provides a stage for the appearance of the cardinal virtues. The artist wanted those who looked at his painting to participate in a cosmic event.

Admittedly, the atmosphere and substance that make figures and objects truly credible are absent from Mantegna's great painting. This required not only a revolution in draftsmanship, but also an upheaval in painting technique: it was achieved as a result of the introduction of oil paint. The fine glazes made possible by this new medium resulted in delicate shading, which gave materials substance and rendered atmosphere perceptible. Such coloristic effects bypassed the eyes, instead appealing to the tactile sense feelings, while geometrically constructed perspectives addressed the intellect. Discovered by early Netherlandish painters such as Jan van Eyck (see p. 254 f.), introduced via works imported from the Netherlands, and subsequently practiced in Italy itself by Italian painters such as Antonello (see p. 290 f.), the new technique captured the imagination of the young Leonardo and his circle in Florence. The small panel from *The Annunciation*, again from a predella, shows the extent to which geometry is not important, provided that the atmosphere and the substance can be adequately conveyed by light and shadow.

Andrea Mantegna (1431–1506), Minerva Chasing the Sinners from the Garden of Virtues, 1497/1502, tempera on canvas, 159 x 192 cm, second floor, room 8

The Grande Galerie and the End of the Early Renaissance

Andrea del Verrocchio (1436–1488), it is now regarded as an early work of Ghirlandaio, who later worked much more systematically. The debt to Verrocchio, Leonardo's teacher, and to early Netherlandish masters such as Hugo van der Goes, is palpable. The still life featuring books, an hourglass behind the infant Jesus, and a glass of water containing flowers are a particularly charming touch.

Domenico Ghirlandaio,
Old Man with Grandson
Wood, 62 x 46 cm

These two anonymous persons were painted by Ghirlandaio, an experienced portrait painter, in a timeless illustration of the intimate relationship between old age and youth. The same old man is captured with his eyes closed in an individual drawing in the Nationalmuseum, Stockholm, possibly a posthumous portrait of a Florentine aristocrat, and so the work in Paris may have been painted as a memento or as an allegory. It has proved to be of interest, not only to students of art, but also to members of the medical profession, who diagnosed the condition apparent on the older man's nose as the skin disease hypertrophic rosacea (rhinophyma).

Domenico Ghirlandaio (1449–1494),
Mary with Christ Child, ca. 1475–1480
Wood, 79 x 56 cm

This magnificent picture of the Virgin Mary heralds a particularly fertile phase in painting from Florence. Formerly attributed to

Andrea Mantegna (1431–1506), *Mary with Christ Child,* known as the "*Madonna della Vittoria,*" ca. 1496
Canvas, 285 x 168 cm

This canvas, enormous in size, was commissioned by Francesco Gonzaga II for the chapel of S. Maria della Vittoria in Mantua, as a votive picture to commemorate the battle of Fornovo on July 6, 1495. It shows the duke of Mantua in a bold variation of what was called the *Sacra Conversazione.* In a viewpoint from above, he is kneeling in his armor on the left of the picture, while the knights Saint Michael and Saint George hold the cloak of Mary, who, like Jesus, is stretching her hand out protectively to the general. Only the heads of the patron saints of Mantua, Andrew and Longinus, are visible. Also on the podium, to the right of the throne, is John the Baptist, whose mother Elizabeth is kneeling. She is diametrically opposite the general and represents the patroness Isabella d'Este, his wife.

Andrea Mantegna,
Calvary, 1457–1460
Wood, 76 x 96 cm

Mantegna began his creative career with several revolutionary pictures, including the retable commissioned by the important Venetian notary, Gregorio Correr, for the high altar of Saint Zeno in Verona. The predella was shared between Paris and Tours, while the pala remained in Verona. The monumental nature of this work is indicated by the Crucifixion, with its stone panorama of the hill of Golgotha, being approached by a soldier in the foreground, and the crosses towering high into the sky. When compared with the paintings of Pisanello and Jacopo Bellini, the perspectival composition and the sculptural quality of the bodies, which are modeled on antique marble statues, show the extent of the aesthetic revolution that took place during the Early Renaissance.

Antonello da Messina (ca. 1430–1479),
The Flagellation of Christ,
Venice or Sicily, ca. 1476–1478
Oil on wood, 29.8 x 21 cm

The moving effect of this picture, which was only acquired as recently as 1992, is produced by the concentration on one aspect of the events portrayed. Painted to serve as a devotional picture, it focuses on the suffering Christ. The place and date of origin are uncertain; the picture may have been painted after the artist moved to Messina, where he spent the remainder of his life.

Antonello da Messina, _Portrait of a Man_, "_Il condottiere_," 1475
Oil on wood, 35 x 28 cm

The anonymous subject is shown in three-quarter profile at a time when Italy still favored the full profile. Background and clothing are distinguished only by a few nuances of light. Painted in oil, this picture represents a new type of portrait, originating from the Netherlands, of which Jan van Eyck (ca. 1390–1441) was the progenitor. Antonello da Messina skillfully imitated his technique and his way of seeing things. He signed and dated

the Paris picture on the cartellino with the words: "1475/Antonellus messanens(is) me pinxit". The resolute gaze of the man and the scar on his lip have led to his being dubbed "The Mercenary Leader". During the time of the Renaissance, Italian politics were very influenced by these military leaders. Cities such as Florence and Venice have erected monuments to them, but we do not know for certain whether the man painted by Antonello was among their ranks.

The High Renaissance

Piero di Cosimo (Piero di Lorenzo) (1461/62–1521),
Mary with Christ Child and a Dove,
known as the "*Dove Madonna,*" ca. 1490
Oil on wood, 87 x 58 cm

Piero di Cosimo was a solitary painter of genius, as this picture with its unusual coloring shows: the reredos is modest, like a woven mat, and Mary's clothing and the stiff blue cloth covering her head also appear extraordinarily simple. The importance to the artist of the Virgin Mary's humble poverty is likewise demonstrated by the prayer book, which is in plain script picked out in red. Simple threads serve as bookmarks. The infant Jesus points at the less than perfectly white dove that is also sitting on the balustrade, which appears tilted toward the onlooker; the tiny halo of the dove signifies the Holy Spirit.

Leonardo da Vinci (1452–1519), Portrait of a Woman, known as "*La Belle Ferronnière*", (1495–1499)
Oil on wood, 63 x 45 cm

Leonardo's painting, which perhaps depicts Lucrezia Crivelli or Cecilia Gallerani, both of whom were mistresses of Duke Ludovico il Moro of Milan, or possibly even his wife Beatrice d'Este, soon entered the possession of Francis I (1494–1547). The picture first became famous under a false name, because the subject was confused with a mistress of Francis I, wife of a certain M. Le Ferron. The "ferronnière" adorning her forehead did nothing to dispel the confusion. The play on words merely shows how little names mean. Although the woman who once turned her expressive gaze to the artist is long since dead, her open countenance survives in the Louvre in an unusually subtle light, turned suddenly toward the onlooker, it is reserved and at the same time mysterious.

Lorenzo di Credi (ca. 1458–1537),
*Mary with Christ Child and Sts. Julian
and Nicholas of Myra*, **before 1494**
Oil on wood, 163 x 164 cm

On the left stands the pilgrims' friend, Saint Julian, completely devoid of attributes. Nicholas is recognizable by his three golden balls, which he has placed on the ground at the bottom right side of the picture as if they were mere trifles. The resem-blance between the naked Christ child and Saint Nicholas is due to the Mannerist treatment of their hair. The status of the figures is reflected in the architecture: Mary is seated on a throne in front of an alcove, while a view of the sky suffices for the saints. Glowing colors, deep red and blue, were used by the artist, a pupil of Ver-rocchio, in this picture; dated 1494, it was painted for the Mascalzoni chapel of San Maria Maddalena dei Pazzi in Cestello.

**Cima da Conegliano (Giovanni Battista Cima)
(1459/60–1517/18), *Mary with Christ Child
between John the Baptist and Mary
Magdalene*, ca. 1511–1513**
Oil on wood, 167 x 110 cm

Mary is seated on a high stone throne on a terrace, separated by a balustrade from the landscape beyond. The reredos rises high into the sky. On the left, John the Baptist is bending down and facing the Christ child, whom he identifies with the writing on his scroll as the Lamb of God. Mary Magdalene, who is holding her jar of ointment, does not meet the others' eyes, but seems lost in contemplative meditation. These figures occupy only a small part of the pictorial space. The landscape, captured in clear colors with a bright, glowing evening sky, creates a very peaceful atmosphere. Mountain ranges are visible on the distant blue horizon through the tall crags to the right. This panel, signed "JOANIS BAPT CONEGLANE(N)S(IS) OPUS" on the cartellino on the step in front of the throne, is from the Dominican church in Parma. The artist can be identified by his brilliant rendering of light. Cima's painting, one of the artist's most famous, is one of the surprisingly few examples of Venetian painting in the Louvre before Titian.

Mary is pictured to be kneeling underneath some rocks, accompanied by two naked infants and an angel. She embraces one of the boys gracefully with her right arm, while she holds her outstretched left arm protectively over the other. An angel supports the back of the somewhat smaller, and hence younger child; this is Jesus, raising his small right hand in a sign of blessing to the infant St. John. The bodies, sculpturally molded by the use of light and shade, look as if they have been placed in front of a dark screen. The rocky ground is adorned with flowers, which the artist also studied in nature. On the left, the view opens out into an inhospitable mountain landscape of steep, high rock formations. The harmonious pyramidal composition with the delicate gradations of color and the *sfumato* that is characteristic of Leonardo in the background all combine to make this painting unforgettable. It was originally the center panel of a winged altar that Franciscan monks in Milan commissioned from Leonardo da Vinci, the de Predis brothers, and the sculptor Giacomo del Maino for a chapel of the Confraternity of the Immaculate Conception. A second version can be seen in the National Gallery in London, England.

Leonardo da Vinci (1452–1519)
The Virgin with Christ Child and St. John **known as the** *Virgin of the Rocks* **(with detail), ca. 1483**
Oil on wood, transferred to canvas, 199 x 122 cm

Leonardo da Vinci (1452–1519),
St. Anne with Virgin and Child
(with detail), ca. 1508–1510
Oil on wood, 169 x 130 cm

The group of figures is pictured against a rough and rocky background, opening out into a desolate landscape beyond the tree to the right. Saint Anne is holding her daughter, Mary, on her lap; the latter is bending down to restrain her son, who is pulling away from her and climbing onto the back of the lamb. Jesus is pulling the ears of the lamb playfully. Leonardo has incorporated the ancient theme of the three generations in a narrative describing mankind's redemption through the Passion, with the lamb as a symbol of sacrifice. The panel was destined for the high altar of Santissima Annunziata, one of the most important churches in Florence. Although begun in 1500 and revised in countless sketches and drawings, like many of Leonardo's paintings it remained unfinished and was never delivered. It was still in Leonardo's possession when he spent the final years of his life in France as court painter to Francis I. It was not until the reign of Louis XIII (1610–1643) that the work entered the royal collection.

Andrea Mantegna (1431–1506),
Mars and Venus, known as *"Parnassus"*, 1497
Canvas, 159 x 192 cm

Isabella d'Este (1474–1539), countess of
Mantua, commissioned five paintings for her
first *studiolo,* of which the best two were
painted by Mantegna. The more famous of
these is now known as *Parnassus*, the central
feature of which is the dance of the muses to
the strains of Apollo's lyre. The earliest

inventory, however, names the principal figures as Mars and Venus, who was actually
married to Vulcan. Cupid is aiming at the
latter, who is seen gesticulating furiously in
his forge, not with a bow but with a blow-
pipe. The painting does not commemorate
the adultery of the goddess of love, but celebrates the harmony engendered by her
alliance with the god of war. The question of
whether Apollo, or his son Linus, or even
Orpheus, as was thought in 1547, is playing

to muses or mere nymphs, remains unresolved. In any event, the notion of Parnassus as the home of Apollo and the muses definitely recedes into the background. The immense freedom with which Mantegna treats mythology is also evident in the figures of Mercury and Pegasus; their juxtaposition is perhaps simply an allusion to the astrological constellations in ascendancy at the time of the marriage of the royal couple.

Lorenzo Costa (1460–1535), *Allegory on the Court of Isabella d'Este,* **known as** *"The Crowning of Isabella",* **1505/06**
Oil on canvas, 164.5 x 197.5 cm

Lorenzo Costa, who was from Isabella's native city of Ferrara, was commissioned to continue the series of pictures for her *studiolo*. His slender figures in airy spaces are in keeping with a more atmospheric rendering of nature, but Mantegna's humanistic discipline is absent. Pictorial structure with elements of a relief gives way to looser composition, again with figures that are difficult to identify. Following on from Mantegna's *Parnassus* (1497), Costa's painting represents more civilized pleasures in the garden of Harmonia, the daughter of Venus and Mars, who for this reason, personifies the equilibrium of virtue.

Perugino (Pietro di Cristoforo Vannucci) (shortly after 1450–1523), *The Struggle between Love and Chastity,* **1505**
Oil on canvas, 156 x 192 cm

The unforgettable quality of Mantegna's painting also outstrips that of Perugino. Even Isabella d'Este had made disparaging remarks concerning the latter's picture in a letter. This shows the battle between virtuous and sinful deities, with Athene in full armor triumphing over Cupid, a naked youth distinguished only by the blindfold on his eyes from the other small cupids around him.

Should Works of Art be Returned to their Place of Origin? The Theft of the *Mona Lisa* in 1911

Leonardo's *Mona Lisa* has always occupied a place of honor in the Louvre; this was no less the case on August 23, 1911, the Monday night on which Vincenzo Peruggia locked himself in the Louvre. A mirror maker, he had worked in the museum and therefore knew his way around the Grande Galerie, with its numerous mirrors, and the Salon Carré, where Leonardo's painting hung between Titian and Correggio. At that time the museum was closed on Mondays, and so Peruggia was able to remove the picture unnoticed.

Fictional illustration of Vincenzo Peruggia's theft of the Mona from the Louvre in 1911, contemporary lithograph

This was in the days before the introduction of cabling or alarms, when large areas of the museum did not even have electric light. A contemporary cartoonist drew a sequence of fictional illustrations of the crime, in which he imagined the scene as follows: despite Peruggia's voluminous coat, the picture frame will not fit inside it, and therefore the thief is obliged to dispose of it; he carries the painting through the Grande Galerie and the Salle des Sept-Mètres and down a small staircase that is closed to the public, and then crosses the courtyard containing the sphinx to the quayside on the Seine.

It was precisely during this period that people had begun to express the view that the most important works of art should be protected against vandalism, and a program of glazing was begun, in connection with which Peruggia had been engaged. Louis Béraud, who was a painter employed by the Louvre, had designed something especially for the *Mona Lisa*, but when he went to look at the painting on the museum's weekly closing day, it was gone. A futile search in the photographic studio ensued. There was no trace of the painting for some time: Peruggia kept it in his lodgings at 5, rue de l'Hôpital St.-Louis, in the false bottom of a suitcase. What Peruggia intended to do with "his" Leonardo remains a mystery. In a naive response to an advertisement by Geri, a Florentine art dealer who wished to purchase Italian works of art, he wrote offering the *Gioconda*, as the work is

G. Léonnec, Le Clou du Louvre, caricature from La Vie Parisienne, September 1911, containing a play on the word "clou" (French for both "nail" and "main attraction").

Raymond Langlois introducing his new alarm system in June 1941, in the frame of a reproduction of the Mona Lisa.

called in Italy. Geri invited Peruggia to Florence, where he received the painting in the presence of Poggi, the director of the Uffizi. It was identified on December 11, 1913. In the following weeks it was briefly exhibited in Florence, and then in Rome and Milan, before being returned to Paris on January 1, 1914, where it was first exhibited at the Ecole des Beaux-Arts to raise funds for charitable works in Italy. On January 5, it returned to the Salon Carré in the Louvre, where Raphael's *Castiglione* (see p. 323) had acted as a worthy substitute. In the following year, legal proceedings began against the thief. Born in 1881, Peruggia claimed to be a patriot who had wanted to return the painting to Leonardo's birthplace. Why, though, had the

Paris police already taken his photograph and fingerprints on January 25, 1909? Before Peruggia was arrested, the Louvre had to endure the embarrassment of being left with nothing but the nail on which the painting had hung.

A whole generation was to pass before the problems of security became better understood. With a certain amount of irony, Raymond Langlois, a pioneer of alarm systems in the Louvre, was photographed during the Second World War with the *Mona Lisa* in his hands. During this period, however, the real *Gioconda* was in hiding.

303

The Salle des États

Leonardo da Vinci (1452–1519),
***Mona Lisa*, also known as**
***"La Gioconda"*, 1510–1515**
Oil on wood, 77 x 53 cm

To this day we still cannot identify the subject of the most famous portrait in the history of painting. It was christened *La Gioconda* by Giorgio Vasari (1511–1574), the artists' biographer, whose play on words immortalized her smile: *La Gioconda* simply means "the joyful one". Having the dignity of one who knows how to keep a secret, this figure who is firmly anchored in the picture, distances herself from all attempts to identify her as the wife of a Florentine silk merchant, the mistress of a prince, or even as an androgynous self-portrait of the artist. It is not the legends surrounding this picture, which was once stolen and found again, that give the *Mona Lisa* the power to triumph over an unworthy rabble, but the artistic distancing from the realms of daily life, which most visitors to the Louvre remember more clearly than anything else.

This enigmatic woman is seated before a backdrop of rocky landscape, in which it seems possible to gaze beyond the rivers and mountains to the distant Alps; the horizon behind her appears unobtrusive.

This scene does not correspond with a real landscape, but with a bifocal view of a figure placed in front of the horizon. Despite the anecdotal evidence, *Mona Lisa* is not really smiling at all. The artist has left the areas that determine facial expression, the corners of the mouth and eyes, open to interpretation. As a direct result, every individual whose attention is engaged by this countenance can bring to it something of their own experience and expectations, and it is this effect that gives the painting an immensely vital quality. Yet when one steps back, imagining one has understood the figure, all that remains is the majesty of an impenetrable gaze, which seems to be acquainted with more of the secrets of the world than the crowds that flock to see the enigmatic *Mona Lisa*.

Titian (Tiziano Vecellio)
(1488/1490–1576),
***The Man with the Glove*,**
ca. 1520–1522
Oil on canvas, 100 x 89 cm

The art expert Bernard Berenson once said in relation to this and other comparable pictures that they were the real offspring of the Renaissance, taught no

fear and nothing in commonly life. The likeness of a young Venetian of good standing and, given the indistinguishable coat of arms on his ring, aristocratic pretensions, has become the epitome of noble youth. Delicate and yet bold, his true identity remains a mystery. Titian spreads the figure, viewed from the front and turned almost casually to the right, expansively over the pictorial surface. The significance of the gloves still remains a matter of great debate among art historians today.

Mona Lisa visits Jackie Kennedy

When he painted the *Mona Lisa*, Leonardo created not only a portrait but also a global symbol of womanhood. At present, she receives visitors in the Salle des Etats in the Louvre, and is due to move to a new room, the design of which is already complete, in 2003. At the end of 1962, beginning of 1963, however, she went on her travels to visit the New World and to pay her respects in Washington to the most famous American presidential couple. Shortly before this was decided, in 1962, the Paris newspaper *Libération* published a vituperative article: "*La Gioconda* will stay in Paris. One does not summon a beautiful woman to one's house. One goes to see her".

Nevertheless, *Mona Lisa* did travel, with global repercussions. Edward T. Folliard, Pulitzer prizewinner and correspondent of the *Washington Post*, was responsible for putting the idea into the head of André Malraux in 1962. The French culture minister, a writer and adventurer who did not take the anxieties of the professional museum curators all that seriously, proved open to such a suggestion. The painting had given cause for concern on several previous occasions: in 1911 it was stolen by a patriotic Florentine (see p. 302 f.), and in 1957 a mentally disturbed person threw a stone at it. The extensive report by the experts, which decisively rejected the undertaking, was praised as an outstanding achievement by Malraux, who promptly gave unequivocal orders to the person then responsible, Madeleine Hours, to eliminate all risks.

The effort was enormous; an aluminum box, weighing over 80 kg (176 lbs), with relative humidity of 48% and a constant temperature of 17 degrees Celsius (63 degrees Fahrenheit), was dispatched from Le Havre to New York, not by air but on the luxury liner *France*. The painting spent the Christmas of 1962 in the storeroom of the National Gallery before emerging on January 8, 1963, following the first session of the Senate in the new year, to honor an illustrious company: President Kennedy, who was to be assassinated under a year later, had at that point achieved the height of adulation. Jacqueline Bouvier, his wife, was regarded throughout the world as the ideal Frenchwoman; after all, she had French ancestry, had studied in Paris, and was elegance personified.

Jackie's ancestral land was at that time undergoing historic upheavals: General de Gaulle had granted independence to Algeria. The entire political Right rose up against the conservative French Resistance hero of the Second World War; he was rebuked for abandoning national territory, demoralizing the nation, and violating the constitution. For this reason, the strengthening of international friendships made much sense – even with America, a nation General de Gaulle disliked.

Seldom has France sent a better ambassador into the world. The lines of people anxious to view the painting were endless: Four visitors at a time climbed a small staircase in order to

The Mona Lisa on display in the National Gallery, Washington, January 8, 1963. President Kennedy, Mme Malraux, the French culture minister André Malraux, Jackie Kennedy and Vice-President Lyndon B. Johnson

spend around five to seven seconds in front of the picture. On January 9, maximum security was already in force: Madame Hours from the Louvre, suddenly anxious, bent down under the barrier to inspect the monitoring devices. In her excitement, she forgot safety measures; a Marine immediately tried to stop her at bayonet point, but was pre-empted by a Secret Service agent who laid her out on the floor with a karate blow. She fell sideways, unconscious, and the point of the bayonet fortunately did no more than cut the strap of her brassiere.

In Washington, the French and Americans had arranged a poetic reunion for *Mona Lisa*, placing her alongside Botticelli's *Giuliano de' Medici* from the National Gallery. According to one story, Leonardo is supposed to have immortalized in the *Mona Lisa* an unfulfilled love for the prince, who was sadly murdered. In Washington, therefore, *Mona Lisa* visited her beloved, or, as Madame Hours wrote: "Les amants désunis … se trouvaient réunis aux Etats-Unis". (The disunited lovers were reunited in the United States.)

Giorgione (Giorgio da Castelfranco) (1477/78–1510), or more probably Titian (Tiziano Vecellio) (1488/1490–1576), *Concert Champêtre*, ca. 1510
Oil on canvas, 110 x 138 cm

This picture was attributed to Giorgione for a long time, but is now regarded as a major work from Titian's early period of creativity. Even the genre of the painting is impossible to establish beyond doubt: the attire of the distinguished lute player in the center looks far too contemporary if an allusion to mythological or to historical themes from Antiquity was intended. It remains unclear what the two clothed men and two naked women are doing. Even the gesture of the woman on the left is paradoxical, as she appears to be pouring water into the well, rather than taking water from it. However, her gesture acquires a surprisingly poetic

quality precisely due to its evident point-lessness. In the absence of any concrete definition of the content, the picture conveys the mood of a pastoral scene, a rural idyll; it excites the imagination, as if offering a view of an enchanted, magical world.

Titian (Tiziano Vecellio) (1488/1490–1576),
Madonna with Rabbit, **1530**
Oil on canvas, 74 x 84 cm

Along with the arrival of the new concept of the rural idyll or pastoral scene, religious themes also underwent changes in Titian's painting. Perhaps this work is intended to depict the rest during the flight into Egypt, though Mary is sitting on the ground in a manner typical of the Virgin of Humility of an earlier date. A young woman is handing over her the child; we can see from her clothing that she is probably not a virgin, but the attributes of a saint are missing, which likewise shows a certain amount of freedom as regards convention. From his own imagination, the artist paints figures that might also represent pious onlookers. The painting may have been intended for the aristocrat Federico Gonzaga; indeed, it has even been suggested that the shepherd on the right in the middle ground, is a portrait of the nobleman.

Titian (Tiziano Vecellio),
***Entombment of Christ,* ca. 1523–1526**
Oil on canvas, 148 x 205 cm

The Louvre, unlike practically any other museum, is able to show widely differing facets of Titian's revolutionary contribution to the visual arts. The powerful landscape format of this picture of the entombment of Christ, drawn from life, as it were, shows the unbridled grief of Mary, Mary Magdalene, and John, and the gentleness of those who are laying him to rest. It is typical of this expressive artist, who was able to disregard aesthetic rules when necessary. Dramatic use is made by Titian of darkness and light in the foreground and in the sky.

Titian (Tiziano Vecellio),
***Penance of St. Jerome,* 1531**
Oil on canvas, 80 x 102 cm

It was, ironically, in the watery world of Venice that a feeling for landscape developed during the 16th century. The picture

of the Father of the Church, St. Jerome, plays an important role in this, his penance in the wilderness in Thebes in Upper Egypt providing a stimulus for the imagination. Having first led the eye over the distant countryside, Titian shows virtuosity in expressing the inner turmoil of the penitent St. Jerome in a wild part of the forest: the almost impenetrable darkness signifies the state of his soul, straining in the direction of the few rays of light that illuminate the scene from above. The traditional attributes of his sainthood recede into the background; his lion is sheathed in darkness. What is new is the intensely subjective experience. This picture, in particular, remained artistically challenging until the arrival of Romanticism in the 19th century.

Titian (Tiziano Vecellio),
***Jupiter and Antiope*, known as the *"Pardo Venus,"* 1535–1540, reworked ca. 1560**
Oil on canvas, 196 x 385 cm

Titian frequently worked for the Spanish Habsburgs, a fact that gave rise to the traditional name of this picture from the El Pardo palace, where the painting was kept for a long time. Once again, the poetic license in the Venetian artist's approach to antique mythology distorts the view of the actual subject of the picture: the reclining nude is not, as the original name suggests, the goddess of love, Venus, but Antiope, daughter of the king of Thebes. Jupiter, who is in love with her, comes to her in the form of a satyr, and is seen uncovering the body of the sleeping girl, with Cupid hovering above. In a wondrous landscape,

which again resembles a pastoral idyll, we see a mythological event played out that is very seldom depicted in such monumental paintings. The purpose of the large figures on the left is not entirely clear; huntsmen are involved in encounters with satyrs and peasants, while more hunters are chasing a deer to the rear of the main figures.

Lambert Sustris (ca. 1520–after 1591),
***Venus and Cupid,* ca. 1554**
Oil on canvas, 132 x 184 cm

During the 16th century, Venice and the areas on the mainland that were conquered by the Venetians attracted artists from all over the world. Lambert Sustris came from Amsterdam and painted landscapes in Titian's studio. In this large-scale picture of a familiar mythological theme he adds an unusual note to the depiction of Venus, a subject painted more frequently by his master: although the Dutchman's application of color follows the tradition that was customary in Venice until Tintoretto, the composition, featuring the studied articulation of the limbs of the elongated nude figure and the curious motif of the union of two doves, apparently at the behest of the goddess of love, is without precedent in Venice. While native painters seem to have lacked the will to define objects and forms clearly, Sustris was inclined to excessive clarity, as this painting demonstrates. The artist wallows in detail, painting the carvings on the bed, the drapes, and the braid with great care. He not only places the principal figure of Venus next to the infant Cupid, but shows Mars, the god of war, striding up in full armor. As a result, the humanist idea of the birth of harmony from love, in particular that between Mars and Venus, emerges more clearly from the works of Sustris than from works by his contemporaries Giorgione and Titian.

Lorenzo Lotto (ca. 1480–1556),
Christ bearing the Cross, 1526
Oil on canvas, 66 x 60 cm

Lorenzo Lotto, a Venetian, was the most perceptive "psychologist" of all the northern Italian Renaissance painters. As if a picture, now in Ghent, by the Dutch painter Hieronymus Bosch (ca. 1450–1516) were directly in front of him, Lotto focuses on the silent suffering in the countenance of Christ, gazing out from a scene on which night has apparently fallen. The detail in the other figures is radically curtailed, their faces distorted by light and shade. The colors are still bright, but against the dark background there is already a feeling for the chiaroscuro that Caravaggio (1571–1610) and his followers were about to disseminate throughout Europe on the threshold of the Baroque, in their paintings that were just as dramatic in nature as those of the Venetian.

Lorenzo Lotto, *Christ and the Woman taken in Adultery,* **between 1529 and 1539**
Oil on canvas, 124 x 156 cm

Although a Venetian, Lotto does not quite fit in with the other painters from his native city; significantly, he painted more on the mainland than on the lagoon. His *Christ and the Woman taken in Adultery* was painted in glowing colors and using powerful chiaroscuro effects. The subject matter, which was unsuitable for altarpieces, was not discovered until the 16th century, and was subsequently employed on both sides of the Alps. As was customary after Mantegna, Lotto's half-length figures are placed in front of a dark background. The faces of those gathered around Christ to hear his judgment on the woman who has committed adultery are reminiscent of the wild, distinctive features depicted in works by Leonardo, Bosch, and Dürer.

Veronese (Paolo Caliari) (1528–1588),
***The Marriage at Cana,* 1563**
Oil on canvas, 660 x 990 cm

This monumental oil painting is from the refectory of the Benedictine order at San Giorgio Maggiore. Instead of the Last Supper, Veronese has painted Christ's first miracle. A servant in the foreground on the right indicates that the last jug of wine becomes almost empty; Christ is asked by Mary to perform the miracle, and the bride and groom appear at the wedding. Little of this is apparent in the Veronese painting. Instead, the artist seems to have taken as his starting point an idea for the *Last Supper,* with Jesus in the center of the painting, accompanied by the Apostles, but without the Virgin Mary. Whether or not Christ takes any interest in the matter of the wine is lost in the hurly-burly of events.

Ten years later, at an interrogation before the Inquisition regarding a similar painting, which was initially intended to portray the Last Supper, but was then subsequently changed and renamed the *Feast at the House of Levi* (this is now in Venice, in the Accademia), Veronese said that in large-scale paintings such as this, the artist, like the poet, needs freedom to invent other characters alongside the key figures, a freedom of which he made full use in *The Marriage at Cana.* The basic tendency of Venetian painting to disregard wherever possible the requirements of the subject matter was reinforced by the attitude of the master from Verona.

The Louvre during the Second World War

A Room in the Egyptian Section during the Evacuation and Securing of the Inventory at the end of 1939.

War shaped the Louvre in different ways, filling its rooms with Napoleonic loot, but also threatening its continued existence. The Franco-Prussian war of 1870/71 might have meant the end, for civil war broke out in Paris after the defeat at Sedan. This Commune uprising destroyed the Tuileries palace, because it had been the residence of the deposed emperor, and came close to destroying the museum to which Napoleon III had given such magnificent support. If armed security guards, supported by the National Guard, had not defended the Louvre against the masses in 1871, more treasures would have gone up in flames.

In the 20th century, war brought even worse devastation. Both sides have remained largely

The Venus de Milo in its packing case, autumn 1939.

The Nike of Samothrace is lifted ready for transport in 1939.

silent concerning the extent of the unspeakable damage during the First World War, especially during the final push by the Germans toward Rheims. Today – after the bombing that reduced almost all German cities to rubble and ashes – German dreams of destroying Paris from the air have been forgotten. The title page of an anonymous German pamphlet dated 1926 shows

German bombers swarming around the spires of Notre-Dame. However, such barbarism was expected in the autumn of 1939, when France entered the war following the German invasion of Poland.

The Louvre reacted immediately. In an unprecedented operation, the museum was evacuated, and the works were loaded onto freight trains taking them to no fewer than 72 storerooms at locations far from Paris. Castles were requisitioned for this purpose, and it seemed sensible to move many art treasures to sites as distant as possible from the northeastern flank of the country, in other words in a southerly direction, often as far as the Pyrenees.

There was a dearth of trained staff of course; the packers and drivers, like the trucks, came from the large Paris department stores. Very few of them had ever driven across the country, let alone without lights. The headlamps were blacked out and off they went. The truck containing Géricault's gigantic *Raft of the Medusa* (see p. 438 f.) became entangled in the overhead cables of Versailles and cut off the power supply to the entire town, and the truck full of Watteau's paintings was temporarily lost in thick fog, but all finally arrived at their destination. In

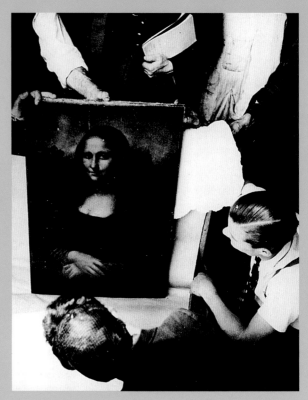

Leonardo's Mona Lisa, its frame removed, being packed in September 1939.

the Louvre itself, plaster casts and similar exhibits were skillfully arranged in order to be able to offer something to soldiers sent to recuperate in Paris from the eastern front. Immense efforts were devoted to hiding the most famous large sculptures. The monumental size of the *Venus de Milo* is still evident: despite the urgency

of the situation, it looks as though it is bursting out of its wooden packing case. A marble sculpture such as the *Nike of Samothrace* could only be moved using heavy lifting equipment.

The rooms of the Louvre were deserted. It was not possible to dismantle everything, nor could everything be accommodated in the transport reserved for the most precious works. Sandbags were piled up in the various rooms to protect heavy stone sculptures. Picture frames lay on the floor in the Grande Galerie with an air of bleak desolation that was actually not that far removed from Hubert Robert's gloomy vision of the destruction of the Louvre (see p. 265). Without its frame, even the acclaimed *Mona Lisa* seems humbled; nevertheless, a photograph taken as the picture was being packed shows the majestic impression it was still able to convey, even under these less than perfect circumstances. The enigmatic phrase of: *La Joconde a le sourire*, or "the Mona Lisa is still smiling," served as a coded message during the war years, meaning that all was well with the works of art in storage.

Not until July 1949 was the museum able to open its doors again. The dreadful events of the war had never reached Paris in its full force, and the nightmare of bombing campaigns and destruction of the nation's treasures had not come to pass. Little had been lost. By contrast with Berlin, no work of critical importance to global culture that was entrusted to this museum went missing, and over the past few decades, only the London museums have been able to compete with the Louvre in Europe in terms of continuing to expand their already priceless collections of treasures.

The Grande Galerie, showing the empty picture frames following the removal of the paintings in 1939.

**Raphael (Raffaello Santi; 1483–1520),
Mary with Christ Child and St. John,
known as "*La Belle Jardinière*", 1507/08**
Oil on canvas, mounted on
wood, 122 x 80 cm

Mary is sitting on a stone
bench against a green backdrop, with a great voluminous blue cloak over her red
gown. She is holding the
small Christ child by the
hand; he is leaning against
her legs, gazing up at her. The
two figures are linked by
glances and by gentle tou-
ches. The infant Saint John,
clothed in animal skin in an
allusion to his future life as a
hermit, fulfills two functions
in the picture: the cross he
holds is a reference to the
Passion, and in addition his
devoted worship of the infant
Jesus is exemplary. The Virgin Mary, in this particular
painting, called "*La Belle Jardinière*", is the most charming
of the Florentine Madonnas
by Raphael, and reveals the
extent to which the young
master had studied Michelangelo and Leonardo (see p.
296 f.). The painting is signed and dated on
the hem of Mary's cloak. The identity of the
person who commissioned it is not known,
neither is the date that it entered the royal
collection. Perhaps Max Ernst and Paul Klee
had this painting in mind when they painted
their versions of the *Belle Jardinière*, one as
Eve, the other as a real gardener.

Raphael (Raffaello Santi),
Baldassare Castiglione, **1514–1515**
Oil on canvas, mounted on wood, 82 x 67 cm

Baldassare Castiglione (1478–1529) was a leading statesman and writer of the Italian Renaissance; he traveled in England and France as an envoy. His major work, *The Courtier* (*Libro del cortegiano*, 1528), was a treatise on the ideal qualities required by a courtier in that era. It was partly for this reason that Raphael's extraordinarily noble portrait of this man made such an impression. It shows various stylistic influences from older paintings, as far back as the *Mona Lisa* (see p. 304 f.), and was probably painted in Rome while Castiglione was ambassador of the duke of Urbino.

full, which has the effect of increasing the dynamism of the composition. The landscape in the background is painted from above and is a rather unusual feature for Raphael. Although the panel is signed and dated (RAPHAEL VRBINAS. PINGEBAT M.D. XVII. 1518), for a long time it was thought to have been painted by assistants in his studio. It was commissioned by Pope Leo X at the suggestion of Francis I; Leo's nephew, Lorenzo de'Medici, presented the painting to the king at a later date, in order to strengthen the alliance with France in view of the wars against the Turks.

Sebastiano Luciani, known as Sebastiano del Piombo (ca. 1485–1547),
***The Visitation*, 1519, dated 1521**
Oil on canvas, 168 x 132 cm

The Louvre does not possess any paintings by Michelangelo himself, but he is represented by his friend of many years, Sebastiano del Piombo, in this painting with its effective use of light. The setting sun lights up the sky dramatically, as if the painter were aware of Mary's arduous journey over the mountains to visit her cousin Elizabeth. The artist reveals his Venetian origins by concentrating on the state of mind of the youthful Mary and the elderly Elizabeth, who was to give birth to John the Baptist. Like Giorgione and the young Titian, he had turned to landscape and understood the emotional power that the figures in his paintings could derive from it.

Raphael (Raffaello Santi), *St. Michael*, called *The Great St. Michael*, ca. 1518
Oil on wood, transferred to canvas, 268 x 160 cm

The archangel occupies the center of the picture like a strong pillar, and yet appears as light as a dancer. He is standing on the fallen angel Lucifer, whom he condemns to eternal damnation in hell. Neither the weapons nor Michael's wings are shown in

Il Pontormo (Jacopo Carrucci; 1494–1557),
***St. Anne with Four Saints*, 1528/29**
Oil on wood, 228 x 176 cm

This painting is in the tradition of pictures depicting the Virgin Mary with saints, and focuses on the three generations represented by St. Anne, Mary, and Christ. Commissioned by the Signoria, the municipal authority of Florence, the painting was intended for the high altar of the San Anna monastery in Verzaia. A procession took place here every year, as depicted on the medallion at the bottom of the picture, commemorating the feast day of St. Anne on July 26, 1343. On this date, the tyrant Gaultier de Brienne, the so-called duke of Athens, was ousted. The saints – Sebastian, Peter, Benedict, and Philip – are also featured.

Louvre is the only known individual panel painting from his stay in France between 1530 and 1540. The cushions on which the body of Christ is laid bear the coat of arms of the chief of the household of Anne de Montmorency, in whose castle the painting hung until it was acquired by the Louvre in the 18th century. The bodies of Christ and

Saint John the Evangelist show traces of a different, earlier composition, later painted over in black as can be seen through the craquelure. Mary is the real focus for any prayer uttered in front of this picture; in her suffering, turned toward the onlooker, she seems to be asking, like Enguerrand Quarton's Provençal Mary (see p. 368 f.), whether any pain was ever as great as hers.

Rosso Fiorentino (Giovanni Battista di Jacopo;
1495–1540), *The Mourning of Christ*
Oil on wood, 127 x 163 cm

An outstanding representative of the Mannerist movement, Rosso came to France from Florence to work for Francis I at the castle of Fontainebleau. This painting in the

Correggio (Antonio Allegri) (1489–1534),
Venus and Cupid, Watched by a Satyr,
1524–1527
Oil on canvas, 188 x 125 cm

A beautiful woman, lying asleep at the edge of a forest, is approached by a satyr emerging from the darkness; The woman was originally thought to be Antiope, whom Jupiter seduces disguised as a forest creature (cf. Titian's *Pardo Venus*, p. 312). But the infant Cupid sleeping beside her,

identifies the woman as Venus, her beauty intensified by the curiosity of the satyr. He appears at the edge, as an onlooker rather than a main figure. However, pure physical pleasure does not seem quite appropriate in the era of the Mannerist Correggio: for this reason it is thought that it might be a complex allegory of love, possibly a pendant to *The School of Love* in the National Gallery in London. The Paris picture would then represent earthly desire, the London painting heavenly love. The paintings may have been the result of a royal commission for Duke Nicola Maffei of Parma.

Giuseppe Arcimboldo (1527–1593),
Spring, **1573**
Oil on canvas, 76 x 64 cm

No matter how famous the paintings by the unique Mannerist artist Arcimboldo might be, they belong to the category in which little is gained by seeing the original work as compared with reproductions. The Louvre owns the well-known *Four Seasons* series, commissioned by the Habsburg king Maximilian II for Duke August of Saxony, whose Meissen coat of arms appears on the scene depicting winter. With great virtuosity, the painter incorporates heads in his depiction of the fruits of nature brought forth in each season, which are thus capable of allegorical interpretation. The splendid frame of flowers magnifies the impression of opulence; it may have been added later, perhaps in the 17th century.

The Italian Baroque

**Michelangelo Merisi de Caravaggio
(ca. 1571–1610), *The Fortune Teller*, ca. 1594/95
Oil on canvas, 99 x 131 cm, originally 89 x 131 cm**

This particular painting by the young Caravaggio epitomizes a new kind of painting; it is the most beautiful genre painting by this artist. During the course of a discussion about the best teacher a painter could choose, Caravaggio apparently nominated nature, in all its infinite variety. In a quite spontaneous gesture, he is supposed to have singled out a Gypsy from the crowd, in order to paint her while she was telling fortunes. The resulting genre picture, since its subject was considered to be humble and mundane, was unlikely to fulfill the theoretical criteria defining great art. Whether all this really happened is questionable: however, what is beyond doubt is the breakthrough that produced a radical style of painting based on the model, focusing primarily on what was visible rather than on the teachings of Antiquity and tradition. It is frequently supposed that the artist led his life on the fringes of society, desperately struggling for recognition, but this is contradicted, not least by the history of the picture in Paris. Despite the ridicule directed at art of this kind by theoreticians, this painting, in particular, was deemed by the Florentine Medicis in 1637 to be a suitable gift for Louis XIII. Once in the possession of the French king, additions were made to the top and left-hand side of the canvas for decorative purposes; originally, the life-size figures had more substance and immediacy.

**Michelangelo Merisi da Caravaggio,
The Death of Mary, 1601/1602
Oil on canvas, 369 x 245 cm**

Attitudes to Caravaggio oscillated wildly between contempt and the highest recognition. This moving picture of the dead Virgin Mary was painted by the great artist for the barefoot Carmelite order located in the poor quarter of Trastevere in Rome. She has apparently been callously laid on a small bed in a cellar, with signs of her death throes still evident. The Apostles, all aghast, weep silently over her, and the graceful young woman in the foreground, filled with grief, neglects her duty to wash the body. All that appears above this depressing scene is a triumphal red drape; there is no emissary from heaven. According to malicious rumors, the body of a prostitute that had been fished out of the River Tiber served as a model for Caravaggio. The paupers and monks saw this work merely as an affront, but it did find favor with Flemish painter Peter Paul Rubens, who recommended that the prince of Mantua acquire it immediately for a handsome price after its rejection by the Church. As a result, shortly after the scandal, this strikingly serious picture, which,

it is true, makes no allusion to the celestial glorification of the Mother of God, found a place in a royal picture gallery instead of a church. With its life-size figures, this painting constitutes one of the first of the great Baroque altarpieces, despite the fact that it was immediately removed from the church for which it was destined.

Orazio Gentileschi (1562–1647),
Rest on the Flight into Egypt, **1628 or 1637**
Oil on canvas, 157 x 225 cm

Caravaggio was by no means alone in his affinity for uncomplicated life. Orazio Gentileschi, interest in whom has recently been renewed owing to his unfortunate daughter Artemisia (1597–after 1651), was also inspired by the simple life in his pictures such as this *Rest on the Flight into Egypt*. The contradiction between chiaroscuro as a fundamental principle for style, and the necessity of depicting the scene in the open air is resolved by Gentileschi, who places an almost completely black wall behind the harshly illuminated figures with a somber, cloudy sky above. Joseph's uncouth slumber and the eagerness with which the child attaches itself to its mother's full breast are derived from the life and behavior of common people. Pictures such as this enjoyed success far beyond Rome. The example in the Louvre may have been painted for Charles I of England, or alternatively it could be a replica painted in 1637.

Domenichino (Domenico Zampieri) (1581–1641),
St. Cecilia, **ca. 1617/18**
Oil on canvas, 160 x 120 cm

Contemporary artistic theory was far more in tune with painters from Bologna than with Caravaggio and his followers in Rome. Among those promoting the works of the former were the Bolognese Ludovisi family, from whose ranks came Pope Gregory XV (1621–1623). This picture was painted for the great patron Cardinal Ludovico Ludovisi, and found its way to France as early as the mid-17th century. The saint's upward gaze was inspired by the only major work by Raphael that remains in Bologna, which also depicts Saint Cecilia. Yet, in its composition against a dark background and its bold use of chiaroscuro, this painting reveals that even the Bolognese painters, although perpetually regarded as starkly contrasting with the style of Caravaggio (see p. 330 f.), were nevertheless representative of the same era. Both share a common inclination toward pared-down still life and a desire to master the paradoxical task of surpass-

ing the effect of music in a silent medium. In competing with this other art form, Caravaggio and the Bolognese painters had precedents in Venice, where Giorgione (1477/78–1510) had already attempted something similar. St. Cecilia is also the subject of frescoes by Domenichino.

In the Light of Venice

The Grand Canal in the last rays of the evening sun.

Venice, located in the middle of a lagoon, is unique; moisture from the sea and radiant light combine to bestow on the city an atmosphere that is beyond compare. Owing to the effects of the climate, paint applied directly to walls in this lagoon city hardly lasted any time at all, and wood warped all too frequently. For this reason, cloth became established as a surface for painting earlier and more decisively in Venice than elsewhere. Oil paint brushed lightly onto canvas became the epitome of the Venetian style of painting, to some extent paving the way for the French Impressionists, who did not emerge as a group until 1870.

Although water was the principal element in Venice, the very remoteness of the city from the mainland unleashed the imagination with regard to landscape painting, as if the Venetians were constantly yearning for a shady bower or a world of pastoral grace. The rural idyll, which Giorgione and Titian populated with worldly as well as with spiritual themes (see p. 308 f.), was

biblical subjects is demonstrated by Titian's *Supper at Emmaus*, which invites comparison with Tiepolo's *Last Supper*. The great master of the Renaissance is content to show his figures in

F. Guardi (1712--1793), Feast of Corpus Christi in the Piazzetta, 1782, oil on canvas, 67 x 100 cm

initiated in Venice, as was the possibility of painting gloomy landscape, both as a background to and as an expression of somber states of mind. Light, even when merely illuminating darkness, plays a prominent role; it even fills the Early Renaissance paintings – of which the Louvre possesses few examples – of Giovanni Bellini and Cima da Conegliano (see p. 295). The power of light to transform our view of traditional

natural light against a landscape in which night is gradually falling. A bright area is provided by the white expanse of the tablecloth. The light sculpts the figures, which at first glance appear undifferentiated, casting the youth on the left, seemingly arbitrarily, into sharp relief; in fact, however, these additional figures merely provide a frame for the main group. The two disciples who are dining with Christ the day after Easter are illuminated in a way that assuages their numb grief at the death of their master, and enables them to recognize the risen Christ.

Titian is content with a careful use of light in order to achieve this effect. Tiepolo, by contrast, is unwilling to forego a trick of light that verges on the supernatural: the crucial moment in his depiction of the *Last Supper*, a picture in which the figures depicted are small, shows the head of Christ surrounded by an ethereal white cloud

Giambattista Tiepolo (1696–1770), The Last Supper, ca. 1745/1750, oil on canvas, 81 x 90 cm

Titian (Tiziano Vecellio) (1488/1490–1576), The Supper at Emmaus, ca. 1535, oil on canvas, 169 x 244 cm, second floor, room 25

that also encompasses his shoulders. Even in the work of this late Baroque Venetian painter, however, the events are intensified by the use of light as observed in nature, contrasting dramatically with the darkness of the pillars and the rear view of the figure of Judas in the foreground. The light seems to penetrate the scene with force from above, while at the same time singling out the principal figure of the Redeemer from those surrounding him. A picture such as this acquires an inherent greatness.

Secular themes were also captured in Venetian light: the city on the banks of the lagoon has a penchant for festivals, for the wild excesses of the carnival as well as for splendid state and religious festivals (see illustration on p. 335, second floor, room 21). Paintings of occasions like these were already popular abroad by the 18th century, simply because of the wonderful opulence they depict. They not only provide a documentary record of the city, but also of the stylish structures that were constructed for such festivals.

Salvatore Rosa (1615–1673),
The Ghost of Samuel Appearing to Saul, 1668
Oil on canvas, 273 x 193 cm

Salvatore Rosa seems, by virtue of his radical subjectivism, to be a precursor of 19th-century Romanticism. At first glance, this massive picture, dated 1668, evokes images of Henry Fuseli or even Goya (see p. 356 f.). In a manner that is far removed from the aesthetics of the Bolognese painters and the proponents of the Roman Baroque among Caravaggio's followers, (see p. 332 f.), Salvatore Rosa uses a chiaroscuro effect in order to create a ghostly vision emerging from the shadows of a landscape background, with vaguely defined forms that deprive the bodies of any solid unity. The subject matter is also ghostly: on the day before his defeat in the battle against the Philistines and then his subsequent suicide, King Saul sought out the Witch of Endor. She conjured up the ghost of Samuel to appear before him in a white shroud, presaging the king's death.

Giovanni Battista Piazzetta (1683–1754),
The Assumption of the Virgin Mary, 1735
Oil on canvas, 517 x 245 cm

Clemens August, archbishop of Cologne, commissioned this awe-inspiring painting of light in Venice for the church of the Teutonic Order in the Sachsenhausen district of Frankfurt. Now in Paris, this picture invites comparison with Caravaggio's *Death of the*

Virgin Mary (see p. 330 f.), painted in Rome. Piazzetta's version is filled with wonder at the physical ascent of Mary into heaven.

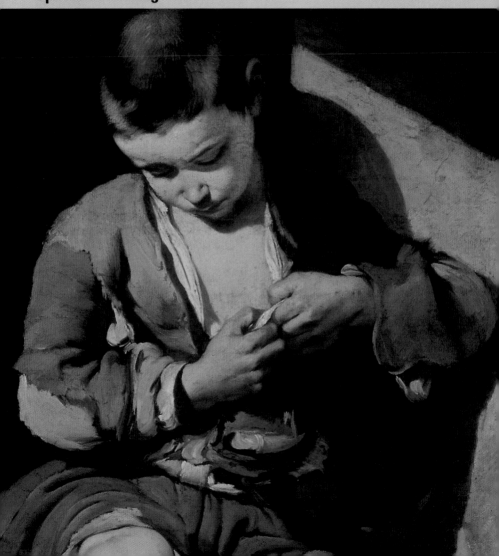

It was not just the reputation of Italian painting that was promulgated in France; the profile of art from the Iberian Peninsula was also raised by its French admirers. The volume of Spanish paintings in circulation in the art market was, of course, smaller. The famous images of Velázquez remained at court in Madrid, and, as family gifts, in Vienna; the altarpieces, insofar as they survived adversity during anticlerical phases in the country's history, are for the most part still to be found in their original locations or in Spain's incomparable treasure trove of national art, the Prado museum in Madrid. In view of such constraints the Louvre, despite its relatively small department, offers an outstanding collection with which few institutions outside Spain are able to compete.

One enters a strange world via the Gothic painting of the Iberian Peninsula. In most churches, a vast wall of painting, consisting of a number of individual panels termed *guardapolvo* in Spanish, obscured the view behind the altar. The Louvre has an excellent example in the *Retable of St. Vincent* by Bernardo Martorell (ca. 1400–1452). However, closer acquaintance with this work also reveals the problem posed by the late-Gothic period in Spain: when confronted with paintings containing unusually large quantities of figures, there is a tendency to create nothing more than a general impression. For this very reason, and also because

of the propensity for gruesome scenes of martyrdom, for example in *The Flagellation of St. George* (see p. 346), the delicate sensitivity with which bodies, materials, and faces are painted is lost.

Sacred painting in Spain gained considerable momentum as a result of the Counter-Reformation. New religious orders were founded, and monasteries needed sacred paintings in order to reinforce Catholicism, in the spirit of the Council of Trent (1563). The piety that is typical of the Spanish, that survives even today and finds expression in the magnificent feast-day processions during Holy Week, was probably defined during that period. It was at that point that the path taken by art divided, either to follow the intense desires of the popular imagination or to be harnessed by a small circle of highly cultured nobles, to whom a certain ambiguity is also attributable. Practically no old master has reflected upon the differentiated tasks facing him to the same extent as the royal court painter Velázquez, and with Goya Spain gave birth to an artistic temperament that expressed in a revolutionary way the sense of fear on the threshold of the modern era — something Goya was able to achieve through paintings that were in fact intended merely as commissions.

Louis XIV did not rate Spanish art highly, and so it was not until 1838, with the opening of the Spanish gallery, that there was a surge of genuine enthusiasm in France for the paintings of its neighbor, resulting in the creation of an unusually rich collection. Following the revolution of 1848, however,

Bartolomé Esteban Murillo (1618–1682),
Young Beggar (detail), ca. 1650, see p. 354

the 412 paintings that had been acquired with the funds belonging to the king, Louis Philippe, which were claimed by him as private possessions, were sold and cast to the four winds. Despite the gaps left as a consequence, all the Spanish painters of the *siglo de'oro*, the golden age, are very well represented in the Louvre. The extent of the controversy surrounding many Spanish paintings is shown by Jusepe de Ribera's *Clubfooted Boy* of 1642. The subject's extraordinarily hideous appearance caused the Italian painter Salvatore Rosa (see p. 338 f.) to express the opinion that the quality of good painting should be evident without the need to portray beggars.

Jusepe de Ribera (1591–1652), Clubfooted Boy, 1642, oil on canvas, 164 x 93 cm, second floor, room 26

Juan Carreño de Miranda (1614–1685), Mass for the Foundation of the Order of the Holy Trinity, 1666, oil on canvas, 500 x 315 cm, second floor, room 26

Spanish Painting

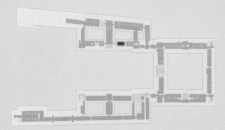

Second Floor

Francisco de Zurbarán,
St. Apollonia, p. 352 f.

Francisco de Goya,
Christ on the Mount of Olives,
p. 356 f.

Other works:

1   Master of St. Alfonso, 2nd half of the
    15th century, *Mary Giving the Chasuble
    to St. Alfonso*, room 28, p. 347

2   Luis Meléndez, *Still life with Figs*,
    ca. 1770, room 32, p. 356

Francisco de Herrera the Elder,
St. Basil Dictating his Rule, p. 349

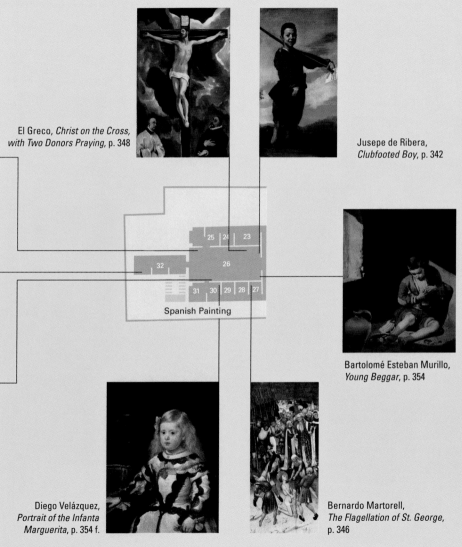

El Greco, *Christ on the Cross, with Two Donors Praying*, p. 348

Jusepe de Ribera, *Clubfooted Boy*, p. 342

25 | 24 | 23

32

26

31 | 30 | 29 | 28 | 27

Spanish Painting

Bartolomé Esteban Murillo, *Young Beggar*, p. 354

Diego Velázquez, *Portrait of the Infanta Marguerita*, p. 354 f.

Bernardo Martorell, *The Flagellation of St. George*, p. 346

Bernardo Martorell (documented from 1427–1452), *The Flagellation of St. George*, ca. 1435
Wood, 108 x 53 cm

According to the legend, Saint George was subjected to many dreadful tortures and torments in his martyrdom, before he was finally beheaded. He is seen here as the victim of flagellation by four thugs who are brutally beating him with their whips and fasces. Although the stake at which he is martyred might also be found in a picture of the flagellation of Christ, it is of unique construction. Hordes of spectators have come to watch, forming a cluster that stretches away to the horizon. The groups of onlookers are strictly segregated, and it is interesting to observe how the silver helmets of the soldiers, the white headdresses of the women, and the brightly colored headgear of the men are seen as juxtaposed areas of color. Part of the altar with its scenes from the life of St. George is in the Louvre, while the remainder is in the Art Institute in Chicago. These pictures were originally attributed to the "Master of St. George," however stylistic comparisons with the *Altar of Púbol* (Gerona), the authorship of which is well documented, have identified the painter of the panels as Bernardo Martorell. His painting is still largely characterized by the international Soft Style.

**Master of St. Alfonso,
second half of the
15th century,
*Mary Giving the Chasuble
to St. Alfonso*, Castile**
Wood, 230 x 167 cm

The subject of this painting is the episode constituting the actual miracle in the life of St. Alfonso, a writer who venerated the Virgin Mary. Instead of the servers, it is the Virgin who hands him the chasuble. The scene, painted anonymously, is played out on a tiled floor that would be appropriate in a church, but the scene is exposed to the sky, and as a result of this, one interprets it as an imaginary episode in heaven.

Mary, enthroned as Queen of Heaven, invests Saint Alfonso assisted by the angel on the left, and watched by other saints on the right. This type of painting from Spain was inspired by Dutch precedents: the reproduction of the material quality and the treatment of light and shade can be traced back in particular to Jan van Eyck (see p. 454 f.). The gently flowing draperies that are characteristic of the Soft Style have been superceded. In this painting, and others like it, the folds are crisp, and the faces are clearly defined. Gravity has ousted weightlessness from painting, and bright colors are bleached by harsh light.

El Greco (Domenikos Theotokopoulos) (1541–1614), *Christ on the Cross, with Two Donors Praying*, ca. 1585–1590
Oil on canvas, 260 x 171 cm

acquire a celebrated composition by him, and so this Crucifixion scene was repeated several times, but donors are only included in the panel in the Louvre.

The cross – which appears to have no means of support – is standing against the background of a dark, blustery sky painted in somber colors. The Greek artist (El Greco), who was originally from Crete and who came to the ancient royal city Toledo via Venice, is less concerned with reproducing realistic clouds, than expressing heightened emotion. Christ, who is painted with an elongated body in the Mannerist style, is looking up in an ecstasy of suffering to the Father in order to utter the words "It is finished" (John, ch. 19, v. 30) just before he expires. Although the title was faithfully reproduced in three languages, the principle aim of the painting is not to satisfy the antiquarian interests of scholars, but rather to evoke emotion in an unprecedented way. The example in the Louvre is from the Hieronymite monastery in Toledo. Many other collectors of the art of El Greco evidently wished to

Francisco de Herrera the Elder (1576–1656),
St. Basil Dictating his Rule,
(?)1654
Oil on canvas, 243 x 194 cm

As the father figure in the monastic order, Saint Basil is seated, quill in hand, in the center of the picture, and looks up reflectively from his writings. He is surrounded by clerics, varying in age and in ecclesiastical rank, all engaged in the task of writing. St. Basil, one of the three great ecumenical teachers of the Greek Church, is dictating, inspired by the Holy Spirit.

The laws of gravity and probability have been suspended, for the men appear to float ethereally in space, and the actual setting is not clearly defined. For a long time, this painting was the only picture in the Western world featuring the saint. As a result of the revival of spirituality during the Counter-Reformation, a monastery dedicated to St. Basil was founded in Seville, and it is from there that the painting originates. The individuality of the heads and the lively brushwork combine to make *St. Basil* one of the artist's best works.

Herrera, who lived almost exclusively in Seville, was the true founder of Spanish painting of the Golden Age, which later came to be centered on the city of Madrid. Velázquez was one of his pupils. Herrera was considered irascible, and the young genius is said to have left his tutelage in order to escape his mood swings.

From Spanish Civil War Veteran to De Gaulle's Culture Minister – André Malraux

The Intellectual Left at the Writers' Congress in Paris: Tristan Tzara (front, with legs crossed), Madeleine Paz speaking, with Nizan, Malraux, and Gide next to her, 1935

optimism. In André Malraux's most famous work, *La Condition Humaine* (Man's Fate), which he wrote in 1933, revolution amounts to no more than the struggle to maintain dignity in the face of life and death. Fascinated by Chou En-lai and by Trotsky, Malraux joined the communists. He participated in the Soviet Writers' Congress in Moscow in 1934 and in 1935 played a leading role in the congress in Paris. After fighting Franco during the Spanish Civil War, he led the Alsace-Lorraine clandestine units in their underground struggle, but distanced himself from the communists during the Second World War and campaigned for de Gaulle after 1945. At the same time, this political literary figure wrote in an extremely original manner about art, dealing with global art up to the present day and singling out El Greco as a particular hero. Three volumes were produced between 1947 and 1949, the first and most famous of which is the work *The Imaginary Museum*, which was published in revised versions as *The Psychology of Art* (1951) and *Voices of Silence* (1963), and exerted a global influence on modern art. They are still very important in the history of aesthetics.

"Once a communist, always a communist" is one of the unfortunate catchphrases from the era of the Cold War. In France, however, there was far more tolerance of freedom of thought among intellectuals. André Malraux, one of the individuals responsible for breathing new life into the Louvre, is an example of radical transformation of political ideas. Born in 1901 in Paris, he studied archeology and went to Asia in 1923. In his first novel, entitled *Conquérants* (The Conquerors), Malraux sketched a character who was typical of his heroes: a revolutionary, fighting without political passion or real

In 1958, de Gaulle appointed his former comrade-in-arms as minister for cultural affairs – at a time in which colonial power was in final collapse, and even Algeria had to be relinquished. Instead of imaginary museums, Malraux was now responsible for the Louvre. He is one of the first to have given new status to the tradition of cultural heritage: for him, art and cultural institutions were "the cathedrals of the 20th century". On the outside, this erstwhile revolutionary arranged for the sooty facades of large monuments to be sandblasted, while conducting a campaign on the inside against the torpor of the museums. He was fascinated by modern technology, especially television, which he opened up to high culture. It was part of his per-

Writer and Politician in front of the Writer in the Louvre (see p. 124 f.): the Minister of Culture, André Malraux, giving a guided tour to Léopold Sédar Senghor, President of Senegal, 1960

sonal tragedy that one of his decisions almost brought France off the rails in the spring of 1968: in March of that year, the minister dismissed Henri Langlois, director of the Cinémathèque in Paris, because of financial irregularities. Those who had remained on the Left joined forces with the youth movement in solidarity against Malraux. Even though de Gaulle survived the crisis, he was obliged to depart after losing the referendum of 1969. André Malraux also resigned. He died in 1976 in Créteil, outside the gates of Paris.

De Gaulle and Malraux visiting the Exhibition of Mexican art in 1962

Francisco de Zurbarán (1598–1664),
St. Apollonia, ca. 1636
Oil on canvas, 134 x 67 cm

The saint is walking toward the left of a stage, in a space that remains undefined. She is turning, as if by chance, directly toward the onlooker, at whom she gazes with interest but apparently without any emotion. In her left hand she is gracefully holding the palm frond that signifies her martyrdom, while in her right she holds the instrument that has made her a martyr to her faith: a pair of pliers and a tooth. According to legend, all her teeth were pulled out. The real attraction of the painting lies in her garments. The costly, luminous fabrics fall in crisp folds, catching the changing nuances of light. This picture was painted with other pictures of saints for the monastery of San José de la Merced Descalza in Seville. Zurbarán worked mainly as a religious painter, and was able to bring to his work both ascetic discipline and mystical inspiration. As well as completed paintings from Spanish monasteries such as this, the Louvre also possesses six of the 23 sketches by Vicente Carducho, born in Florence (1576/1578–1638) for the Carthusian monastery of Paular in Castile. Sketches like these were used as starting points for discussion between artists and patrons.

Jusepe de Ribera (1591–1652), *Adoration of the Shepherds*, 1650
Oil on canvas, 239 x 181 cm

The Christ child is radiant, lying on a bed of straw in the crib. In contrast with the other figures, his complexion is rosy and resembles porcelain. Mary is kneeling behind the crib and praying to God; around her are gathered three shepherds and an old woman, who is gazing steadfastly out from the picture on the right-hand side. The clothing of the shepherd kneeling in the foreground is extremely eye-catching, providing a study of sheepskin in all its various manifestations. All the figures below the line of the horizon remain in darkness, but the angel announcing the birth of Christ to the shepherds in the fields shines brightly in the sky. Jusepe de Ribera ran a busy workshop in Naples in which Italian, Flemish, and Spanish artists were employed. He worked as a court painter under the Spanish viceroy of Naples. This work shows him to be moving away from his original radical, Caravaggiesque style, and he demonstrates a mastery of light that is characteristic of this painter.

Bartolomé Esteban Murillo (1618–1682),
Young Beggar, ca. 1650
Oil on canvas, 134 x 100 cm

The boy is sitting in a bare, dirty room, devoid of furnishings. The arched window is covered in dust. There are shells of crustaceans on the floor, apples are visible in a wicker basket, and a large jug of water on the left completes the picture. The boy's clothes are so ragged that various layers are needed to form a jacket. His dirty feet and engrossed search for a flea on his chest turn this picture into the embodiment of social deprivation. Painted using muted earth tones and chiaroscuro in the manner of the followers of Caravaggio, the artist's observation in this genre scene is extraordinarily fresh, despite the way in which the objects are arranged.

Spanish painting during the period known as the Golden Age featured still lifes and genre paintings of young beggars and cripples, as well as numerous religious subjects and portraits.

Diego Rodriguez de Silva y Velázquez (1599–1660), *Portrait of the Infanta Marguerita*, ca. 1655
Oil on canvas, 70 x 58 cm

Dressed in a magnificent robe and adorned with jewels like an adult, the young girl gazes at us forlornly from the picture. The child's round eyes are so serious in the delicate face that the section of the chair which is visible on the left serves as a measure, reminding us how small the princess actually is. In this portrait of the daughter of Philip IV (1605–1665), Velázquez shows himself to be an astute portraitist who succeeds in conveying status by means of courtly pomp and circumstance, but also in capturing the state of mind of a lonely child. As well as the psychological perceptiveness, his technique is worthy of note. The paint is applied coarsely in places, and the brushstrokes remain very visible. This lively painting was later to be of great interest to the Impressionists, but it seems not to have been very appealing to King Louis XIV, who consigned it to be hung in his wife's bathroom.

Luis Meléndez (1716–1780),
Still Life with Figs, ca. 1770
Oil on canvas, 37 x 49 cm

Very few people are aware of the remarkable part played by Spanish painting in the history of the still life. On a table bearing the marks of age and use are three large objects: a loaf of bread, a plate of figs, and a basket containing ham. Although the foods are differentiated in terms of their surface characteristics, it is the vital coloring of the

green figs that is foremost. Like his father, the Neapolitan-born artist initially worked as a miniaturist during the reign of Kings Ferdinand VI (1713–1759) and Charles III (1716–1788), and then as a court painter in Madrid. It was not until later in his career

that he devoted his attention exclusively to still life painting.

Francisco de Goya y Lucientes (1746–1828),
Christ on the Mount of Olives, 1810/1819
Oil on wood, 47 x 35 cm

Although in his early designs for tapestries, which today survive as paintings, Goya succeeded in once again conjuring up the great beauty of courtly Europe prior to the Enlightenment and to the Revolution, the ambiguity in his art and its psychology are already apparent. His treatment of subjects in the Christian tradition seem especially alien. In this small-scale sketch for a scene on the Mount of Olives, possibly for the Escuelas Pias in Madrid, the onlooker is transported into an icy cold nocturnal atmosphere; it was here that Christ sweated blood in the Garden of Gethsemane when he was no longer able to turn away the cup of suffering. Although the way his physiognomy is rendered may be attributable to the coarse brushwork of an oil sketch, awareness of the dog in the foreground leads one to wonder what has become of Christ in the work of this artist.

French Painting

It is impossible to imagine the modern fine art world without France, even though Paris is no longer the decisive epicenter, as it was around the year 1900. The museum played a huge part in this, for the avant-garde used the Louvre as a benchmark, despite their desire to break with all conventions: the older works of art there ultimately embodied the standards against which they were fighting. Painters such as Paul Cézanne (1839–1906) maintained, however, that the Louvre had been their true place of education.

For centuries, the old royal palace housed the Royal Academy, which strictly imposed its artistic dictates on many generations of artists and determined the success or failure of the talents in its exhibitions or Salons. However misguided the criteria for judging art might have been at that time, recent art theory is subject to the same fate as art itself. However irritating the narrow-minded standards of the spokesmen of art in Paris, their frequently justified invective leaves its mark on discussions about art, even for those who do not submit to their yoke.

Jean-Antoine Watteau (1684–1721), The Embarkation for Cythera (detail), 1717, *see p. 401*

As a repository for royal treasure since the time of Charles V (1338–1380), as the home of the Academy from 1648 onward, and as a museum (and often an artist's residence) from 1793, the Louvre itself played a decisive part in the history of art. The transformation in the artist's profession, from princely patronage to the way artists live today, is linked to the palace and is most clearly reflected in French painting. For this reason the French section deserves close attention when visiting the museum, especially since it occupies most space – 73 rooms lit from above in the Richelieu wing together with the monumental rooms in the Denon wing.

Claude Lorrain (Claude Gellée; 1600–1682), Campo Vaccino in Rome, ca. 1636, oil on canvas, 56 x 72 cm, second floor, room 15

Early French painting was almost completely destroyed because of the iconoclasm in the 16th century, leading to quite a striking disparity between the countless examples of manuscript illuminations and the rare panel paintings. France is frequently regarded as having merely been subjected to a variety of foreign influences until well after 1500, with a failure to recognize even the unique achievements of the artists of

Nicolas Poussin (1594 –1665), Echo and Narcissus, 1625/1630, oil on canvas, 74 x 100 cm, third floor, room 13

Fontainebleau and Paris during the Renaissance and Mannerist periods. In the Louvre, however, independence in terms of coloring and application of paint is just as evident as the astonishing pictorial imagination of the many French painters, especially those from Provence.

France had already become a leading authority in the world by the 17th century, although it exerted greater influence from Rome than from Paris. Indeed, it was in Italy that Nicolas Poussin and Claude Lorrain painted the poetic pictures in which ancient mythology and the influence of Antiquity shaped Europe's feeling for history. The route is no more direct from here to the era of gallantry, in which France defined the fashions of the 18th century, or to the more spontaneous style of painting with which Chardin is still perfectly able to astonish us even today.

It was only the great divide marked by the Revolution in 1789 that made possible the freedom with which French painters of the early 19th century captured great themes from the past, as well as contemporary history, on monumental canvases. The private collections bequeathed to the Louvre thus still give us great insight into a phase, no longer really appropriate here, in which the view of the world changed: the French galleries culminate in the Impressionist works of Claude Monet. The collection in the Louvre served many generations of painters as an essential stimulus, for it was while competing with the early French masters that they found their own style.

Jean-Baptiste Siméon Chardin (1699–1779), The Brioche, 1763, oil on canvas, 47 x 56 cm, third floor, room 15

French Painting

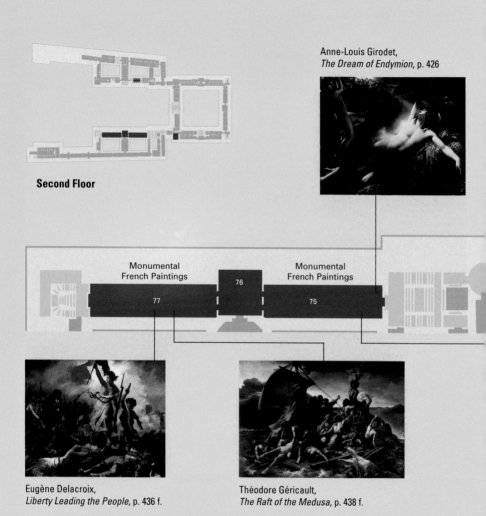

Second Floor

Anne-Louis Girodet,
The Dream of Endymion, p. 426

Monumental
French Paintings

Monumental
French Paintings

76

77

75

Eugène Delacroix,
Liberty Leading the People, p. 436 f.

Théodore Géricault,
The Raft of the Medusa, p. 438 f.

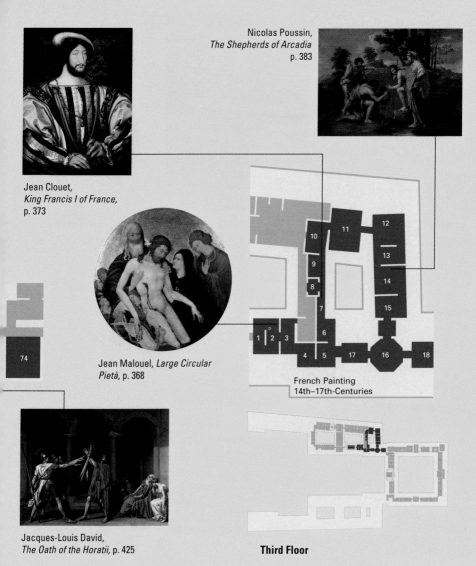

Nicolas Poussin,
The Shepherds of Arcadia
p. 383

Jean Clouet,
King Francis I of France,
p. 373

Jean Malouel, *Large Circular
Pietà*, p. 368

French Painting
14th–17th-Centuries

Jacques-Louis David,
The Oath of the Horatii, p. 425

Third Floor

Jean-Antoine Watteau,
Pierrot, p. 400

Third Floor

Marie-Guillemine Benoist,
Portrait of a Black Woman,
p. 408

Camille Corot,
The Bridge at Mantes, p. 415

Jean-Auguste-Dominique Ingres,
The Turkish Bath, p. 410 f.

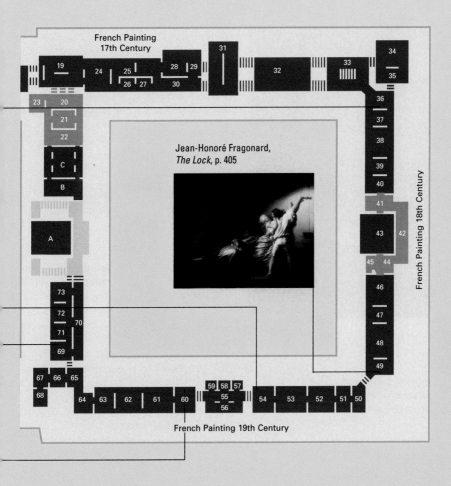

French Painting
17th Century

19 24 25 28 29
26 27 30

31 32 33 34
35

23 20

21

22 36

37

C 38

B 39

40

A 41

43 42

45 44

73 46

72 70 47

71 48

69 49

67 66 65

68 59 58 57

64 63 62 61 60 55 54 53 52 51 50
56

Jean-Honoré Fragonard,
The Lock, p. 405

French Painting 18th Century

French Painting 19th Century

more, it depicts a contemporary figure, and not even in a religious context. There is quite a visible tension between stylization and painting from observation in this portrayal. The inscription on the gold ground reads "Jehan Roy de france" (John, King of France). John II, called "The Good" for his simple-mindedness, lost his wife in the great plague of 1349, had to renounce his kingdom and throne in the Hundred Years' War against England, and generally had a reign filled with such misfortune, that no king of France subsequently bore the name of Jean.

Parisian painter, (?Jean d'Orleans),
Parament of Narbonne **(detail), ca. 1375**
Silk, 77.5 x 286 cm

Another unique example is provided by this silk painting from the precious paraments in the cathedral in the southern French town of Narbonne. Over the Easter period, the silk panel was spread over the front of an altar; for this reason the crucified Christ is central. In accordance with the reverence that was required, no colors were used, but only shades of black – in other words, grisaille. The themes of the passion – Christ's arrest, flagellation, his bearing of the Cross, the Crucifixion, the entombment, descent into hell, and the meeting between the resurrected Christ and Mary Magdalene – form a complete cycle.

Around the main scene are smaller sections, featuring a group of royal donors, as

The Late Gothic Period

Parisian painter, *John II (the Good),*
***King of France*, before 1350**
Wood, 60 x 44.5 cm

This portrait of John the Good (1319–1364), which welcomes the museum visitor from a distance, is probably the oldest surviving French panel painting; further-

well as a prophet and a synagogue showing King David. The crowned "K" at the edge signifies King Charles V (1338–1380), the son of John the Good. It is clear from the profile of the queen, Jeanne, that a number of corrections were occasioned by her vanity: the size of the nose, chin, and breasts was reduced retrospectively, no doubt to present an image that was much more flattering.

Jean Malouel (documented 1397–1415), *Large Circular Pietà*, ca. 1400–1410
Wood, diameter 64 cm

Philip the Bold of Burgundy (1342–1404), the youngest son of John the Good (1319–1364), was a patron of the arts, particularly in respect of a religious foundation, the Carthusian monastery of Champmol near Dijon. Philip the Bold furnished the monastery with works of art from all over the world, and he summoned painters from the Netherlands including the painter of this picture, whose name, Jan Malwell, literally meant "paint well". Malouel's *Large Circular Pietà* is a perfect example of the style known as International Gothic. Central to the picture is the body, sculpted in delicate colors, of the dead Christ. The reddish hair of the Redeemer merges with the color of the small angels, while the figure of God the Father consists entirely of dark blue and bluish gray. The tiny dove is interposed between Father and Son, completing the Trinity. The Virgin Mary looks yearningly at the eyes of her son, closed in death, while John stands behind her. Rather than illustrating an episode from the Gospels, this *Pietà* (from the Latin *pietas*, pity, in the sense of devout empathy) appeals to the compassion of the onlooker.

Enguerrand Quarton (active 1444–1466), *Pietà of Villeneuve-lès-Avignon*, ca. 1455
Wood, 163 x 218,5 cm;
with original frame, 195 x 255 cm

This retable is the most striking example of early French panel painting. The work was probably donated to the collegiate church of Notre-Dame in Villeneuve-lès-Avignon.

Quarton, who was a native of Picardy and worked in Provence, has left few paintings. His other main work is a large-scale altarpiece. The "Vespers picture" of Mary with her dead son on her knees appeals to the onlooker in its inscription on the gold ground: "All ye who pass by here, look on me and see, if ever was suffering as great as mine?" The main group is flanked by John and Mary Magdalene. It is tempting to recognize the brilliant light of Provence in such a painting. Despite its poor condition, there are details that are fascinating: blood and water flow vertically in drops from the wound in the side of the dead Christ, while the traces of dried blood remain as a testament to his hanging on the Cross. While the faces of the saints are modeled in thickly applied paint, the portrait of the donor is crisscrossed with many fine white lines. This technique of adding fine lines is used to show the bristles of the beard, the eyebrows, and the lines and creases to the furrowed countenance.

Unknown painter in Paris (André d'Ypres?), retable in Paris parliament, ca. 1455, wood, 145 x 270 cm, third floor, room 6

England is regarded throughout the world as the cradle of parliamentary democracy, for it was there, in 1215, that a criminal and incompetent king was forced to sign a great charter. As a result of this Magna Carta, which he abhorred, King John Lackland (1167–1216, king from 1199) achieved unwanted fame. From that time, the crown ceased to have authority over taxes. These were instead a matter for a permanent council, in which speeches were made. This is the literal meaning of the word "parliament," derived from the Latin *parlare*, to speak. Parliaments also date back to the 13th century in France, but the "place for speaking" had an additional function there: from the time of St. Louis onward (Louis IX, 1214–1270, king from 1226), the parliament in Paris served as the supreme court. Taxation was determined by the States-General, who were rarely, or in some cases never, convened by the highest authority in the land. The last occasion on which a king did so, it cost him his head: the summoning of the States-General was the beginning of the end for Louis XVI (1754–1793), who was removed from power by the Revolution in 1789 and beheaded in 1793.

The major Parisian courts are all now located on the site of the Paris parliament building. The Sainte-Chapelle was built by St. Louis in the 1240s at the end of the Ile de la Cité, facing the Louvre; it was here that Philip IV (Philip the Fair, 1285–1314) built a palace; and it was here, too, that Charles V (1338–1380, king from 1364), while he was crown prince, witnessed the killing of his closest advisers in 1357, during the rebellious uprising led by Etienne Marcel. Since then, kings have avoided the Ile de la Cité; a concierge was left in charge of the palace, which is why it is now called the Conciergerie. In 1431, Charles VII assigned the entire area to the parliament. In

order that the judges could swear their oaths by Christ and by saints with political significance, a sensational painting was installed in the main chamber in around 1455. This links Christ's death on the Cross with St. John the Baptist, the legendary founder of the St.-Denis monastery near Paris (see p. 526 f.), as well as St. Louis, and the emperor Charles the Great. Louis IX is standing on the left, in front of a view across the Seine to the Louvre, while Charles obscures the view of the royal palace on the Ile de la Cité. The paint-

View over the Conciergerie with the Sainte-Chapelle facing the Louvre, photograph from 1863/1865.

ing is by a great artist, who also illuminated manuscripts. To the rear of the saint, one can see the Louvre as it appeared in the 15th century. On the right, the palace on the Ile de la Cité, the seat of parliament, appears closer to the onlooker.

Jean Fouquet (ca. 1415/1420–1478/1481),
King Charles VII of France, **ca. 1453 or after 1461**
Wood, 86 x 71 cm

Jean Fouquet, *Guillaume Jouvenel des Ursins,*
Chancellor of France, **ca. 1460**
Wood, 96 x 73.2 cm

On his return from a journey to Italy, Jean Fouquet, the nation's highest ranking artist, combined influences from Italy and the northern Alps in manuscript illuminations and panel paintings, and at the same time succeeded in achieving a new, monumental quality in panel painting. This artist of genius painted the powerful portraits of the chancellor and king that hang side by side. The aristocratic Parisian, Guillaume Jouvenel des Ursins, whose prayer book lies on a cushion bearing a coat of arms in glowing colors, is portrayed as a well-built figure. Pictured as though he is at a window, the curtain of which has just been drawn to reveal him, is King Charles VII of France (1403–1461), who is possibly also praying. He is puny and somewhat bloated in appearance, with padded shoulders. While a Madonna or a devotional image was undoubtedly linked to the picture of the chancellor, the purpose for the portrait of the king is unspecified. The inelegant inscription "The especially victorious king of France, Charles, the seventh of that name" is original. Since the king was only dubbed "victorious" after his death in 1461, the portrait must have been painted posthumously. Beneath the visible layer of paint, X-ray photography reveals a Madonna alongside Charles VII, painted earlier in around 1450.

Jean Clouet (documented 1516–1540/41),
King Francis I of France, **ca. 1530**
Oil on wood, 96 x 74 cm

Continuing the tradition of Fouquet, Jean
Clouet portrayed Francis I (1494–1547) in
magnificent Renaissance finery. As in Jean
Fouquet's portrait *Charles VII*, the king is
pictured half-length, behind a parapet, but
occupying considerably more of the pictorial space. His shoulders are padded and he
seems to be breathing deeply. Rather than
praying, his left hand reaches for his dag-
ger. Cold and brilliant, this picture was
painted for a court competing with those of
Italy and King Henry VIII in England.

Jean de Gourmont (ca. 1483–after 1551),
***Adoration of the Shepherds*, ca. 1525**
Oil on wood, 93.5 x 115.5 cm

Hardly any religious pictures in the strict sense of the word were painted during the period of the Huguenot wars. The few that survived the turmoil testify to a deep crisis in art and its content. Architectural fantasies from Italy, and elements from the German Danube School are supposed to be identifiable in this stirring panoramic view of the stable in Bethlehem. The figures give the impression of staffage: Mary and the Christ child are minute, although they are surrounded by hovering angels that fill the fantastical ruin with their Christmas message. As a concept, the picture is a virtuoso performance, but as a work of art the effect is somewhat strange.

Antoine Caron (1521–1599), *Augustus with the Tiburtine Sibyl*, ca. 1575–1580
Oil on canvas, 125 x 170 cm

Antoine Caron worked for Catherine de' Medici (1519–1589) and Charles IX (1550–1574). His few paintings are characterized by a magnificently decorative spirit: of particular note here are the turned pillars of the altars, while the architecture to the rear resembles fantastic models. The notion of the sibyls was kept alive in Christendom, since the pagan prophecies referred to Christ. The scene in which the Tiburtine sibyl prophesies the birth of the Savior and the decline of the pagan world is almost incidental. On the banks of the Anio, Caesar Augustus shows the female oracle a circle in the sky in which Mary appears with the Christ child. The painting probably reproduces one of the scenes celebrating the return to Paris of King Henry of Poland in 1573, hence the resemblance between Caesar Augustus and Charles IX of France.

First School of Fontainebleau,
Diana Hunting, **ca. 1550–1560**
Oil on canvas, 191 x 132 cm

Italian art became more accessible to France as a consequence of the campaigns in Italy. Francis I (1494–1547) summoned masters such as Leonardo da Vinci (1452–1519) to his court. Between 1534 and 1537, with the founding of the gallery in Fontainebleau, French art came under the influence of the Mannerist style. The goddess of hunting, who is painted here by an unknown artist, is an allegorical portrait of Diane of Poitiers, who is the mistress of Henry II (1519–1559). She is stalking, naked, with bow and arrow, her dog chasing an invisible quarry. Diana is striding along, and seems perfectly at ease, she turns and glances almost tenderly over her shoulder at the onlooker.

tub. The attitude of the women and the provocative manner in which one is reaching toward the nipple of the other leads one to suppose that there is more to this than the usual bathing scene. To date, however, it has proved impossible to establish its symbolic significance. It might be an allegory referring to the birth of one of the children of Henry IV, perhaps César de Vendôme, born in 1594. The impression

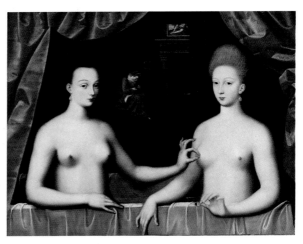

Second School of Fontainebleau, ***Gabrielle d'Estrées and one of her Sisters***, **ca. 1594**
Oil on wood, 96 x 125 cm

Framed by a red curtain, this scene was not intended for public view, which is the secret of its appeal today. The favorite of Henry IV, Gabrielle d'Estrées (1573–1599) is sitting naked with her sister in the bath-

left by the picture is one of pleasure in the extraordinary self-assurance conveyed by the women, who are painted like porcelain, combined with a feeling of irritation at their behavior. This painting has repeatedly captured the imagination of artists, and it is astonishing that it has never fallen victim to any pious moral crusade in light of its pronounced eroticism.

The Great Century

Valentin de Boulogne (1594–1632),
The Fortune Teller, ca. 1628
Oil on canvas, 125 x 175 cm

When Caravaggio (ca. 1571–1610) arrived in Rome around 1588, new subjects and new lighting effects appeared on the stage of art. Valentin de Boulogne was one of the younger painters to be attracted by the stimulating climate in Rome. In this picture he has painted a scene in a hostelry: an old man is playing the harp, while a woman plays a guitar. A youth is having his palm read by a woman, whose face is in shadow. Whereas in Caravaggio's treatment of this subject the man is so hypnotized by the fortune teller's beguiling eyes that a ring is stolen from him, in this case it is the woman who is robbed. The chiaroscuro painting of Caravaggio's followers was as popular with art lovers as it was despised by theoreticians – not least because of the straightforward nature of the subject matter.

Simon Vouet (1590–1649), *The Presentation in the Temple*, ca. 1640/41
Oil on canvas, 393 x 250 cm

The fate of French painters during the 17th and 18th centuries was all too frequently decided in Rome, rather than in their own capital, Paris. Simon Vouet soon became an important figure in Rome; upon returning to France in 1627, he worked as court painter to Louis XIII. He lived at the Louvre and decorated the king's palaces, but also embellished churches with his art. Cardinal Richelieu donated this picture to the Jesuits in Paris in 1641. The Circumcision of Christ might have been a more suitable subject, for it was during this ceremony that the child was given the name Jesus, from which the name of the order derives. In the kind of room that was most admired in Rome at that time, beneath pillars resembling those with which Gianlorenzo Bernini (1598– 1680) would later surround St. Peter's Square, Mary brings the Christ child to present him to the aged Simeon. The figures on the left show that even this rigor-ously academic painter was interested in Caravaggio (ca. 1571–1610). Light and color, however, testify to Vouet's independence.

Philippe de Champaigne (1602–1674),
Portrait of Cardinal Richelieu,
ca. 1639
Oil on canvas, 222 x 165 cm

The slim, rather vain man who is the subject of this painting directed the affairs of state during the reign of King Louis XIII. The artist painted several portraits of Cardinal Richelieu (1585–1642), and probably stayed in Paris on the journey from his native Brussels to Rome. He was part of the first generation of academic painters who, far away from Italy, typified the increasingly independent classicist movement in France.

Nicolas Poussin (1594–1665),
The Inspiration of the Poet,
ca. 1630
Oil on canvas, 182 x 213 cm

Although this painter, who was a native of Normandy, had spent most of his life in Rome, he was nevertheless the great master of French classicism. His pictures were enthusiastically received in France and were held up to young painters as examples alongside the art of Raphael (1483–1520). The Louvre now has in its possession some 38 pictures that are representative of the entire spectrum of the artist's creative work. Cardinal Mazarin (1602–1661) was the owner of this very

early picture of a writer with quill and paper, next to whom we see the Muse, Euterpe, and the god of the arts. Apollo, who accompanies the feast of the gods on his lyre, is also regarded as the leader of the Muses. Euterpe, identifiable by her flute, represents lyric poetry accompanied by flute music. Winged Genii bear laurel wreaths, with which to crown the poet. The picture is constructed like a relief. Poussin departs from the antique precedent by virtue of his grandiose manipulation of the light and by embedding the scene in a landscape, showing the degree to which the Venetian Titian (1488/90–1576) was able to influence such an uncompromisingly Roman painting.

Nicolas Poussin,
Self-portrait, **1650**
Oil on canvas, 98 x 74 cm

Those who are familiar with the colorful pictures of the artist must be astonished by the extreme seriousness of his monumen-

tal self-portraits in Paris and Berlin. Merely a hint of Poussin's mythological painting appears in the background of the picture in the Louvre, but the attention is focused entirely on the dignified man, who posed in Rome as the thinker for the French collector Paul Fréart de Chantelou.

Nicolas Poussin,
The Shepherds of Arcadia, ca. **1638–1640**
Oil on canvas, 85 x 121 cm

This is one of Poussin's most famous works. The mountainous highlands of the Peloponnesus were a showcase for pastoral poetry by the Hellenistic period. Virgil (70–19 B.C.) wrote about a tomb in Arcadia, but discussion of the inscription *ET IN ARCADIA EGO* did not emerge until the 17th century. The question as to whether it refers to mortality (in which case it is death who says "I too am in Arcadia") or to the thoughts of the deceased as he remembers happy times ("I too was once in Arcadia") remains unresolved. Three shepherds, turning to a figure who is probably a priestess, consider the message with apparent amazement. The sculptor and master builder Gianlorenzo Bernini (1598–1680) said of Poussin's landscapes that they were born, not of the heart, but of the intellect. In no way was this detrimental to their effectiveness; indeed, they remained models for many subsequent artists.

Claude Lorrain (Claude Gellée; 1600–1682),
The Disembarkation of Cleopatra at Tarsus,
1642/43
Oil on canvas, 117 x 148 cm

Almost as significant for classicism as Nicolas Poussin was Claude Lorrain. He too had spent most of his life in Rome, where he developed the ideal landscape. The golden light, which Lorrain used to epitomize Italy or landscapes of the south, and in which the grandiose, imaginary architecture was bathed, continues to exert its fascination. The principal motif in this painting is a sunrise over a harbor. We are far too absorbed by the reflected light on the sea, the rigging of the magnificent vessels, and the architecture, to pay any attention to the figure of Cleopatra, clad in blue. Historical accuracy is likewise of no account when one is confronted with a backlit scene, in which the human figures seem almost incidental.

Nicolas Poussin,
Winter, or the Deluge, **1660–1664**
Oil on canvas, 118 x 160 cm

The *Four Seasons* cycle constitutes Poussin's artistic and religious testament. Executed for Richelieu (1585–1642), the series came into the possession of Louis XIV following the death of the cardinal in 1665. Different concepts are subtly connected in these four paintings: seasons, times of day, and both biblical and mythological ideas.

A storm with torrential rain rages on a somber, moonlit night. The foreground is illuminated from an invisible source. People can be seen attempting to save themselves by boat from rocky crags. Although they are assisting one another, they nevertheless appear isolated. A second boat has capsized at a waterfall; one of its occupants is praying to heaven, but a massive sheet of lightning appears instead of God. A huge snake is winding its way over the rocks – probably signifying evil.

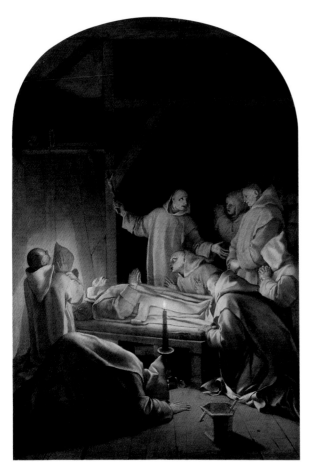

in 1628, were all painted for the monastery to the south of the Palais du Luxembourg, where they hung in cloisters that were open to laymen. The effect of these paintings in the Louvre is disconcerting, for their pale colors and the penetrating blue that recedes into night look incongruous among the surrounding works. Le Sueur was a pupil of Simon Vouet, and his contemporaries in art referred to him as the "French Raphael".

Lubin Baugin (ca. 1612–1663),
Still Life with Pastries,
ca. 1630–1635
Oil on wood, 41 x 52 cm

The painting shows pastries and wine that are displayed on a cool blue tablecloth, on a table in front of a bare wall of large square stone slabs. The costly and fine wineglass provides a curious contrast with the wickerwork wine bottle. The arrangement of the rolled waffles on the plate, which itself overhangs the edge of the table, is complex in terms of perspective. This simple ensemble is given mysterious vitality by the light and shadow, which also introduce clear, calm lines into

Eustache Le Sueur (1616–1655),
***The Death of St. Bruno,* 1645–1648**
Oil on canvas, 193 x 130 cm

The 22 pictures from the life of the founder of the Carthusian order, who was canonized

the composition. The famous panel is signed at the bottom on the right-hand side. Baugin, an early still-life painter who worked in Paris with Simon Vouet (1590–1649), frequently restricts himself to a small number of objects, which he disposes geometrically in a clear composition of circles and planes. In the French art world, which was increasingly influenced by the Académie Royale, still-life painting, as an inferior genre, was in a difficult position; the significant achievements of minor virtuosos in this sphere in France are all the more astonishing. The stock held by the Louvre and the role played by the museum in educating artists in the 19th century partly explain the extremely lively interest in the structure of Baugin's paintings shown by artists such as Gustave Courbet (1819–1877) and Paul Cézanne (1839–1906).

A Mysterious Thief in the Louvre

Modern museums are high-security areas, thanks to the imagination shown by technicians behind the scenes. They have to prevent patriots from taking works of art home with them, lunatics from defacing them, and the criminal fraternity in general from helping itself to the stock of an establishment such as the Louvre. Before all the modern aids were introduced, documentary evidence shows that there existed a thief whose name is now forgotten, and of whom there remains no trace. The thief in question lived in the era before photographic records were made of all the paintings, when artistic and forensic science were in their infancy – in short, when it was possible to do things that criminals can only dream about in this day and age.

The realization that something was missing from the Louvre dawned gradually, for

The deserted Hieroglyph Gallery in the Louvre

the clever machinations of our anonymous hero ensured that there was no empty nail to draw attention to an empty space previously occupied by a picture. At first, when experts studied

certain still-life paintings, they thought they were hallucinating. Surely the Flemish style had been imitated, leading to a similar abundance of robust fare in French paintings? Suddenly, all the rich and sumptuous food seemed to have vanished. One old master, who had always been overshadowed by de Heem, among others, and whose unusual name was rarely noted – Lubin Baugin (see p. 386 f.) – was particularly affected, having apparently embarked on a sudden diet after all the feasting. In one of his paintings, there remained little more than a half-full glass, a bottle, and a light snack.

It looked as if someone in the pictures had cleared the table. Once alerted, the curators in charge were constantly coming across other unexplained losses. This much was known: the paintings were only defaced at night. Secondly, the thief seemed concerned exclusively with food, for one or two items to do with food went missing from the Egyptian collection; as a result, reliefs from the Old Kingdom, and the New Kingdom wall paintings assumed an increasingly

Attendant in the Louvre courtyard, ca. 1910

Jan Davidsz. de Heem (1606–1683/84), Still-life Showpiece, 1640, oil on canvas, 149 x 203 cm, third floor, room 6

tidy appearance. Thirdly, it was obvious that the thief had style, was most probably pedantic, and wanted to use the pictures to change the history of art, by restoring hieroglyphics to the Egyptians, and by making a very sharp distinction between the French and their northern neighbors.

The police initially disclaimed responsibility for this matter, but they were later ordered to take action by higher authority.

There followed some very lonely and eerie nights for the officials (the *flics*), lit only by

Handling works of art has become much more complex today. The prospect of a museum employee examining a picture in such an intimate manner is now unthinkable.

moonlight, since they were obliged to keep their flashlights switched off. In the end, however, the thief gave himself away. He had by then pared down all the French still lifes, but when, as a true connoisseur, he moved on to Jan Davidsz. de Heem's *Still-life Showpiece* of 1640 (see p. 389), he stumbled against a lute, creating sounds that led to his instant capture. Our suspect confessed what he had done. One of those employees with what is now termed a service contract, he had worked all his life for the Louvre, and was now being threatened with retirement without receiv-

ing a pension – a fate that his parents had long since warned him about. As a true art lover, the idea of art leaving him penniless was uncongenial, and he decided to see whether art might relent. It did: he lived off the pictures for a while, and was at last able to do what no official museum curator would have been allowed to do, namely to create some order and impose his own standards in the museum. He turned out to be quite important, because without him, Lubin Baugin would have remained a mere imitator of the Flemish style.

Adrian Brouwer (ca. 1605–1638), Landscape at Sunset, ca. 1635, oil on wood, 17 x 26 cm, third floor, room 23

The ultimate fate of our thief is open to dispute. To the poor policeman who saved de Heem's picture for us in its present form, all the works and their creators were nothing more than a passing shadow, and so he too was unable to say what had really happened. The thief evaded the police, stepped into a landscape painting, and disappeared forever. It was said by some to be a painting by Watteau, but they were too far away to see. However, if you look at the unkempt *Landscape at Sunset* by Adrian Brouwer, you will see that the unidentified thief still had unfinished business with the Flemish artists.

Georges de la Tour (1593–1652),
Jesus and Joseph in the Carpenter's Workshop,
ca. 1642
Oil on canvas, 137 x 102 cm

Georges de la Tour, a native of Lorraine who worked in Lunéville, was not burdened by the need to strive for an ideal imposed by Antiquity and Raphael's Renaissance. He probably never even visited Italy, so his strikingly Caravaggiesque qualities (see p. 330 f.) were not the result of direct influence. Despite the fact that his creative work did not comply with any of the criteria of contemporary art criticism, his works seem to have had considerable impact. Visiting Paris for the first time in 1639, Georges de la Tour is said to have presented King Louis XIII with his painting of *St. Sebastian* (now in the Louvre), and the king was so impressed with it that he had all the other paintings taken down in order to give this one his full attention. The painter strayed from the traditional paths of iconography to find subjects for his pictures, and created a kind of religious genre painting. He brilliantly conveys nocturnal scenes that are illuminated by candlelight, such as that in which the Christ child is immersed in this picture. Clothed in petic raiment,and according to legend rather than to biblical accounts, he holds the candle for Joseph while the latter works on a piece of carpentry, a deliberate allusion to the making of the Cross at Golgotha.

Georges de la Tour, *The Card-sharp and the Ace of Diamonds*, ca. 1625
Oil on canvas, 106 x 146 cm

The paintings in the Louvre by Georges de la Tour were acquired after 1926 following his rediscovery; this artist was ignored for centuries and has only attained global fame in more recent times. Because of their late emergence, the originality of some is occasionally disputed, especially in the case of this mysterious picture. The subject matter concerns the parable of the prodigal son, represented by the smartly dressed youth on the right, who is surrounded by three sinful temptations – wine, women, and gambling. Following in the tradition of Caravaggio's genre paintings, Georges de la Tour executes this picture with his own particular style of exaggerated chiaroscuro, in which smooth surfaces are drastically foreshortened, only to vanish again immediately into the black background. The effect of such contrasts is almost supernatural.

Louis (or ?Antoine) Le Nain (1600/1610–1648),
The Peasant Family, ca. 1642
Oil on canvas, 113 x 159 cm

A family is pictured staring out from a dark interior. On the floor there are artistically arranged objects from everyday life; even the two women seem artificially posed. Yet the people in front of the huge grate on the left are paying no attention to what is going on in the foreground, with the result that artificiality is contrasted with the arbitrary. The bread and wine in the hands of the old people allude to the holy sacrament. The seriousness of the theme, to which one might almost ascribe an underlying social agenda, and the strong contrasts between darkness and light are characteristic of the three Le Nain brothers from Laon, who painted according to the principle of the division of labor, as was customary in the old tradition of craftsmanship. This creates great difficulties when trying to distinguish between their work. The brothers Louis and Antoine fell victim to an epidemic and died within two days of one another.

Philippe de Champaigne (1602–1674), so-called
Portrait of Arnauld d'Andilly, ca. 1650
Oil on canvas, 91 x 72 cm

This portrait features a popular trick that tests the artist's skill. The unidentified subject of the painting is leaning slightly out from the reveal of a stone window, in such a way that one could almost believe he were reaching out beyond the picture frame. The gray of the stone has been cleverly chosen with the man's iridescent clothing in mind, while the gray tones of the background are also echoed in the color of his hair. The slightly ruddy face and hands stand out all the more vividly for this. A comparison with the engraving by Gérard Edelinck (1640–1707) of Arnauld d'Andilly (Louvre, Département des Arts Graphiques) shows the original attribution to be unsustainable. This painting is more spontaneous than the portrait of Richelieu (see p. 380).

The Academy of Fine Arts and Standards in Art

The Académie de Peinture et de Sculpture was founded in 1648 by Anne of Austria and Cardinal Mazarin, and was initially housed in the Salle des Caryatides, followed by the Salon Carré (see p. 265 ff.). Charles Le Brun (1619–1690) was the instigator of its foundation, following the example of the Académie Française, which was founded in 1635 for literature and the sciences; in 1671 the scope was widened to include architecture, which resulted in the creation of the Académie des Beaux-Arts. By contrast with the Académie de St.-Luc, which like the old painters' guilds, was dedicated to the Evangelist and painter, St. Luke, and which remained in existence until 1774, the Académie Royale distanced itself from the guilds and from the shackles of religion in art. Training in craftsmanship was systematically linked to theoretical discourse.

The Academy had the power to award public contracts, and membership was a prerequisite for financial success as an artist. The most recent works of members were exhibited on a very regular basis, and were awarded prizes; this took place firstly in the Palais Royal, then at a later date in the Salon Carré in the Louvre, which gave these exhibitions the name "Salon".

The contemporary reports on the Salons, provide a continuous record of both good and bad aspects of art criticism right up to the threshold of the 20th century; many of the texts relating to avant-garde work reflect only the lack of understanding of backward-looking critics.

As a fundamental contribution to the evaluation of art, the Academy formulated categorical concepts of painting, based on the degree of difficulty as well as the content. According to the institution, pictures of people painted from the imagination were rated much more highly than a faithful reproduction of merely static objects. Historical painting stood at the head of a hierarchy in which still life was consigned to the very

Charles Le Brun, studies of expressions: left, Terror, Musée du Louvre; right, Head of a Fugitive, Royal Library, Windsor

Charles Le Brun, drawing taken from an essay on human physiognomy and animals

lowest position. The remaining categories fell between the two extremes: portraiture suffered because it was imitative; the image of man, which constituted the highest purpose of artistic creation, was absent from landscape painting; and genre scenes were charged with the offence of portraying man not engaged in worthy actions.

The new feeling for categorization led artists such as Charles Le Brun to catalog the vocabulary of gesture and facial expression, and he was able to draw upon physiognomic sketches to convey a range of expressions, even in religious paintings such as the *Adoration of the Shepherds* (1689). However, even these images were not created from observation of nature, but from theoretical work and study of the old masters. Consequently, the skillful way in which Le Brun conveys nocturnal effects is born of the intellect rather than observation. When confronted with Jesus' humble birth in the stable, the theoretically important question of appropriateness arises: the artist faces the problem of conveying the inner significance of the event by means of monumental ruins and grandiloquent gestures.

Hyacinthe Rigaud (1659–1743),
Louis XIV, King of France, **1701**
Oil on canvas, 277 x 194 cm

Hyacinthe Rigaud, *Portrait of the Artist's Mother, Marie Serre,* **1695**
Oil on canvas, 81 x 101 cm

The individual features of the 63-year-old king (1638–1715), dressed in ornate coronation robes that fall to the floor in heavy folds, are scarcely recognizable. Details of fashion, such as the red and white high-heeled silk shoes and the opulent wig, have an alienating effect. The subject of this picture is the absolute power of the monarch. As the official portrait of Louis XIV, it is without doubt the most famous work by Hyacinthe Rigaud. Originally intended for Philip V of Spain, it nevertheless remained in France.

The originally elliptical portrait of Hyacinthe Rigaud's mother, showing two aspects, demonstrates well the accuracy of the artist's portraiture, if the task permitted. At the same time, it explains why for the most part he painted men: women, he said, could not be painted with too good a likeness, because it was not flattering to them; and, if one were to flatter them, the likeness would not be good. This portrait was painted during a visit to Perpignan, in order that Antoine Coysevox could make the marble bust for the Louvre in 1706.

The 18th Century

Jean-Antoine Watteau (1684–1721),
Pierrot, known as "Gilles," **1718/19**
Oil on canvas, 184.5 x 149 cm

The young man is pictured standing in curious isolation, dressed in a Commedia dell'Arte costume, on a narrow strip of land.

There is a gap between him and his companions, who are standing some distance away in the background. While they push a donkey to induce it to move, the white-clad fool remains alone and melancholic, looking at the viewer. The pierrot is actually a clown, a type of jester from the Commedia dell'Arte. Watteau penetrated below the veneer of humor that was applied with the make-up, and was successful in capturing a human dimension, henceforth always discernible in pictures from the world of the traveling entertainer. Later on, Edouard Manet (1832–1883) and Pablo Picasso (1881–1973) both studied this unique painting. Born in the town of Valenciennes in Flanders, Watteau came to Paris for the first time in 1702; people in the capital city were so unreceptive to his art that he was given only decorative work to do, and so he returned to his beloved birthplace. It was not until 1712, following his return to Paris in 1710, that he was finally admitted to the Academy as a painter of *fêtes galantes* – courtly paintings in a parkland setting – and was eventually given the recognition due to him, as one of the greatest colorists of all time.

Jean-Antoine Watteau,
The Embarkation for Cythera, 1717
Oil on canvas, 129 x 194 cm

A couple in the foreground on the right, pictured beneath a statue of Venus, are rising to their feet. They are at the end of a procession of people, some of whom carry a pilgrim's staff – but this is no religious pilgrimage. These are lovers, in various stages of readiness to board the ship lying beside the shore, who are paying homage to the goddess of love. Whether they are leaving Cythera, the island of love, in order to sail away into the infinite distance of the landscape, or whether they are waiting on the landing stage to be ferried across to the island, remains deliberately uncertain. Cupid is hidden, his bow and arrows hanging on the plinth of the statue of his mother, Venus. This picture led to acceptance by the Academy of the genre of painting invented by Watteau and known as the *fête galante*. He repeated this composition with more vivid coloring in another version (Berlin, Charlottenburg), in which the lovers are reluctant to leave the sanctuary of Cythera, lending it a slight melancholy.

Jean-Baptiste-Siméon Chardin (1699–1779),
Still Life with Ray, 1725/26
Oil on canvas, 114,5 x 146 cm

Various sea creatures – oysters and fish – are spread out on stone slabs in front of a bare wall. Alongside them, half-hidden beneath a cloth, lie items of cutlery that reflect the light to different degrees. Not yet gutted, the ray is hanging from a hook. The effect of the friendly "facial expression" of the fish's stomach is disconcerting, given its actual condition. Even the cat seems to be aware of this, for it is arching its back. This picture was submitted, together with the *Buffet* in the same room, for Chardin's admission to the Academy. Although they occupied the lowest rank in the hierarchy of painting, Chardin's still lifes swiftly gained admirers, and were celebrated by the philosopher Diderot (1713–1784) in his literary salons.

François Boucher (1703–1770),
Diana Bathing, 1742
Oil on canvas, 57 x 73 cm

Diana, the chaste goddess of the hunt, is sitting naked on the bank of a river with a companion, following a successful stalking episode, indicated by the booty in the foreground. Boucher skillfully plays on contrasts: the rude hunting implements with

the red band on the quiver add an important accent of color and are juxtaposed with the delicate figure of the woman, adorned with a diadem and seated on exquisite blue fabric. In his portrait of Diana, the artist has recourse to a popular subject, not just with regard to Fontainebleau (see p. 376 f.) but also in respect of Louis XV's passion for hunting. The picture enjoyed success following its exhibition at the 1742 Salon.

Maurice Quentin de La Tour (1704–1788),
Madame Pompadour, ca. 1751–1755
Pastel on blue paper, with the face inserted,
175 x 128 cm

As the mistress of King Louis XV, Madame
Pompadour (1721–1764) was an influential

power in politics from 1745 onward. This
almost life-size pastel portrait celebrates her
role as a patroness of the arts; in it, we learn
of her attempts at drawing and engraving,
and the spines of the books show them to
be volumes published under her patronage.
She is pictured holding a large notebook.

Jean-Honoré Fragonard (1732–1806),
***The Bolt*, 1777**
Oil on canvas, 73 x 93 cm

The two figures in this picture have been caressing one another, but suddenly resistance is awakened in the young woman; she wants to extricate herself from the situation before things get out of hand, but the young man is bigger and stronger, and he alone can reach the small bolt with which he now locks the door. An apple on the table in the foreground on the left is an allusion to the Fall. According to an account dated 1816, Fragonard had intended this picture as a counterpart to the *Adoration of the Shepherds* (in the same room), as a representation of earthly love. The long-lost original, with its porcelain-smooth surface, has only recently been acquired by the Louvre. Overlooked by Parisian art dealers, it was identified by Pierre Rosenberg.

Diderot and Greuze

A page (on confectioners and pastry cooks) from Diderot's Encyclopédie, published between 1750 and 1780

Denis Diderot (1713–1784) was one of the greatest intellects of the Enlightenment, and it is one of the most astonishing phenomena in the history of ideas that such a person nearly succeeded in creating havoc on a national scale by the publication (jointly with d'Alembert) of an encyclopedia. The mere knowledge of the way in which nature and society function was sufficient to shake the monarchy and the Church to their very foundations. Consequently, this man and his important project have come to epitomize the age of Enlightenment, in which pure knowledge entailed political consequences that endangered both the monarchy and the Church. The fine arts were not spared from this barrage; indeed, the fundamentals are contained in Diderot's critical accounts of the Salons for the years from 1759 to 1781. The whole world was aware of Denis Diderot, whether they were supportive or critical of him; in Germany, for instance, he had become known as a result of Goethe's tendentious analysis of the *Encyclopédie*. The rigid rules of the Academy, which supposedly governed the classical and therefore

Jean-Baptiste Greuze (1725–1805),
The Broken Jug, 1785, oil on canvas, 110 x 85
cm, third floor, room 48

Jean-Baptiste Greuze, The Father's Curse:
The Punished Son, 1778, oil on canvas,
130 x 163 cm, third floor, room 51

absolute ideal of beauty, were countered by Diderot with the notion of perceived beauty. Diderot's dictum that every onlooker was able to make judgments on the basis of his feelings deprived the custodians of the Academy of the prerogative of judging works of art.

The philosopher had an important influence over the blossoming of a new kind of art held in low esteem by the Academy, because it occupied a place between history pictures and genre scenes, in defiance of the hierarchy of categories. This new type of painting, that featured anonymous figures, was embraced by Jean-Baptiste Greuze (1725–1805), for a long time Diderot's favorite painter. Pictures such as *The Broken Jug* (1785) occupy a curious position between Rococo and sentimental portrayal of emotions; in this case, the image of the broken jug, also used by Kleist, is an allusion to lost innocence, in the form of a beautiful child who is now in trouble. Alongside this painting, which resembles a portrait, *The Father's Curse* (1778) looks more like a grand historical picture: children are mourning an old man lying on his deathbed. Standing upright, a woman is pointing, turned toward the young man who has just entered; this is *The Punished Son*, who in the previous scene, painted in 1777, was depicted as *The Unworthy Son*. In the earlier painting he had taken his leave, against his father's wishes, to serve in the army. "Moralizing art," Diderot's term for these pictures, was extremely popular with his contemporaries. Such subjects achieved the status of a new category between history and genre painting on the threshold of the great Revolution. Consequently, the painter also became an instrument of the Enlightenment.

though the painter exposes the black woman to the gaze of the voyeur, at the same time she endows her with a dignity that renders her unapproachable. Jacques-Louis David, of whom this artist was a pupil, was obliged to defend Benoist against the voices of certain critics who found the presence of women in the studio unseemly.

The 19th Century

François Gérard (1770–1837),
Cupid and Psyche, 1798
Oil on canvas, 186 x 132 cm

Cupid, igniter of human love, is himself in love. But he can only visit Psyche – the human spirit personified as a butterfly – by night. He is banished as a result of her curiosity to see his face. However, Zeus eventually rewards her love by granting their eternal union. Gérard shows the moment in which the astonished Psyche receives Cupid's first kiss, without looking at him. A fertile meadow provides the setting in which their love is awakened. Gérard's Neoclassicism is as far removed from the style of the _fête galante_ as it is from Greuze's genre scenes (see p. 407). The return to Antiquity is accompanied by abstraction, which once again aims at the ideal of beauty.

Marie-Guillemine Benoist (1768–1826),
Portrait of a Black Woman, 1780
Oil on canvas, 81 x 65.1 cm

In a three-quarter length view, her face turned toward the onlooker, sits a young woman with bared breast, her dark skin standing out against the white cloth. The arms are relaxed, the head held erect with self-assurance, while the eyes look down on the onlooker, unfathomably gentle. Even

Pierre-Paul Prud'hon (1758–1823),
Portrait of the King of Rome, 1811
Oil on canvas, 46 x 56 cm

A boy, lying on opulent fabrics in a small clearing, is sleeping sweetly in the shade of a shrubbery. The flowers of the crown imperial lily bend their heads toward him, as if ambassadors of the light in the background; they also allude to the boy's future life. This is Prud'hon's celebration of the birth of the supposed heir to the throne, Napoleon II, known as the king of Rome or the duke of Reichstadt, the son of the emperor and of Maria-Louise of Austria. He was only treated as the heir during the confusion of the retreat in 1813/14, and was dead by 1833. The surface of the paint has the appearance of lacquer, and the light and dark values are subtly applied. In 1803, Prud'hon painted two ceiling paintings in the Louvre. The artist, who worshiped Leonardo da Vinci (1452–1519) and admired Correggio (1489–1534), was also a friend of the sculptor Canova.

Jean-Auguste-Dominique Ingres (1780–1867),
The Turkish Bath, 1862
Oil on canvas, diameter 110 cm

A nude figure, viewed from the rear, a variation on the *Baigneuse Valpinçon* (1808) in the same room in the Louvre, is the focus of attention. On the right, next to the lutenist, a woman lying in a relaxed pose is gazing out of the picture, while her companions are unselfconsciously enjoying the atmosphere of the hammam. They are all in different poses, as though the painter had included all the studies he could find in this picture. Although the womens' bodies radiate a warmth, the predominant atmosphere is one of coolness. In 1859, Prince Napoleon bought the picture as a rectangle, but returned it to the elderly painter, who had the panel sawn down to make a tondo.

Théodore Géricault (1791–1824),
The Epsom Derby, **1821**
Oil on canvas, 92 x 122.5 cm

Four horses at full gallop, with their jockeys standing in the stirrups, are flying like arrows across the fields; not a single hoof is in contact with the ground. The speed is emphasized by the dark clouds, and the pole that appears on the right of the picture is the only vertical. It was not until Eadweard Muybridge (1830–1904) photographed the movements of horses that it became clear that horses never move in this way; but for Théodore Géricault, whose magnificent *Self-portrait* (ca. 1815) hangs in the same room, faithful representation was never an issue. It is possible that he found the winning formula for the almost surreal flight from English engravings, because this picture, which is not typical of French Romantic painting, was in fact painted in England. The artist, a native of Normandy, kept several horses and died as the result of a riding accident.

Théodore Chassériau (1819–1856),
Esther at her Toilet, **1841**
Oil on canvas, 45.5 x 33.5 cm

Esther lived in the harem of the Persian king, Ahasuerus. An account of her deeds is given in the Book of Esther in the Bible. A pogrom plotted against her people, the Jews, forced her to enter the king's presence unbidden, even at the risk of death. In a thoroughly Oriental fantasy, the blonde Esther is pictured with two dark-skinned servant girls prior to her courageous action. Her naked torso is brought to life with nuances of light, while the contours of her body are delineated with light shading. Chassériau was a pupil of Ingres at the age of 12, but also an admirer of Delacroix.

Théodore Rousseau (1812–1867),
***Avenue of Chestnuts*, 1837–1842**
Oil on canvas, 79 x 144 cm

The principle of studies made from life became firmly established for the first time in France with the advent of the Barbizon school, which enjoyed great success, particularly during the two decades between the revolutions of 1830 and 1848. It was countered by the conviction of the academics that it was not permissible to confront nature before one had learned the rules of art. Théodore Rousseau retreated with Charles-François Daubigny (1817–1878) and others to the village of Barbizon; however, the technical means necessary to execute large-scale oil paintings in the open

had not yet been developed. Just like the Academic painters, the completion of a major work such as Rousseau's *Avenue of Chestnuts* required time: although begun in 1837, the picture was not submitted to the Salon until 1842 — and was rejected.

The Thomy Thiery and Moreau-Nélaton Foundations

Unlikely subjects to be acquired by the state, the Louvre owes the following treasures to members of the general public who wanted to see contemporary paintings. Works that have long since acquired the status of classics were still controversial in Paris in 1902, when Georges Thomy Thiery (1823–1902) bequeathed his collection of Corots, Millets, and other landscapes painted by members of the Barbizon school to the Louvre. The same was true of the Moreau-Nélaton collection in 1906.

Camille Corot (1796–1875),
***The Bridge at Mantes*, 1868/1870**
Oil on canvas, 38.5 x 55.5 cm

Corot rarely stayed at Barbizon, but was a friend of Daubigny. He valued Italy as an idyllic location and a heroic landscape in the style of Claude Lorrain. His extraordinary paintings combine the freshness of open air paintings with a heightened sense of composition. The view through the trees of a stretch of landscape that fills the picture and offers interest only because of its atmosphere was of great significance for generations of artists to come: Pissarro and Cézanne do not seem so far from a painting such as this one, the gray tones of which are given unusual vitality from their juxtaposition with small red and white dots of color.

Camille Corot,
Woman with Pearl, ca. 1868–1870
Oil on canvas, 70 x 55 cm

Corot found just as much inspiration in the Louvre as on his extensive travels through France and Italy. He adapted famous paintings to his own ends in an astonishing way; one must inspect this picture closely to recognize Leonardo's *Mona Lisa* (see p. 304 f.).

The Carlos de Beistegui Bequest (1942)

Various art lovers have bequeathed their paintings to the Louvre, on condition that they be exhibited separately as a collection. This results in some interesting ensembles based on the interests and also the origin of the donors, and reveals a great deal about the personalities of the collectors. Carlos de Beistegui (1863–1953), for example, had bequeathed his paintings to the Louvre 11 years before his death, although he kept them during his lifetime. With advice from the curators, Beistegui bought further pictures to add to the collection, with the result that various well-known paintings are united in this unlikely location.

Jean Hey, called "Master of Moulins"
(documented 1480–1500),
Dauphin Charles Orland, 1494
Wood, 39.7 x 36.8 cm

The dauphin (1492–1495), the child of Charles VIII of France and Anne of Brittany, who died at a very early age, is pictured at the age of two being presented with a rosary. The light-colored clothing emphasizes the pale complexion of the boy in this half-length portrait. The slightly reddish tinge to the skin, often found in people with red hair, is echoed in the red of the brocade curtain, the opulence of which underlines the noble origins of the boy who was the heir to the French throne. The view from above and the unusual composition, which drastically cuts off the left arm. convey an impression of the child's urge to be active, as yet unconstrained by court etiquette.

Ernest Meissonier (1815–1891),
The Barricade in the Rue de la Mortellerie in June 1848 or *Memorial to the Civil War, 1850/51*
Oil on canvas, 29 x 22 cm

Loose paving slabs are piled up in the foreground, but the dead are lying in rows to the rear. They lie just as they fell; not a living soul is to be seen. The color has ebbed away from the picture, just as life has ebbed away from the combatants, and even the life blood of the blue, white, and red tricolor appears to have drained completely away. Meissonier, however, was not a revolutionary; in 1848 he was an artillery captain in the National Guard.

Francisco de Goya y Lucientes (1746–1828),
The Comtesse del Carpio, Marquesa de la Solana,
ca. 1794/95
Oil on canvas, 181 x 122 cm

Maria Rita Barrencha (1757–1795), wife of the conde del Carpio, count of Solana, wrote many highly regarded plays for the theater. This picture was finished shortly before her death. The painting in the Louvre shows the honesty with which Goya treats the women who gave him commissions, while depicting them in surreal landscapes. In pictures such as this, the old order of Europe and its divisions according to rank appear to have been shaken to the core. The individual, however, despite the veneer of nobility, acquires a positively modern aspect.

The Collection of Princess Louis de Croÿ (1930)

Samuel van Hoogstraten (1627–1678),
The Slippers, ca. 1670
Oil on canvas, 103 x 70 cm

The bequest of Princess Louis de Croÿ, born Eugénie de l'Espine (1867–1932), is one of the most comprehensive in the Louvre, comprising 3800 drawings and paintings. In fact, only a cross-section of the paintings is on display, taken from the genre in which her father Oscar de l'Espine (1827–1892), a great lover of 17th-century Dutch painting, was a collector.

This large picture, with no human presence, is puzzling; it affords a view through three open doorways into intimate surroundings, in the manner of a picture within a picture. We can see from behind the figure of a beautiful woman, who is depicted in several paintings by Gerhard Terborch (1617–1681), such as the *Father's Warning* (1654/55) in Berlin. The onlooker is left in doubt as to what she is doing. Someone apparently has removed their shoes in order to eavesdrop, but the events will remain an eternal mystery.

The Hélène Loeb and Victor Lyon Collection (1961)

The collection of Hélène Loeb (1883–1946) and Victor Lyon (1878–1963) did not arrive in the Louvre until 1977; it encompasses large expanses of the history of painting. Because the donors wished their collection to be preserved as a whole, the Impressionist pictures it contains are the only ones that remain in the Louvre following the transfer of other paintings dated after 1848 to the Musée d'Orsay. Visitors therefore have the pleasure of seeing the delightful *Hélène Loeb with a Flower Basket* by Paul Merwart (1855–1902), as well as two magnificent Canalettos.

Claude Monet (1840–1926),
Honfleur in Snow, **1867**
Oil on canvas, 41 x 55 cm

Landscapes in snow are among the most wonderful images conveyed by Impressionist painting. In their pictures of snow, Monet and Pissarro observe the variety of color in white, especially the blue in the shadows. Pictures such as these provide evidence of the com-

pletion of the revolutionary process within French painting that had its foundations in the Barbizon school. We leave French painting with the fresh quality of nature in snow, as portrayed in three paintings by Monet, at a point at which painting from nature triumphs over art in the tradition of the old masters. There are changes both in composition and the view of the painter, and the coloration becomes more important.

Monet's Motif in the Louvre

Although the state museum has outlived its role as a school for the nation's young painters, one still stumbles over easels in the picture galleries of the Louvre. Ever since the founding of the Académie des Beaux-Arts, artists in France have been taught to copy the old masters as part of their training. For most theoreticians, but also for painters as recent as Paul Cézanne (1839–1906), the study of works by an artist such as Nicolas Poussin (1594–1665) was considered preferable to working from a model. The paintings of Hubert Robert showed copying of pictures by Raphael, and of ancient sculptures in the ruins of the Grande Galerie (see p. 265).

The avant-garde artists of the late 19th century were the first to attempt to lift the yoke imposed on contemporary art by tradition and the museum. Even as recently as the beginning of the 20th century, however, the relative merits of the old masters for the purpose of training young artists were still being disputed. At the same time, the museum and the established models were emancipated by means of a movement that was, in the first instance, concerned solely with capturing nature itself – or more accurately, the impression given by nature in changing light conditions, when painted quickly. Most painters who called themselves Impressionists had begun in the conventional manner, and so the Louvre had been their most important teacher too. Even Manet's *Déjeuner* is a variation on Titian's *Concert Champêtre* (see p. 308 f.).

On April 27, 1867, when Monet (1840–1926) requested permission from the curator of the museum to paint there, it was already clear that he did not wish to be part of the traditional scheme of things. Unlike countless students and artists who copied paintings professionally, this Impressionist painter, who was granted his request on April 30, was not concerned with the works of the old masters; indeed, Monet ignored the famous paintings. Continually reflecting upon his professional calling as an artist, he threw open the windows of the museum and allowed fresh air to stream in from the world outside. In order to paint his best picture, now in Berlin, he actually went outside, beneath Perrault's colonnade, to commit to canvas his breathtaking view of St.-Germain-l'Auxerrois in brilliant sunshine. Monet succeeded in capturing the view that can be seen today from the Egyptian rooms.

This view of real life, painted from the museum, finally overcame the reservations of the Academy, whose objective was to train the eye in exclusively traditional ways. In his depiction of inconsequential comings and goings beneath the trees in front of the church, Monet ennobles his subject matter. He breaks free from the system of categorizing types of painting by painting a landscape that includes people, but without becoming a painter of genre scenes. This painting is one of the earliest views of the city, and undoubtedly one of the most beautiful, far superior to the two other views, in which the

Claude Monet (1840–1926), View from the East Side of the Louvre of the Church of St.-Germain-l'Auxerrois, 1867, oil on canvas, 79 x 98 cm, Nationalgalerie, Berlin

painter looked out over the Seine from his vantage point in the Louvre (now in Oberlin, Ohio, and The Hague). When faced with the picture of St.-Germain-l'Auxerrois, it is easy to suppose that Monet is using light to pay homage to the style of the Venetians: artists such as Guardi (see p. 334 f.) and Canaletto in the 18th century, who were, after all, also giving a pictorial account of life in their city in large *vedute*, featuring tiny figures.

Monet, however, gave no thought to such precursors. In fact, it is his critics who deserve reproach; in attacking Monet, they appeared totally ignorant of the fact that earlier generations of artists, who were by that time greatly admired, had taken similarly radical steps.

The Great Rooms on the Second Floor – the Salle Mollien

Jacques-Louis David (1748–1825),
Napoleon Crowning Josephine (detail), 1806/07
Oil on canvas, 621 x 979 cm

The moment chosen by David from the ceremony of the imperial coronation of 1804 is that at which Napoleon, having already been crowned himself, crowned his wife, Josephine. The artist avoided showing the scandalous act in which the ruler himself, watched by the pope, placed the crown on her head. In order to include as many dignitaries as possible in a recognizable form, David, like Rubens in his *Médicis Cycle* (see p. 488 ff.), forms distinct groups of figures on a small scale, but ensures that they benefit from the monumental architecture. The artist had originally intended a series of four paintings, but only the *Distribution of the Eagles* was completed. These paintings saw David at the height of his fame. He was the leading painter of the Revolution and in the court of Napoleon.

Jacques-Louis David,
The Oath of the Horatii, **1784**
Oil on canvas, 330 x 425 cm

The three Horatii stand braced alongside one another, their arms raised to swear the oath on three swords held in the air by their father. To their right are women seated with their children, and overcome with grief. The quarrel between Rome and Alba Longa is to be decided by a fight between the three Horatii and the three Curatii brothers. Two Romans died in the battle, but the third emerged the victor; returning to Rome, he killed his sister because she was mourning one of the Curatii, to whom she was betrothed. Corneille's tragedy, *Horace*, which was performed in 1782 at the Comédie Française, is said to have inspired David's sketches. Enthusiasm for the painting was based on ideological rather than artistic grounds: on the eve of the Revolution, emotions were stirred by the ideal of sacrifice for the sake of one's country and by the sight of the grieving women.

Anne-Louis Girodet de Roussy-Triesen (1767–1824), *The Dream of Endymion*, 1792
Oil on canvas, 198 x 261 cm

Pierre-Paul Prud'hon (1758–1823), *Josephine in the Park at Malmaison*, 1805
Oil on canvas, 244 x 179 cm

Endymion is lying naked on his bed, his faithful dog sleeping at his feet. Girodet portrays the handsome shepherd in a scenario reminiscent of the story of Danae, the lover of Zeus, who appeared to her in a golden shower. Diana, the chaste goddess of the moon, who is not visible, has to be content with a kiss via a ray of light that seems to be bearing the shepherd away.

The empress is seated on a stony bank in the middle of a landscaped garden. She is contemplative, relaxed, and rather loosely attired. Whereas the plants in the foreground are clearly delineated, the foliage appears blurred by the light. Prud'hon learned this technique of using several layers of paint to produce a lacquer-like surface from the renowned Leonardo da Vinci (1452–1519).

Elisabeth-Louise Vigée Lebrun (1755–1842),
Self-portrait with Daughter, **1786**
Oil on wood, 121 x 90 cm

Jacques-Louis David (1748–1825),
Madame Récamier, **1800**
Oil on canvas, 173 x 243 cm

This artist, the wife of a prominent art dealer and the ultimate painter of women in the 18th century, knew how to portray the joys of motherhood and children in a manner befitting the era characterized by the philosophy of Jean-Jacques Rousseau. Whereas pictures treated in a similar vein had frequently evoked the Madonna, this feature was absent from the work of Vigée Lebrun.

Until she was banished from France in 1811, Julie Récamier (1777–1849) presided over elegant society in Paris. The Empire is personified in this portrait, painted in 1800: clothed in antique robes, she is pictured reclining on an exquisite piece of furniture, which is still linked with her name. Next to her are an oil lamp and a footstool. David indicates the surrounding space by use of dashes of color.

Jean-Auguste-Dominique Ingres (1780–1867),
Caroline Rivière, 1804/05
Oil on canvas, 100 x 70 cm

Ingres had worked with Jean-Louis David on *Madame Récamier*; in this case, however, he now turned for inspiration to Raphael (1483–1520). In the lower part of the picture, he maintains a dark background and without form, in order to generate a contrast in the radiance of the white garments against the cool tones. Caroline Rivière (1790–1807) is seen wearing furs, suede, and fine fabrics, all painted with mastery. Her head is turned to gaze at the onlooker.

Théodore Chassériau (1819–1856),
The Artist's Sisters, 1843
Oil on canvas, 180 x 135 cm

The fascination of things that are similar, but not quite identical, is the source of charm in this double portrait. Alice and Adèle are wearing the same clothes and have the same hairstyle, but the high cheekbones and rather gaunt neck of one of the sisters contrasts with the rosier cheeks and more rounded shoulders of the other. In this feast of sumptuous color, their pale skin shines luminously against the brightly colored wall covering in a dark corner of the room. At the same time, a painting such as this testifies to the magnificence of the colonial period. The women are wearing cashmere shawls over the finest French silks.

Restoration in the Louvre

The public likes to see paintings in a good, clean condition, and as much as possible in uniform splendor. However, these objects are hundreds, and sometimes thousands, of years old, and are subjected to stress in the form of constant exposure to huge crowds of visitors, even if they do no more than stream past obliviously, perspiring and wearing damp jackets. Preservation of the treasures with which it is entrusted is therefore one of the most monumental tasks facing a museum such as this.

Museums have seen great changes in this field during the past two hundred years. In London, the National Gallery formerly closed its doors to the public for one week each year, so that the soot from the London smog could at

View of the restoration workshop with Dutch paintings on the test stand.

least be washed off the pictures. Nowadays there is a great deal more refinement; for example, it soon became painfully obvious how quickly a wooden panel warps, with the result that the paint simply becomes detached. It is hard to imagine that the first floor rooms in the Louvre did not have electric lighting until shortly before the Second World War, and that work is still under way to equip all the rooms of this huge building to a uniform standard.

Although some people in the museum world dread progress, the Louvre welcomed innovation long before the current enthusiasm for computers and new media. As long ago as 1931, a pioneering laboratory was established. From 1934 onward, the patron Carlos Mainini made it possible for the X-ray specialist Fernando Perez, who was also the Argentine ambassador in Paris, to carry out sensational investigations in a newly founded department in the Louvre. In the face of opposition, including some from within the ranks, art experts learned how to use X-ray methods from teachers who included doctors. Since that time, thanks to the Louvre, remarkable knowledge has been acquired on all possible aspects of the care of works of art. The innovator Madeleine Hours, an archeologist who set about exposing restoration to the influence of scientists as well as to those of a purely artistic persuasion, will never be forgotten. After assuming responsibility as director for the entire museum, she showed, in an exhibition in 1980 entitled *La vie mystérieuse des chefs-d'oeuvre, La science au service de l'art,* the fascinating way in which science is able to discover the "secret life of the major works," as promised by the title of the exhibition.

Pioneer Madeleine Hours, 1961

Of course, it would not have been possible to harness technical innovation with its considerable costs for the exclusive benefit of the Louvre. For this reason, the history of the restoration workshops is closely linked to the national administration of the arts, and André Malraux, minister of culture in de Gaulle's government from 1958 to 1969, had his finger on the pulse of the modern era.

For Malraux, scientific analysis was a byway between the major routes of history writing and poetry, but nevertheless a path that was in keeping with the times, and so prospects for the nationwide collaboration between museums, in conjunction with the conservation of monuments, were considerably improved. The workshops in the Louvre were at the heart of the art conservation movement throughout France. Since those days, however, circumstances have continually changed: the establishment of the Grand Louvre in 1993 entailed the reorganization of all the services, culminating in the final years of the 20th century in a new national organization called C2RMF (Centre de Recherche et de Restauration des Musées de France), a body which is under the aegis of the Direction des Musées de France, but is housed in the Pavillon de Flore of the Louvre. The workshops are divided into sections; the headquarters are in the Petites Ecuries in Versailles, but there are also studios located in the Louvre itself in order to avoid the need for transportation of works of art.

Four large departments of varying size deal with the fundamentals. The starting point for every intervention is the analysis provided by the Département de Recherche with its laboratory, which has at its disposal a particle accelerator, and radiography and infrared equipment – in short, everything necessary for nondestructive examination. The Département de Conservation/Restauration comprises all the workshops providing security, cleaning, and similar services. Well over a hundred independent restorers with service contracts work alongside the staff employed by the Louvre, where the importance of documentation was understood at an early stage; France is, in any event, fascinated by information technology. France also lives by the motto that a nation that forgets its monuments has forfeited its greatness, so the C2RMF naturally has easy access to computerized records in a formidable Département de Documentation

Laboratory investigation in the 1950s.

Informatique. There is renewed awareness of the environmental conditions in the exhibition rooms themselves, where the works of art are subject to stress from the crowds of people, as mentioned earlier, and glazing and cabinets are also being introduced to provide miniature self-contained rooms with regulated climatic conditions. The smallest department to date, the Département de Prévention, combines experience with the need for research.

It is impossible to describe in general terms the way in which this department functions, for each work of art has its own particular problems, and each intervention costs money. Two groups of people work in tandem in this area: the conservators, mostly experts in archeology and art history, are responsible for the inventory, while the conditions in the exhibition rooms are constantly monitored by the restorers with their technical expertise. If anything is noticed in a work of art that requires action, the conservators air the problem with their colleagues. Discussions are held with the C2RMF regarding the course of action to be taken, and the work is then dispatched via the analytical laboratory in the Département de Recherche to the Département de Conservation/Restauration. Everything that happens on the way is documented as a matter of course; the Louvre takes particular pride in the collection of files that are systematically kept on as many works as possible.

The scientists and restorers are particularly busy when there are new acquisitions or exhibitions, whether the Louvre itself is staging the exhibition or whether loans are being dispatched elsewhere in the world. The laboratories are the first and last port of call when the works leave and are returned to the Louvre.

It is not absolutely essential for the public to understand what goes on behind the scenes, in case it detracts from their pleasure in viewing the works, but there is a type of exhibition which is becoming increasingly common, and from which those who are interested in such matters can learn a great deal. Small presentations are held, and they are usually accompanied by excellent catalogs, in which the Département de Peintures, for instance, opens its archives. Pictures are then displayed alongside photographs

Carlos Mainini and Fernando Perez

from the laboratory, showing the sensational discoveries that are sometimes made. In principle, however, there is a sensible rule that should be observed: the extremely variable condition of the pictures should not be perceived as a crass contrast. No attempt is made to conceal from the expert what has been perfectly preserved and what has been lost; meanwhile, the general public is offered a rational juxtaposition in aesthetic terms of impressive works.

The Salle Daru

Antoine-Jean Gros (1771–1835),
*Napoleon Visiting Victims of the Plague
at Jaffa (March 11, 1799)*, **1804**
Oil on canvas, 523 x 715 cm

The paintings of Baron Gros are typical of Napoleonic propaganda, which attempted to portray its heroes as being as invulnerable as saints. The emperor evokes Christ and hopes of a miraculous cure for France as he fearlessly lays his hand on a lesion caused by the plague; by contrast, one of his companions is seen covering his mouth, fearing infection. In the fantastical, half Gothic, half Oriental architectural setting, costume is also used to maximum effect to heighten the exotic and yet gruesome atmosphere.

Gros follows the Italian tradition in his portrayal of Napoleon as a "doubting Thomas" feeling the wound in Christ's side after the Resurrection, and the figure seated on the left with his head in his hands bears a resemblance to one of the damned from Michelangelo's *Last Judgment* in the Sistine Chapel in Rome.

Eugène Delacroix (1798–1863),
Liberty Leading the People, **1830**
Oil on canvas, 260 x 325 cm

The glorious days of the July Revolution inspired Delacroix to paint this picture, described as the "first political composition in modern painting." A formidable woman is striding energetically forward, holding a gun in her left hand and the tricolor in her right hand. Her simple robe has fallen from off her shoulder, revealing her bare breasts, and she is wearing the Phrygian cap of the Jacobins on her head. She represents the idea of liberty, and is preceded by the boy, resolutely swinging his pistol, whose fearlessness cost him his life as he led the breakthrough across the Seine to the town hall. Dead bodies are lying in the foreground, but the injured

are still looking up with hope at the figure of "Liberty." The artist, who remained in hiding during the unrest, has left a memorial to himself in the shape of the formally dressed leader on the left which is not entirely honest. Notre-Dame is visible in the background, as is the burning city, the smoke from which seems to form a halo around the personification of liberty. This painting, which aroused much interest – and a certain amount of derision – among both the public and critics such as Heinrich Heine (1797–1856) when it was exhibited in the Salon, was considered to be politically dangerous even in the reign of bourgeois king, Louis Philippe, whom the revolution had brought to the throne. He arranged for it to be bought for the Musée du Luxembourg, where it remained under lock and key until the next revolution in 1848.

Théodore Géricault (1791–1824),
***The Raft of the Medusa,* 1819**
Oil on canvas, 491 x 716 cm

This, Géricault's only major historical picture, shows a contemporary disaster: the *Medusa*, a frigate, ran aground off the coast of Senegal in 1816. While the ship's officers, led by an incompetent royalist captain, commandeered the lifeboats for themselves and 86 people were consigned to a single raft until the 15 remaining survivors were eventually picked up by the *Argus*. The new kingdom was rocked by a political crisis as a result. The craft in Géricault's painting is sailing in stormy seas toward the minute rescue ship that reveals itself on the horizon. The stronger members of the crew are waving garments in the air to attract attention. In the foreground, however, the scene is filled with the bodies of the sick and the dead, the realism of which caused a great deal of controversy after the painting was exhibited at the 1819 Salon. The composition contains no defining hero as in Gros' *Napoleon Visiting Victims of the Plague at Jaffa* (see p. 436); instead, human misery is portrayed as heroic. Géricault made a large number of studies for this painting; during the course of the studies he observed the cramped bodies of victims of execution as well as sick and dying people in hospital. The painting was despised by Ingres (1780–1867), but admired by the younger Delacroix (1798–1863). However, the state, plunged into crisis by the *Medusa* affair, did not purchase the painting during Géricault's lifetime, as he had hoped.

Eugène Delacroix (1798–1863),
The Death of Sardanapalus, **1827/28**
Oil on canvas, 392 x 496 cm

The confusion of women's bodies, jewels, excited stallions, smoke, and gruesome murders contrasts starkly with the ruler, reclining impassively on his red couch. The legend of the Assyrian king Sardanapalus, who, besieged in his palace, burned himself and everything that had ever given him pleasure, was familiar in medieval times; Boccaccio had painted the downfall of the king in 1360/75. Delacroix may have been inspired by Lord Byron's tragedy, *Sardanapalus*, written in 1821. As a painter, using intense color and brushwork that owe a great deal to Rubens (1577–1640), he succeeded in transforming the horror of one particular moment into what is now considered one of the most important paintings of French Romanticism.

Eugène Delacroix,
The Massacre of Chios (detail), 1824
Oil on canvas, 419 x 354 cm

Lord Byron (1788–1824) is also associated with this painting, for the great English Romantic found the event depicted here so shocking that he went to fight for the liberation of Greece from Turkish rule. After resisting for a year, the Greek inhabitants of the island of Chios were obliged to admit defeat in April, 1824; 23,000 of the inhabitants were killed, and 47,000 sold as slaves. From the desolate, empty center of the picture, Delacroix portrays the atrocities inflicted by the Turkish cavalry. Like the same artist's *Liberty Leading the People* (see p. 436 f.), the picture was painted immediately after the news of the atrocity broke out, but, by contrast with Géricault's *Raft of the Medusa* (see p. 438 f.), it is completely devoid of any hope.

English Painting

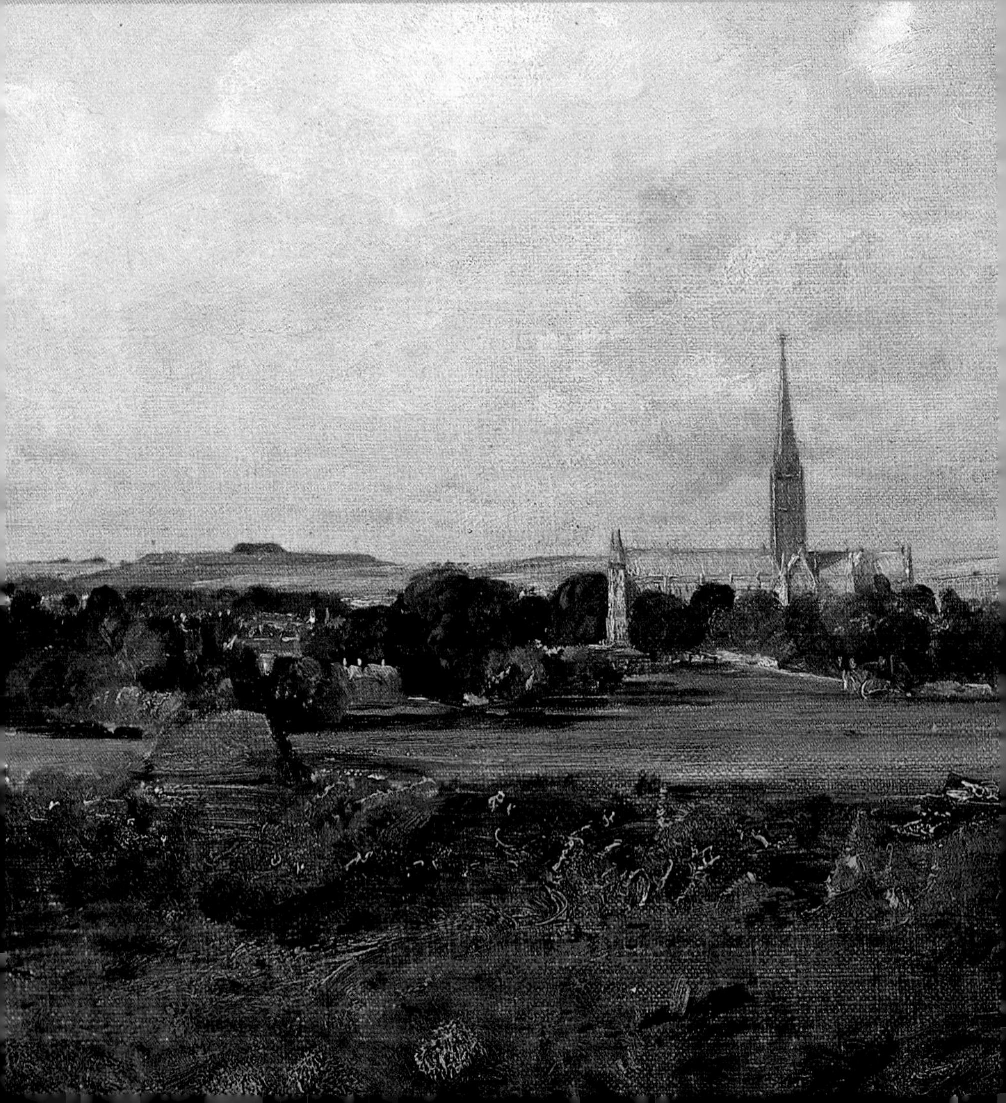

As a result of the Reformation during the reign of Henry VIII (1491–1547) and the Church's subsequent hostility to painting, important spheres of activity were lost to painters in England. Great masters from the Continent who settled in London for a time, such as Holbein and van Dyck (see p. 500 f.), painted portraits of important personalities in English history, such as the unfortunate King Charles I, for the benefit of later generations. This suggests that the contribution made by the island nation to European painting was not immense, and may explain why there is no museum in Continental Europe that is able to offer a representative selection of such paintings; even the collection of around 100 English paintings in the Louvre contains gaps. The satirical genre paintings executed by William Hogarth (1697–1764), for example, are not represented at all.

It is precisely because it is so difficult to gain any idea of the crucial achievements of English painters on the Continent that the material on display at the Louvre is so welcome. The brilliance of the great portrait painters is revealed, and the revolutionary initiatives that English landscape painters carried over into the 19th century are also prominent. A selection of English paintings has been on temporary display in the Salle Denon. The new hanging arrangements will give higher priority to English painting.

John Constable (1776–1837), View of Salisbury (detail), 1820?, oil on canvas, 36 x 52 cm, Musée du Louvre

Sir Joshua Reynolds (1723–1792),
***Master Hare,* ca. 1788/89**
Oil on canvas, 77 x 63 cm

Oblivious of the onlooker, a child is captured in a spontaneous movement, with his clothes in disarray. Showing sensitivity to color and surface texture, the painter contrasts the white of the fabric with the child's complexion and the brown of the sash with his hair. This charming portrait was painted for the boy's aunt, Anna Maria Shipley, Lady Jones. As the founding president of the Royal Academy of Arts in London in 1768, Reynolds' discourses on art were to have worldwide influence on artistic theory and aesthetics in their published form.

Thomas Gainsborough (1727–1788),
Lady Alston, ca. 1760
Oil on canvas, 228 x 168 cm

Against the backdrop of a gloomy pine forest, a woman is standing with her body turned slightly to the right and her head to the left as she gazes into the distance. The blue-gray silk fabric of the dress undoubtedly influenced the painter's choice of background, as the irregular structure of the folds is perfectly reflected in the branches of the pine trees. The picture conveys an impression of cool elegance and a restrained passion. The face with its rosy cheeks shines out from the darkness and the cool, pale gray wrap, with echoes in the reddish tones in the background. The setting can also be regarded as significant; the woman wants to appear as mysterious and as impenetrable as a pine forest. With this portrait of Lady Alston, Gainsborough proved his worth as a painter of portraits as well as of landscapes.

Sir Thomas Lawrence (1769–1830),
The Children of John Angerstein, 1799/1800
Oil on canvas, 195 x 146 cm

Four children are pictured in a dark parkland setting. The three girls are engrossed in remembering dance movements, while the boy gazes fixedly at the onlooker. In terms of color, the composition is defined by the glowing red of the silky, shimmering velvet in which the boy is clothed, and which is echoed in the shoes of the two younger girls. Even if family resemblance were responsible for the similarity in the features of the children, the uniformly sweet expression of their large, dark eyes and apple-red cheeks, seems rather cloying. The painter was the friend and artistic adviser of the children's father, John Julius Angerstein; the Louvre also has in its possession a double portrait of Angerstein and his wife. Sir Thomas Lawrence is considered the leading English portrait painter of his day alongside the theoretician, Sir Joshua Reynolds (see p. 443), whom he greatly admired.

Wright of Derby (Joseph Wright; 1734–1797),
View of Lake Nemi at Sunset, ca. 1790
Oil on canvas, 100 x 128 cm

Better known as a painter of the wonders of the early industrial age, Joseph Wright devotes himself here to the golden light of Italy, viewed through English eyes. Travels in Italy in 1773 inspired in Wright a love of landscape in various lighting conditions. This picture, the foreground of which is in darkness, is conceived as a classical composition. The spreading branches of a tree on the right obscure the bright late-afternoon sunshine. However, a striking effect is produced by the horizon, which appears as a straight gray stripe between the uplands and the rather washed-out blue of the late summer sky.

Wright of Derby was the first English artist to distance himself from the artistic life of the capital, working wherever possible at a distance from London, in his native Derbyshire; it was there that he painted this picture, which gives concrete form to his memories of Italy. It is an example of a landscape painting executed from studies in the artist's studio.

Richard Parkes Bonington (1801–1828),
The Parterre d'Eau at Versailles, **ca. 1826**
Oil on canvas, 44 x 55 cm

A stormy sky of unusual color dominates the picture. Owing to the perspective chosen, little of the topographical location in Versailles is recognizable; the veduta-like nature of the painting is subordinate to the observation of the people and their random comings and goings. Bonington, who lived in France most of his life, was responsible for the introduction into France of the realistic landscape painting of England. The artist was a friend of Delacroix, and had left his parental home at an early age; the Louvre provided him with a valuable training ground. Bonington made open-air sketches from nature, which he then turned into paintings during the winter months in his Paris studio. The Impressionists had a profound understanding of his art; they were the first painters to go out into the open to paint their motifs directly from nature.

Joseph Mallord William Turner (1775–1851),
Landscape with River and Distant Cove
Oil on canvas, 93 x 123 cm

An undulating mountainous landscape, apparently treeless, opens out to the rear of a high plateau in the foreground and descends to a low-lying riverbed. Whether the river flows into the sea or into a lake is not discernible from the bay that lies just in front of the horizon. A revolutionary view of the physical properties of color, which is the sole vehicle of light, is essential in order to translate landscape into painting in this way. Although the effect is of open-air painting, the picture was apparently created in the studio. Alongside Monet's pictures in the Loeb-Lyon collection (see p. 420 f.), this important work by Turner is one of the few examples in the Louvre of the new radical style of painting leading into the modern era.

Henry Fuseli (Johann Heinrich Füssli) (1741–1825), *Lady Macbeth Sleepwalking*, Oil on canvas, 221 x 160 cm

This painter, born in Switzerland, immigrated to England at an early age, where he caused uproar with his paintings of poetic and literary subjects. The plays of William Shakespeare (1564–1616) in particular, in addition to the well-known *Paradise Lost* by John Milton (1608– 1674), provided the artist, a friend of Reynolds, with subject matter for many of his paintings. *Lady Macbeth Sleepwalking* is portrayed with Romantic horror by Fuseli, who takes as his theme a monologue from Shakespeare's tragedy; Lady Macbeth is distraught, having become deeply entangled in her husband's murderous hunger for power. The nocturnal chiaroscuro conveys the impression that the central character is on a stage; the figures looking on from behind, however, are from the painter's imagination. Fuseli was not yet interested in using clothing and accessories to evoke a medieval atmosphere. The classical garments transport

the onlooker to a period between remote Antiquity and the period in which the artist was living. The conservation of Fuseli's paintings has proved to be quite problematic, as he never really learned to use oil paints properly and some deterioration over the years has become apparent.

Early Netherlandish and Early German Painting

Burgundy, with its capital, Dijon, lies at the heart of France; and yet the art of the southern Netherlands, with the proud cities of Ghent, Bruges, Brussels, Louvain, and Malines, is today also regarded as Burgundian. The Parisian metropolis attracted artists from the north, with the result that the tour of the Louvre starts logically in Paris and then branches into the Early Netherlandish-Burgundian and French routes.

It is significant that the most beautiful painting, which belonged to an important official in the service of the duke of Burgundy, came from Autun in France, but was painted by Jan van Eyck in Bruges: it is the *The Virgin of Chancellor Rolin* (see p. 454 f.). It depicts the world in a new way, hints at physical sensations, and at the same time causes the gaze to wander, as if the artist were remembering his own journey in the snow-clad Alps in this bold miniature format. Exquisite pictures such as this one are simultaneously open to Christian interpretation; they can be seen as extolling God as the creator of the world by virtue of their meticulous reproduction of nature.

Precedents for this form of art are to be found in illuminated manuscripts in Paris in the early 15th century, based on a revolutionary technique that remains a mystery. The first pioneer of the new realism, Jan van Eyck, was also regarded as the inventor of oil painting. It was due to the influence of his creative work, and to an even greater extent that of his contemporary Rogier van der Weyden (ca. 1399–1464), that painting also developed in Germany.

Art gained decisive momentum from Italy in the period of radical change around 1500; more important than this, however, were different expectations of art: secular themes began to appear along with the religious motifs. With Jan van Eyck, the portrait achieved special status; the illusionism that made it possible to depict landscape and interiors provided the stimulus to give such phenomena a central position in painting. As a consequence, the first pure genre pictures were painted, and people in these "global landscapes" were used as staffage.

Quentin Massys (ca. 1466–1530),
The Money-changer and his Wife (detail),
1514, see p. 472 f.

Master of the Bartholomew Altar (active
1480–1510), The Descent from the Cross
(detail), ca. 1500–1505, see p. 466.

Early Netherlandish and Early German Painting

Third Floor

Hans Holbein the Younger,
Erasmus of Rotterdam,
p. 470 f.

Quentin Massys, *The Money-changer and his Wife*, p. 472 f.

Hans Memling, *Triptych*, p. 462

Other works:

Albrecht Dürer, *Self-portrait with Thistle*, p. 468 f.

Master of the Holy Family,

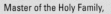

Germany

Netherlands

12 | 10 | 8
11 | 9 | 7
6
5
4

Jan van Eyck, *The Virgin of Chancellor Rolin*, p. 454 f.

Rogier van der Weyden, *The Annunciation*, p. 456

The Early Netherlandish Masters

Circle of Jan van Eyck (ca. 1390–1441),
Wooden Book as Diptych, *St. John the Baptist*
and *Mary with the Christ Child*, ca. 1440
Wood, overall dimensions 37.5 x 22.8 cm, painted
surface 31.5 x 17.3 cm

With this wooden book, which opens to
show the Virgin and John the Baptist, the
painter competes with sculpture by imita-
ting alabaster statuettes, as in the *Ghent Altar*
of 1432. What appears to be a prayer book is
in fact a piece of wood, in which is concealed the most exquisite oil painting,
resembling an altarpiece and appearing to
be sculpture.

Jan van Eyck,
***The Virgin of Chancellor Rolin*, ca. 1434**
Oil on wood, 65 x 62.3 cm

Hardly any painting can compare with this
in terms of visual wonder – it is almost possible to feel the air and touch the objects. A
lone worshipper ventures to approach the
Deity, in the person of the child on Mary's
lap. The kneeling supplicant, having confessed his sins, asks to leave his own world
on the left and to go into the heavenly city
filled with churches on the right. The eye is
drawn from the hands clasped in prayer to
the bridgehead where access is granted or
denied to the domain ruled by Christ. The
painter has depicted the world with such
immense realism that the onlooker is drawn
through the room in the palace and out to
the rear of the battlements
to join the people looking
out over the river and cities
to the snow-covered moun-
tains. Even for one of van
Eyck's works, this painting
remains without equal. It
was found in 1793 in the
chapel of Chancellor Rolin
(1376–1462) in Autun. It is
not known precisely whom
it represents, but the subject
might be John the Fearless,
duke of Burgundy, who was
slain on a bridge in 1419, an
occasion on which Nicolas
Rolin proved his courage.

Rogier van der Weyden
(ca. 1399–1464),
The Annunciation, ca. 1450
oil on oak, 86 x 93 cm

In comparison with Jan van Eyck, even such a subtle picture as this one by Rogier van der Weyden appears subdued: the gestures are more heavily stylized, and the material quality, despite the amazing effects produced by the glass vessel and the metal jug, is less pronounced. Emulation of the Master of Flémalle, who is frequently and erroneously equated with his contemporary Robert Campin (before 1380–1444), proved deci-

sive for paintings of interiors, since the painter transposes the Christian miracle into his own times; Mary is surprised by the angel while at prayer, not in bourgeois surroundings, but in a regal setting.

Conceived as the center panel of a triptych, the *Annunciation* has since become separated from the picture of the donor and the picture of the Visitation of Mary. Both wings remained in Turin, while the main panel was requisitioned by Napoleon and was not returned in 1815. The attribution to Rogier van der Weyden, who was apprenticed to Robert Campin in Tournai in 1427 and was later appointed official painter to the city of Brussels, is in dispute.

Rogier van der Weyden, *Mary Magdalene*,
right wing of the Braque triptych, ca. 1452
Oil on oak, 41 x 34 cm

The Braque family triptych, featuring four saints surrounding the Savior, is one of Rogier's most important works. The most beautiful is Mary Magdalene, an idealized open-air portrait, clothed in the finest fabrics, tangible but at the same time remote in all her noble finery. The picture was painted for Katharine of Brabant, who came from a prominent bourgeois family in Tournai, for her deceased husband, Jehan Braque, whose coat of arms bearing a skull and inscription decorate the outer edges.

On the Value of Character Portraits –
the Urbino *Studiolo*

Banknotes all over the world bear portraits of characters from bygone eras which are intended to guarantee their value. People once joked that the mathematician Carl Friedrich Gauss (1777–1855), whose head used to appear on the old German ten-mark note, was encouraging them to economize. However, there must be an underlying explanation for the fact that people are more reassured about the value of a note when the countenance of some worthy deceased person appears on it.

This association between worth and faces can be traced far back to classical Antiquity; conversely, there also exist

Justus van Gent (ca. 1430–?1474) and Pedro Berruguete (1450/1455–1504), Famous Men, 1472–1476, wood; Dante 111 x 64 cm; Plato 101 x 69 cm, third floor, room 6

recorded instances of such images attracting ridicule. In a prank in the 5th century B.C., Alcibiades, an Athenian scholar of the philosopher Socrates who later became a great general, defaced the marble heads of an entire gallery of civic dignitaries by smashing the noses. This did nothing to discourage the fashion for accumulating ancestral portraits, even if one were ignorant of the appearance of these forebears. The Louvre possesses 14 of the 80 pictures that formed the most noble and scholarly portrait

gallery in the history of painting. They are from Urbino, Raphael's birthplace, where the military leader Federico da Montefeltro had realized a humanist dream: he had moved his extremely valuable library, the manuscripts of which now belong to the Vatican, into a gallery of *homines illustris*, or famous men, from both the antique and modern eras, in the ducal palace built between 1466 and 1472. He united three artistic worlds in Urbino; the only Italian was Melozzo de Forii (1438–1494). The visionary portraits, however, were executed by Justus van Gent (no dates), a virtuoso from Flanders, and the Castilian painter Pedro Berruguete (1450/1455–1504). Recent investigations have demonstrated the difference in their painting techniques in panels that the two painters worked on in turn; insignia granted to the duke in 1474 appear only in the more recent paint layer, and so the work carried out subsequent to that can be attributed to the Spaniard Pedro Berruguete.

On the threshold of the Renaissance, the early Netherlandish painters Justus van Gent and Pedro Berruguete painted amazing pictures of Greek philosophers and church fathers in late Antiquity. Plato is depicted as an extremely sensitive bearded figure, with the head of an Apostle rather than a pagan thinker's forehead; Augustine appears fragile and spiritual, a contemporary of the late-Gothic period. The memory of Dante's face, by contrast, remained very much alive. Pope Sixtus IV, the youngest in the gallery, reigned from 1471 to 1484, so his picture could have been a genuine portrait if the painters had been in Rome at the time. This pope shared a love of humanism with the duke of Urbino, having founded the Vatican library in 1475.

The portrait of Augustine was completed by Justus van Gent; Dante was partly retouched; and Plato appears with an extra layer of paint, the preliminary sketches for which were painted in without changes by Berruguete. Sixtus IV, however, has been superseded by a completely different, considerably younger figure, so it is possible that the pope at the time was received into the studio only after he had appointed Federico de Montefeltro as military leader of the Papal States.

Justus van Gent (ca. 1430–?1474) and Pedro Berruguete (1450/1455–1504), Sixtus IV, 1472–1476, wood, 116 x 56 cm, third floor, room 6

Juan de Flandes (active 1496–1519),
***Jesus and the Samaritan Woman,* 1496/1504**
Oil on wood, 24 x 17.5 cm

It is only rarely that episodes from the life of Jesus not featuring in church services or private worship are portrayed. Pictures such as this one, depicting Christ with the despised woman from Samaria, are found almost exclusively in ensembles consisting of several different scenes.

The Spanish queen Isabella the Catholic (1451–1504) owned an altar comprising many small panels; it is one of the most exquisite in Early Netherlandish painting and demonstrates the importance for the Netherlands of patrons from the Iberian peninsula. Albrecht Dürer (1471–1528) admired the work in 1521 when he saw it at the residence of Margarete of Austria in Malines in Belgium.

Most of the pictures in the ensemble, which are now divided between Madrid and major museums throughout the world, were painted by an artist known in Spanish as Juan de Flandes. The painting by this artist in the Louvre reveals a feeling for air and atmosphere; it is as though he had thrown off the constraints that were more oppressive in the Netherlands, than when he served in Spain. The fact that a French painter, none of whose works is in the Louvre, also worked on this painting shows the extent to which commissions from the royal courts broke down the barriers of national artistic productivity. Michael Sittow also worked on this altarpiece.

Michael Sittow (ca. 1468–1525/26),
***The Coronation of Mary,* 1496/1504**
Oil on wood, 24.5 x 18.3 cm

This panel from the *Altarpiece of Isabella the Catholic* illustrates the importance of distinguishing the work of different artists in a single painting. The picture by Michael Sittow from Talinn in Estonia is executed with greater precision than Juan de Flandes' *Jesus and the Samaritan Woman,* and the figures have an impressive sculptural quality. The painter arrived in Spain via the Netherlands; his paintings are now, sadly, extremely rare.

Hans Memling (ca. 1435–1494),
Triptych of the Resurrection of Christ with the Martyrdom of St. Sebastian (left) and *The Ascension of Christ* (right), ca. 1490
Oil on oak, center panel 61.8 x 44.6 cm;
side panels 61.8 x 18.5 cm

The resurrected Christ, a slender figure in the sequence by Rogier van der Weyden (see p. 456 f.) appears in a Renaissance setting supported by stone-colored *putti*. It is typical of Bruges around 1500, for the city was a trading center for works of art and artistic ideas. Probably born in Seligenstadt near Aschaffenburg, and named after the neighboring town of Mömlingen, Memling arrived in Brussels via Cologne to become a pupil of Rogier van der Weyden, and later worked independently in Bruges. The triptych in the Louvre is one of his best paintings, showing the Apostles closely grouped together on the occasion of Christ's Ascension, while a plague healer is pictured on the left, being honored with St. Sebastian. The painter can be easily identified by his graceful figures, the exquisite use of color, and the hazy landscape beneath a crystal-clear sky.

Gerard David and studio (ca. 1450–1523),
***The Marriage at Cana*, 1500–1505**
Oil on wood, 100 x 128 cm

When Louis XIV began to collect pictures, the very first one he owned was this early Netherlandish painting. In 1683, the painter Charles Le Brun attributed it to Jan van Eyck, for reasons that had more to do with the Sun King's desire to own a painting by the "inventor of oil painting" than with the truth. In Gerard David's depiction of Christ's first miracle, the biblical account is eclipsed by civic pride, expressed through the donor and the view of a magnificent city on the left. This work is more like a genre painting featuring early 16th-century marriage customs than a scene from the life of Christ. At Mary's request, Jesus turns the water into wine; at around 1500, the subject matter was relevant to the growing controversy surrounding the Mass.

Hieronymus Bosch's *Ship of Fools* – Drawing and Painting of the Early Netherlandish Artists

Many visitors to the Louvre miss out on one of its most fascinating aspects: the museum possesses drawings for a number of its paintings that are so sensitive to the light that they are hardly ever exhibited. Although the painters drew first and painted afterwards, the work they did prior to the final execution of their paintings was regarded for a long time simply as preliminary material which was of no interest.

When we encounter drawings that correlate largely with surviving pictures, our instinctive response is to assume that these are sketches for the final painting. In fact only very few of these early drawings can really be seen as studies that allow us to chart a work's progress through to the final picture. The value that most of the surviving drawings – particularly in the case of the Netherlandish painters – held in their day was that they were records of successful compositions at a time when there were no better means of reproduction available. It was through such copies, and also through written descriptions, that pictures could become known over a wide geographical area. A close examination of these drawings often helps us gain a better understanding of paintings as they existed in their original form.

One example of this kind of drawing in the Louvre is of one of Hieronymus Bosch's most artful pictures: the painter from the town of 's-Hertogenbosch in the Duchy of Brabant, today forming an island of Catholicism within the

Protestant Netherlands, adopted and realized in small format an idea which existed around the beginning of the modern era in a wide variety of

Drawing after Hieronymus Bosch's The Ship of Fools, beginning of the 16th century, black brushwork with white highlights on gray prepared paper, 25.7 x 16.9 cm, Musée du Louvre

forms. Mankind is sailing around on a ship of fools indulging in all the gluttony of the land of Cockaigne. *The Ship of Fools* was also a book written by the German moralist Sebastian Brant (ca. 1457–1521), published in several different languages after 1494. The book contains the verse (given in a modern rendering below):

"We sail around through every land/ we scour all the harbors and shores/ we sail around at great injury to ourselves/and yet cannot find a/ suitable place to land."

The ship relates to the bushes in an unreal way and seems to stand still as it comes into view, heavily laden with food and drink, with a goose in its mast and the sign of the moon on its banner. A nun and a monk sing a ditty while taking their turn with the others to take bites out of a swinging morsel of food. Without changing any details, the draftsman of the sketch has transposed Bosch's composition into two colors and has successfully reproduced the painter's wit. In Bosch's original the top of the tree has later been considerably enlarged. What Bosch originally intended can be seen better from the early 16th-century copy.

Hieronymus Bosch (ca. 1450–1516), The Ship of Fools, beginning of the 16th century oil on wood, 58 x 32.5 cm, third floor, room 5

(Madrid, Prado), into the stylistic language of the Lower Rhine region. Its gold background and decorative elements give it the appearance of a carved altarpiece with a tracery veil, in whose shrine the figures seem to be alive. The skin tones are skillfully contrasted, the body in its deathly gray against the hands of the men who are taking Christ's body down from the cross, and the faces of the mourning women, red from crying, with Mary's pale countenance. Mary Magdalene on the right, recognizable from her jar of ointment, is clutching her breast with grief. The symbols of St. Anthony in the gold border on the top right, the T-shaped cross and little bell, tell us that the work, completed by an anonymous artist who probably came from around Utrecht, was commissioned by a branch of the brotherhood of St. Anthony.

Early German Painting

Master of the Bartholomew Altarpiece (active 1480–1510), *The Descent from the Cross*, ca. 1500–1505
Wood, 227.5 x 210 cm

Even the most impressive paintings in our museums are not necessarily based on an original composition of their own: thus this splendid altarpiece transposes the most celebrated painting of Rogier van der Weyden, the Escorial Deposition from around 1440

Master of the Holy Family (active 1470/1480–1515), Triptych depicting the *Seven Joys of the Virgin*, ca. 1480
Wood, 127 x 182 cm

The middle panel of this work depicts the presentation of Christ in the Temple. Here, the artist was following a famous model from the preceding generation: Stephan

Lochner's Darmstadt picture of the same subject from 1447. The Virgin Mary brings her son up to the altar at Candlemas (February 2), 40 days after his birth. Her son is received by the aged priest Simeon, who reveals that he will be the bringer of true light to the world. The naked Christ child has already been passed to Simeon and Mary is holding two doves as offerings. Although the altar in the picture is decorated with scenes from the Old Testament (on the middle panel Moses with the commandment tablets, Cain slaying Abel next to it, and on the antependium Moses by the

burning bush), it is nevertheless clearly intended as a place for worshiping Christ. Simeon is wearing a brocade chasuble and the other figures are all dressed according to the fashions of the time. The left panel shows the Adoration of the Magi and the right shows Mary and the risen Christ as bride and bridegroom in the Song of Songs. The retable had originally belonged to the Benedictines in Cologne. It demonstrates how persistently gold backgrounds were adhered to. The leaves on the middle panel as well as the plant group on the left at the front are strikingly lifelike.

Albrecht Dürer (1471–1528),
Self-portrait with Thistle, 1493
Parchment on canvas, 56.5 x 44.5

The young man is holding a sprig of eryngium or sea holly. This thistle-like plant was regarded as a symbol of love and was very widespread in the Upper Rhine area, where Dürer stayed in 1493. The painting is therefore widely regarded as an engagement present from Albrecht Dürer to his fiancée Agnes Frey. Their union was decided upon by the two fathers. The thistle can also symbolize the Passion of Christ, which would be consistent with the quotation on the upper edge: "My sach die gat / Als oben Schtat. 1493" (freely translated as: "my affairs will go as ordained on high"). This self-portrait, acquired in 1922, is the only painting by Dürer in France.

Hans Baldung, known as "Grien" (1484/85–1545),
Knight, Young Girl, and Death, ca. 1505
Oil on wood, 33.5 x 29.6 cm

The knight's powerful bay tries to rear up as the youth does all he can in his attempt to save his female companion, sitting on the horse behind him, from the inevitable. Death tugs at her dress with his teeth, bracing himself strongly against a stone with a bony leg covered in leathery skin. His entrails are spilling from his body and his genitalia are covered by a cloth.

The theme of "death and the maiden" was popular in German art of the early

16th century. Its origins lay in the "dance of death" and it developed into a very enthralling subject for pictures, soon being used as an opportunity to produce more or less lascivious paintings of nude bodies. In graphic terms, however, the interest lies more in the figure of Death himself and his habit of lying in wait for lovers.

This Paris picture is held to be one of the earliest works produced by the artist. Hans Baldung, who was no doubt given his nickname as a "greenhorn," came from a family of scholars. Having studied in the Upper Rhine area, from 1503 he spent time with Dürer in Nuremberg before running the studio when Dürer was in Venice.

of the decline of patronage in Basle. The portrait of the 41-year-old scientist also depicts the tools used in the making of astronomical instruments for measurement. Kratzer is constructing a sundial of ten sides, the unfinished body of which he is holding in his left hand.

Hans Holbein the Younger,
Erasmus of Rotterdam Writing,
1523
Wood, 42 x 32 cm

Hans Holbein has chosen to depict the humanist Erasmus of Rotterdam (1467–1536) in the process of writing. The paper, which is creased around the edges, rests on a desk; the writing on it is illegible. The small desk alone calls to mind a scholar's study. The background consists of a curtain and paneling, but does not conjure up the illusion of being a real room. The artist painted this uncommissioned picture before his trip to France. This portrait of the humanist is one of three in existence by Holbein; there is also a study by him of the scholar's hands (silverpoint and chalk on white prepared paper, 20.6 x 15.3cm) Musée du Louvre).

Hans Holbein the Younger (1497–1543),
Nicholas Kratzer, **1528**
Oil on oak, 83 x 67 cm

Nicholas Kratzer (born in 1487) worked from 1519 as astronomer to the English king, Henry VIII. Holbein had made the journey to England, where he later became court painter to the king, in 1526, because

Netherlandish Renaissance

Jan Gossaert, known as "Mabuse"
(ca. 1478–1532), *Carondelet Diptych*, 1517
Oil on wood, each panel 43 x 27 cm

Only the face and hands of Jean Carondelet stand out against this picture's dark
background. The wealth of the Burgundian
prelate, who was archbishop of Palermo in
the service of Charles V, is displayed dis-
creetly in his rings and the fur trimming of
his coat. The idea for the picture is taken
from an older tradition, but Jan Gossaert
makes the relationship between the praying man and the divinity astonishingly
vivid, at the same time real and intimate.

The "Madonna" panel bears a coat of arms
on its back, while the reverse of the portrait of Carondelet depicts a foreshortened
skull painted from below. When the diptych was closed, which would have been
the way it was most frequently seen, a
proud reference to status and a reminder of
life's transience would have been visible, as
with Rogier van der Weyden's *Braque Triptych* (see picture on page 456).

Quentin Massys (ca. 1466 – 1530),
***The Money-changer and his Wife*, 1514**
Oil on wood, 70.5 x 67 cm

The viewer peers into a room across a felt-
covered tabletop, where a money-changer

weighs coins while his wife looks up from her prayer book. Massys demonstrates his skill through the books, writing implements, and precious objects. The parchment above the woman's head is signed and dated 1514. Painters have been playing with mirrors, like the one in the foreground, ever since Jan van Eyck first used them.

Joachim Patenir (ca. 1475/1480–1524),
St. Jerome in the Desert
Oil on wood, 78 x 137 cm

One particular episode in the life of St. Jerome caught people's imagination. The Church father withdrew to the desert of Chalcis in order to devote himself to a life of asceticism. In fact he did not live alone there, but in a monastery, of which most paintings show nothing. Joachim Patenir also depicts him as a hermit in a world landscape, and shows him penitent before a crucifix. He is scourging himself with the stone in his hand and the whip that lies on the floor. We are given a bird's-eye view of a scene an enormous distance away to the left, comprising a river with houses and a windmill, not at all typical of the Orient. This landscape is connected to the foreground by the blue robe, and the figure of Jerome is accentuated by the cardinal's purple of his cloak and hat. Brightness plays about him like a spotlight and this is to be understood as the Holy Spirit itself.

Pictures of this sort are known as "world landscapes" because they embrace all types of geographical formation from the high Alps to coastal lowlands. The depiction of such diversity relieves a fairly high horizon, allowing the silhouettes of mighty cliffs to tower over it. An aerial perspective that bathes the horizon in an icy light blue helps to make the distancing effect believable.

**Antwerp or Leiden Master,
first half of the 16th century,
Lot and his Daughters, ca. 1520**
Oil on wood, 48 x 34 cm

The viewer is witness to an amorous encounter in a tent encampment that takes place amid the eerie atmosphere of a judgment from heaven. A richly clothed man turns to a younger woman who is holding a glass drinking bowl, while another young woman in the foreground fills a jug. Genesis 19 tells the story of the daughters of Lot, who seduce their father in order to have their children by him rather than by the heathens. In his anger, their God has just razed the city of Sodom to the ground because of the godlessness of its inhabitants. It is only the obedient Lot who is given the opportunity to escape, but his wife fails to obey the command not to look back toward Sodom and is turned into a pillar of salt, as can be seen at the right-hand edge of the picture. The work impresses through its delicate light effects, which create strong contrasts, its luminescent colors that emerge from the darkness, and its fascination with costume. It was for a long time mistakenly attributed to Lucas van Leyden (1494 – 1533), and could have been painted in either Antwerp or Leiden. With paintings of this type a tendency developed, which remained popular beyond 1600 into the early Baroque period, for many painters to specialize almost exclusively in virtuoso compositions representing fires and scenes of the Apocalypse.

Pieter Bruegel the Elder (ca. 1525–1569),
The Beggars, **1568**
Oil on wood, 18.5 x 21.5 cm

Five crippled men perform a dance wearing costumes of hats and capes with animal tails attached to them. The only one of them still with his own feet is wearing bells around his calves. None of them pays any attention to the viewer. A woman with a bandaged head in the middle of the picture is holding out a plate for alms from spectators who are not shown. Brick walls frame the view to a gateway, beyond which an open landscape can be glimpsed. The work is signed in the bottom left hand corner. On the reverse a Flemish saying urges: "Have courage, you blind! Your lot will improve!"

Lucas van Leyden (1494–1533),
The Fortune-Teller, ca. 1508–1510
Oil on wood, 24 x 30.5 cm

The "lesser" genres of painting almost all date back to the period when the late Middle Ages gave way to the modern era, when "drolleries" became independent works of art in their own right. Thus genre painting was already developing around 1500 with the appearance of small panels like this one, whose story is not entirely clear: a young woman with a generous décolleté turns up one of a few cards on the table while a well-dressed man hands her a carnation. He doffs his hat in greeting, but she doesn't look at him. Several other faces loom out of the dark background. Pictures like this, which depict unspecified occurrences in contemporary dress, were popular in the Netherlands. Just like Dürer, Lucas van Leyden, was regarded as something of a child prodigy by his contemporaries, and was also a talented engraver.

Anthonis Mor van Dashorst (1519–1575),
Cardinal Granvelle's Dwarf, ca. 1560
Oil on wood, 126 x 92 cm

The court jester, sumptuously dressed, stares sternly out of the picture, holding the fool's scepter in his right hand. The mastiff by his side emphasizes his small stature. The coat of arms on its collar is that of Cardinal Antoine Perrenot of Granvelle (1517–1586), archbishop of Malines and official of Philip II in the Netherlands. The Cardinal made the acquaintance of the painter from Utrecht, in Antwerp in 1547, and took him into his service. The painting is one of the few pictures by any of the so-called "primitives" to have been designated by its correct name in France's old royal collection.

Cornelis van Haarlem (1562–1638),
The Baptism of Christ, 1588
Oil on canvas, 170 x 206 cm

Positioned on one of the gallery's visual axes, this large-format painting astonishes even the experts: few will be familiar with the work as it only arrived at the Louvre in 1983. The theme of the baptism of Christ is not immediately discernible: powerful, naked figures, including a man with barely concealed genitalia, move into view like river gods or like antique nature spirits. The Mannerist reversal of emphasis forces the viewer to look at the

painting much more closely: in the distance, although at the center of the painting, we see Christ standing in the river Jordan with John the Baptist, with God the Father above them, just visible between the tops of the trees. The men at the front of the picture have also come to witness the baptism. The dirt under the foot at the bottom edge of the painting indicates that they have come a long way and are now waiting, undressed, to experience God's recognition of his son Jesus. As with landscape, genre, and still life that appear in other religious paintings of the late 16th century, the painting of the nude here assumes an independent quality of its own. The painter finds freedom and expression in the free arrangement of the male forms.

Flemish and Dutch Baroque Painting

In the Louvre's new high-windowed galleries, visitors are hardly aware of the classical division of the art gallery into painting of different periods, and the problem of Franco-Flemish art from around 1400 is solved by the brilliant device of making the routes from the entry area to the Flemish and French sections diverge. Equally fluid are the transitions that occur between the artists known in many European languages as the "primitives" and those classed as exponents of a modern classicism. The major royal galleries excluded the older style of painting, which only began to be considered worthy of display in museums from around the year 1830 onward.

The Louvre's fluid transitions are entirely in keeping with the historical reality, which has all too often been concealed beneath misleading "certainty." In the 14 volumes of his *Early Netherlandish Painting*, for example, the great expert on early Netherlandish painting, Max J. Friedländer (1867–1958), set himself the task of going back as far as Pieter Bruegel the Elder, who died in 1569, while Erwin Panofsky, who wrote the most intelligent book about this period – *Early Netherlandish Painting*, 1953 – goes back beyond Hieronymus Bosch and therefore before 1500. The Northern Renaissance is rarely encountered without the presence of some traces of late-Gothic painting culture, and the beginnings of the Mannerist style

are already becoming apparent north of the Alps as early as the late 15th century.

If the prevailing political conditions are taken into consideration when setting these boundaries, it becomes clear that major changes did not occur in the Netherlands until toward the end of the 16th century. This is when the decisive transformation took place that determined the region's future: in 1581 the 14 Northern Provinces broke away from the Habsburgs, whose Spanish line had inherited them from the

Jan Vermeer (1632–1675), The Lacemaker (detail), ca. 1670/71, see page 516

Ambrosius Bosschaert (1573–1621), Vase of Flowers in a Window, ca. 1619/1621

Burgundians. Although Madrid did finally recognize the sovereignty of the new state in 1648, the resulting Netherlands, or Holland, defined itself as a Protestant land standing in stark opposition to Catholic Spain. The Southern Provinces, however, including Antwerp, remained Catholic.

Economically and culturally, the two regions, whose languages only differ from each other to a small extent, went separate ways, and great technical and economic innovations became more the preserve of the North, which made use of its trading might to operate all over the world.

For art, the division into Catholic and Protestant regions represented a break that could hardly have been any greater: a tide of iconoclasm, which had raged equally fiercely in the South, swept many of the churches clean of their pictures. In the North, altarpieces could only be erected in secret Catholic places of worship, as they were no longer tolerated by the dominant reform churches. Picture propaganda in the South, following on the heels of wounds inflicted by a civil war fueled by religion, ensured that the churches were decorated all the more sumptuously. But devotional painting remained alive even in the North, simply adapting itself to circumstances by changing its character. While Peter Paul Rubens (1577–1640) praised the might of the Lord and the glory of the Mother of God in brilliant colors in Antwerp, painters such as Rembrandt (1606–1669) in Amsterdam discovered quiet tones and new subjects, and devoted themselves to the Old Testament and to events that had little or no place on the altar.

The role played by Paris in the debate must not be underestimated. It attracted painters such as the Catholic Rubens and the Protestant Willem Kalf (1619–1693), who worked either for the kings themselves or for the metropolis's rich art market. The visitor making a fleeting visit to the Louvre is given a peculiar impression: a single royal commission, Rubens' *Médicis Cycle*, takes up more picture space than all the Dutch masters put together.

Visitors usually stop in front of a monumental work painted by a certain Cornelis (1562–1638) from Haarlem in Holland, who experienced his greatest triumphs while at the court of the Habsburg emperor in Prague. Rubens freed the Catholic painting of the South from the Mannerism found in this kind of art. Together with the work of Anthony van Dyck (1599–1641) and Jacob Jordaens (1593–1678), his paintings occupy the enormous rooms which follow. After these, however, visitors find themselves almost immediately face to face with the great diversity of the Dutch masters, incorporating landscapes and still lifes, genre and portraits, and are able to recognize what a wealth of life artists in the Protestant areas were able to tap as a result of their being barred from the contemporary market for religious commissions.

Peter Paul Rubens (1577–1640),
Village Fair (detail), ca. 1635, see p. 498 f.

Flemish and Dutch Baroque Painting

Anthony van Dyck,
Charles I at the Hunt, p. 500

Third Floor

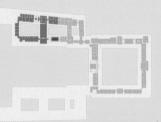

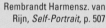

Rembrandt Harmensz. van
Rijn, *Self-Portrait*, p. 507

Gerrit Dou, *The Dropsical
Woman*, p. 515

Other works

1   1. Sébastien Stoskopff, *Still Life*,
    room 14, p. 487

2   1. Adriaen Brouwer, *Twilight Land-
    scape*, room 23, p. 391

Jacob Isaacksz. van Ruisdael,
The Ray of Sunlight, p. 519

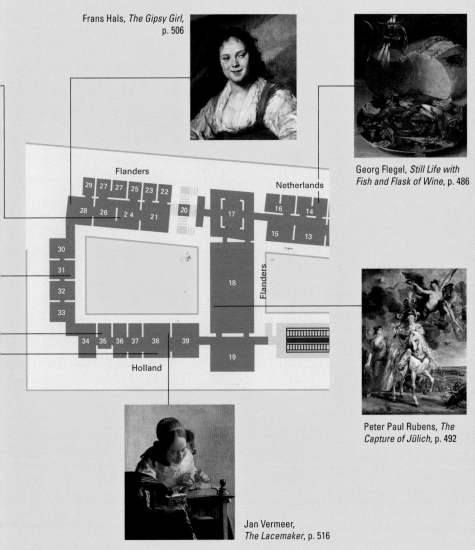

Frans Hals, *The Gipsy Girl*, p. 506

Georg Flegel, *Still Life with Fish and Flask of Wine*, p. 486

Flanders

Netherlands

Flanders

Holland

Peter Paul Rubens, *The Capture of Jülich*, p. 492

Jan Vermeer, *The Lacemaker*, p. 516

Flemish and Dutch Baroque painting **485**

German Still Life

Georg Flegel (1563–1638),
Still Life with Fish and a Flask of Wine, 1637
Oil on wood, 19 x 15 cm

This delightful picture shows small fishes arranged with leaves and petals on a pewter plate, a glass carafe containing light red wine, and a loaf of bread against a very dark background. The random nature of the view is emphasized by the fact that the plate and loaf are cut off by the edge of the picture. The reflection of windows in the glass draws in the outside world. A surprising effect is the fly, life-size in scale, which sits hungrily on the painted bread as if also tricked by the skill of the artist. Flegel, who was one of the most significant pioneers of still-life painting, came from Olmütz (Olomouc) in Moravia, and was principally active in Frankfurt am Main. He shone particularly in small-format work. It is easy to forget the contribution to this field made by artists from other regions in the light of the achievements of the Netherlandish painters, of which this is a fine example.

Sébastien Stoskopff (1597–1657),
Still Life with Books, Candles and a Bronze Statuette, after 1622
Oil on canvas, 51 x 69 cm

This picture by the painter from Alsace, who was trained by Dutch immigrants and, like Georg Flegel, was active for a long time in the Frankfurt area, shows a nighttime view of a study table. Various different bookbindings and types of metal are depicted: the candlestick on the left appears to have been

polished until it shines, and the bronze statuette of a naked soldier drawing his sword on the right is gleaming dully.

The picture hints at an interpretation somewhere between the domains of science, literature, and art.

The *Médicis Cycle* (1622–1625) by Peter Paul Rubens

Not only is the Louvre a former royal palace itself, it also contains large ensembles from other royal palaces. One of these is the cycle painted for Marie de Médicis, moved to the Louvre from the Palais du Luxembourg in Paris. In the cool, completely un-Baroque atmosphere chosen for the refurbishment in 1993, the Rubens room creates an astonishing impression that only increases when one examines the paintings

On February 26, 1622, the artist accepted a commission to produce 24 paintings depicting the deeds of the French queen, Marie de Médicis (1573–1642), member of the powerful Medici family of Florence, based on existing sketches. The fee was 60,000 *livres*, and the works, which were to be completed within four years, were to hang in the west wing of the Palais du Luxembourg. A matching series was to hang in

the east wing to honor her assassinated spouse, King Henry IV (1553–1610). The first 12 paintings were supposed to be completed in just a year. While the paintings of the king were not executed in the end, the painter from Antwerp took a great deal of trouble over his heroic portrayal of the queen. The subjects as stipulated in the contract almost correspond to the actual titles today. The formats of the paintings were calculated to fit the intended space; the way they are hung today follows the same pattern as the original, although they are considerably more cramped.

Marie de Médicis did not return to Paris, having been banished by her son, Louis XIII, until 1620. No one would really have expected genuine events to have been depicted in this cycle. In the allegorical world it creates for the mother of Louis XIII, it already displays a great splendor that prefigures the absolute monarchy of Louis XIV.

Peter Paul Rubens (1577–1640),
The Birth of Marie de Médicis in Florence
***on April 26, 1573,* 1622–1625**
Oil on canvas, 394 x 295 cm

The mythological framework prevents the biography of the future queen of France from beginning with pictures of her birth. It is not her natural mother, but the personification of the city of Florence that holds the naked child in her arms on the steps of a mighty palace. The newborn baby appears

third holds in its hands a cornucopia that contains the insignia of royal power. The mythological beings are very scantily dressed, while the little princess is wrapped in precious cloth.

Peter Paul Rubens,
Henry IV Receiving the Portrait
of Marie de Médicis,
ca. 1622–1625
Oil on canvas, 394 x 295 cm

After the *Education of Marie de Médicis* comes a landscape scene. The smoke is a sign of the war between France and Savoy. Jupiter and Juno look down from the heavens. The god of marriage, Hymen, and Cupid together hold Marie's portrait, which Henry gazes upon, in delight, just as Tamino later looks at the portrait of Pamina in Mozart's opera *The Magic Flute*. Behind the king stands Gallia as the personification of France; two amoretti play with the king's helmet and shield, as a sign that he has laid down his weapons and peace is now to reign. In fact it was no marriage of love, but a union of dynasties, following the annulment of Henry's marriage to Margaret of Valois on the grounds of childlessness.

as radiant in the dark night as the torch of Lucina, the Roman goddess of childbirth. The Archer, Sagittarius, not Marie's zodiac sign, but that of her future husband Henry IV, appears in the heavens. In front sits the river Arno with his lion, and two *putti* play with the Medici coat of arms. Three spirits hover in the sky: two scatter flowers and a

Peter Paul Rubens,
The Coronation of Marie de Médicis at St. Denis on May 13, 1610, ca. 1622–1625
Oil on canvas, 394 x 727 cm

The Coronation is one of the three paintings whose importance is emphasized by their monumental transverse format. The stage for the coronation was the Gothic abbey church of St. Denis. Although Rubens was in a position to have known the church, he renders its interior – except the window – with just a few details that are not particularly characteristic of it. The altar is framed by mighty columns and candles, and the splendor of the robes is breathtaking, the cardinals' purple being especially impressive. An allegorical element is also intro-duced by the inclusion of two hovering spirits. This historical painting has always been admired for the remarkable variety of authentic portraits it contains; their inclusion was of political significance. For example, Margaret of Valois leads the ladies' procession; Henry's illegitimate sons from his relationship with Gabrielle d'Estrées are carrying scepters and other royal insignia; Marie and Henry's son, the future King Louis XIII, stands next to the queen; and their daughter kneels on the other side of her. Henry IV follows the ceremony from a gallery above the queen. The two dogs in the foreground are generally understood to be symbols of prophetic doom, because, just a day after the coronation ceremony, the king was assassinated.

continuity under Marie's regency. But the depiction of a battle would have been quite out of place in Marie's program of celebrating her role of peace-bringer. Rubens instead presents Marie's triumph: the royal commander rides toward the viewer side-saddle, in a female version of the equestrian statue. The helmet and marshal's baton are carried by male commanders, but the mane of the white horse is long, thick, and curly. Below the hill is shown the actual event, the surrender of the town of Jülich.

Peter Paul Rubens,
The Flight of the Queen from the Château of Blois on February 21/22, 1619,
ca. 1622–1625
Oil on canvas, 394 x 295 cm

The architectural elements that had already been used in the *Birth* of the queen serve here to represent a palace. The rather tragicomic incident of the not exactly slim 46-year old having to make her way out of a window and down a rope ladder is transformed in the picture into a dignified nighttime event. The goddess Minerva leads Marie to the troops who are to bring her to safety from the soldiers of her son Louis XIII. A woman behind them simply indicates the uncomfortable descent from the palace with a gesture.

Peter Paul Rubens,
The Capture of Jülich on September 1, 1610,
ca. 1622–1625
Oil on canvas, 394 x 295 cm

After peace comes war: Henry IV was no longer able to participate in the Lower Rhine campaign, and thus the capture of Jülich represents an important proof of

The Storming of the Louvre

by Herbert Köhler

A glimpse into the CyberLouvre.

When the train pulls into the Palais-Royal metro station this particular Sunday afternoon, everything seems calm. It should be, after all it is Sunday. There is no sign of the bustling weekday mix of people on their way to work and people in a state of excited pre-museum anticipation. In spite of this, the station makes it clear that the largest collection of art treasures in the world is close by. Museum pedagogues have certainly had a hand in designing the boards that indicate

how to get there, for there is a traffic system in operation that is geared to ensuring a smooth flow of massed visitors. No one need ask how to get to the Louvre. Here you are simply carried along, until you see a pyramid forming a source of light from above. Now the storming of the museum can begin.

This is the museum's nerve center, located in the rooms of the Salle Napoléon under the glass pyramid. The symbol of the pharaohs provides a cryptic reference to the special relationship enjoyed by the French rulers with the people of North Africa. What was once regarded as legitimate spoils on campaigns of conquest is today described rather differently as "art theft." In spite of this, it would not only be wrong to assume that the museum's 300,000 or so exhibits are nothing but stolen property, but it would not be a sensible attitude with which to approach the collections either. And certainly no visitor to the museum has the feeling of having to walk through a labyrinth of burial chambers in order to arrive at the real treasures. A better comparison would be with an anthill.

The Louvre today is an enterprise with economic ambitions. Apart from the optically and didactically skillful presentation of the collec-tion, the many structural changes carried out in the 1980s and 1990s had just one thing in mind: the museum visitor. It is the visitor who helps to finance it all. The days when the state used to make a gift of culture to the people are long gone. The "fun culture evangelists" of the Disney World Trusts and the sky-high superiority of the Americans in terms of service have shown how things ought to be done. No program of state subsidy and no sponsorship by private business could replace this. For this reason the Musée du Louvre is not just a temple of culture, but also a temple of cuisine and merchandising. Souvenir stands and coffee machines have turned into bookshops and very good restaurants. Postcard stands have turned into the CyberLouvre. This room which is designed for

A hall containing Greek sculpture showing the staircase that leads to the Nike, photograph ca. 1975

interactive computer access and for a virtual tour of the exhibits, is not, however, simply a way of accommodating weary visitors. It allows the computer-literate, which are mostly younger visitors, with the requisite zapping skills, to do what they do all day long: watch television! Touring a virtual Louvre by mouse click? Where is the uplifting experience of coming face to face with the original work? What has happened to that steely determination to follow signs for mile upon mile that will eventually bring you to a halt in front of the Mona Lisa? But then – why bother going to the Louvre at all? Those who feel incapable of moving around even in their youth might as well stay at home and look at http://www.Louvre.fr. With a virtual museum visit on the World Wide Web you are left in peace, there are no crowds in front of the highlights, you don't have to drag yourself around the collection, and potato chips are within reach at all times. The only danger is of possible tendonitis in the mouse hand.

But isn't it amazing? In spite of all this digital convenience,

the Louvre is always full of "real" people, of whom – we can suppose – half already have access to the Internet at home. Is it only old viewing habits that draw these people to the mammoth museum show? Yes! Viewing goes with visiting and visiting means allowing oneself to experience the general aura. You have to stand face to face with the *Mona Lisa*, *Nike of Samothrace*, the *Venus de Milo*, or the *Sphinx of Tanis*. Only then will it become clear what visiting really means. After all, let's be honest, you can't visit a sick friend or relative on the Internet. A proper work of art requires the same degree of personal contact. The visual aspect alone is not enough. Simply looking and seeing may allow you to notice certain things and memorize them, but the real experience occurs face to face. For this reason, slightly older visitors see the main advantage of the CyberLouvre in the fact that they can leave their children there safely while they enjoy their own experience of art unaccompanied. The childish question of: "How much more is there to go?" is more nerve-racking than quietly putting up with the loss of access to art and its aura when there are young children around. This is not what the museum pedagogues want to hear at all. They see the CyberLouvre as a presentational aid, not a replacement for art.

But real confrontation with sculpture from across the millennia is not always easy. It is well known that connoisseurs prefer to internalize silently. They want to be alone with the work, allowing it to be absorbed deep within. On the other hand, Esoterics are inclined to meditate in front of their favorite subject and hate the "channel breaks."

Fortunately these kinds of museum visitor are rare. And the idea of an intimate situation between viewer and work of art in such a gigantic operation is rather comical. The majority of visitors are crowd-friendly and talkative. It is possible to hear comments here that give you a lively insight into real private worlds. The best way of doing this is to stand for a while in the middle of the ever-present, yet moving throng in front of Leonardo's *Mona Lisa*. If the subject of the painting could ever have heard what has been said about her during the course of her time hanging there, she would long ago have stopped smiling and started crying until her tears washed away the very paint. The worst comment heard recently was made by a 13-year old, claiming that she would never have thought Leonardo di Caprio capable of something so old-fashioned. One boy was visibly disappointed by the small format of the painting and also declared that on his poster at home she had a duck's bill, which suited her better. A gentleman appeared pleased with the successful restoration of the painting. He had never agreed with Marcel Duchamp's addition of a mustache even at the time … When will *Mona Lisa* finally break her silence?

What Madame Récamier does with her visitors… photographs ca. 1975

Jacob Jordaens (1593–1678),
The Four Evangelists, ca. 1620
Oil on canvas, 134 x 118 cm

The Louvre possesses far fewer prominent pictures by the second greatest master of Antwerp Baroque, but these include one of his simplest and most beautiful works: three old men and a young man stand around a heavy table with books on it. They are probably discussing a passage of text together, and hold different opinions. The youthful John is radiant in his white cloak. He gives the impression of being almost naively helpless except for his nervous hands, which betray the scholar in him. Only he can be identified, because of his youth (which is widely documented within the tradition of representing him). The others remain nameless, and Jordaens was trying to depict the Evangelists as a group without individual attributes, in dispute together over the Holy Scriptures. He has succeeded in creating the faces of honest men who look for this quality in others.

Peter Paul Rubens (1577–1640),
Village Fair, ca. 1635
Oil on wood, 149 x 261 cm

Among the work of the greatest Flemish Baroque painter, the Louvre does not only house the rather pompous pictures painted for Marie de Médicis (see p. 448). Here we also meet Rubens as an admirer of Bruegel (ca. 1525–1569), the painter of peasants, whose work he attempts to surpass in this *Village Fair*. A country group has gathered in front of a large house to hold a party. Rough tables have been set up, and some heavy drinking seems to be taking place.

Some peasants have already fallen asleep, drunk in the bright evening light. A band plays under the tree in the middle of the picture. People are dancing boisterously, and the rhythms of the music can really be felt in their swinging movements. We are not being shown a particular type of dance here, but rather an atmosphere of exhilaration, and this is the element that constitutes the unusual quality of this picture. Rubens does not depict the Dionysian behavior going on between the couples, and their kissing in complicated bodily contortions, in a morally disapproving way, but as a natural phenomenon in the landscape. Numerous individual observations invite the onlooker to study the painting in detail: a dog snuffles at

the tub that forms part of the still-life group to the front right of the picture. Rubens follows the older tradition in the basic concept as well as the richness of detail, but as a whole, goes beyond it, however, through his painterly vision of the whole. The shadows on the left softly enfold the trees and farmhouse, whose details no longer interest the painter and whose contours have become indistinct in the chiaroscuro. A bright clearing opens out to the right, ending eventually in relatively ordinary hills which have no claim to the concept of world landscape. Our eye is led away across the groups of figures, each of which initially appear dense and dark, and then shine out and flicker in the light.

Peter Paul Rubens,
Hélène Fourment and her Children, ca. 1636
Oil on wood, 113 x 82 cm

The second wife of Rubens, Hélène Fourment, has her arms around the youngest of her children, Frans. The youngster holds a toy in his right hand and is looking back at the observer. He seems to be the pivot of the composition, with his slightly older sister, Clara-Johanna (born 1632), and his mother both looking at him. The addition of little Isabella-Helena (born 1636), who is just learning to walk, seems to have caused so much difficulty that only her clumsy little hand, at the front, was roughly executed. An additional figure has been sketched out on the left of the picture.

Anthony van Dyck (1599 – 1641),
Charles I at the Hunt, ca. 1635–1638
Oil on canvas, 266 x 207 cm

Anthony van Dyck depicts the English king standing on a hill in a pose combining relaxation with dignified majesty and shows him looking back at the observer with a delicate smile. Although Charles I (1600–1649) is leaning on a stick, he appears to have just got off his horse, to which a squire is attending. Behind them a page brings a cloak. This work creates an atmosphere that is at once majestic and intimate. The view from a hilltop into the distance, the emergence from a forest, and the magnificent white horse are all traditional features of a leader's portrait, but Charles appears not to feel that he is being observed. The English king who is presented in this ambiguous way was led to the scaffold by Oliver Cromwell in 1649. Van Dyck's Paris painting is the noblest reminder of the unlucky man.

Gerrit van Honthorst (1590–1656),
The Concert, 1624
Oil on canvas, 168 x 178 cm

Utrecht Caravaggism is represented in the Louvre not by a nighttime scene from the Bible, but by a splendid, brightly lit painting that brings together female musicians and winged creatures, and is therefore not really a genre painting at all. The young women appear against the warm tones of the wooden beamed ceiling in cold, clear colors. Their red cheeks stand out strongly against their pale skin. The two *putti*, bringing along a laurel branch and garland in happy flight, are painted in a similar way.

Celebrated in Italy as Gherardo delle Notti, Honthorst painted the picture as a fireplace decoration for Governor Frederick of Orange-Nassau in The Hague.

**Hendrick Terbrugghen
(1588–1629),
The Duet, 1628**
Oil on canvas, 106 x 82 cm

Unlike Honthorst's *The Concert*, this painting by Terbrugghen, the most subtle of the Caravaggisti of Utrecht, offers true genre without the inclusion of any classical elements. A singing lute player sits in the foreground, while behind him stands a young woman singing from a book of music. The concert was a popular subject even before Caravaggio (ca. 1571–1610), offering painting the opportunity to show itself in competition with another art form. Terbrugghen, who may even have got to know Caravaggio personally on his Italian journey of ca. 1604–1614 (see p. 330), uses the Italian master's sand-colored background and spotlight-like lighting effect, but creates a quite different tonality. The man's pink and light-blue suit upon closer inspection transforms into a surface composed of apparently chaotic dots. In its detail, the picture invites the observer to make comparisons between the reddened skin of the man's face and the delicate complexion of the woman, between the inner surface of the hand, lying in shadow, and the fingertips bathed in light, and also between the man's hand placed on the neck of the lute and the delicate curvature of the décolleté.

Jan van Goyen (1596–1656),
River Landscape with Windmill and Ruined
Castle, **1644**
Oil on canvas, 97 x 133.5 cm

Holland greets visitors to the Louvre with
contrasting pictures from various different
schools of painting. It reveals its true self in
a monumental flat landscape by one of the
most important painters of the 17th century. A wide river, its left bank cut off by
the edge of the picture, takes up the whole

of the width of the painting in the foreground, like the sea. There are two fishing
boats on it, containing barely discernible
people overshadowed by a dark cloud. On
the right-hand bank stand the ruins of a
fishing house and windmill. The low horizon helps create a strong impression of
depth. The largest area of the picture is
taken up by the sky: powerful cloud formations travel across the picture diagonally, poorly lit by the weak sunshine. This
creates an impression of damp sea air.

Pieter Claesz. (1597/98–1661), *Still Life*, **1623**
Oil on canvas, 69 x 122 cm

This composition is like an over-extravagant collection of themes for a still-life painting.

of the oval dish at the front and the double bass are not entirely clear. A sumptuous still-life painting such as this depicts a great diversity of pleasure. In terms of meaning, the transitoriness of life and hidden erotic

The flutes and stringed instruments represent music and pleasure, the pocket watch indicates the passing of time as well as ingenious technology, the books stand for extensive knowledge, and so on. The mastery of the artist is displayed in his reproduction of the various objects: he depicts silver plates, dull horn, shiny metal receptacles, and a gleaming wine glass with its truncated reflection showing in the mirror. Although the objects are distributed about the table in a convincing way, the positions

allusion could also be mentioned. But perhaps more importantly, a still life like this is an arrangement created by the artist that groups together inanimate things, including in this case a live tortoise, in such a way that the whole is made interesting to paint. On the one hand this picture is about vision itself, as the mirror indicates; on the other it is about solidity and the daily experiences of the public.

Frans Hals (ca. 1581/1585–1666),
The Gypsy Girl, **1626**
Oil on wood, 57.8 x 52.1 cm

Holland's greatest portrait painter presents us with an unknown young woman in this half-length portrait, which he almost certainly intended as a character study rather than a proper portrait. Her loose hair and

careless dress both indicate that she is not a member of the middle class, hence her general description as a courtesan. But social class and profession are of less importance than the tremendously lively style in which this mischievous and self-confidently smiling individual is painted. We can even appreciate the wild brush strokes with which her blouse is applied on her. It is also worth noticing how few colors have been employed, without it appearing drab. Here, unlike Rembrandt's warm gold effect, the coloring is based on shades of gray illuminated by white light.

Rembrandt

Rembrandt Harmensz. van Rijn (1606–1669),
Portrait of the Artist at his Easel, **1660**
Oil on canvas, 111 x 90 cm

A half-length Rembrandt, on the verge of his old age, stands holding a mahlstick, brush, and a palette in front of a dark wall. The easel can be discerned as a narrow strip on the right-hand side. He is wearing a white cap onto which most of the light in the picture falls. The painter looks into the light at the observer pensively and with a neutral expression, as if he is seeing what to paint on the canvas. But the artist is playing a double game: in order to paint a self-portrait, he has to look into the mirror (which the observer has become). His eyes and the paint on the palette are accentuated by the light. Interestingly, his extended hand, holding the mahlstick in a resting position, has not been highlighted in the same way as the artist's eyes and the palette.

Only a few artists have painted as many self-portraits as Rembrandt did. Originally the artist depicted himself wearing a different cap, which can still be picked out by the naked eye. On the right, a 5 cm (2 in) length has been added on to the painting to replace a missing strip.

Rembrandt Harmensz. van Rijn,
The Holy Family, 1640
Oil on wood, 41 x 34 cm

Rembrandt Harmensz. van Rijn, The Archangel
Raphael Leaving Tobias and his Family, 1637
Oil on wood, 68 x 52 cm

When the artist painted *The Holy Family*, he took the radical step of giving it a contemporary setting, with the same attention to detail and light displayed in his 1660 self-

Rembrandt reveals himself in this small-figure picture to be a devoted storyteller, depicting this particular scene in a completely new way: two couples and a dog are

portrait. Thus, in the 18th century, the painting was considered to be a genre painting of a carpenter with his family. This carpenter, however, is Christ's foster-father Joseph, and a tranquil study of everyday life becomes an intimate depiction of the Holy Family. Also portrayed is Mary's mother Anne, who recognizes in the boy a saviour.

taking leave of a guest, who has just revealed himself to be the Archangel Raphael, in front of the door of a house. Tobias looks up and seems confused, having just undertaken a long and difficult journey with the angel. Sent abroad by his blind father to reclaim some debts, he weds Sarah and returns with her to restore his father Tobit's sight with the bile from a fish. As the traveling companion takes his leave, father and son prostrate themselves in gratitude, and Sarah and Anna also show themselves to be deeply moved, as if all those present had suddenly understood with great certainty the meaning of the name Raphael: "God heals." The small dog reflects the emotions of the people, which lie between fear and curiosity. In this composition the contrast that is created between the mortals, set firmly on the earth, and the angel, who is rising toward heaven in ordinary clothes, is particularly beautiful.

Rembrandt Harmensz. van Rijn,
The Supper at Emmaus, **1648**
Oil on wood, 68 x 65 cm

This work is a perfect example of the religious picture in the post-medieval period, whose great power lies in its portrayal of the apparently everyday. Christ sits facing the onlooker, and is holding

reveals his identity to two of the disciples in the way he breaks the bread. In the vertical format, the figures all appear small. The figure of Christ with his beautifully painted halo, is positioned centrally in front of an alcove within an asymmetrical composition. The servant enters from the kitchen on the right. This work is an example of a

a loaf of bread; two of his disciples, also barefoot, react with astonishment; and the young servant, waiting to serve the meat, is unsure as to what to make of the situation. This scene depicts the meeting at Emmaus, where following the Resurrection, Christ

"religious genre painting" that takes its inspiration from the Italian artist Caravaggio (ca. 1571–1610). However, in contrast to Rembrandt's disciples, Caravaggio would have painted the figures life-size in scale, and half-length.

Rembrandt Harmensz. van Rijn,
St. Matthew and the Angel, **1661**
Oil on canvas, 96 x 81 cm

In his later years, Rembrandt knew how to penetrate into secrets such as the divine inspiration of the Gospels, by concentrating on the painting of individual faces, the depiction of awkward movements, and the use of light that fills his roughly executed pictures with a spiritual quality. Even those who no longer believe can be deeply moved by a painting such as this one, as it deals with the simple phenomenon of youth and old age.

Rembrandt Harmensz. van Rijn,
Bathsheba with King David's Letter, **1654**
Oil on canvas, 142 x 142 cm

A naked woman sits on a bench that is not very clear to the viewer. The room is equally obscure. An old woman, clearly a servant, possibly the nurse, dries her toes, indicating that she has just been bathed. The naked woman's right hand has been painted with particular attention and has been enlarged as a consequence; in it she holds a piece of paper that will lead to dramatic events. Her presentiment of this makes her pensive under the weight of destiny. She is Bathsheba, whom King David has seen bathing and now invites to his palace. But the beauty is married to Uriah, a soldier in the king's service, who is away fighting for him in battle. Rembrandt does not show David, he only depicts

Bathsheba, lit from the left, reminding us of the king's voyeuristic observation. He is also showing the loneliness of the woman at this important moment during which she is still free to withstand temptation, yet knows that she will give in to the letter and become David's mistress, thus committing carnal sin.

an ox, which hangs on a rack. Its hoofs have already been hacked off, its lungs and innards removed, and its thorax propped open with a large leg bone. But the butchers themselves have disappeared and with them all traces of their work. The only person to be seen is a woman, apparently looking at the same scene as the viewer, and leaning in a relaxed fashion over the upper part of the door. This type of subject in painting was considered an outrageous challenge to traditional art criticism for very many years, whereas later generations learned to appreciate the purely painterly qualities of the work.

Aelbert Cuyp (1620–1691),
Landscape near Rhenen, ca. 1650–1655
Oil on canvas, 229 x 170 cm

Painters and collectors in Holland already appreciated unfeigned views of their own countryside. When a so-called Italianate painter such as Cuyp bathed them in a southern light and transformed the countryside scene into a pastoral idyll, their value increased tremendously. At the front left of this picture, but not illuminated by the warm sunshine, sits a shepherd playing a pipe. Behind the cows stands his audience, which consists of a boy, a girl, and a dog standing in a group. Behind the cows to the right of the picture the countryside climbs up, and we see shepherds scattered about it with their flocks. The town of Rhenen, which was popular with many landscape painters because

The Lesser Genres of Painting

Rembrandt Harmensz. van Rijn,
The Slaughtered Ox, 1655
Oil on wood, 94 x 69 cm

Few pictures have frightened art theoreticians with their subject matter as much as this painting by Rembrandt. In the dark of a slaughterhouse room, light falls on the almost completely disemboweled carcass of

The hides of the cows are dappled with the very distinct interplay of light and shade, which is particularly noticeable on the red-brown animal on the right.

Michael Sweerts (1624–1664), *The Young Man and the Procuress*
Oil on copper, 19 x 27 cm

The visitors to the Louvre often just notice in passing the display case containing this small painting by a little-known artist. A young man and an old woman emerge out of the chiaroscuro, as with Caravaggio (see p. 330), but are painted in a more fluid style and in a much smaller format. Sweerts had spent a long time in Rome, where he was part of the so-called *Bamboccianti* colony, the apparently dissipated young painters from the North, who drew attention to themselves with their

of its characteristic silhouette, emerges in the background. A string of clouds drifts over from the direction of the town and seems to catch in the trees towering over the scene. cheeky pictures. During his early creative period, he favored subjects with a folk-like character and no great depth of meaning. Sweerts later became a missionary.

On the Value of Pictures

For millennia, art has attracted fascination and mockery in all matters relating to money. That an artist, through his own skill, can turn an object of little value into a highly prized treasure is not always looked upon kindly. Wealth during an artist's lifetime is seen as equally as questionable as record prices on the art market following the death of a master. We know only too well how values fluctuate from generation to generation, and are often able to observe the monetary value of a work dramatically collapsing or rising to dizzy heights for no obvious reason.

The Dutchman Gerrit Dou (1613–1675) offers an impressive case. He was the most subtle of the masters of the Golden Age. His method of working reveals his sense of the precious that expresses itself in the glowing splendor of the colors he uses in his usually highly polished pictures. His brush strokes are invisible, the surroundings of his small figures are noble, and the individual works are exceptionally exquisite in every respect. The subjects of his paintings are often glimpsed through precious textiles. As in Rembrandt's early work (see p. 508), light is

treated in such a way as to greatly increase the effectiveness of the composition. This is why hardly any attention is paid to the rather ordinary subject matter of most of these pictures, taken as they are from the everyday lives of prosperous people: the great value of the work becomes apparent when it is taken as a whole.

Gerrit Dou (1613–1675), Still Life with Clock, 1663, oil on wood, 86 x 68 cm, third floor, room 35

The art market has also valued paintings of this kind highly during times when genre painting, as a lowly form of art, was out of favor with art critics. Dou's pictures were valuable during his own time as well as during later periods. In the 19th century the painter achieved astonishingly high prices that put many of his more famous colleagues in the shade.

A polemic survives from the year 1642, written by Philip Angel, a fellow citizen of Dou's from Leiden, called "In Praise of Painting." For the author, the unique regard in which Dou was held is illustrated by the fact that he had a contract with the most important patron of the time, a Mr. Spierings. For an enormously high annual sum, this patron had secured the option to purchase the entire output. of the painter. Veronese (1528–1588) is also supposed to have had a financial guarantee of this sort. Angel regarded this as the most important proof that artists were still valued and honored for their art.

Dou's most significant work in the Louvre shows that even the presentation of a painting can contribute to its enhanced value: while previously people had been accustomed to a precious sacred painting or to even a portrait being hidden behind shutters, this painter from Leiden presented genre scenes in a case that could be closed by folding another painting over

it. Pictures that today hang separately on the wall of the gallery once formed a curious ensemble: closed it displayed a *Still Life with Clock*, large-scale and without figures, and only when opened did it reveal the real focus of the ensemble in the form of a stunningly beautiful full-figure scene with sophisticated lighting effects. The cover, as with those of holy pictures, had a double function: to protect the real work from the light and general wear and tear, but also to make people eager to see the main painting that was hidden behind.

Gerrit Dou, The Dropsical Woman, 1663, oil on wood, 86 x 68 cm, third floor, room 35

Jan Vermeer (1632–1675),
The Lacemaker, ca. 1670/71
Oil on canvas, transferred to wood, 24 x 21 cm

A table on which there are needlework accoutrements, is pushed up close to the observer. Red and white threads, which have been dripped onto the picture in pure color, extend from a sewing cushion. The

lacemaker is bent over her work in complete absorption. She is illuminated on her left side by the incoming light, and the mullion and transom of the window cast their shadow onto the white wall. Appropriately enough for its intimate subject and small format, this is one of Vermeer's most popular pictures. This may stem, on the one hand from the lack of distance between it and the viewer, and on the other, because we are especially able to enjoy the way it is painted. The grain of the coarse canvas has been used to give the tablecloth and dress their structure; to this end the paint has been applied dryly and coarsely. But other sections, such as the tassel of the sewing cushion, have been painted with wetter paint in order to produce a more blurred effect. Much enthusiasm has already gone into explanations of the optical characteristics of Jan Vermeer's paintings based on his skillful use of a camera obscura. The painter then ingeniously transposed what he observed using this aid into his own medium.

Jan Vermeer,
The Astronomer, **1668**
Oil on canvas, 50.8 x 46.3 cm

A young man sits at a table in front of a window in his blue-green scholar's cloak. He has just raised himself up and is supporting himself with his left hand in order to turn the astronomical globe with his right hand. The astronomer – for this is what the instruments on the table reveal him to be – seems to be checking something he has just read in his open book. Vermeer turns this piece of research into an agile gesture by using the diagonal shadow to emphasize the man's movement, as if wishing to depict a thirst for knowledge. The lively flower pattern of the woven carpet, which lies in folds on the table, also fits into this scheme.

Although not corresponding exactly in size, this painting has always been regarded as a companion piece to the *Geographer* of 1669, which is in Frankfurt. Both show the same man as scientist, whereas most of Vermeer's other subjects consist of women in a domestic milieu. Nothing is known of the person who commissioned these pictures, and this has given rise to speculation that each is a kind of disguised portrait, which

Vermeer is not otherwise known to have painted. The Paris picture was already well known by 1800. How little the signature meant at that time, though, is demonstrated by an old reproduction of the *Astronomer* on which Vermeer's name has been removed and the work passed off as that of his fellow Dutchman Terborch because such a good picture needed to have a good name attached to it.

Pieter de Hooch (1629–1684),
Soldiers and a Young Woman, Drinking, **1658**
Oil on canvas, 68.6 x 60 cm

A young woman is having wine poured for her by a soldier, to whom an older woman is speaking from behind. He is holding his hat in his hand and is therefore no more at home here than the seated man, who is still wearing his hat. It is unclear whether the two of them are in search of an erotic adventure. A picture on the wall depicts Christ and the adulteress, associated with Christ's words: "Let he who is without sin cast the first stone." The light has been painted with great accuracy. Outside it is gleamingly bright, the furniture in the room is casting shadows, and the room next door is apparently lit by a large window that is not visible.

Jacob Isaacksz. van Ruisdael (1628/29–1682),
The Ray of Sunlight
Oil on canvas, 83 x 99 cm

Jacob van Ruisdael, who was also a practicing physician, achieved the most monumental effects of any of the Dutch landscape painters. His masterful use of light transforms this scene of a simple cornfield with a few trees and bushes into a powerful and dramatic landscape. This major work, which is part of the Louvre collection, is also influenced by the tendency toward heroic landscapes; the river, bridge, and ruins beneath a high mountain all evoke an Italianate atmosphere. The ground was prepared for eventful pictures such as this by Rembrandt's experience with chiaroscuro, and the Baroque pathos of the Golden Age of Dutch painting.

Decorative Arts

Objects made of metal or gemstones, glass or ceramics, as well as textiles and furniture, all of which are primarily designed to serve a practical purpose, can mean little to those whose artistic appreciation does not place much value on the decorative, and prefers the pure in art to the applied. In the current neglect of applied arts museums there is a historical paradox, however, as these collections form the core of what used to be gathered and displayed in art cabinets centuries before the development of the modern museum. Princely collections, out of which the great libraries also emerged, brought together everything, from rare natural finds to the more extravagant work of jewelers, which was unusual from the point of view of form, and which challenged the imagination. As medallions also formed part of these collections, they simultaneously became a sort of ancestral portrait gallery in bronze.

The decorative arts were also fundamental to the origins of our museums in another respect: as the bourgeois society of the 19th century started establishing its own museums, these collections played an essential role as a treasure trove of inspiration to craftsmen who had to make furniture and various other practical objects that satisfied a taste for the historical. In Paris the enormous Musée des Arts Décoratifs was founded for this very purpose, as a sep-

arate entity from the Grand Louvre, in the northwest wing of the palace.

Many people will not be aware that the Louvre has a large department devoted to arts and crafts. But for previous visitors, those who are familiar with the *Mona Lisa* and the *Venus de Milo,* and above all those who wish to avoid the stream of visitors, the decorative arts department offers not just peace and quiet, but also an insight into an undreamed of world of creation and invention. Both Christian and heathen stories are played out here, often in miniature, and frequently executed in a manner revealing how earlier epochs combined materials with subject matter. For example, one reliquary bears tiny thuggish fellows striking blows against its central receptacle, and is made of rock crystal once containing a relic associated with Christ's flagellation (see p. 536).

Other rooms, on the other hand, require viewing from less close quarters, as their walls are decorated with enormous Gobelin tapestries, named after the factory in Paris, and also the tapestries of their Flemish predecessors from Arras, Bruges, and Brussels. Following this, visitors can walk through the suites of rooms of an imaginary palace whose interiors and furniture, vessels, and other practical objects, as well as the occasional valuable painting, provide an entire overview of former ways of life.

From Late Antiquity to the Carolingians

Serpentine Paten, 1st century B.C. or A.D. and (?)late antique (paten), and second half of the 9th century (surround)
Serpentine, gold, precious stones, colored glass, diameter 17 cm

The eight golden fishes were probably inlaid in the dark-green serpentine bowl in late Antiquity. The gold work surround was added when Charles the Bald (843–877) gave the paten to the abbey of St. Denis. Large stones have been set within the band bordered by semi-circular garnet batons, using the cloisonné technique.

Lapis Lazuli Icon: Christ Giving a Blessing, reverse: Virgin Mary Praying, Constantinople, first half of the 12th century
Lapis lazuli with inlaid gold, silver-plated gold, and precious stones, 8.3 cm high

Here we have an example of a precious object that is fashioned from unusual found objects such as jewelry or pictures, in which the intended subject matter is subservient to the materials at hand. Available to the Byzantine artist who made this icon was a lapis lazuli cameo, at 8.3 cm high one of the largest of its type. Using a technique hardly used even in Constantinople, the artist inlaid the stone, in relief, with gold in such a way as to depict Christ and the Virgin Mary. On the front the artist has shown the Redeemer standing with a book in his left hand and giving a blessing with his right. On the reverse, Mary appears in an act of intercession, both arms raised in prayer.

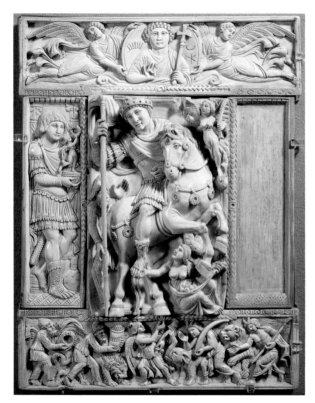

both as representations of the secular and as pictures of heavenly glory. Here an emperor, possibly Justinian (527–565), gallops victorious out of the background. In the upper part of the relief, Christ, inside a halo carried by angels, gives a blessing. The emperor forces back a defeated barbarian or Scythian behind his lance, while an allegorical representation of the earth holds onto the horse's hoof as a symbol of subjugation. In the left side panel, a general pays homage to the emperor holding in his hand the goddess of victory. In the lower field, the vanquished also pay tribute to him. While the very three-dimensional design and master craftsmanship are impressive, the horse's right hoof has been worked in such a way that it appears almost completely detached. The difference in size between the elephant tusk and the elephant is delightful. The panel originally consisted of five parts, but its right-hand side panel is now missing. The whole would once have formed a diptych with another panel of equivalent size, although the very three-dimensional middle part of this side would have made it impossible to close the two together.

Panel of a Diptych: *The Emperor (?Justinian) Triumphant,* known as the "Barberini Ivory," Constantinople, first half of the 6th century
Ivory, traces of glass beads, 34.2 x 26.8 cm

The western rulers orientated themselves toward the antique world and the Christian emperors of Byzantium. Depictions of triumphant emperors worked on two levels:

Equestrian Statuette of Charlemagne or Charles the Bald, 9th century, Horse possibly late Roman
Bronze with traces of gilding, 23.5 cm high

This horseman is the only fully three-dimensional figure that survives from the Carolingian period. He sits upright on his horse and wears a crown decorated with milkwort. In his left hand he carries the imperial orb, while the attribute in his right hand would have been a sword or scepter. His shoes, with numerous buttons, have been worked with lavish detail. They are decorated with a clasp in the form of milkwort, like the decoration on the crown. The rider is without beard, but has a broad mustache, which reveals how different the appearance of the Carolingians was to that of the kings of the later Middle Ages (see p. 533). It unclear whether this ruler is Charlemagne (768–814) or Charles the Bald (843–877). The horse, which is more convincingly three-dimensional, is rather small for its rider, and is possibly a reworking of a late-Roman piece. Until the Revolution, the sculpture belonged in the cathedral treasury in Metz, the city in Lorraine that afforded the Carolingians easy access to both the East and West Frankish empires. The model for this statuette was the equestrian statue of Marcus Aurelius, believed at the time to be an image of Constantine.

A Neoplatonist Philosopher as Christian Martyr and the Abbey of St. Denis

Everyone knows Montmartre, but hardly anyone is still aware that it is literally the "hill of martyrs," where St. Denis and his companions were beheaded in the 5th century. According to legend he carried his own decapitated head 10 kilometers (six and a quarter miles) north in order to choose the site for the building of a monastery that bears his name: St. Denis. Religious tradition conflated three individuals into this one figure: St. Denis himself, a heathen philosopher called Dionysius who was converted by St. Paul on the Areopagus in Athens, and Dionysius, author of the treatise "On the Celestial Hierarchy." This work describes God's creation of the world as the conversion of divine light into matter in order to combine the neoplatonist idea that goodness is embodied in light with Christian doctrine.

St. Denis was patron saint of the French kings, who endowed the abbey over a period of many centuries with crown estates (see p. 556) and from the time of the Merovingian Dagobert onward, made it their place of burial. Even the kingdom's war standard, known as the Oriflamme, was kept in the abbey and sent for when war broke out, for St. Denis was the refuge of peace and war alike.

For as long as the traditional Catholic faith was dominant, the fame and power of the abbey also rested on its tombs and its wealth of adored relics. Relics are either the bodies of saints, small portions of which were often distributed throughout Christendom in a way which we find

Charles Alexandre Lesueur (1778–1846), Alexandre Lenoir defending the Tomb of Louis XII and his queen, Anne of Brittany, in St-Denis, pen-and-ink drawing with wash

very hard to understand today, or else the objects they used. Relics attracted pilgrims, who spent heavily wherever holy artefacts were to be found, and needed to be stored in vessels whose sumptuous appearance did justice to their indescribably valuable contents. On this point, the treatise of St. Dionysius ensured that no doubt remained as to the divine significance of gold

and of precious stones: if goodness is embodied in light, then it is
best communicated through the
gleam and sparkle of precious
materials. Abbot Suger (1122–
1151), who began to reconstruct
the church in the early Gothic
period, describes the same thing
shortly after 1140: what is most
important is not the untold riches
per se, but the presence of God in
the gold, enamel, pearls, and precious stones that are the material
embodiment of the ultimate spiritual value. Umberto Eco, too, uses
this explanation in his novel *The
Name of the Rose* (1980), when his
abbot talks about riches.

When the Revolution broke out,
the treasure of the Benedictines of
St. Denis was taken away, still on
the orders of King Louis XVI, and
brought to Paris in 1791. What was
left behind is now shared between
the Louvre and the Bibliothèque
Nationale. Although the church
was ravaged by the iconoclasts,
the fight to preserve the most
important royal tombs led to a
change of thinking within France.
Alexandre Lenoir (1761–1839) became a hero because he was
nearly killed by the mob while
ardently defending the works of
art in the church.

*St-Denis, view of the choir, constructed by Abbot Suger after
1141, and the nave of the abbey church, built in the 1250s
under St. Louis*

time of office entitled: *De rebus in administratione sua gestis.* He found the porphyry vase in a coffer and had it transformed it into an eagle by the addition of the gilt surround. An inscription at the base of the neck explains: "This stone is worthy of being set in gold. It is made of marble, but this will make it even more valuable than marble." The extraordinarily realistically worked eagle's head and the finely chased feathers make it one of the most important works of medieval art.

**Charlemagne's Coronation Sword,
known as the "Joyeuse"
Sword: 10–11th centuries,
Cross-guards: 12th century, Handle: 13th century**
Gold with glass and lapis lazuli pearls
Sheath: end of 13th century and 19th century
Gilded silver, copper, precious stones, and velvet, 105 cm high

St. Denis not only housed the sacred treasures; one of the abbey's most important functions was also to look after the coronation regalia or crown jewels belonging to the king. Apparently the sword, which legend held to be the famous "Joyeuse" sword of Charlemagne (768–814), was initially made for the coronation of Philip Augustus in 1179. It was last used for the coronation of Charles X in 1825. In the same display case are the coronation spurs (end of the 12th century, 16th and 19th centuries).

**Eagle-Shaped Vase,
Egypt or Imperial Rome and St. Denis,
before 1147**
Porphyry and silver gilt, 43.1 cm high

In the 12th century, Abbot Suger (1122–1151), an adviser to Louis VII, added some important pieces to the treasury of St. Denis, among them this eagle-shaped vase. He mentions it and three other vessels of precious stone in his writings about his

Gothic Art Treasures

**Madonna from the Treasury of Ste-Chapelle,
Paris, before 1279**
Ivory with traces of paint, 41 cm high

This figure is very large for a statuette
carved from the tusk of an elephant. The
posture of the figure has been elegantly,
but not exaggeratedly, taken from the natural curvature of the material. Paris was
the center of Gothic ivory carving in the
13th and 14th centuries, and the Ste-
Chapelle Madonna is considered one of its
most beautiful and important works. It is
mentioned in the chapel's inventory of
1265–1279 and is supposed to have been
donated by St. Louis. This would make it a
representative in small-scale sculpture of
the felicitous period of high Gothic, to
which the Ste-Chapelle itself, built in the
1240s, also belongs.

Descent from the Cross, **ca. 1260–1280**
Ivory with traces of paint, Christ and Joseph of
Arimathea: 30 cm high, Mary: 23 cm, Ecclesia:
23 cm, Nicodemus: 19.8 cm

Although composed of individual fragments, this group of figures is impressive in
its use of space. In the middle is the Deposition: the powerfully built Joseph of Arimathea is holding Christ's corpse on his
shoulder. Christ's body takes the form of
an elegant sweeping curve that matches

the shape of the figure bearing it. This stems in part from the nature of the material, and was also in part the deliberate intention of the artist, as one can see from the way Christ's arm reaches out to Mary. The personification of the church, on whose other side its counterpart the synagogue, was previously depicted, is smaller, and would apparently have stood further back in the arrangement. Finally, because of its stylistic affiliation, the figure of Nicodemus must also belong to the Deposition. While in the possession of the Rothschild family in the 19th century a restorer added hands and a scroll, thus interpreting him as a prophet.

Madonna of Jeanne d'Evreux, Paris, 1324–1339

Silver gilt, *basse-taille* enamel on silver gilt, precious stones and pearls, 68 cm high

Mary stands holding the Christ child on a rectangular base that is supported by a lion at each of its four corners. In addition to her stunning golden glow, she once had a crown that would almost certainly have been decorated with jewels. Separated by pillars, which are all decorated with the small figures of prophets, the enamel plates on the base depict episodes in Christ's life on earth, and are of great significance in the history of Gothic enameling. They are: the Annunciation, the Visitation, the birth of Christ, the adoration of the shepherds, the adoration of the three Magi, the presentation of Christ in the Temple, the flight into Egypt, the massacre of the innocents, the Resurrection, and Christ in hell. The inscription (Ceste ymage donna ceans ma dame la Royne Jehanne devreux, Royne de France et de Navarre Compaigne du Roy Challes le XXVIIIe jour d'avril l'an MCCC XXXIX) designates the benefactor Jeanne d'Evreux (died 1371) as queen of France and Navarre, wife of the last Capetian king, Charles IV "The Fair" (reigned 1322–1328), whom she had married in 1324, and names 1339 as the year in which she donated the statuette to the abbey of St. Denis.

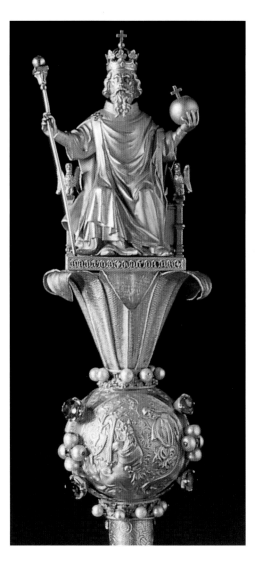

Scepter of Charles V, known as "Charlemagne's Scepter," Paris, (?)1364–1380
Gold, silver, precious stones, blue and green glass and pearls, 60 cm high

Enthroned on the end of this scepter is the figure of Charlemagne (768–814), who bears little resemblance to the rider in room 1 (see p. 525), and in fact follows the 14th-century ideal, as represented by Charles IV and King Wenzel in Germany, in terms of hairstyle and dress. In his hands he holds the imperial orb and scepter, decorated with the same lily as the large scepter itself to which the statuette is attached. This lily flower constitutes the base on which the seated figure rests, and was once coated with white enamel. The lily, or fleur-de-lys, also, of course, features on the royal coat of arms of France. Beneath a ring of pearls there is a pommel on which are depicted the three appearances of the Apostle St. James the Great supposedly witnessed by Charlemagne. The scepter was deposited in the treasury of St. Denis in the year of Charles VI's coronation, 1380. Along with the sword and spurs, it belonged to the crown jewels of the French kings, whose crowns, however, were specially made for each coronation, and incorporated the most important gemstones in the royal treasury. We can imagine the king who held this scepter enthroned exactly as depicted.

Retable from Poissy,
Embriachi workshop, northern Italy,
ca. 1400, perhaps 1397
Bone, traces of paint and gilding, *alla certosina*
marquetry, 276.5 x 236 cm

The enormous wealth of pictures presented
by this altarpiece, which is divided up into
small sections, seems rather alien to us
today, but work of the Embriachi workshop
was highly valued in France around 1400,
particularly by the Duc de Berry (1346–
1416), the greatest patron of his day. The
material used – bone – did not permit larger
forms to be made. Scenes from the life of
Christ in the central panel are flanked by
episodes from the life of John the Baptist on
the left and John the Evangelist on the
right. On the predella are depicted the
benefactors and their patron saints: Jean de
Berry and his wife Jeanne
de Boulogne. The Duc de
Berry had donated the
retable to Poissy abbey,
possibly in 1397.

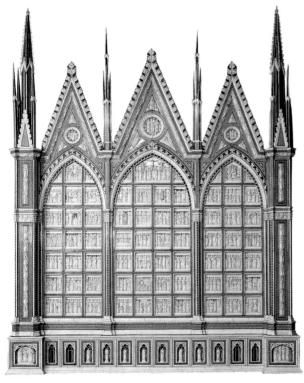

Reliquary from the Chapelle
de l'Ordre de St-Esprit,
(?)London, before 1412
Enameled gold, 44.5 x 15 cm

The art of coating figures
that are completely three-
dimensional with enamel,
known as *émail en ronde-
bosse*, had been mastered
with great virtuosity by
around 1400. Only a few
individual pieces that are
architectonic in structure
survive today. The tiny figures with golden beards
and hands are placed in
niches. The middle part is
now only occupied by God
the Father because a small

crucifix is missing. The original depiction of God showed the Holy Trinity with God presenting his son on the cross with a dove. Above appears Mary, relatively large, with a standing Christ as *Salvator mundi* right at the top. Four Apostles and three female saints occupy the remaining niches of the reliquary, in which a piece of the crown of thorns was kept. The reliquary was given by the English queen Joan of Navarre to the dukes of Brittany in 1412. For this reason it is suspected that it was made in England rather than France or the Netherlands. Items such as this piece of gold work, which satisfied the need for embellishment as well as serving a sacred purpose, and also appealed to man's instinct for play, were probably relatively numerous. In the event of financial difficulties they were often melted down. One of Duc Jean de Berry's goldsmiths is said to have lost his mind and to have ended up in a monastery as the result of one such case of vandalism.

On the Threshold of the Modern Age

Flagellation Reliquary, Venice, 15th century
Rock crystal, gilt copper, enamel, 32.5 cm high

This reliquary from S. Alvise in Venice is particularly impressive. The central part is formed by a vase made of rock crystal, carved with great virtuosity, which contained two thorns from Christ's crown. Two thugs, resting on their own plinths that extend from a shared base, flank the goblet that once contained the relics. The conspicuously uncouth individuals are raining blows on the Redeemer, represented by the thorn relics, in seemingly eternal repetition. It seems not to have been necessary to depict Christ himself in order for the meaning of the reliquary to be understood. In this, the Venetian work is a further example of the peculiarly medieval type of reliquary known as the talking reliquary.

Jean Fouquet (ca. 1415/1420–1478/1481), Self-portrait from the Melun Diptych, shortly after 1450
Enameled copper, 6.8 cm in diameter

The work of the greatest French artist of the 15th century can be seen in three places in the Louvre: two portrait panels hang with the paintings (see p. 372) and some very delightful miniatures are owned by the Department of Graphic Arts. Jean Fouquet's most intimate work, however, is to be found with the objets d'art as it has been classified, not as painting,

but as precious metalwork. The artist created a self-portrait in black-enameled copper and included it with other medallions set into the frame of a large-format diptych. This monumental painting (divided today between Antwerp and Berlin) was commissioned for Melun by Etienne Chevalier, who was the treasurer of Charles VII. Jean Fouquet, the first artist from the North to return transformed from a journey to Italy, apparently had some antique portraits in mind while carrying out this work and was looking for a technique that made it possible for him to reproduce their dark ground and golden drawing. The rather coarse, still very youthful head that Fouquet presents to the viewer is all the more striking as it is that of an ordinary child of his time without any recognizable Humanist stylization.

Workshop of Catharina Hasselet and Jan de Wilde (French: Sauvage), *Scenes from the Life of St. Anatole of Salins*, **Bruges, 1502–1506**
Gobelin

The art of tapestry weaving flourished in Bruges and other towns in Flanders and Brabant. Wool of the finest quality was available as a result of the trade with England. High standards had been set as a result of the patronage of the dukes of Burgundy and of their court. Orders came in from all over the world. Among the oldest examples from the Bruges workshops are 14 pieces for the cathedral of Salins. Three tapestries from this series commemorate the miraculous intervention of the patron saint Anatole during the Burgundian war of succession. Salins was part of Franche-Comté, and as such belonged to the Burgundian inheritance of Emperor Maximilian that was under the control of the German Empire. Salins, like Dole, was attacked by troops of the French king. That both towns were spared any damage was attributed to Anatole. Even at the time of their design, consideration was given to the fact that the life and miracles of this saint were not well known, and inscriptions are thus provided that give detailed explanations.

leidis anathonile baron

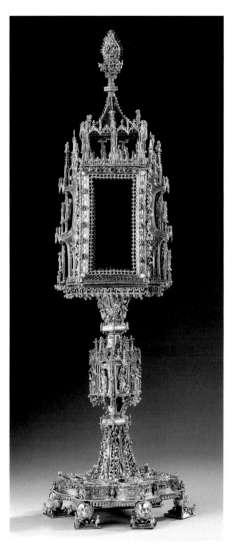

**Giovanni Leon,
Hand Reliquary of St. Martha,
Venice, 1472/1474**
Silver

This reliquary came from the convent of St. Martha in Venice, and testifies to the fruitful artistic interchange between Italy and the North. Designs for items of gold work were made widely available through German prints, and work of this kind was especially highly valued in Venice around 1500. This is probably the reason why Giovanni Leon, from Cologne, received the commission to make this receptacle for the hand of St. Martha in the German style. He placed the figures in late-Gothic niches.

**Master of the King Louis XII Triptych,
Coronation of the Virgin, Limoges, ca. 1500**
Enamel

Mary sits in prayer on a chair, decorated with jewels, in front of a blue background interspersed with gold points. Christ bends over to her and places the crown on her head. Mary's blue cloak has a braid trimming studded with precious stones, and displays a pattern featuring the golden initial "m" for Mary. Along with the painted enamel made of opaque metal oxides, the gemstone effect produced by the transparent enamel also plays an important role here. Enamel work from Limoges made use of a store of models taken from book illumination and prints.

Decorative Arts

Second Floor

Flap: *March* from the series of tapestries known as *Emperor Maximilian's Hunt* (detail) p.546

Jean Fouquet, Self-portrait, p.536

Workshop of Catherina Hasselet and Jan de Wilde, *Scenes from the Life of St. Anatole of Salins*, p.538

Galerie d'Apollon, p.554

Madonna from the Treasury of Ste-Chapelle, p.530

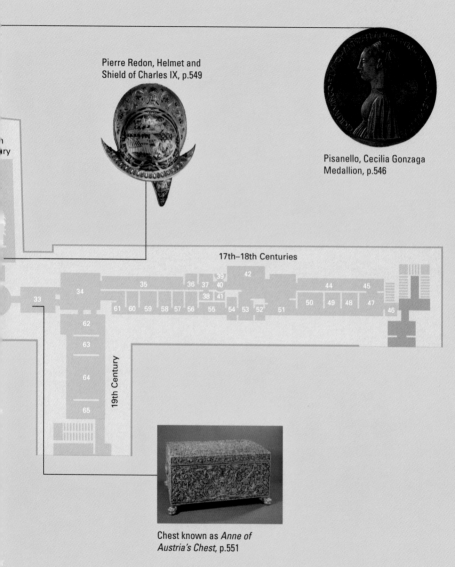

Pierre Redon, Helmet and
Shield of Charles IX, p.549

Pisanello, Cecilia Gonzaga
Medallion, p.546

17th–18th Centuries

19th Century

33 34 35 36 37 38 39 40 41 42 44 45
61 60 59 58 57 56 55 54 53 52 51 50 49 48 47 46
62
63
64
65

Chest known as *Anne of
Austria's Chest*, p.551

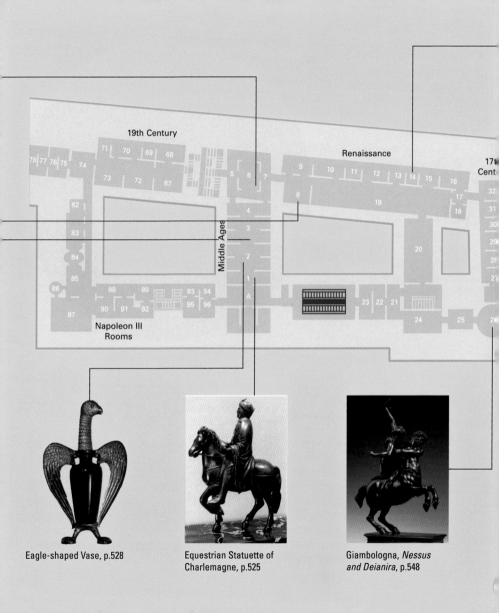

19th Century

Renaissance

17t Cent

78 77 76 75 74 73 72 67 71 70 69 68 66

82 83 84 85 86 87

Middle Ages

Napoleon III Rooms

5 6 7 4 3 2 1 A

8

9 10 11 12 13 14 15 16 17 18 19 20

32 31 30 29 28 27 26 25 24 23 22 21

88 89 90 91 92 93 94 95 96

Eagle-shaped Vase, p.528

Equestrian Statuette of Charlemagne, p.525

Giambologna, *Nessus and Deianira*, p.548

**Pisanello (ca.1395–1455),
Cecilia Gonzaga Medallion, 1447**
Bronze, 8.2 cm in diameter

The circular, half-length portrait of this young woman takes the form of a strict profile in bas-relief. The folds of her garment as well as her hair are brought out in minute detail, while her facial features are only lightly worked. On the reverse is a picture of the girl with the unicorn, an allusion to chastity and to innocence, which were apparently, particularly prominent aspects of the character of the young woman. Medallions developed during the Renaissance following an antique model, and were soon being minted in many European capitals. Pisanello portrayed a number of different princes and military commanders on medallions, thus closely following the antique tradition. There were fewer opportunities for portraits of young women, and this is why he seldom depicted them in this medium. The same Cecilia Gonzaga (1425–1451) was possibly the subject of the artist's Paris portrait of a woman in which the tradition of the portrait in profile is taken from the art of the medallion and transposed into painting. Depicting the whole bust, however, is a technique borrowed from painting and produces a rather artificial effect on a medallion.

March **from the Series of Tapestries known as**
Emperor Maximilian's Hunt, **Brussels,
1531–1533**
Wool, silk, gold and silver thread, 400 x 750 cm

A year's cycle of 12 tapestries depict the hunt during each of the 12 months. This series, for which the room in the Louvre that houses it was specially adapted, was produced shortly after Flemish tapestry-weaving had received its most significant international commission: the weaving of Raphael's designs for the Sistine Chapel in Rome, large compositions that illustrate stories from the lives of the Apostles.

The important panel painter Bernard van Orley (ca.1488–1541) adopted the principle used by them, which was modeled on monumental painting, in his own tapestry designs for this cycle. The astrological sign relating to each month is emblazoned in the middle of the border above the scene, and executed in closely related shades. In March, which as the beginning of spring, opens the cycle, the astrological sign is the ram (Aries). Numerous historical figures belonging to the Habsburg dynasty are repeatedly portrayed in these scenes of princely life, including the Emperor Maximilian I (1459–1519), Charles V (1500–1558), Ferdinand I (1503–1564) and Maria of Hungary (1505–1558). In addition to this, the tapestry astonishes with its topographically accurate depictions of the landscape around Brussels. In *March* Brussels itself forms the backdrop to the hunting scene. Bernard von Orleys' series was only associated with Emperor Maximilian in later inventories; it is more likely that it was carried out for Ferdinand I or for Maria of Hungary.

Metalwork of the 16th Century

Giambologna (in the Louvre: Jean Boulogne, 1529–1608),
Nessus and Deianira,
Florence, end of the 16th century
Bronze, 42.1 x 30.5 cm

Nessus carries travelers across the river Euenus. When Heracles tries to use his services with his wife Deianira, the centaur assaults her and is killed by Heracles with an arrow. This most famous small bronze of the artist born in Douai, but who worked in the service of the Medici family, simply shows Deianira's frightened cry for help. One of its main points of interest is the way the two bodies are turned in relation to each other, twisting upward in serpentine fashion. Giambologna, whose name derives from the town of Boulogne in northern France, ran a flourishing workshop in Florence, with many assistants producing bronzes that were distributed throughout the whole of Europe using his designs. These served as diplomatic gifts and, alongside antique sculptures, provided a model for the tradition of small bronze sculpture that endured into the 19th century. This sculpture is worthy of particular attention because of its meticulous execution and the signature on the centaur, although some people believe this was not all the artist's own work.

the Teutons. His adventures in Africa are of interest for the maritime wars against the Turks and Tunisian pirates. Grotesques, fruits, and other ornamental elements, in both transparent and opaque enamel, are set into the gold background around this scene. That this splendid ensemble of shield and helmet was made for King Charles IX (1550–1574) is evident by his monogram "K," which, alternating with small medallions, forms the decoration of the rim of the shield.

Pierre Redon,
Helmet and Shield of
Charles IX, ca. 1570
Hammered iron, gold plating, enamel
shield: 68 x 49 cm

Along with grotesques and masks, the sides making up this helmet, which was originally crowned with a helmet decoration, bear two scenes depicting antique battles. In the middle of the shield the victory of Marius over Jugurtha is depicted, a story that was well known throughout the Middle Ages in France. Marius was a Provençal hero due to his defeat of the Cimbri and

Cloak of the Order of the Holy Spirit, France, late 16th or early 17th centuries
Gold and silver embroidery on blue velvet

Among the most impressive of the reconstructed interiors at the Louvre is the one that contains the apparel belonging to the Order of the Holy Spirit. This order had been founded by Henry III, third son of Catherine de Médicis and the last in the male Valois line, on New Year's Eve, 1573 to commemorate his two royal proclamations, each made at Whitsun, in Poland in 1573 and in France in 1574. In addition to the king, 100 knights also belonged to the order, whose gatherings were held in Paris in the church of the Grands-Augustins. A blue velvet cloak with an orange satin lining, around four meters (13 feet) in length, was made for King Henry III (or his successor Henry IV). It is decorated with the flames of the Holy Spirit embroidered in gold in a pattern that decreases in size toward the top. These magnificent robes are complemented by a cape made of green silk, which is almost completely hidden by the lavish gold embroidery that adorns it.

Chest known as *Anne of Austria's Chest*, Paris, ca. 1660
Wood covered with gold and lined with blue velvet

In terms of its materials, one of the most precious pieces in the Louvre is this chest, which rests on claws, and is named after Anne of Austria (1601–1666) the mother of the Sun King, although it never actually belonged to her. The outer walls and lightly domed lid are decorated with foliage that flows into rose flowers. The rectangular surfaces are framed by a narrow leaf-design trim. In order to create variety in the decoration, the gold was hammered, to produce elevation, and pierced in order for the individual leaves to be separated from one another. Finally, the forms have been chased and decorated with filigree. This luxuriousness is typical of the taste for ornament that prevailed during the early years of Louis XIV's reign (after 1661). The first mention of the chest is in the "inventaire des diamants de la couronne" that was compiled in 1791.

Domestic Interiors of Different Periods

An extensive suite of rooms of different periods follows, predominantly displaying the French art of interior decoration up to the early 19th century, and revealing the private worlds of distinguished citizens and nobility. In terms of walls and furniture, many of these rooms were conceived from the outset as units exactly as they are exhibited today. In addition to these, other ensembles have been created, that bring together works of art, including some valuable paintings, with furniture and objects from different periods. Narrow corridors in this area, moreover, allow an almost incalculably large number of precious individual objets d'art to be exhibited. Space for the rich treasures of this department was only created under the reorganization that followed the finance ministry's departure from the Richelieu wing. Up to now, however, word has not really got out that the extension has also allowed a spectacular princely apartment, which had not been accessible for generations, to be integrated into the museum. Napoleon III not only gave the Denon wing opposite a new space housing rooms of state, such as the Salle des Etats, but also had a stately apartment with a terrace, overlooking the large inner courtyard of the Louvre, built for himself.

Before entering the 11 rooms, visitors should take a brief look at the cabinets in the entrance. They contain the relatively modest treasures accumulated during his lifetime by historian and politician Adolphe Thiers (1797–1877, head of the Cabinet under Louis Philippe and state president from 1871). They show how little his espousal of capital brought this exponent of anti-republican, anti-Napoleon III and anti-Commune bourgeois politics.

The imperial domestic interiors await the visitor in all their lavish splendor and are the epitome of the Second Empire. They were created between 1856 and 1861 by Hector Lefuel, the same architect who built the additional galleries and the state rooms on the opposite side of the Louvre. Their stylistic orientation was taken from the Sun King, whose model had already turned the Second Empire into a period of neo-Baroque. Their high point is the enormous corner room with its over-extravagant decoration by Louis-Alphonse Tranchant. The room could be rearranged into 11 rows of seats from which performances being given in the theater salon next door, from which it is separated by a real theater curtain, could be enjoyed. How the apartment, admittedly private in name only, fitted into the grand tradition of the Louvre is explained in the paintings: the one in the center celebrates Napoleon III's uniting of the Louvre with the Tuileries, and there are four other pictures in which Francis I, Catherine de Médicis, Henry IV, and Louis XIV are being shown plans for the Louvre by their respective architects.

A glance out of the windows onto the Cour Napoleon is rewarded with a view of the area, (with the exception of the glass pyramid exactly as it was during the Second Empire), and reveals that although Hector Lefuel was the architect in charge, this courtyard really belongs to the Paris of Georges Eugène Haussmann (1809–1891). Historically, this space offers a foretaste of the radical new layout of the metropolis conceived of under Napoleon III, which was to be intersected by broad streets whose facades were all made of the same stone and all bear witness to the same neo-Baroque and neo-Renaissance spirit.

Napoleon III's apartment, grand salon

The Galerie d'Apollon

In 1566, construction of what was known as the "Petite Galerie" began under Charles IX. With an attractive facade facing east, which took its present form in 1850, the wing, which stands at right angles to the Seine, leads to the Grande Galerie. After an interruption during the Huguenot war, building work resumed under Henry IV, as his monogram on the facade indicates. Just as the wing was about to be redesigned for the young Louis XIV, a fire broke out which gave the Sun King's great architect, Louis Le Vau (1612–1670), all the freedom he wanted for his own refurbishment.

Plans for the decoration were drawn up by the painter Charles Le Brun (1619–1690). He established a connection for the first time between the antique sun god Apollo and the Sun King in this gallery. Hence the sun was supposed to crown the stars with the signs of the zodiac during the course of the year. Earth and water, the seas, and the continents are all among its subjects. Apollo rules over the company of nine muses and, as the sun, also presides over the birth of the cosmos.

Only the stucco reliefs in a light ocher color, which had to be put into place before the painting, could be largely completed, in 1663/64. The south portion, above the end wall facing the Seine, depicting the "Triumph of the Water" was completely finished, but hardly any of it still survives in its original form. The composition is organized around the *Neptune* of François Girardon (1628–1715). At the end of the 18th century, the unfinished Apollo gallery was assigned to the Académie Royale de Peinture et de Sculpture. In order to finish off the decorative work, new members of the academy were given blank areas of ceiling to paint as their admission piece.

The Galerie d'Apollon and the whole of the area that surrounds it owes its present appearance to the activities of Félix Dubans (1797–1870), following the 1848 revolution. The concept of the Baroque ceiling offered the opportunity for a colossal ceiling painting. In 1851, therefore, Delacroix (1798–1863) painted his *Apollo Vanquishing the Python* with its sun chariot appearing in a majestic blaze of light above the female dragon that guards the treasure on Mount Parnassus. This spirited and fiery work provides a stark contrast with the worthy wall paneling from the same time, which incorporated "respectable" pictures illustrating the history of the Louvre. The Galerie d'Apollon is also a treasure chamber displaying objets d'art that, unlike the historical sequence adopted in the Richelieu wing, are arranged in the wall cupboards and in free-standing cabinets, organized by type of (precious) material.

Eugène Delacroix, Apollo Vanquishing the Python, 1851, oil on canvas, 8 x 7.8 m

Page 558/559: Hubert Robert (1733–1808), View of "Antique Rome" (detail), after 1800, oil on canvas, 65 x 81 cm, Musée du Louvre

Revolutions and Crown Jewels

Crowns still possess important symbolic value today, as can be seen, for example, from the practice of referring simply to the "crown" when the British state is meant. Even before the French Revolution of 1789, this mode of expression was largely inappropriate in France. Unlike Germany, for example, whose imperial crown, kept today in the treasure chamber in Vienna, can lay claim to almost mythical antiquity, the custom in France was for two crowns to be made for the coronation of each king, in which the most precious individual gems, the crown jewels, were set. What happened later to these coronation mementos depended on the individual monarch. The most precious diamonds, however, were returned to the dynastic treasure, while the crown itself was given away or melted down.

The treasury of St. Denis (see p. 526), however, can be thanked for ensuring that at least the crown of one French king survived. Louis XV donated the silver-gilt crown made for his coronation to the abbey in 1722, and it eventually made its way into the Louvre with the rest of the abbey's collection. It was designed by Claude Rondé and executed by the goldsmith Augustin Duflos under his supervision. The king deposited it with the Benedictines in 1729, after the diamonds had been replaced by rock crystal. The crown was restored for the first time in 1780. That enormous value was incorporated into it for the brief moment of the coronation is not really

Augustin Duflos, following the designs of Claude Rondé, Louis XV's crown, 1722, silver and silver gilt, precious stones replaced with copies, 24 cm high, 22 cm in diameter, Galerie d'Apollon

indicated by the crown in its current form, which does not perhaps correspond to its original appearance. For the coronation, 161 large, and 121 small diamonds, were worked into it, as well as 64 colored gemstones comprising equal numbers of rubies, sapphires, emeralds, and topaz. Two of the most famous diamonds in the world lie today in the display case next to the crown: the Régent and the Sancy, which were also previously set into it.

The fate of such pieces provides some of the most fascinating stories in history: since there was no traditional crown around which legends could grow, as was the case with Hungary's St. Stephen's crown, there was no need for anyone to undertake any symbolic action against such an object following the Revolution, which desecrated so many of the symbols of the old regime. What happened to individual pieces was, like so much else during that time, a question of finance and good or bad management of the exchequer. The most famous stones remained in French possession, which is why the Louvre gallery is able to exhibit its collection of huge unset diamonds.

The jewels that fell to the state following the collapse of the Second Empire were dealt with in a rather more radical way. In 1853 a diadem, and two years later a crown, were made for Empress Eugénie by Gabriel Lemonnier. Both items were sold in 1887. The diadem, set with 22 pearls and 1,998 diamonds appeared as one of the main lots in the famous auction held in 1982 by the royal house of Thurn and Taxis.

This gave the "Friends of the Louvre" the opportunity to reacquire the incredibly valuable object for France and to deposit it in the museum, which was founded before the first Revolution, shortly before its bicentennial celebrations. The crown had been donated to the Louvre four years previously by a private individual, Roberto Polo.

Jacques-Louis David (1748–1825), Napoleon crowning Josephine (detail), 1806/07, see p. 424

Appendix

A Short Explanation of Techniques

Casting Bronze

The most common method of producing statues in bronze, which was also widespread during classical Antiquity, is the so-called lost wax technique. The sculptor models the wax as precisely as possible into the form of the desired sculpture over a roughly shaped core made of clay or plaster. For this he or she uses a variety of differently shaped wooden and wire modeling tools. The model, which is now identical to the final bronze cast in terms of the width of its outer walls and its surface features, is packed with heat-resistant material (clay), which forms the mold. Before this is done, small rods (also made of wax) are fitted. These allow the wax, which has liquefied during firing, to flow out, and the bronze alloy to be poured into the hollow space that has thus been made. Fixing pegs are inserted to prevent the model from slipping. Once the cast has cooled off completely, the outer shell of the mold can

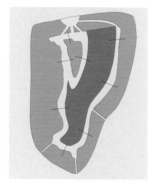
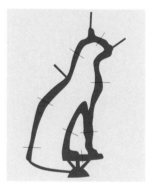

Making bronze sculptures using the lost wax technique

■ *Core and wax model*
  Small channels allow the wax to flow out and the bronze to be poured in
■ *The model is packed in a clay casting mold with pegs inserted to hold it in place*
■ *The bronze cast after the clay surround has been broken off*

be knocked away. Because the outer shell is destroyed in the process, it is not possible to make another identical cast. A procedure that preserves the mold and therefore allows several identical casts to be made was not perfected until well into the 15th century.

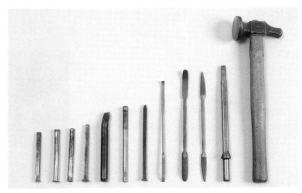

Tools used in the finishing work carried out on the cast bronze

Chasing and Completion of the Cast Sculpture

The cast that emerges when the clay shell is knocked away still needs various types of careful work doing to it, known as chasing or cold work. Firstly the casting channels, also filled with bronze, must be sawn off. Larger sculptures, frequently cast in several sections, need to be fitted together and erected. Joins need to be filled and smoothed off with a hammer. Finally, the surface of the sculpture will be polished with abrasive paper or a grinding stone and sometimes given a punched finish with special metal punches or stamping tools (ital. *punzone*), which can be either patterned or smooth.

François Girardon (1628–1715), bronze model for an equestrian statue of Louis XIV, cast by Desjardins, 17th century, see p. 246

(Stone) Sculpture

Creating a sculpture in stone is fundamentally different to creating one in bronze. While the artist making a bronze sculpture works from the inside out using a soft material (wax), the sculptor of stone is confronted at the beginning of the process by a raw, unworked block. Starting with this solid block of stone, the artist works their way toward the contours of the sculpture they are aiming for from the outside in. This requires careful planning, using preparatory sketches or drawings, for example, as a single unintentional blow with hammer and chisel can often lead to irreparable damage and ruin a piece of work completely. A mobile punching machine allows the most important reference points to be marked out on the stone.

During the working process the artist can chip away superfluous material to reveal the contours of the final sculpture either from a single side, or by working continuously and equally all the way round. In order to discard the material that is not required, the sculptor initially uses coarser, heavier tools, and then turns to a range of different pointed and toothed chisels for the finer contouring of the surface. With regard to the artistic working of a particular stone – the choice of material was often restricted in the past by geographical availability – it was important to take into account the inherent possibilities and aesthetic qualities that it offered.

Michelangelo Buonarroti, St. Matthew, ca. 1503–1505, marble, 271 cm high, Galleria dell'Accademia, Florence

Evidence of Michelangelo's Artistic Methods in his Unfinished Marble Sculptures

Michelangelo's unfinished works provide us with an insight into the sculptor's artistic methods. The way the artist crafted the bodily contours of his subject little by little from the stone was memorably compared by Giorgio Vasari (1511–1574) to the gradual draining of water from a bath. In many cases, various different stages in the work process can be seen in the marble. The surface of Michelangelo's *St. Matthew*, for example, attests his use of a variety of tools. Different sizes of toothed chisel were used by the artist in various places to create the inner structure within the stone.

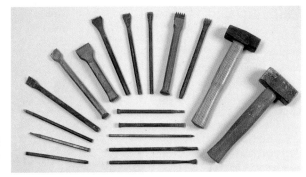

The sculptor's tools

Amenemonet and his wife Taka (detail), end of the 18th dynasty (1337–1295 BC), bas-relief with sunken hieroglyphic inscription, *see p. 132*

The Art of Relief

The art of relief is an independent form of sculpture subject to its own specific rules. Compared to fully three-dimensional sculpture, relief has a fundamentally more graphic-like quality. A special form of relief, known as sunken relief, was developed by the Egyptians. This is the opposite of low relief, also known as bas-relief, in which the image stands out against a flattened background. Depending on the degree of three-dimensionality and modeling that has taken place, a further distinction is often made between half and high relief.

Painting with Tempera

In order to produce a traditional egg tempera, which was the type of paint used almost exclusively in the Middle Ages, pigments were dissolved in an oily, watery liquid, and then mixed with egg in order to produce a form of color that could be used for painting. The specific properties of paints mixed in this way and their uses depended on the proportions of individual ingredients that went into their composition. As their liquid component evaporated quickly as a rule, tempera paints (from the Latin *temperare*, to mix or moderate) dried extremely quickly and therefore allowed the painting process to proceed swiftly. Tempera also enabled painters to use the finest possible brush strokes. In contrast to the more radiant oil paints, tempera paints have a thicker consistency and duller shine, which can, however, be heightened through the use of varnish (a coating material that produces a luster). Fluid tran-

The constituents of egg tempera

sitions between different colors are hard to achieve with tempera paint, which is largely a surface-covering paint, and an impasto (thick, lumpy) application of paint is not possible at all. The fact that the paint lightens during the drying process makes it difficult to calculate color effects in advance, and makes it more or less impossible to achieve an identical color tone during any subsequent painting over of the same areas.

Mixing the paint

Barnaba da Modena (known to have lived ca. 1361–1383, Madonna and Child, ca. 1362, tempera on wood, 109 x 72 cm, Musée du Louvre

Michelangelo Buonarroti (1475–1564), Mary with the Boy Jesus, John the Baptist, and Angels, known as the "Manchester Madonna," ca. 1500, tempera and oil on wood, 105 x 77 cm, National Gallery, London

The matt, deeper-lying paint layers and extensive surface-covering properties of tempera can be seen in Barnaba da Modena's *Madonna*. A shading effect is achieved through the use of close-hatched brush strokes.

Michelangelo's "Manchester Madonna" is an example of the combining of tempera and oil paint that was widespread in the 15th century and also explains some of the work processes used in the creation of a panel painting. Parts of the initial sketching-out can be seen on the white grounding. The fleshy areas were under-

painted with green and the robes of Mary and the angels to the side with dark gray and red tempera. Effects of light and shadow were also laid down in the underpainting, and certain areas that were to be light in the finished picture were painted white. Beneath the central group of figures, the surface can be seen to have already been coated with a transparent oil-based glaze that greatly heightens the intensity of the colors.

Oil Painting

Painting tools, brushes and spatulas

For the production of oil paints, pigments are ground together with a binding medium consisting of drying oils or semi-drying oils (flax, poppy, or walnut oil). In the 16th century, oil painting on canvas almost completely replaced the use of tempera paint on wood, which had been the norm during the Middle Ages. The increasing popularity of oil paint was primarily due to the fact that this medium provided artists with an extremely versatile and diverse range of creative possibilities and effects. The drying process with oils, which was slow by comparison with tempera, may frequently have held up the execution of the painting, but it also allowed for the easy merging of colors into one another, which could thus be mixed together even on the painting surface to create subtle transitions. In addition, oil paint did not change shade as it dried. An oil painting could be carried out by

means of the application of several thin, transparent layers of paint that merged with one another, or else by using the *alla prima* method, which involved the swift single application of surface-covering pigments. From the Renaissance onward, artists also made use of the opportunity oils gave them of applying oil paint using the impasto technique, using a spatula or palette knife to build the paint up to a considerable thickness. Characteristic of oil painting is the radiance of its vivid, shining colors.

The so-called glaze technique was perfected by the Venetian Titian. He obtained the subtlest of color effects in the depiction of flesh tones and drapery through the careful application of transparent layers of color that showed through one another.

Rembrandt demonstrated his virtuoso mastery of the different effects that could be

Titian (Tiziano Vecellio), Madonna with Rabbit (detail), 1530, see p. 309

achieved using the impasto technique in numerous late works. Here he did not limit himself to use of paintbrushes and spatulas, but also rubbed the paint with his fingers in places. The face in the Louvre's *Self-Portrait* is virtually modeled in paint. This vehemently applied mass of paint contributes to the creation of a mysterious vividness in this impressive portrait, which has lost nothing of its immediacy even several centuries after it was painted.

Rembrandt Harmensz. Van Rijn, Portrait of the Artist at his Easel (detail), 1660, see p. 507

Glossary

Abbasid (Arabic *Al Abbasijjun*): caliphate dynasty (749–1258) that came to power as the result of an organized revolt under the leadership of Abu Muslim in Chorasan in 747. After the seizure of Al Kufa in 749, Abdul Abbas came to power as the caliph. Mongols took over the city of Baghdad in 1258, after which a branch of the dynasty continued to live as mock caliphs in Cairo at the court of the Mamelukes until 1517.

Abbey church (from Hebrew *abba,* "father;" Medieval Latin, *abbatia,* "abbey"): also minster or conventual church: a building that is closed to its surroundings and houses a community of monks or nuns and place of common prayer. Set down in the spirit of the ordination rules compiled in Monte Cassino in the 6th century by St. Benedict of Nursia (ca. 480–before 553 A.D.), the Benedictine structure of the medieval abbey church with the adjoining cloister has a fixed place in the south of the abbey.

Académie Royale (French "Royal Academy") official name Académie Royale de Peinture et de Sculpture: state-run academy of art set up in Paris by Anne of Austria with the support of Cardinal Mazarin, that maintained an academy with the Ecole des Beaux-Arts and continues to do so today. In 1666 it was expanded to include the Académie Française in Rome.

Acropolis (Greek "high city"): ancient Greek name for the citadel of a town (*polis*), and especially for the Acropolis of Athens which became famous for its magnificent buildings; as long ago as the Mycenaean times (ca. 1600–1150 B.C.) it was the entrance to the city as well as palace, stores, treasury and armory, holy temple, and refuge on a hill or mountain in a strategically favorable position.

Akkad: Semitic-speaking occupants of a former city of northern Babylon (exact location unknown) that was founded in 2300 B.C. by Sargon I of Akkad as the capital of the first Semitic imperial center on Mesopotamian soil ("the land of the Akkad").

Almagest: Latinized originally Arabic term, in common use since the Middle Ages, for the "mathematical syntaxis," the main work by the Greek astronomer and geographer Claudius Ptolemy (ca. 100–160 A.D.); soon famous as the "great syntaxis" (megale syntaxis), the "Almagest" was the first systematic handbook on mathematical astronomy.

Amarna age (Arabic *Amarna, Tell el-Amarna*): term derived from the ruins of the residence built ca. 1380 B.C. by King Amenhotep IV, Ikhnaton (1351–1334 B.C.), in central Egypt on the eastern banks of the Nile; refers to the brief cultural heyday of the capital Akhet-Aton, which was soon deserted. Major finds included a number of clay tablets found in 1888 (the "Amarna tablets") in cuneiform writing, most in Akkadian.

Amun-Ra (Egyptian "the concealed"): one of the main Egyptian gods who was of special importance in the early Middle Empire (ca. 2100 B.C.). Originally the god of wind, who was honored by river boatmen, then later merged with Min of Koptos, the god of fertility. Usually appeared as a human wearing a high crown of feathers and with a whip, falchion, or scepter in his hand. The 11th dynasty (2119–1978 B.C.) saw him in Thebes, where he merged with sun god Ra and became king of the gods as the city ascended. For the Greeks and Romans Amun was the god of the oasis at Siwa, and the site of their oracle.

Amor (Latin "love"): Eros in Greek mythology. The god of love, according to Simonides the son of Mars and Venus. Originally a winged youth in the poems and visual art of Antiquity; later a mischievous, playful boy

Edme Bouchardon, Amor Drawing his Bow, 1746–1750, Musée du Louvre

with a bow and arrows who, half in fun and half in wickedness, shot his arrows into the hearts of gods and mortals to make them fall in love.

Ancien Régime (French "old government"): name mainly of the form of government of absolutism in the 17th and 18th centuries against which the French Revolution turned in 1789.

Aphrodite: the goddess of love and beauty in Greek-Roman Antiquity (Roman: Venus)

Apocalypse (Greek *apokalyptein*, "reveal, expose"): text that deals with the end of the world, such as the Revelation of St. John the Divine, the last book of the New Testament.

Apollo: Greek-Roman god, son of Jupiter and Leto and twin brother of Diana. Apollo assumed the shapes of many local gods and adopted their features, so manifold religious impressions flowed into his person. Among others, he was the god of prophecy, music and the arts, and of the muses (Apollo Musagetes), light and sun (Phoebos Apollo), and for centuries embodied Antiquity's idea of beauty.

Apotheosis (Greek *apotheoun*, "to deify, declare"): deification; the placing of a living being among the gods.

Apse (Latin; Greek *hapsis*, "connection, rounding, arch"): a niche, constructed over a semicircular or polygonal base and topped with a semi-dome; usually houses an altar. Choir room adjoining the main choir room or that reserved for the clerics; also known as the exedra. Small ante-apses are often located on the lateral or side aisles.

Archivolte (Italian *archivolto*, "front arch;" Greek *archein*, "to begin, to dominate," Latin *volutus* "turned, rolled"): profiled or decorative arch that is applied as a semicircular architrave (main beam that bears the load of the superstructure) across the tops of columns.

Ariadne: in Greek mythology the daughter of King Minos of Crete who used the so-called "Ariadne's thread" to help Theseus escape from the infamous Labyrinth after he had been abducted to Crete, and accompanied him on his

Aton: the royal family – Ikhnaton, Nefertiti, and two daughters, altar relief, ca. 1345 B.C., limestone, Egyptian Museum, SMPK, Berlin

flight. She was later abandoned by Theseus on Naxos, then rescued by Dionysus, who later took her for his wife.

Assyrians: in Antiquity, the inhabitants of Assyria, the country around the city of Ashur on the Tigris, where a mighty empire was founded in the 2nd century B.C. (now part of Iraq). The origins and early history of the Assyrians, who worshiped the goddess Ishtar and the god Ashur, are unknown.

Athena also Pallas Athene, and Minerva to the Romans: the virginal goddess of the city of Athens, and later the main goddess of Greece. Is said to have sprung fully grown from the head of Zeus, whose favorite daughter she was; goddess of wisdom and war, and the protector of women's work and the arts and crafts; inventor of ship-building, the flute, and weaving. Her chief cult center was the Acropolis in Athens, where numerous festivals were held in her honor including the Panathenaea.

Aton (Egyptian "sun disc"): Ancient Egyptian name for the sun disc. Elevated to main god under Amenhotep IV,

Ikhnaton (1351–1334 B.C.), in Amarna, and worshiped since then as the sun god; depicted as a sun disc with rays emanating downward and ending in hands.

Baal (Semitic "lord" or "owner"): title for countless Syrian and Palestinian gods, also the name of Hadad, the Canaanite god of the weather. There are myths from Ugarit that tell of Baal's appointment and deeds; there he was also known as Alijan ("the powerful"). Symbolic animal is the bull, and Baal is frequently shown either standing on one, or in the shape of one.

Babylonians: in Antiquity the inhabitants of Babylonia, which was much praised for the fertility of its soil, situated on the lower Euphrates and Tigris.

Bacchus: see Dionysus

Baroque (Portuguese *barocco* "small stones, not round"): European style period between the end of Mannerism (ca. 1600) and the beginning of Rococo (ca. 1720/30). Originally a goldsmithing term, where a "barocco" is an uneven pearl.

Belle Epoque (French "beautiful period"): the term for the period between 1890 and 1914 in France when there was an increased enjoyment of life.

Cameo (French *camée*): semiprecious gem with a relief, usually of a figure.

Capriccio (Italian "caprice"): name for all kinds of fantastic representations, usually collated randomly under a particular theme. In addition to paintings by Giuseppe Arcimboldo (1527–1593), the capriccios of Francisco da Goya (1748–1820) are the most important.

Carmelites, Order of (Latin *Ordo Fratrum Beatae Mariae Virginis de Monte Carmelo*, "Order of the Brothers of the Blessed Virgin Mary of Mount Carmel"): order of mendicants dating back to 1247 whose members lead a life of religious meditation and are committed to missionary work and mystical theology. Started as a mermitage on Mount Carmel near Haifa in Israel.

Carolingians: Frankish and European dynasty of noblemen from the Moselle/Maas area; named after Charles the Great (768–814) and resulting from an agreement made between the leading families of the French nobility.

Cartellino (Italian "note, sign"): strip of paper often included in religious historical pictures or portraits as a trompe l'oeil with an inscription bearing the artist's signature and the year of painting or a motto.

Capriccio: Giuseppe Arcimboldo, Winter, 1573, oil on canvas, Musée du Louvre

Carthusian (Italian *certosa*): a special form of abbey developed by monks of the Carthusian order. The cloister is flanked by individual houses with small gardens, each one of which is inhabited and tended by a monk. They share the chapterhouse; however the church, abbot's quarters, and guesthouse are all outside the enclosure.

Caryatid (Greek *karyatides*): building supports or pillars in the shape of a female form with baskets or cushions as head ornaments that are used instead of a column or other tectonic element to carry the entablature. The name is probably derived from the name given to the females, in particular the temple dancers, of the Laconian city of Karyai near Sparta. Because of the treacherous behavior by the populace during the Persian Wars (500–479 B.C.), the village girls ended up as slaves.

Cathedral (Greek *kathedra*, "seat"): term widely used in France, Spain, and England to refer to the main church of a bishopric.

Centaur (Greek *kentauros*): mythical being of Greek legend with a human upper body and the lower body of a horse.

Centralized building: a structure, every part of which is designed equally in line with a central point. Popular in the Renaissance following examples from Antiquity; e.g. the Pantheon in Rome.

Central perspective (Latin *centralis*, "in the middle," and *perspectiva [ars]*, "looking through [art]"): a scientific-mathematical method of perspective representation from Filippo Brunelleschi (1377–1446) to the beginning of the 15th century. To the observer, all the lines that lead deep into the picture cross at a central point, the vanishing point. The three-dimensional illusion is represented on a two-dimensional surface by the precise reduction and proportionalization of the represented objects, landscapes, buildings, and figures in accordance with their spatial layout.

Francis I (1515–1547) orders the rebuilding of the Louvre as the king's palace. Work begins in 1546

Henry II (1547–1559) embarks on the repression and persecution of the Huguenots

Thousands of Huguenots die in the St Bartholomew's Day Massacre (24.8.1572)

Charles IX (1560–1574) ascends to the throne as a minor, though his mother Catherine de' Medici remains the regent

1500   1550   1600

Under Francis I the main tower is dismantled in 1528 and the building restored. From 1546 rebuilding of the Louvre under Pierre Lescot with the Caryatid room as the main hall. Finished under Henry II

Catherine de' Medici orders Philibert de l'Orme to plan a palace in the Tuileries (1564)

Extension of plans presented by Lescot (Cour Carré) under Henry IV; building of the Grande Galerie (1595–1600)

Albrecht Dürer, *Self-portrait with Thistle* (1493)

Leonardo da Vinci, *Mona Lisa* (1510/1515)

Rosso Fiorentino, *The Mourning of Christ* (ca. 1530-1540)

Titian (Tiziano Vecellio), *The Supper at Emmaus* (1553)

Pieter Bruegel the Elder, *The Beggars* (1568)

Michelangelo Merisi da Caravaggio, *The Fortune Teller* (ca. 1594/1595)

Tilman Riemenschneider, *The Annunciation* from the church of St. Peter in Erfurt (ca. 1495)

Michelangelo Buonarroti, *The Rebelling Slave* for the tomb of Julius II (ca. 1513)

Germain Pilon, Domenico Barbiere, *The Three Graces*, from the tomb housing King Henry II's heart in Paris (1561/1566)

Adriaen de Vries, *Mercury Robbing Psyche* (1593)

Dietrich Schro, *Count Palatine Ottheinrich* (1556)

High Renaissance (ca. 1500–1530): Raphael, *Self-portrait with a Friend* (ca. 1518/1519)

Francis I sets up an art gallery in the Fontainebleau Palace (basis for the Louvre collection: *Mona Lisa*, Raphael's *Michael*, Michelangelo's *Slaves*)

Catherine de' Medici's Tuileries gardens, laid out in an Italian style (1564)

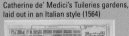

The Edict of Nantes brought the religious wars in France to an end (1598)

Baroque (end 16th –beg. 18th centuries): Rembrandt, *Bathsheba* (1654)

History

The politics of King Philippe IV (1285–1314) leads to the dissolution of the Order of the Knights Templar and to the election of the French pope, Clement V

Charles V (1364–1380) used the Louvre as his royal residence

Hundred Years War (1337–1453), depiction of the battle of Crécy, miniature from the *Grandes Chroniques des Jean Froissart*

France becomes a strong European power under King Philippe Auguste II (1180–1223). After 1190 building of a fortress on the right shore of the river Seine

1200   1300   1400

Architectural History

Under Philippe Auguste II the fortified tower (Donjon) and the rampart that surrounds the Louvre are built. It is mainly used as a vault and as a prison (after 1190)

Extension of the Louvre under Charles V, the tower is surrounded by walls; miniature from the October picture of the duc de Berry's *Très riches heures* (mid 15th century) by Barthélemy d'Eyck

Painting

Master of San Francesco, *Christ Crucified* (ca. 1265/1270)

Parisian painter, *John II (the Good), King of France* (before 1350)

Jan van Eyck, *The Virgin of Chancellor Rolin* (ca. 1434)

Rogier van der Weyden, *Mary Magdalene* (ca. 1452)

Giotto di Bondone, *The Stigmatization of St. Francis* (ca. 1300)

Botticelli, *Mary with Christ Child and John the Baptist* (ca. 1470/1475)

Sculpture

Stonemason's Yard at St. Denis, Figures from Corbeil, Essonne

Nino Pisano, *Mary*, taken from an Annunciation Group (mid 14th-century)

Donatello, *Madonna of the Villa Vettori*, Florence (ca. 1440)

Head of Christ, Burgundy (ca. 1295/1300)

Unknown Parisian Sculptor, *Jeanne de Bourbon* (Wife of Charles V) (ca. 1375)

Culture

Seal of the Knights Templar

Early Renaissance (ca. 1420–1500): Fra Angelico, *Coronation of Mary* (ca. 1430)

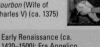

Gothic (ca. 1150-1400): Chartres Cathedral, western portal (1145)

Popes in Avignon (1309–1415): Palace of the Pope

Jeanne d'Arc (1412–1431), Painting by Jean-Auguste Dominique Ingres (1854)

Timeline

4000	3000	2000		1000

Ancient Orient

Beaker, Susa (4200/3800 B.C.)

Stele of Ur-Nanshe Sumerian (2500 B.C.)

Head of a king, possibly Hammurabi, Babylon (1792–1750 B.C.)

Goddess Feeding Goats, Port of Ugarit (?end 2nd century B.C.)

Demon Pazuzu, Assyria (?9th/7th century B.C.)

Winged Bull with Human Head, Chorsabad (ca. 706 B.C.)

Islam

Egypt

Old Kingdom (ca. 2640–2134 B.C.) Sphinx (?ca. 2600 B.C.)

Middle Kingdom (2134–1650 B.C.) Pharaoh Senusret III (1872–1853/52 B.C.)

New Kingdom (1552–1070 B.C.) Nefertiti and Ikhnaton (1351–1346 B.C.)

Third Intermediate Period (1070–712 B.C.) Triads of Pharaoh Osorkon II (874–850 B.C.)

Late Period (712–332 B.C.) Statue of Nachthoreb (595–589 B.C.)

Greece

Head of a Female Statue, Kéros in the Cyclades (2700–2300 BC)

Proto-Attic vase, Athens (ca. 690 B.C.)

Archaic Period (ca. 680–480 BC) "Dame d'Auxerre," (?)Crete (ca. 630 B.C.)

Execias, black-figured amphora, Athens (ca. 550–540 B.C.)

Rome

Tombs of an Etruscan Couple, Cervotori (ca. 530/510 B.C.)

Ancient Orient

Stylized Head, Southern Arabia (?1st century B.C.)

Bust of a Sassanid King, Iran (6th/7th century B.C.)

Female Nude Statuette Babylonia (ca. 300 B.C.)

Islam

Pyxis, Spain (368)

Mohammed's flight from Mecca to Medina, from when Islamic dates are calculated (A.D. 622)

Portrait of Fath Ali Shah (1797–1834), painted silk

Egypt

Christ and Abbot Mena of Bawit (6th/7th century)

Mummy Portrait from Antinoë (2nd/3rd century)

Greece

Classical (ca. 480–323 B.C.) Nike from the West Gable of the Parthenon, Athens (438–432 B.C.)

Venus de Milo (ca. 120 B.C.)

Hellenistic (323–31 B.C.) *Nike of Samothrace* (ca. 190 B.C.)

Rome

Goblets with Skeletons from Boscoreale (1st century B.C.)

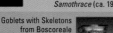

Fragment from the *Ara pacis* (13–9 B.C.)

Nine Muses on the Outer Wall of a Sarcophagus near Rome (mid-2nd century)

Napoleon Bonaparte, 1799 coup
d'état, imperial crowning, 1804

After the Second Republic
(1848–1852), Napoleon III is
emperor until 1870 (Versailles)

Liberation of Paris
in August 1944

The Paris Commune
1870/71 (Musée d'Orsay)

The 1830 Revolution

François Mitterand,
French President
from May 1981–1995

History

1800   **1850**   **1900**   **2000**

Building of
the north
wing on the
Rue de
Rivoli
(1810–1814)

Joining of the north wing to
the Cour Carré. Closure of
the "great square"
(1852–1857)

Evacuation of the
Louvre during World
War II (1939)

Napoleon orders construction of
the triumphal "Carrousel" arch, as
entrance to the Tuileries (1806)

Fire in the Tuileries
Palace (1871)

Opening of the Grand
Louvre (1998): pyramid
by I. M. Pei (1993)

Architectural History

William Turner, *Landscape with River
and Distant Cove* (ca. 1845)

Jean-Baptiste Camille Corot,
Woman with Pearl (1868-1870)

Francisco de Goya y Lucientes, *Christ
on the Mount of Olives* (1810/1819)

Jean-Auguste-Dominique
Ingres, *The Turkish Bath*
(1862)

Painting

François Rude, *Young Neapolitan
Fisherman Playing with a Turtle* (1833)

Claude Ramey, *Napoleon in
Coronation Robes* (1833)

Sculpture

Charles Baudelaire
(1821–1867), poet and
art critic

Impressionism (from ca. 1870), named after
Claude Monet's painting: *Impression
Sunrise* (1872), Musée Marmottan

Re-planning of Paris
under Baron Georges
Haussmann (1809–1891),
he was major prefect of
the Seine under
Napoleon III

Auguste Rodin, *Honoré de
Balzac* (1891/1897), Musée
d'Orsay

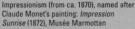

Gustave Eiffel, Eiffel Tower (1889)

La Grande Arche
(1989), part of the
"Grands Projets" of
the Mitterand era

Culture

Henry IV (1589–1610) founder of the absolute monarchy, married to Maria de' Medici. Died in the Louvre due to an assassination.

Louis XIII (1610–1643) employs Cardinal Richelieu as first minister

Under Louis XIV (1643–1715), also known as "The Sun King", France becomes the model of an absolute state; introduction of court culture in Versailles

Louis XVI (1774–1798/92), last monarch of the Ancien Régime

Storming of the Bastille, 14th July 1789. Beginning of the French Revolution (Musée Carnavalet)

Continuation of the absolute state under Louis XV (1715–1774)

1650   1700

Under Louis XIII the west wing is extended and the central clock tower is built (today the Sully wing)

Petite Galerie converted to Louis XIV's Galerie d'Apollon (1661–1670)

Louis XIV orders the building of the colonnades (1667–1674) under Claude Perrault

Louis XVI plans to set up a museum in the Grande Galerie

Opening of the Musée Centrale des Arts under the direction of Vivant Denon (1793)

Rubens, *The Médicis Cycle* (1621/1625)

Nicolas Poussin, *Shepherds in Arcadia* (ca. 1638/1640)

Jan Vermeer, *The Lacemaker* (ca. 1670/1671)

Hyacinthe Rigaud, *Portrait of the Artist's Mother, Marie Serre* (1695)

François Boucher, *Diana Bathing* (1742)

Thomas Gainsborough, *Lady Alston* (ca. 1760)

Giambologna, *Nessus and Deianira*, Florence (end of the 16th century)

Gianlorenzo Bernini, *Cardinal Richelieu* (1640)

Pierre Puget, *Milo of Crotona* (1670-1682)

Louis XV's Crown (1722)

Pigalle, *Voltaire Naked* (1776)

Antonio Canova, *Cupid and Psyche* (1793)

Wing of Louvre named after royal court minister Duke of Sully 1560–1641)

Versailles Palace, painting by Pierre Denis Martin (1772)

Rococo (ca. 1700–1750): Jean-Antoine Watteau, *The Embarkation for Cythera* (1717)

Classicism (ca. 1760–beg. 19th century): Jaques Louis David, *The Oath of the Horatii* (1784)

Denis Diderot, editor of the *Encyclopédie* (1713–1784)

Romanticism (19th century): Théodore Géricault, *The Raft of the Medusa* (1819)

Chiton (Greek): important element of Ancient Greek clothing; a shirt-like garment, either with or without sleeves, worn down to the knee or calf and usually tied with a belt.

Choir screen (Latin *chorus*; Greek *choros*, "round dance, dancing and singing group"): the railings or wall that separate the choir area of a church from the church congregation.

Classical Greece: in the stricter sense, the term for the world of Greek art from the 5th to the 4th centuries B.C., during the course of which sculpture and architecture were released from Archaic severity and strictness, moving to a harmonious, nature-based form of design.

Classicism (French *classique*; and Latin *classicus*, "exemplary, first-rate"): style of between 1750 and 1840 that was based on the example of classical Antiquity (5th–4th centuries B.C.).

Cloister: a corridor around the rectangular courtyard of an enclosure, usually arched with decorated openings toward the courtyard.

Colonnade: on a building, a row of columns bearing an architrave, as opposed to the row of arches that characterize an arcade.

Contrapposto (Italian, from Latin *contrapositus*, "opposing," from *ponere* "to place, to set"): stationary motif in classical Greek sculpture that received its name from the sculptor Polyclitus (ca. 480–415 B.C.) and subsequently became a binding principle in European art, in which the various directions of force and movement in the human body are brought to a harmonious balance. The distribution of the loading and supporting, resting, and driving forces of a figure are balanced between the supporting and free legs. The contrapposto was reassumed in the Renaissance.

Corps-de-logis (French): main building of a Baroque palace, raised above the side wings and pavilions and used for residential and representational purposes.

Council of Trent also "Concilium Tridentinum" (1545–1563): the 19th ecumenical council. After several failed attempts, Pope Paul III (1534–1549) summoned a gathering of the church to Trent (Trento). The main tasks were to put an end to fighting in the name of religion (Reformation), the general reform of the Church, and the release of Christians from suppression by nonbelievers. In three sessions, the Council introduced substantial changes and improvements.

Citizen king, Louis-Philippe (1773–1850): he and his father, the count of Orléans, initially joined the Revolution of 1789, but then in 1793 crossed over to the Austrians with General Dumouriez. After spending some time abroad, he returned to France in 1827, where his court became a meeting place for the liberal opposition. When Charles X was forced to abdicate in 1830, Louis-Philippe ascended the throne as "King of the French."

Counter-Reformation: standard term for measures adopted by the Roman Catholic Church against the Reformation since the time of Leopold von Ranke (1795–1888). The protestant split promoted the Catholic restoration, in the first instance the work of church-political activities by the Jesuits, who became influential with Catholic rulers and universities.

Crater: in Greek ceramics the name for a wide, open, pot-bellied container with two handles. Made on a potter's wheel and painstakingly decorated with a black glaze, the crater is used in Greece both to blend wines and as a cooler.

Crypt (Latin *crypta*; Greek *krypte*, "covered walkway, archway"): underground chapel or tomb room, usually situated beneath the priest's chancel in a church.

Diana: in Greek mythology Artemis, the goddess of hunting and virtue. Originally probably the goddess of death, she was also one of the goddesses who eschewed harm and brought blessings; merged with countless local deities in the course of time. Deer (in the Actaeon legend), boar, dogs, the red mullet, and lobster are some of the animals dedicated to her.

Diderot, Denis (1713–1784): French writer, universal scholar, and occasional publisher and author of the French *Encyclopédie* (1751–1727). In addition to aesthetic and literary-theoretical works, he also wrote erotic novels and short stories; introduced the "tearjerker" and bourgeois tragedy to France, and frequently appears in paintings.

Dionysus, also **Bakchos** (Latin *Bacchus*): the god of wine and fruitfulness in Greek mythology; son of Jupiter and Semele, spouse of Ariadne; was brought up in a cave by nymphs.

Dioscuri (Greek *dios*, genitive of *Zeus*, and *kuros*, "lad, boy"): in Greek mythology the inseparable twin brothers Castor and Pollux, sons of Zeus or Tyndareus and Leda, and brothers of Helena and Clytemnestra. Worshiped especially as helpers in battle and to those in distress at sea.

Diptych (Latin *diptychum*; Greek *diptychos*, "folded double"): an ancient folding writing tablet; in medieval art a two-winged opening altarpiece (sculpture or painted) with no fixed centerpiece.

Dynasty: the chronological division of Egyptian history into a number of periods of rule. The 30 dynasties are gathered into several major periods: the early dynastic periods (1st and 2nd dynasties, ca. 3100–2700 B.C.); the Old Kingdom (3rd–8th dynasties, ca. 2700–2200 B.C.); First Intermediate Period (7th–11th dynasties, ca. 2200–2033 B.C.); Middle Kingdom (11th–13th dynasties, ca. 2033–1710 B.C.); Second Intermediate Period

Figura serpentinata: Giambologna, The Rape of the Sabine Women, 1581–1583, marble, Loggia dei Lanzi, Florence

(14th–17th dynasties, ca. 1710–1540 B.C.); New Kingdom (18th–20th dynasties, ca. 1550–1069 B.C.); Third Intermediate Period (21st–26th dynasties, 1069–664 B.C.); Late Period (26th–30th dynasties, second Persian rule and Ptolemaic rule, 664–30 B.C.).

Enamel (French *émailler*, "to cover with a coating"): the act of applying a colored glass-based coating to a decorative item.

Encrustation (Latin *incrustare*, "to coat with a rind"): to cover walls and floors with colored polished stone sheets, usually marble or porphyry, that are made into patterns, thereby giving structure to and decoratively enlivening the surface.

Enfilade (French "lining up"): a succession of rooms, the doors of which are all in one axis so that when they are open it is possible to see through all of them. Developed in France ca. 1650, the enfilade is a typical design feature of Baroque palaces and houses.

Engraving: working metal with a chisel, cutting tool, and file; the carving of figured and ornamental decorations in gold and silver.

Enlightenment: an intellectual movement that began at the end of the 17th century and continued until the 19th century; based on humanism, philosophy, and the liberating possibilities of rational and scientific knowledge in which "reason" (Latin *ratio*) governs human nature. Started in western Europe and supported and developed increasingly by a more self-confident bourgeoisie, it was the leading spiritual movement of the 18th century and had a strong influence on every aspect of cultural life; the active centers of Enlightenment were cities and universities.

Erechtheum: temple on the north side of the Acropolis in Athens dedicated to the mythical King Erechtheus, probably planned under Pericles and executed at the time of the Peloponnesian War (431–404 B.C.). According to legend, the temple contains a number of old cult sites that cause irregularities in the Attic-Ionic building, including, in the east cella a cult picture of Athena that fell from the sky, the imprint of Poseidon's trident in the northern vestibule, Kekrops' grave in the southwest corner, and in the west, Athena's sacred oil tree.

Etruscan (Latin *etrusci, tusci*; Etruscan *rasna*): member of an ancient, non-Indo-Germanic people that ruled Etruria and occasionally the Po plain and Campania. The culture of the Etruscans, which differed in language, religion, and customs and had its own wholly independent style of art that was strongly influenced by the Orient and Greece, flourished between the 7th and 4th centuries B.C. The ascent of Rome led to the downfall of Etruscan power in the 4th century.

Exedra (Greek "isolated seat," plural *exedren*): niche with a bench at the end of a line of columns; name for the apsis, the altar niche at the end of the choir area reserved for the clergy; any other semicircular niche.

Faience (French): fired earthenware; porous, yellow-gray or red to brown, often covered with a white or colored, usually painted, zinc glaze. Named after the town of Faenze, the capital of Italy's faience producing area. The history of the technique goes back to the 4th century B.C. (Egypt); found all over the Middle East in the 2nd century B.C.

Figura serpentinata (Latin *figura*, "figure, shape," and *serpens* "snake") also statua serpentinata: a form of design that was found in Antiquity, and later especially in the painting, drawing, and sculpture of the Italian High Renaissance and Mannerism in which the human form is shown in a spiral, often exaggerated position.

Filigree (Latin *filum* "thread," and *granum* "corn"): a metal-processing technique in which fine metal threads, usually gold or silver, are soldered onto a metal

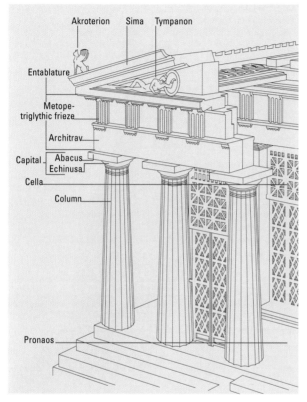

Akroterion Sima Tympanon

Entablature

Metope-
triglythic frieze

Architrav

Capital
Abacus
Echinusa

Cella

Column

Pronaos

Greek temple

base to make jewelry, or woven together to create an independent decorative work. Filigree work found in Troy and Mycenae testify to the great age of this technique, which was also of great importance in Byzantium and in Carolingian goldsmithery.

Franco-Prussian War (1870/71): staged by the Prussian Germans as a political national war. The German victory at Sedan (with the capture of Napoleon III on September 2, 1870) spelled the end of the French Second Empire. The Frankfurt peace treaty of May 10, 1871 called for large amounts of compensation from France and the ceding of Alsace and Lorraine.

Fresco (Italian "fresh"): wall painting that is applied to a lime wash while it is still wet.

Frieze (mid-Latin *frisium*, "fringe, peak"): sculpted or painted strip of continuous horizontal wall decoration that serves to enliven or give structure to a wall surface.

Generic terms in art: terms that differentiate between the subjects of various types of art. In medieval and Renaissance painting, we differentiate between religious and profane picture subjects. In Dutch art there was a marked development in the variety of subjects after the beginning of the 17th century. The repertoire of subjects deemed worthy of representation increased dramatically in line with the specializations of individual artists, and gradually their work was ordered according to type (architectural, sea, flower, kitchen, social, interior, landscape, still life, historical, etc.). A hierarchy of types formed in Italy in the 15th century, in which the historical picture – the representation of religious and mythological subjects or historical events – was regarded as the most discerning and elegant task of the painter; this remained very much the case until well into the 19th century.

Genius (Latin "creator"): in Roman mythology the god-like power found in man that is related to his ability to procreate. The female counterpart to the male's genius is the goddess Juno, revered for her ability to bear children. The honoring of genius became an early form of the cult of rule, when the *Genius Augusti* was elevated from the ranks of private geniuses under the Emperor Augustus (63–14 B.C.). Today's more common form of usage, *genius loci*, is usually a reference to the characterization of the spiritual climate and the charisma of a local unit.

Glass flux also glass paste: strong refractive lead glass used in the manufacture of imitation gems, especially imitation diamonds.

Guild (Low German): a cooperative association that has existed in Germanic countries and northern France since at least the 8th century A.D. Membership ensured legal protection for the individual, followed at a later stage by mutual welfare aid.

Gobelin (French) also wall tapestry: general term used since the 19th century for a tapestry carpet. The word "Gobelin" goes back to the Flemish carpet-making family of the same name, who worked in Paris in the 17th century and whose flourishing workshop was acquired by Henry IV (1553–1610) and became the royal Manufacture des Gobelins under Louis XIV in 1682.

Gothic (Italian *gotico*, "barbaric, not antique"): European style epoch of the Middle Ages that started in northern France ca. 1150, where it also ended ca. 1400, although it continued to the early 18th century elsewhere. The name is derived from the Germanic Goths. Specific architectural features were the peaked arch (an arch that is split at the apex) and the ribbed vault (right-angled intersection of two barrel vaults of the same size), and the repositioning of the flying buttresses (arches and supports that help to support the pressure on the abutment and roof load) to the outside. The build-

The god Horus as a falcon, 7th century B.C., Museo Gregoriano Egizio, Vatican, Rome

ings give the impression of soaring upward; the splitting up and lighting of walls and brick surfaces are other typical features. The cathedral (bishop's church) defines this style of building. The sculpture is largely linked to architecture. Another key feature is an idealized interpretation of nature. The interplay between bodies and vestments, usually shown as an elongated representation, is fundamental for the expression. Panel and glass painting are key items of Gothic art.

Greek temple (Latin *templum*, "area, room"): constructed to house the image of a deity in the cella; access was given only to the priests. Usually rectangular in construction, and based on a three-tiered plinth. Columns support a horizontal entablature consisting of a metope-triglyphic frieze which may be repeated on the cella. The cella is separated from the columns by a vestibule (pronaos). Topped by a flat gable roof, the pediments are decorated with reliefs. The layout is determined by the arrangement of the columns: Doric, Corinthian, or Ionic.

Griseille (French *gris*, "gray," and *grisailler*, "to paint gray"): gray-on-gray painting that deliberately dispenses with colored gradations and uses only stone colors or shades of brown or gray. It is particularly suited to the artistic representation of sculptural works.

Hathor (Egyptian *Ht-Hr*, "dwelling of Horus"): Egyptian goddess of ecstasy, inebriation, and joy, in the form of a cow or a woman with a cow's horns. Main cult site is Dendera. Hailed as the goddess of dance and love since the Middle Kingdom (2119–1794/1793 B.C.); also as the goddess of mining areas in Sinai, Byblos, and Nubia.

Hera: in Greek mythology the daughter of Cronos and Rhea, sister and spouse of Zeus, and mother of Ares, Hephaestus, and Hebe. Tormented by Zeus' infidelity, she opted for marital revenge. Generally seen as a statuesque, mature woman, she is the protector of marriage and birth.

Heros: usually translated as "hero;" in Greek a person who performs extraordinary deeds, later also a synonym for demigod. Probably dates back to primeval times. Heroes and the cult of Heros are first mentioned by the poet Hesiod (ca. 700 B.C.).

Hieroglyphics (Greek "sacred carved writing"): the Greek term, consisting of the words for "sacred" and "carved," for the Ancient Egyptian picture writing of the 2nd/3rd centuries B.C. The direction of writing results from inverting the representations of animals and humans. When the resemblance to writing is lost, the symbol becomes a character representing a word, syllable, or letter.

Hijrah (Arabic "flight") also Hegira: Mohammed's flight from Mecca to Medina on July 15 or 16, 622 A.D. The Muslim calendar dates from this event (anno hegirae).

Himation (Greek): usually an outer garment or coat, also worn by Roman gods. A long rectangle of cloth that is draped, perhaps with a tip on the left side of the chest and the remainder of the fabric wound over the left shoulder across the back to the right side of the body; the exact arrangement could vary according to the particular occasion.

Hittites: Indo-European tribes who in the 17th century B.C. from the fortification Hattusa (now Bogazköy) in northern Anatolia set up their first short-lived Hittite empire. In the 14th century B.C. the Hittite state became a major power that ruled Anatolia and Syria, and soon had the empire of Mitanni under its control. The Hittites became one of the most serious competitors with the Egyptians in their battle for control over Asia Minor in the 14th and early 13th centuries B.C. Under Ramesses II, and after serious battles, they finally reached a peaceful, treaty-based agreement. The Hittite Empire fell in the 12th century B.C.

Horus (Egyptian "distance"): name for a variety of usually hawk-headed gods. The history of the Horus cult goes back to pre-dynastic times. The last god to reign over Egypt according to Diodorus Siculus, who wrote a history of the world in Julius Caesar's time. Son of Isis and Osiris. Regarded by the Greeks as identical to Apollo. Supposed to have helped humanity with wise oracles and by healing the sick.

Humanism (Latin *humanus*, "human"): literary force developed in Italy from the mid-14th century which, with its basis in Antiquity, had human existence at its core. A key feature at the time of the Renaissance was man's emancipation from God. This was associated with a striving for new spiritual and hard scientific findings based on worldliness. Humanists commit themselves especially to the rediscovery and maintenance of the Greek and Latin languages and literature. Even today, the term refers to the supposedly ideal link between education based on traditional learning and a humanity that stems from a proximity to and close observation of reality.

Hundred Years War: name for the conflict between England and France, which took place on French soil, for supremacy in western Europe. Interrupted by the peace treaties of Brétigny (1380) and Troyes (1420) and countless cease-fires, it lasted from 1337 to 1453. First broke out when King Edward III of England (1312–1377) claimed the French crown from the house of Valois when the direct line to the Capets died out.

Hyksos (Greek form of the Egyptian *Heka-Chasut*, "chief of the nomadic tribes"): the term refers to the kings of Asian origin who ruled over Egypt for about 100 years as the 15th dynasty (ca. 1650–1540 B.C.). Based in the eastern Nile delta, where Syro-Palestinian tribes had long been living, they ruled over Egypt in the form of a number of satellite states. The Theban 17th dynasty (ca. 1650–1551 B.C.) drove the Hyksos from Egypt after a number of long battles and set up the New Empire.

Iconoclasm: during the Reformation, the battle against religious pictures in churches and the reverence with which they were treated. Opposing Karlstadt ("Von Abtuhung der Bilder" 1522), Martin Luther tried to balance Zwingli and Calvin, who radically rejected the admiration of pictures. The hatred of pictures developed most fiercely in the Netherlands (1588).

Iconography (Greek *eikon*, "picture," and *graphein*, "to describe"): the study of the content, sense, and symbolism of pictorial representations, especially in Christian art; originally the study of the portraiture of Antiquity.

Ikhnaton ("useful to Aton"): the name the Egyptian king Amenhotep IV (1351–1334 B.C.) gave himself after he introduced the monotheistic cult of the sun god Aton. The latter's temple was the center of Ikhnaton's residence Amarna in Middle Egypt. Relics unearthed there testify to the fundamental changes that took place in the style of art at the time.

Impressionism (French): a pictorial form of expression that flourished in France in the last quarter of the 19th century as a reaction to the rigid doctrines of the Academy and of studio, historical, and genre painting. The name is derived from a painting by Claude Monet entitled *Impression, Sunrise* (1872, Musée Marmoton, Paris), and was initially used in art criticism as a derogatory term for a group of artists that were excluded from the official Salon, who had their first group exhibition in the studio of Parisian photographer Nadar in 1874. As a new form of naturalism, Impressionism negates traditional picture means and, in a wholly revolutionary way, interprets the natural object solely through color.

Index fossil (mid-Latin *fossa*, "grave"): in geology, any fossil of wide geographical distribution and a short range of time, used to correlate and date rock strata and their associated fossils.

Inquisition (Latin *inquisitio*, "inquire"): instituted by the medieval Church for the persecution of heretics and as punishment; papal inquisitors were appointed after 1231 (Dominicans and Franciscans were preferred). The Inquisition became a papal institution (Sanctum Officium) under Pope Gregory IX (1227–1241) and with the decree issued in 1234; later extended to include other offences such as sorcery, witchcraft, and fortune-telling. Lifted by Napoleon in 1808, and finally abolished in 1859.

Isis (Greek version of the Egyptian name for *Iset*, *Ese*): Egyptian goddess who hailed from the Nile Delta; sister and spouse of Osiris and mother of Horus; first named in the 5th dynasty (2504/2454–2347/2287 B.C.). A polymorphic goddess, from the New Empire (1550–1070/69 B.C.), she was put on a level with Hathor, and was often represented with a headdress of cow's horns and a sun disc. She was regarded as the protector of the dead, the bringer of fertility, and the guarantor of the kingdom, and in time she became a powerful universal goddess.

Joan of Arc (1410/1412–1431) also known as the Maid of Orléans: saint and French national heroine who, from the age of 14, heard voices telling her to lead the French army against the English and secure the coronation of Charles VII (1403–1481) in Reims.

July Revolution: uprising by the residents of Paris that lasted from July 27 to 29, 1830. The height of the conflict between the Bourbon restoration and the liberal parliamentary majority, it ended with the deposition of Charles X (1757–1838).

Kaunakes (Babylonian): long-looped woven material used for a skirt; typical of the Mesopotamian sculptures of the so-called Early Dynasty to the Akkad era (ca. 2600–2200 B.C.).

Kore (Greek "girl"): more common name in Athens for Persephone; architectural name for caryatids.

Kouros (Greek "young man"): in ancient Greek sculpture the name for the figure of a naked youth.

Kunstkammer (German "art room"): a type of collection popular in the early modern period especially among

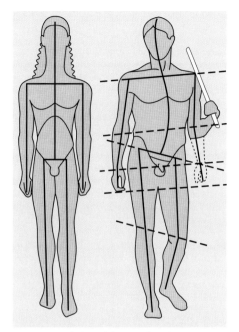

Contrapposto: balanced division of weight in an Archaic sculpture as compared with a Greek classic

high-ranking nobility, wealthy patricians, and scholars. The typical Kunstkammer collection had an encyclopedic character. Depending on the owner's intent and specialties, the Kunstkammer might include paintings, drawings, sculptures, books, and antique works of art, but also natural history objects, automata, and scientific equipment, and was meant to be a miniature reproduction of the world.

Lapidarium (Latin *lapis*, "stone"): a collection of stone memorials, tombstones, altars, and epitaphs – sometimes housed in the cloister of an abbey – or excavation findings left *in situ*.

Loggia (Italian): open archway supported by pillars or by columns.

Luster painting (French *lustre*, "shine," and Latin *lustrare*, "to make light"): extremely thin, metallic shimmering painting on glass, faience, or porcelain in different shades resulting from the particular copper or silver used. Red luster paint has been found on Egyptian sarcophagi. The luster technique was used in painting until well into the 17th century.

Lutrophore: term used in Greek ceramics to describe a type of vase that is used for the transportation of water, and in particular for the bridal bath. The lutrophore is identified by its long neck with correspondingly formed vertical handles that may be attached to the neck of the vase by crosspieces.

Maestà (Italian "majesty, throned in majesty"): term for the strict form of representation of the Mother of God and the Christ child surrounded by angels and saints. This motif is found predominantly in Italian art of the 13th and 14th centuries.

Majolica (Italian *maiolica*): the Italian name for faience, derived from that of the Spanish island of Majorca, via which the technique arrived in Italy in the 14th century and revitalized the ceramic craft that had already been flourishing in early times.

Mameluke (Arabic *malaka*, "to possess"): originally military slaves of Turkish, Caucasian, or Slavic origin who, from the 9th century, formed a large part of the armies in Islamic countries; later members of a ruling Egyptian dynasty (13th–16th centuries) under which Egypt rose to become one of the most powerful states in the Middle East.

Mannerism (French *manière*, "manner, way;" Latin *manuarius*, "of the hands"): period of art between the Renaissance and Baroque, approximately 1520/1530–1600. Mannerism dispenses with the ideal, harmonious shapes, proportions, and compositions developed in the Renaissance. Thus this style makes picture scenes more dynamic, and extends the human body and its representation in anatomically contradictory positions. It involves an excessive complication of compositions, an irrational and strongly theatricalized treatment of light, and a dissolution of the strict way in which light is bound to the object.

Marduk (Sumerian *Amar-Utuk* "young steer of the sun god"): first recorded mention ca. 2800 B.C.; after 2000 the Babylon city god, and at the height of its power the Empire god of the Babylonians (second half of the 2nd century). Marduk later became the rival of the Assyrian Empire god Assur, and was revered as chief deity under the name of Bel.

Mars (Etruscan *Maris*; ancient Latin *Marspiter, Maspiter, Mavors*): Italian deity after whom the month of March (originally the first month of the year) was named. Roman god of war (Ares to the Greek), son of Jupiter and Juno; according to Homer, Vulcan (Hephaestus) surprised Mars dallying romantically with Venus (Aphrodite), with whom he conceived the terrible brothers Deimos and Phobos, and according to other legends Amor, Anteros, and Harmonia as well.

Mercury: in Roman mythology, the messenger of the gods, and equivalent to the Greek Hermes. Mercury was the god of commerce, the spirit of godly endeavor and executor and organizer of world order for his father, Jupiter. He is usually represented in art as a handsome young man.

Mercy seat: art-historical term, first used by F.X. Kraus, inspired by Martin Luther, in his *History of Christian art* (1897), for a form of representation, known since the 12th century, of the Holy Trinity linked to Christ's suffering. God the Father is seated on a throne, holding the Cross with Christ crucified in both hands; the Holy Spirit, in the form of a dove, is hovering over His head.

Merovingian: Frankish line of kings whose name is derived from the otherwise unknown Merowech, who began the dynasty. It was not until the time of Clovis I (481–511), who overcame the west Roman rule in 486 by defeating the governor Syagrius, that the Merovingians temporarily assumed the control of the Frankish Empire (the region between the Somme and the Loire). However, it was effectively lost on the death of Dagobert I (reigned 629–639), and Pepin became the sole ruler of the Frankish empire in 751 when the last of the Merovingians, Childeric III, was deposed.

Metope: see Greek temple

Minoan art: Stone, Copper, and Bronze Age art on Crete. The term was coined by the archeologist Arthur John Evans (1851–1941) after the legendary King Minos. From the stratigraphic finds in Knossos, Minoan Art (ca. 2700–1100 B.C.) was divided into three main periods (early, middle, and late Minoan), each of which consists of three phases (I, II, and III). Egyptian vases, small sculptures, and scarabs found with the Cretan objects were used to establish an absolute chronology. The sparse finds of the so-called First Palace Period (ca. 2000–1700 B.C.) did not present any sort of continuous picture, and investigations and descriptions of Minoan art were based largely on finds from the Second Palace Period (ca. 1700–1400 B.C.), which was when Crete peaked economically, politically, and culturally. Palace architecture in Knossos, Phaestos, Malia, and Agia Triada, unfortified and some with wall paintings of great artistic significance, form economic centers of this peaceful culture with its highly developed knowledge and understanding of technology. Ceramics peaked in the late Minoan period I (ca. 1580–1480 B.C.), in which the lack of any form of human representation is a key feature of the so-called floral and sea styles; preferred shapes are the arched pot and funnel-shaped containers.

Minotaur: in Greek mythology the offspring of a bull and Pasiphaë; a hybrid, a human with a bull's head which, according to the legend, lived in the Labyrinth built by King Minos and killed seven youths and seven girls from Athens at nine-year intervals before finally being killed in a fight with Theseus.

Monolith (Greek "single stone"): component, building shape, or monument made from a single block of stone.

Muses: the Greek goddesses of poetry, music, dance, and the sciences, according to Hesiod (ca. 700 B.C.) supposedly the daughters of Zeus and Mnemosyne. Three at first: Melete, Mneme, Aoede, and later nine: Clio, Euterpe, Thalia, Melpomene, Terpsichore, Erato, Polyhymnia, Urania, and Calliope. Under the guidance of Apollo Musagetes, the god of song and music, they were responsible for branches of the arts and sciences.

Mythology (Greek *mythologia, mythos*, "word, talk," and *logos*, "teaching"): the totality of a people's mythological stories.

Necropole also Necropolis (Greek; "city of the dead"): extensive burial area of Antiquity consisting of tomb constructions; also found in the early Christian–Islamic period in Egypt and among Etruscan remains in Italy. In many cases provides an abundance of items of archeological importance.

Neo-Baroque also New Baroque: a historicizing style reflecting the Baroque, most popular during the second half of the 19th century. The French Neo-Baroque had the maximum international effect. It also contained style elements of the Italian-French Early Renaissance and became one of the state styles in the Second Empire under Napoleon III. Other key examples: Louis Visconti's (1791–1853) and Hector Lefuel's (1810–1880) extensions to the Louvre, and Théodore Ballu's (1817–1885) to the La Trinité church (1863–1867).

Neoclassicism also new classicism: term used in northwestern European countries to denote a move-

Hunefer Papyrus: Thoth at the Judgment of Death, 19th dynasty, ca. 1250 B.C., British Museum, London

ment of Western art that was based on Antiquity. Also used to describe historicizing 20th-century architectural trends involving the reappearance of colossal arrangements of pillars. Examples are from National-Socialist Germany (e.g. the Haus der Kunst in Munich) and Fascist Italy (e.g. Milan's main railroad station) and the 1930s architecture of France (e.g. the Musée d'Art Moderne, Paris, 1937).

New Kingdom: one of the main periods of Ancient Egyptian history (see also Dynasties) that encompassed the 18th to 20th dynasties (ca. 1550–1069 B.C.), from when Amenhotep III (1388–1351/50 B.C.), the most illustrious pharaoh of the 18th dynasty (1550–1292 B.C.), ascended the throne. His son, Amenhotep IV (1351–1334 B.C.), who called himself Ikhnaton, introduced various religious and artistic reforms, and built the palace located at Amarna.

Nike: known in literature since Hesiod (ca. 700 B.C.); goddess of victory who was revered especially in Olympia. She is the daughter of the Titan Pallas and the river Styx. Linked to Zeus and Athena following the battle of the Titans. As she resembles the personification of victory and competition, she wears a victor's wreath and is usually depicted with wings. The *Nike of Samothrace* is rightly revered.

Ningirsu ("Lord of Girsu"): main god of the Sumerian city of Girsu and the state of Lagash; his spouse was the goddess Baba, and his sisters included Nanshe and Nisaba. Like Ninurta, to whom he was subsequently frequently compared, Ningirsu was regarded as the son of the chief Sumerian god Enlil, and carried both the features of a warring deity and of a fertility god for agriculture. Ningirsu's symbolic animal is the lion-headed eagle Imgugud.

Old Kingdom: one of the main periods of Ancient Egyptian history (see Dynasties) covering the 3rd to 8th dynasties (ca. 2700–2200 B.C.) and which was an important step toward the classic Egyptian state. The vast pyramids were constructed in the 4th dynasty (2620–2500 B.C.) under Snefru.

Omayyad (Arabic *Al Umawijjun*): Arabian dynasty of the Islamic Empire who reigned as caliphs in Damascus (661–750 A.D.) and Cordoba (756–1030) and who were one of the leading families in Mecca at the time of Mohammed. In competition with Byzantine, an independent Islamic art developed under the Damascus-based branch of the caliphs. This was linked with the foundation of a number of cities (Basra, Kufa) and the construction of mosques (the large mosque in Kairouan) and of many desert palaces, some of which still survive (Quseir Amra).

Open-air painting also plein-air painting: painting outside under the open sky as opposed to painting in a studio, the idea being to capture realistically the natural features of a landscape and its moods. Following the example of English landscape artists such as John Constable (1776–1837) and Richard Parkes Bonington (1801–1828), in the mid-1900s, French artists, including members of the Barbizon School, began to paint in the open air.

Oriflamme (old French "gold flame;" mid-Latin *aurea flamma*): the two-pointed war banner of the French kings from the beginning of the 11th century to 1415.

Osiris: Egyptian god in human form but with an unjointed body; carried a crook and a whip. According to one legend, this god of dying and regenerating vegetation drowned; another has it that he was murdered by his brother. His sister and spouse Isis found his body, performed a number of special rites to bring it back to life, and posthumously conceived a son (Horus). In Egyptian mythology, the hope of reincarnation is linked to Osiris, the absolute god of the dead.

Ottoman Empire: name originating from Osman I Ghasi (1288–1326 A.D.), under whose rule the Byzantines were driven from western Asia Minor; abolished with the establishment of the Turkish republic (1922).

Pala (Italian "table"): altar picture or decoration, either sculpted or painted.

Pantheon (Latin *pantheum*; Greek: *pantheion*, "temple of all gods"): antique religious building with a vast dome and an eight-columned gabled hall. Rebuilt 115–125 A.D. under Emperor Hadrian (117–138) as a temple for worshiping all the gods. In 609 the building was consecrated as a Christian church. Used since the Renaissance as a burial place for men of stature.

Papyrus (from the Greek *papyros*, probably originating from an Egyptian expression meaning "that of the Pharaoh"): vast numbers of papyrus plants grew in Antiquity around the Nile delta; used for a wide range of crafts (mats, baskets, architecture, boats, sandals, etc.), but also for cult purposes (sacrifices). Because of its high symbolic value (freshness, fertility, regeneration), it became a design model for architectural forms and cult objects. However, it achieved its greatest significance when its pulp was processed to produce the writing material papyrus; known since the 1st dynasty (ca. 3000 B.C.).

Parament: (Latin *parare* "to prepare"): the often extremely ornate and valuable liturgical garment worn by the priest for a service and the cloth used for the altar, chancel, and liturgical instruments.

Parnassus (New Greek *Parnassos*): mountains to the east of central Greece falling away steeply toward the Kaphisos valley to the north; divided by a deep cleft near Mt. Giona. Toward the south, the Parnassus falls away to the lower Parnassus (1561 m) south of the pass road from Delphi to the Gulf of Corinth. Revered in Greek mythology of Apollo as the seat of the Muses.

Parthenon: marble Doric temple of Athena Parthenos and main temple of the Acropolis of Athens. Completed under Pericles (461–429 B.C.) and under the supervision of architects Ictinus and Callacrates after a number of earlier attempts that were not completed. The overall supervisor was the sculptor Phidias, who created an 11-meter-high (35 feet) gold-ivory picture of Athena

Parthenos for the structure. Most of the sculptures in this most famous building of classical Greece were sold to the British Museum in London by Lord Elgin in 1818 as the so-called "Elgin Marbles."

Paten (Greek "bowl"): the bowl used to serve the Eucharistic bread in a service, orthodox liturgy, and in the evangelical communion service.

Patron saint: the saint of a country, town, or city, church, profession, or association, or of an individual.

Peace of Westphalia: a peace agreement signed by a deputation of the Empire after initial discussions in separate places (Munster, Osnabrück) on October 24, 1648 to put an end to the Thirty Years' War (1618–1648).

Pegasus: in Greek mythology the offspring of Neptune (Poseidon) and Medusa, who came into the world at the very moment when Perseus decapitated her. A beautiful, sleek horse with mighty wings, Pegasus accompanied Jupiter, Aurora, and the Muses.

Peplos (Greek): woven woolen outer garment worn by Greek women, a cylindrical piece of cloth pinned on both sides of the neck.

Pharaoh: term based on the Egyptian Par-aa, meaning "large house." Known since earliest times to refer to the royal palace and its inhabitants. Has been used since the 18th dynasty (1550–1292 B.C.) to refer to the person of the king, and later as the title of a ruler.

Phoenicians (Greek *Phoinikes*): Semitic people inhabiting the historical land of Phoenicia on the Syrian-Lebanese Mediterranean coast since at least the 2nd century B.C.; important towns Byblos, Tyre, and Sidon, from where they traded with Cyprus, Egypt, and the Aegean area and contributed to active cultural exchanges with the Orient and Greece. Homer called the Phoenicians the Sidonians. Experienced seafarers, they traveled as far as the Atlantic Ocean and, according to legend, they were sent by Pharaoh Nekau to circumnavigate Africa.

Piano mobile (Italian): the main floor of a building, usually situated above the ground floor, containing the reception rooms.

Pietà (Italian "mercy;" Latin *pietas*, "piety") also Vesper picture (Latin "evening, evening star, west"): representation of the grieving Mother of God holding the body of Christ in her arms.

Pilaster (Italian *pilastro*; Latin *pila*, "pillar"): rectangular wall pillar, usually projecting, consisting of a base (foot), a shaft (middle part), and a capital (top part), that divides the wall. Often grooved, i.e. vertical grooves go down the middle.

Pleurant (French *pleurer*, "to cry"): a mourner who uses pathos to express grief over the death of a person. Some of the most impressive mourning figures in Western art are the mourning Pleureurs (also known as the Pleurants) by sculptor Claus Sluter (1355/60–1405/08) at the grave of Philip the Bold (1342–1404) in Dijon – a procession of grieving monks under tracery arcades along the high sides of the tomb.

Polyptych (Greek *polyptychos*, "having many folds"): a set of several panels (sculptured or painted altar decorations) with more than two wings. It is ideal for illustrating programs of extensive content.

Portrait (French *portrait*, "likeness;" from the Latin *potrahere*, "to produce"): in visual art the representation of a person or group of people by artistic, graphic, sculptural, or photographic means. The person being portrayed is usually made recognizable by the representation of certain physiognomic similarities or other attributes peculiar to the individual. Portraits can be idealized, often serving representative purposes, whereas others may reflect the individual's personality and character. There are numerous forms of expression, ranging from the miniature to cameos and minted coins, to paintings and larger-than-life portraits. Depending on the number of people, we speak of single, double, or group portraits, and also make a distinction between types such as full-figure, half-figure, bust, and head portraits.

Poseidon: the Greek god of the sea and waters, identified by the Romans with Neptune; son of Cronus and brother of Zeus, father of the Cyclops Polyphemus and spouse of Amphitrite. As the god of conquerors, he banished several pre-Hellenic deities, including Hera from Argos, Demeter from Arcadia, and Athena from Attica; the trident in the Erechtheion is a reminder of the contest. The Tritons and Nereids formed the retinue for this god, who shattered the earth and made the seas foam.

Predella (Italian "footstool"): plinth-like substructure to a winged altar, used partly for the storage of relics (religious objects or body parts of a saint). Often decorated with pictorial representations.

Psyche (Greek "soul"): often represented in Antiquity as a bird or butterfly. According to the writings of Apuleius (Metamorphoses, 2nd century), Psyche, the beautiful daughter of a king, invoked Aphrodite's jealousy, who then ordered her son Eros to punish her rival. He, however, fell in love with Psyche, but it was only by Zeus' intervention that the two were finally bound to each other forever.

Ptolemy: ruling Hellenic dynasty in Egypt (323–330 B.C.). The politics of the Ptolemys were defined by state monopoly, the promotion of manufacturing and trade, and the conversion of the palace at Alexandria into an important economic and cultural center (including the famous Library).

Putto (Italian "little boy;" Latin *putus* "boy"): a small naked boy, either with or without wings, and an inven-

tion of the early Italian Renaissance, based on Gothic child angels and the example of the antique Cupids.

Pyramid (Greek): name for a four-sided building with triangular sides and built on a square base; the graves of the Egyptian kings at the time of the Old and Middle Kingdoms (ca. 2707/2657–1794/83 B.C.). With an angle of inclination of 52°, the pyramid of Cheops at Giza has the "ideal" shape for a pyramid, and is also the biggest Egyptian construction of this kind.

Pyx (Greek): small cylindrical container, usually made of ivory (occasionally silver or bronze), often with a decorated lid; probably imported originally from Constantinople and Alexandria. The few remaining examples date back to the 4th to 7th centuries A.D., and are decorated with figural reliefs of mythological and biblical content. Used since the 9th century to refer to the box used to store and hand out the wafers of the sacrament; the original shape of the ivory pyx has been retained.

Qajars: a ruling Persian dynasty (1794–1925) founded by Agha Mohammed Khan (1742–1797), a leader of the Turkmen tribe of the Qajars, that reconstituted Iran after the fall of the Safavids and the tumult of the 18th century, although in general it was more a period of political decline.

Reformation (Latin *reformatio*, "renovation, re-formation"): movement initiated (1517) by the theses of Martin Luther (1483–1546) and the subsequent disputations of Heidelberg and Leipzig to reform the Roman Church, which, after major theological discussions, resulted in the dissolution of Western Church unity and the formation of the Protestant Church.

Regalia (Latin *regalis*, "royal, of a monarch"): term that was introduced in the 11th century A.D. to delineate between worldly and spiritual power regarding rights that were reserved for the king. In France, the Régalé, the right to regalia, declared that the king was free to use the income from vacant bishoprics in the crown domain and dispose over their benefices (land, goods).

Relic (Latin *reliquiae*, "remains"): body part of some divine or saintly person or object closely associated with a saint, to which particular reverence is shown.

Renaissance (French; Italian *rinascimento*, "rebirth"): progressive cultural epoch of the 15th and 16th centuries that started in Italy. The later stage, ca. 1530 to 1600, is also called Mannerism. The name refers back to the term *rinascità* (rebirth) coined in 1550 by Giorgio Vasari (1511–1574), which initially referred only to medieval art. The dominating ideal of the *uomo universale*, of a spiritually and physically multitalented, highly educated person, developed through Humanism, which called on the examples of Antiquity to promote the ideal of a new picture of humanity, the world, and nature. The best known example is Leonardo da Vinci (1452–1519). The visual arts moved from being regarded as a craft into free art, which in turn gave artists a higher status and a certain self-awareness. Art and science were directly linked, each affecting the other, as in the discovery of mathematically calculable perspectives or anatomical structures. Architecture referred back to the architectural theories of Vitruvius (ca. 84 B.C.), and was marked fundamentally by the inclusion of Antique building elements and the development of palace and castle architecture. Centralized building design was typical of the period.

Retable (French *retable*, *rétable*; Latin *retabulum* "back"): object with sculpted or painted altar pictures that is set behind or on the back wall of the altar table.

Risalit (Italian *risalto*, "projection"): center part of a facade, highly popular in Baroque and 19th-century architecture, in which one element projects, to its full height, from the building line.

Rocaille (French "scree, grotto, shellwork"): asymmetrical wave- and shell-patterned decorations in the Rococo.

Rococo (French *rocaille*, "scree, grotto, shellwork"): European period of art between 1710/1730 and 1770/1780. Characteristic is a style of decoration that incorporates small pieces and playful designs. This is emphasized in art by the use of a light palette.

Roller seal: cylindrical seal, widely used in the Near East and Egypt, especially during the 3rd century B.C., with cut-out shapes and texts that were rolled onto the object being sealed (frequently clay seals).

Roman Empire: in Antiquity the extent of ruling of the Roman emperor, which included the provinces as well as Rome and Italy, and expanded most under Emperor Trajan (98–117 A.D.) by incorporating the provinces of Dacia, Arabia, Mesopotamia, Armenia, and Assyria.

Romanesque (from the Latin *Romanus*, "Roman"): term introduced in France in the first third of the 19th century for the Western style of building of the early Middle Ages that was based on the forms of Roman architecture (round arches, columns, pillars, vaults). In different countries, it encompasses the period from ca. 1000 to the middle of the 13th century. Replaced by the early Gothic in central France in the middle of the 12th century. Each region developed its own particular version and style features. The Romanesque style was most widely developed in Burgundy, Normandy, upper Italy, and Tuscany. Used mainly in the construction of churches. Typical: the addition of individual sculptural elements and the pure interplay between cylindrical and cubic shapes.

Romanticism: epoch of European, especially German spiritual life, literature, and visual art that replaced the Enlightenment, classicism, and classics at the end of the 18th century and was marked by emphasis on the emotions, the wonderful, fabulous, and fantastica. In art, the revitalization of medieval myths, fairytales, and history opened up new subjects. Landscape painting was one particular expression of the devotion to an inner world. Romanticism arrived in England and in

Germany before it reached France; its main sphere was in fact historical art. Inspired by the colors of Peter Paul Rubens (1577–1640), Eugène Delacroix (1798–1863) highlighted new concerns, enriching art by adding exotic themes from the Orient. By concentrating on pictorial problems, the art of Camille Corot (1796–1875) and

Rotunda (Latin *rotundus*, "round, rounded"): a small construction over a circular base; also a circular room inside a large complex.

Sacra conversazione (Italian "holy conversation"): form of representation of the dignified gathering of

Salvator mundi: Arles, St-Trophime, tympanum of the west portal, end of the 12th century

the School of Barbizon artists revealed a tendency toward the Romantic.

Rood screen (Middle English *rode*, from Old English *rod*, "cross"): a partition between the nave and the chancel of a church with one or more openings and a platform accessible by stairs from which the Gospel is read.

Mary and a number of saints. The term is confusing, since no actual conversation is represented.

Safavid: Persian dynasty (1501–1722 A.D.) that united the Iranian highlands under the Shia branch of Islam, and under which the arts and architecture flourished. It peaked under Abbas I the Great (1587–1629).

St. Anne with Mary and the Child Jesus: a picture motif that occurred in the late-medieval Anna cult depicting St. Anne, her daughter the Virgin Mary, and the baby Jesus.

Salvator mundi (Latin "saviour of the world"): special way of representing Christ in late medieval art that was particularly prevalent in early Netherlandish paintings. The Savior is shown as a half figure, His right hand

Satyr: Sir Anthony van Dyck, Jupiter as a Satyr with Antiope, ca. 1620, Wallrauf-Richartz-Museum, Cologne

raised in blessing and holding a glass globe of the world in his left, following the image of the Vera icon. The image is also common in architecture. The term places Christ's act of saving and his deeds at the center.

Sarcophagus (Greek "meat-eater"): lavishly decorated coffin, made of wood, metal, clay, or stone.

Sassanids: Persian dynasty, descendants of Sasan, a caliph of Persia who presided over the shrine of the goddess Anahita in Ishtar near Persepolis, which goes back to the Achaemenids. Artaxerxes, the founder of the dynasty, centralized the empire's power, and involved the Romans in fierce battles. As the result of his victory over the Roman emperors, Gordian, Philip the Arab, and Valerian, the Sassanid Shapur I (242–271 A.D.), became an ally of Germania. The dynasty was destroyed by the Arabs in 651.

Satyr: playful, lustful, comic creature that attended the god Dionysus (Bacchus). Although seen in human form, satyrs often have the ears, tail, and hooves of a horse or goat. An older satyr is known as a silenus.

Sedes sapientiae (Latin "throne of wisdom"): representation of Mary seated on Solomon's throne – a large armchair with six steps up to it – as the personification of wisdom. According to the description in the Bible (1 Kings 10, 18–20), the chair is made of ivory and upholstered in gold. The armrests are formed by two lions, and the steps flanked by six further pairs of lions.

Seljuks: old Turkish dynasty in northern Asia (1040–1157 A.D., in Anatolia until 1308); founded by Seljuk (ca. 1000), a sultan of the Ogusa.

Seraph (Hebrew *saraph*, "snake"): six-winged being which in Isaiah's vision (chapter 6) surrounded Jehovah. According to unidentified author Pseudo-Dionysus, the seraphim are the highest of the angel choirs.

Shamash: Akkadian name for the sun god, and also the name for the deified sun. According to Akkadian belief, the son of Anu and sometimes of Enil and brother of Ishtar. Shamash was also the term used for the sun, which is still used today in the Arabic word *as-Sams*.

One of the most important gods in the Babylonion-Assyrian pantheon, Shamash was the protector of justice and right, and oracle and recipient of countless hymns, prayers, and invocations.

Shrine: a wooden container or cupboard, or the fixed center part of an altar. Traditionally, shrines also contain holy relics.

Sibyl: a prophetess who, by contrast with a godly oracle, foretells the future, usually misfortune, without having to be asked. Oriental in origin, the best known of the sybils of Antiquity lived in a grotto in Cumae. She is believed to have written the Sibylline Books, a collection of prophecies, which were destroyed in the fire at the temple of Jupiter (83 B.C.), but were continued and moved to the temple of Apollo under Augustus.

Song of Songs also "Canticum Canticorum" (Latin): Old Testament collection of old Jewish love and wedding songs compiled by Solomon.

Sphinx (Greek): a creature with a lion's body and a human head. In the Old Kingdom in Egypt (from 2575 B.C.) there were numerous examples of the sphinx as sculptures, reliefs, and in paintings. In most cases they are representations of the king – which is why the word "sphinx," which is feminine in Greek, is often masculine in Egyptology. The best-known example is the great sphinx of Giza, which dates back to the 4th dynasty (ca. 2620–2500 B.C.). In the New Kingdom, sphinxes were positioned on both sides of a processional route; this was also known as a sphinx alley. Sphinxes of the god Amun were created in Thebes, consisting of a ram's head on a lion's body.

Stele (Greek): upright stone plate (wood was frequently used later), usually rectangular in shape. The top is often semicircular. Steles were often used as the bases for texts and pictures, i.e. for memorials to the dead or for public records of particular events or contracts. Steles are often huge, and were frequently used at the gates and in the courtyards of temple sites.

Sun King (French *Roi soleil*): Louis XIV of France; the name came from the sun emblem adopted by the king in 1682, who was born on a Sunday.

Supraporte (Italian from the Latin *supra* and *porta*, "above the door"): a painting or relief, situated above the door to a room, framed to suit the door surrounds, and often forming a decorative unit with it. Especially popular in elegant Baroque and Rococo living rooms.

Synagogue (Greek "gathering, community"): originally a gathering place and school for Jews rather than a place of worship. Other than the interior fittings used for the religion (chancel, lectern, ark), the synagogue does not fit any particular building type. In the time of the Roman Empire (3rd–7th century A.D.), and especially in Galilee, it was a three-winged flat-roofed building, initially based on the secular Roman basilica, but in the Middle Ages and early modern times contemporary regional style elements were adopted.

Tapestry (French "wall carpet"): the name for woven, embroidered, or knitted wall hangings or furniture coverings with pictorial decorations. The technique of threading the tapestry design into the warp with various shades of yarn to create a picture is one of the oldest textile inventions. Objects found in the tomb of Pharaoh Tuthmosis confirm that this particular technique was known at least as early as 1400 B.C. It was developed further, and the art of carpet-weaving peaked in the major Gobelin and carpet-weaving centers in France under Louis XIV (1638–1715) and Louis XV (1710–1774).

Thermal spring (Greek *thermos*, "warm"): warm baths such as existed in Roman times in almost every town; large, luxurious public buildings. The centers of the Antique thermal spas, which often also included a sports hall, rooms for entertainment, reading, and lectures, were the frigidarium with the piscina (cold water swimming pool), the lukewarm tepidarium, and the hot caldarium.

Tiras (Arabic *tiraz*, "to embroider"): name for the textile workshops in the Islamic countries between the Omayyad and Mameluke periods that served primarily to provide the textiles for the caliph's courts and the aristocracy and nobility. Also the name for the products made in these workshops, especially the embroidered inscriptions.

Toga (Latin): Roman outer garment that after imperial times was worn only on festive and official occasions, and replaced by the pallium. The toga dates back to the Etruscans, who had been wearing coats with a rounded bottom hem since the end of the 6th century B.C. In early imperial times, garments became fuller and longer, consisting of greater amounts of fabrica.

Tondo (Italian "sphere, plate;" Latin: *rotundus*, "round"): a painting or relief (sculptured representation on a flat surface) of a circular form.

Torso (Italian "trunk"): originally an unfinished or incompletely preserved ancient statue. Since the 16th century, the torso has also existed as a sculptural design in which the head or arms have deliberately been omitted. In a structural context, nowadays we also speak of, for example, a building torso.

Triglyph: see Greek temple

Triptych (Greek *triptychos*, "three-layered, three-fold," from *tri-*, "three" and *ptyche*, *ptyx*, "fold, layer, folded object"): a three-part painting with related content in all three parts. Originally a term used for a medieval winged altar with a fixed center panel and side leaves that could be moved.

Triumphal arch: originally an arch of honor constructed for a Roman emperor or military leader in the shape of a freestanding arch construction with one or three

passageways through. Decorated with reliefs, structural sculptures, and inscriptions giving the reason for the dedication. Prominent examples are the Titus arch, the Septimus Severus arch, and Constantine's arch in Rome. Much use was made of this type of construction in Baroque and classicism, especially in France, and

Belvedere Torso, 1st century B.C., marble, Museo Pio-Clementino, Rome

often in connection with routes where parades take place. The main example is the Arc de Triomphe, the Triumphal Arch in Paris, which was built at the time of Napoleon and completed in 1836.

Trumeau (French): originally the name for the central stone pillar of a portal supporting the tympanum; later also used to describe a stone wall pillar located between two windows.

Tympanum (Greek "drumskin, drum"): recessed area over a portal or the surface in a gable.

Veduta (Italian "view"): type of landscape painting. Generally a strict, true representation of a landscape or town, as opposed to the *veduta ideata*, a type of painting which consists of fantasy landscapes or views of a town with imaginary buildings.

Venus: the goddess of horticulture and fertility; later equivalent to the Greek Aphrodite and thus also the goddess of (sexual) love, who emerged victorious from a beauty contest with Hera and Athena (the so-called Judgment of Paris). As the epitome of female beauty, she was the most frequently portrayed female mythological figure from ancient times until the 19th century.

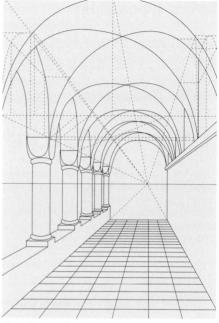

Central perspective

Vizier (Arabic): general term for an Egyptian title denoting the highest minister of state. The vizier was at the top of the Egyptian bureaucracy. Appointed by the king, he deputized for him in every aspect of administration and jurisdiction, managing the royal building works, and so on. A position that has been occupied since the early Old Kingdom, the office was divided into an upper and lower Egyptian vizier's council by the 18th dynasty (1550–1292 B.C.) based in Thebes and Memphis.

Votive picture (Latin *votivus*, "praised, blessed"): picture donated to a saint or to God in thanks for being saved from danger, in support of a plea, or in gratitude for a prayer answered.

Zeus: in classical times the highest and most powerful god of the Greeks, spouse of Hera; his children included Athena, Apollo, Artemis, Ares, and Dionysus. According to legend, he was born and raised in secret on Mount Ida on Crete since Cronus, his father, was prone to murdering his offspring. The adult Zeus deprived Cronus of his power and shared the acquired domain with Poseidon (the sea) and Hades (the underworld), who received the sea and the underworld in turn.

Artists' biographies

Arcimboldo, Giuseppe (1527 Milan – 1593 Milan) studied under his father and worked in his studio until 1559. Court painter in Prague 1562–1587, where he produced his best-known allegorical pictures in which fruit, plants, and similar objects develop stylistically into lively pictures.

Baldovinetti, Alesso (1425 Florence – 1499 Florence) was an important exponent of the early Renaissance in his hometown. He followed the example of his teachers: namely Domenico Veneziano, Fra Angelico, Andrea del Castagno and Piero della Francesca, whose achievements he linked at a high level. Later artists such as Ghirlandaio, Pollaiuolo and Verrocchio were inspired by his works.

Baldung, Hans, known as "Grien" (1484/85 ? Schwäbisch-Gmünd – 1545 Strasbourg) probably trained somewhere on the Upper Rhine and was apprentice to Dürer in Nuremberg 1503/07. Established himself as a master in Nuremberg in 1510. In Freiburg i. Br. 1512–1518. Although his religious paintings were rooted in the Middle Ages, his mythological and allegorical motifs and nudes were evidence of his humanistic thinking.

Bellini, Jacopo Bellini, Jacopo (1400 Venice – 1470/71 Venice), father of Giovanni Bellini. Studied under Gentile da Fabriano. Followed his teacher to Florence from 1423 to 1425. Worked mainly in Venice. His style marked the transition in Venetian art from the soft medieval style to the early Renaissance. Also an important sketcher, as is evident from his books of sketches on display in the Louvre.

Bernini, Gianlorenzo (Giovanni Lorenzo; 1598 Naples – 1680 Rome) studied under his father, a sculptor and painter, and accompanied him to Rome in 1605. Initially sponsored by the Borghese family, then became the papal sculptor and architect under the popes Urban VIII, his main sponsor, and Innocent X, Alexander VII, and Clement IX. His extensive sculptural oeuvre

Gianlorenzo Bernini, Self-portrait as a Youth, 1623, Galleria Borghese, Rome

included works in every style. Played a key role in determining the Baroque appearance of the city of Rome as the designer of St. Peter's Basilica and of other churches and a number of fountains.

Bonington, Richard Parkes (1801 Arnold, near Nottingham – 1828 London), trailblazer of realistic landscape art. Studied watercolor in Calais. He went to Paris in 1818, where he met Théodore Géricault and Eugène Delacroix. Found early success in France, but returned ill from a journey to Italy in 1828 and died a short while later. His feeling for nature and the freshness and the spontaneity of his style influenced Constable and the Barbizon School.

Bosch, Hieronymus (ca. 1450 s'Hertogenbosch – 1516 s'Hertogenbosch), born Hieronymus van Aken into a family of artists. Was famous in his own time, and received important commissions for paintings, stained-glass windows, and decorative works. His usually religious works are noted for an independent, hard to categorize symbolism. They reflect the gray, extravagant fantasies of seriously frightened people. The effect is reinforced by peculiar creatures that turn into grotesques, and are also satirical portrayals of the customs and manners of his time.

Botticelli, Sandro (1444 Florence – 1510 Florence), born Alessandro di Mariano Filipepi; worked mainly in his hometown. Student of Lippi, and strongly influenced by Verrocchio and Pollaiuolo. Botticelli developed an atmospheric, Antique style of mythological pictures. Received important motivation from the circle of Humanists around Lorenzo de' Medici, his main client.

Boucher, François (1703 Paris – 1770 Paris), one of the main exponents of Rococo in France. Influenced most by his teachers Lemoyer and Watteau. His sparkling career at the Academy commenced after a trip to Italy from 1727 to 1731, whose director he also became before being made the king's first painter in 1765. His decorative works with mythological and social motifs and his erotic pictures radiate beauty and a *joie de vivre* that matched the prevailing taste at court, but also found considerable criticism from the populace.

Bruegel (Breugel), Pieter the elder (ca. 1525 ?Breda – 1589 Brussels) joined the Guild of Artists in Antwerp in 1551. Traveled to Italy the following year, returning probably in 1555. Settled in Brussels in 1583 and joined the circle of Humanists around the scholar and poet Dirck Volkertsen Coornhert. His landscapes were reminiscent of Patenir, the grotesqueness of them of Bosch. He made his name with his evocative farming scenes, which earned him the nickname of "Farmer Bruegel."

Canova, Antonio (1757 Possagno/Treviso – 1822 Venice) joined the workshop of sculptor Giuseppe Torretti when only 11 years of age, and later studied at the Venetian Academy of Art under Michelangelo and Gregorio Morlaiter. In 1779 he traveled to Rome, where he spent most of his working life. Canova's sensual figures, cool and elegant in satin-smooth marble, were based on those of Antiquity and were highlights of Italian Classicism.

Caravaggio (ca. 1571 Milan – 1610 Porto Ercole), real name Michelangelo Merisi. Studied under Simone Peterzano in Milan from 1584 to 1588, then worked in Caravaggio near Bergamo. From ca. 1592 he was in Rome, where he soon found sponsors at the papal court. Because of his unconventional lifestyle, he spent the last few years of his life running from the Roman authorities. In addition to the highly realistic figural representation, his works are characterized by a strong element of chiaroscuro and demarcation, and this influenced countless later artists all over Europe.

Caron, Antoine (1521 Beauvais – 1599 Paris) was an important exponent of the School of Fontainebleau. He probably developed his typically mannered style under Abbate and Primaticcio. Catherine de' Medici, who appointed him court painter in 1581, was one of his main patrons. Typical of Caron's decorative style are his groups of figures in expansive scenes, extended and delicately moving bodies, and strong light effects.

Champaigne, Philippe de (1602 Brussels – 1674 Paris) completed his training under Jacques Fouquières, a member of Rubens' studio; then worked in Paris from 1621, where he was influenced by Nicolas Poussin. From 1628 he served Marie de' Médicis, the Queen Mother, and afterwards Louis XIII and Cardinal Richelieu. He created numerous portraits and religious works that combined elements of the French and Flemish styles.

Chardin, Jean-Baptiste Siméon (1699 Paris – 1779 Paris) studied under various different historical artists from 1720. Joined the Guild of St. Luke in 1724 and the Académie Royale in 1728, where he held a number of important offices until 1774. Chardin preferred still lifes and genre works, which were not generally appreciated at the time, but which he helped to make more popular. His style is identified by its finely graded coloring and pared-down compositions.

Jean-Baptiste Siméon Chardin, Self-portrait at his Easel, pastel, ca. 1778/79, Musée du Louvre

Chessériau, Théodore (1819 El Limón, S. Barbara de Samana, Dominican Republic – 1856 Paris) studied in Ingres' studio in Paris from 1830 to 1834. Exhibited at the Salon of 1838 for the first time. Study trips to the South of France, Italy (1840 – 1841), Algeria (1846), and the Netherlands (1856). Produced mainly historical paintings and portraits, but also murals in Paris. Stylistically, his work was between that of Ingres and Delacroix.

Cimabue (ca. 1240 – ?1302), real name Cenno di Pepo. Probably trained at the Baptistery mosaic workshop in Florence, graduating ca. 1260. There is evidence that he was in Rome in 1272 and in Pisa 1301/02. Cimabue tried to break down the stylized formal language of Byzantine art by demonstrating the plasticity and movement of the figures. His thinking made him one of the trailblazers of new Italian art before Giotto.

Cima da Conegliano (1459/60 Conegliano – 1517/18 Conegliano), real name Giovanni Battista Cima. Worked mainly in Venice after 1492. Found his own style at an early stage, one which thematically and artistically resembled Bellini's. The well-balanced composition, emotional moods, brilliant colors, and close observation of nature are characteristic of his representations, which were mainly Madonnas.

Claesz, Pieter (1597/98 Burgsteinfurt, Westphalia – 1660 Haarlem). There is evidence that he was in Haarlem from 1617. After his early still lifes, which consisted of numerous objects in rows, seen from a high point of observation, the artist continued to develop in parallel with Willem Claesz. The name of his "monochrome banketje," a type of breakfast still life, was derived from the brown-gray palette; the content, in contrast to the abundant Flemish type, was pared down to a minimum.

Clouet, Jean (ca. 1480 Brussels or Tours – ca. 1540/41 Paris) worked in Tours first, where he was in the service of Francis I (1494–1547) from 1518. His art, which had a strong Dutch tone to it, combined elements of the Gothic and the Early Renaissance. He was stimulated as much by the School of Fontainebleau as by the Italian Mannerists.

Constable, John (1778 East Bergholt, Suffolk – 1837 London) was self-taught. He worked as a topographer in London before attending courses at the Royal Academy from 1799, becoming a member in 1829. After a trip to Italy in 1819 he concentrated on landscapes, finding inspiration in the works of the Old Dutch masters as well as that of Thomas Girtin and Lorrain. With his uneven, tonal style of painting, he attempted to capture the atmosphere of light in nature. Constable's realistic style of landscape painting provided important inspiration in France for the Barbizon School and later for the Impressionists.

Corot, Jean-Baptiste Camille (1796 Paris – 1875 Paris) studied in the early 1820s under the Classicist landscape painter Victor Bertin, among others. Trained in the style of Poussin, he also worked outdoors. His work was influenced strongly by a long stay in Rome. Corot's landscapes are noted for their strong composition, the detail, and a new understanding of changing light. His later works, produced after the late 1840s and misty in atmosphere, are similar to the Barbizon School.

Correggio (1489 Correggio, Modena – 1534 Correggio), real name Antonio Allegri; worked in Rome and Parma as well as in his hometown. He adopted style elements of earlier artists of the High Renaissance, especially Mantegna's spatial illusionism and Leonardo's sfumato, and was also inspired by Raphael and Michelangelo, combining everything in a highly original manner. In his dynamic style of composition, the soft modeling of the shapes, and the lively yet appealing expressions of the figures, Correggio paved the way for Baroque and later art styles.

David, Gerard (ca. 1450 Oudewater, Gouda – 1523 Bruges) probably trained in his home country of Holland before settling in Bruges (Flanders) in 1484 as a free master. A follower of Momling, he became one of the city's most successful painters, eventually expanding to Antwerp, where he was accepted in the Guild of Artists in 1515. With its highly detailed Realism, his work typified that from the northern Netherlands, although David's later work reflected the confrontation with the Italian High Renaissance.

David, Jacques-Louis (1748 Paris – 1825 Brussels) is the most famous exponent of French Classicism. On the advice of his friend Boucher, he went to study under Joseph Vien in 1766. His studies of Roman Antiquity during his first visit to Rome (1775–1780) provided his main impulses. David was also interested in politics and became an active Jacobin in the Artists of the French Revolution. He later joined Napoleon, who appointed him official painter in 1804. Went into exile in Belgium in 1818 after the emperor was overthrown.

Delacroix, Eugène (1798 St-Maurice-Charenton near Paris – 1883 Paris) based the style of his work on Rubens and Veronese while studying in Paris. Also inspired by Constable. In London in 1825. Traveled to North Africa and southern Spain in 1832. Delacroix was the leading artist of the French Romantics. His concepts developed

Camille Corot, Self-portrait of the Artist at his Easel, (?)1825, Musée du Louvre

from flowing colors, moving away from the "official" Classicism and smoothing the way for Impressionism.

Domenichino (1581 Bologna – 1841 Naples), real name Domenico Zampieri. Worked mainly in Rome before moving to Naples in 1530. One of the leading followers of the Carracci, particularly of Annibale Carracci, with whom he worked in Rome from 1502. Together with Correggio, Raphael, and Caravaggio, he developed an independent style of which Classical purity and monumental expressiveness are typical.

Donatello (ca. 1388 Florence – 1489 Florence), real name Donato di Niccolo di Betto Bardi. Probably studied under Lorenzo Ghiberti and Nanni di Banco in Florence. Worked mainly in his hometown, but also in Sienna, Rome, Padua, and other towns in Italy. Donatello is considered to be the greatest sculptor of the

Quattrocento. No other artist of the age exceeded his extensive oeuvre in variety or innovation. In the early stage of his career he created mainly marble statues; from the 1420s mainly bronze sculptures.

Dürer, Albrecht (1471 Nuremberg – 1528 Nuremberg) learned the goldsmith's art under his father. Moved to Michael Wolgemut in 1488, who introduced him to the art of Schongauer and the Dutch. Was greatly inspired by his trips to Italy in 1494 and 1505/05 by Mantegna and the Bellinis. Dürer became the leading intermediary between the art of southern and northern Europe, creating the foundations for the German High Renaissance at the same time. Not only was his art of importance; so too were his prints and essays on the theory of art.

Dyck, Sir Anthony van (1599 Antwerp – 1641 London) and Rubens were the two leading Flemish artists. Worked in Rubens' workshop from 1617 for several years. First visited London in 1620, and traveled through Italy from 1621 to 1627, where he was inspired by the works of Titian and others. On his return he became court painter of Archduchess Isabella, the governess of the Netherlands. Joined the court of Charles I of England in 1632. Van Dyck developed the type of representation of the nobility that influenced English portrait painting in particular.

Eugène Delacroix, Self-portrait, ca. 1840 or 1860, Galleria degli Uffizi, Florence

El Greco (1541 Phodele, Crete – 1814 Toledo), "the Greek," real name Domenicos Theotokopoulos. Main exponent of Spanish Mannerism. A trained painter of icons, he joined Titian in Venice in 1567. In Rome from 1570, before finally settling in Toledo around 1577. The mystical radiance of his works, which reflect the spirit of Spain's medieval-inspired belief, was achieved by elongating the figures, adopting a strong chiaroscuro, and unrealistic coloring.

Eyck, Jan van (ca. 1390 Maaseyck, Maastricht? – 1441 Bruges) began his career as court painter to John of Bavaria, count of Holland. After the count died in 1425, van Eyck was in service to Philip the Good, duke of Burgundy. Made several trips to Spain and Portugal. Became town painter in Brussels in 1430. Van Eyck's

Italian School, Portrait of Donatello (Detail), 16th century, Musée du Louvre

painting, which had a lasting influence on European art, exhibited a previously unachieved illusionistic forcefulness. Objects were represented down to the tiniest detail of material consistency and light effects, the colors given a new kind of luminescence and depth thanks to further developments in oil technology.

Flegel, Georg (1563 Olomonc – 1638 Frankfurt am Main) was Germany's first artist to specialize in still lifes. By 1594 he was working in Frankfurt with the Flemish artist Lucas van Valckenborch. His early works appear to consist of small pieces, and to be constructed additively, whereas his later ones – paintings of meals and still lifes of flowers – consisted of fewer objects, and were denser compositions in sensitive colors.

Fouquet, Jean (ca. 1415/1420 Tours? – 1478/1481 Tours) was the first painter from the north to adopt the achievements of the Italian Early Renaissance, which he combined with elements of Flemish late Gothic in his works. His paintings were rooted in Franco-Flemish book paintings. During a trip to Italy in ca. 1445/1447, he adapted his work to the styles of Florentine painters such as Fra Angelico. Back in Tours, he worked for the French court under Charles VII and Louis XI, who appointed him court painter in 1475. As well as book illustrations, he produced panel, glass, and enamel paintings.

Fra Angelico (ca. 1395 Vicchio di Mugello, Florence – 1455 Rome) was really Guido di Piero. At 20, already a trained artist, he entered the monastery of the Dominicans in Fiesole. He was renamed Fra Giovanni, later also Fra Angelico or Beato Angelico. In 1436 he moved with the monastery to S. Marco in Florence. In 1447/48 and again from 1452 he worked for the papal court in Rome; also worked in Orvieto. Increasingly, he adopted the new Renaissance shapes in his frescoes and panelings, while the consistency of his sculptures was a key feature of his own style.

Fragonard, Jean-Honoré (1732 Grasse, Provence – 1806 Paris) was a student of Chardin and Boucher. In 1752 he won the Académie's Prix de Rome and became one of the Ecole des Elèves protégés. In addition, he won a

Sir Anthony van Dyck, Self-portrait, ca. 1622/23, The Hermitage, St. Petersburg

scholarship to Rome, and stayed there from 1756 to 1761. On his return he became a member of the Paris Académie. With Watteau and Boucher, Fragonard was considered one of the leading portrayers of the customs and manners of the end of French Absolutism. A Rococo artist, he remained committed to pre-Revolutionary aesthetics throughout his life.

Füssli, Johann Heinrich known as Henry Fuseli (1741 Zurich – 1825 Putney Hill, London). He had to leave Zurich because of his liberal attitudes, and went to England. He worked as a writer before Reynolds persuaded him to turn to painting, and studied in Italy. In 1799 he became a member, and in 1804 the Keeper of the Royal Academy. Füssli preferred literary materials for his Romantic/Classical style of art, which he dramatized using light and an energetic language of form.

Gentileschi, Orazio (1562 Pisa – 1647 London) was born Orazio Gentileschi Lomi. He was trained in the style of Florentine Mannerism and of Pontormo. At the beginning of the 1580s he went to Rome and belonged to the artistic circle around Caravaggio until ca. 1600. In the early 1620s he worked in Genoa before being summoned to Paris by Marie de' Médicis in 1624. He joined the English court in 1626. Gentileschi's work combined Tuscan traditions with Caravaggism.

Géricault, Théodore (1791 Rouen – 1824 Paris) belonged to the beginning of Romanticism in France. He worked with inspiration from his contemporary Antoine-Jean Gros, as well as Michelangelo and Raphael. Géricault broke with Classicism: he preferred contemporary subjects to representative ones. Nor did he follow any particular abstract ideas of shapes, but instead opted for a realistic, artistically emotive style. In addition to paintings of horses, he produced portraits of inmates of mental asylums doing so with a strong sense of pathos.

Ghirlandaio, Domenico (1449 Florence – 1494 Florence) was born Domenico di Tommaso Bigordi. He and Botticelli were the two leading artists of the early Renaissance in Florence. After serving an apprenticeship as a goldsmith, he trained under Alesso Baldovinetti. He received important ideas from Verocchio. In his primarily religious frescoes and panel paintings, which often transposed the events into contemporary settings, Ghirlandaio developed a style that was marked by a strong plasticity and emphasized contours.

Giorgione (1477/78 Castelfranco Veneto – 1510 Venice) was born Giorgio de Castelfranco; also known as Giorgio Barbarelli. He was an important artist of the High Renaissance in Venice. He is believed to have trained under Giovanni Bellini. Giorgione increasingly dispensed with outlines in favor of gradations of color, thereby making the objects come to the foreground of his work. In doing so, he managed to show figures moving freely within the area and to re-create the atmospheric effect of the landscape.

Giotto di Bondone (ca. 1268 Colle di Vespignano, Florence – 1337 Florence) was one of the defining artists of Western culture. He may have been a student of Cimabue. From 1292 he worked in Assisi, then in Rome, Padua, Naples, Milan, and Florence. Giotto broke completely with Byzantine tradition, and with his individualized and physical, three-dimensional view of the human being established a new language of form that was based on reality as it was experienced.

Girardon, François (1628 Troyes – 1715 Paris) as a sculptor played a key role in shaping the style of the time of Louis XIV. After training in his hometown of Troyes and a study trip to Rome from 1648 to 1650 he moved to Paris, where he occupied himself primarily with decorative sculpture. He produced sculptures for the Chambre du Roi and the Galerie d'Apollon of the Louvre, and played an important role in determining the appearance of the Palace of Versailles, frequently working to designs by Charles Le Brun. His work combines Baroque dynamics with Classicist strength.

Gossaert, Jan known as Mabuse (ca. 1478 Maubeuge – 1532 ?Breda) was one of the first Dutch Romanticists. He worked in Bruges until 1503, after which he went to Antwerp. He was in the service of several high-ranking sponsors. He was traveling companion to Philip of Burgundy and visited Italy ca. 1508, but the impressions he gained did not start to influence his work until 1515. In addition to several small Madonnas, he painted portraits and mythological subjects.

Goya y Lucientes, Francisco José de (1748 Fuendetodos, Aragon – 1828 Bordeaux) worked, like his teacher and brother-in-law Francisco Bayeu, for the Spanish court, where he was made official Painter in 1799. On the Restoration of Ferdinand VII, he went into voluntary exile in Bordeaux in 1824. Goya's works were initially influenced by the Rococo style of Tiepolo (1698–1770), and then especially by the natural picture language of Velázquez (1599–1660). Around 1790, when the political situation began to affect him, and as he was impaired by increasing deafness, he adopted a new, somewhat coarse Realism that did not avoid the ugly.

Goyen, Jan van (1596 Leiden – 1658 The Hague) was one of the major landscape painters of the Baroque and a leading exponent of Haarlem tonal painting. He completed his training under Esaias van de Velde in Haarlem before establishing himself as a master painter in Leiden in 1618. He worked in The Hague from 1631. Van Goyen started painting landscapes with folkloric scenes in strong natural colors, but then resumed figural painting and reduced his palette to shades of gray, green, and brown.

Gros, Antoine-Jean (1771 Paris – 1835 Bas-Meudon, Paris) was first trained by his father in painting miniatures, and became a student of Jacques-Louis David in 1785. He worked in Florence and Genoa as a miniaturist and portrait painter from 1793, and accompanied Napoleon on his Italian campaign in 1798. He returned to Paris in 1799 after the French defeat. Gros's pictures of battles and the nobility continued in the classic-

Francisco José de Goya, Self-portrait, 1815,
Academia de S. Fernando, Madrid

academic style, but he impressed the Romanticists with his Rubens-inspired compositions and coloring.

Hals, Franz (ca. 1581/1585 ?Antwerp – 1686 Haarlem) was a sculptor in Haarlem. Around 1602 he studied under the Mannerist artist and writer Karel van Mander. In 1610 he joined the Guild of St. Luke as an independent master painter, and was appointed its president in 1644. Hals developed his own realistic form of representation that was free of any Italian elements. His keen observation and the lively expressions on his models were typical of his portraits.

Heem, Jan Davidsz. de (1608 Utrecht – 1384/85 Antwerp) combined Dutch and Flemish elements in his pictures of flowers, books, and – primarily – magnificent still lifes, and was an excellent exponent of his art. He lived in Utrecht and Leiden before moving to Antwerp as a mature artist in 1635/36. Occasionally between 1667 and 1672 he also returned to the town of his birth.

Hey, Kean (known to have been in France between 1480 and 1500) was also known as the "Master of Moulins." He worked in Moulins from 1483 for the distinguished court of the Bourbons. Although his distinctive Naturalism put him in the Dutch tradition of Hugo van der Goes, his choice of motifs and stylization, which was based on Italian works, was taken from the art of Bourges and the works of Jean Fouquet. His elegant court paintings confirmed him as a French painter who was already committed to the spirit of the Renaissance.

Holbein, Hans, the younger (1497 Augsburg – 1543 London) was the most signficant portrait painter of his time. He first studied under his father Hans Holbein the elder, and then worked as a master in Basel from 1519. He traveled to London for the first time around 1527, and settled there in 1532. From 1538 he painted only portraits, primarily of the nobility at the royal court, and also of Hanseatic merchants. Initially late Gothic in style, Holbein's work gradually became clearer and simpler as the result of his association with Italian art. His works are noteworthy for a cool detachment and precise details.

Hooch, Pieter de (1629 Rotterdam – 1684 Amsterdam) studied under landscape painter Nicolaes Berchem in Haarlem ca. 1647. When he settled in Delft in 1655, he stopped producing his tavern and guardroom scenes, choosing instead his famous interiors and courtyard scenes. Some of these were strongly influenced by Vermeer and showed the everyday life of the bourgeoisie. Another fundamental change in style followed when he moved to Amsterdam around 1681. Influenced by the painting of the French court, he painted only elegant society scenes in magnificent surroundings.

Hoogstraten, Samuel van (1627 Dordrecht – 1678 Dordrecht) was taught by his father Dirck and, from ca. 1642 until 1648, by Rembrandt in Amsterdam. He worked in Vienna and London until returning to Holland and settling in The Hague in 1666, and in his hometown in 1670. In his thematically varied painting, van Hoogstraten initially followed the style of Rembrandt, but later experienced much success with his *trompe l'oeil* paintings. He also designed prints, experimented with optical equipment, constructed peep-show boxes, and wrote a number of important essays on art.

Honthorst, Gerrit (Gerard) van (1590 Utrecht – 1658 Utrecht) was one of the main exponents of Caravaggism in Utrecht. Trained by Abraham Bloemaert, he worked mainly in Rome between 1610 and 1622, where he was delighted by Caravaggio's work, although he lightened his harsh chiaroscuro effects. He specialized in nighttime pieces, which earned him the sobriquet of "Gherardo della Notte." Back in Utrecht, he gradually turned to mythological and Arcadian representations in a Classical style. Honthorst also worked at the English court and for the House of Orange.

Houden, Jean-Antoine (1741 Versailles – 1828 Paris) was trained by various different Parisian sculptors, including Réne Michel Slodtz. During a four-year stay in Rome between 1764 and 1768, he trained himself in the style of Antique sculpture. He then relocated to Paris, and joined the Academy there. His works combine Classicist strength of form and Baroque motion, while his figures are filled with a living Realism.

Hans Holbein the Younger, Self-portrait, ca. 1540–1543, Uffizi Gallery, Florence

Ingres, Jean-Auguste-Dominique (1780 Montauban – 1867 Paris) studied latterly in Paris under Jacques-Louis David. He lived in Florence and Rome from 1808 to 1824, then returned to Paris. In 1853 he followed a call to the Accademia in Rome and taught there until 1841. Initially influenced by David's work, Ingres gradually turned to the Renaissance. He attempted to harmonize ideal forms and naturalness in his style. As an exponent of late Classicism, he was a counterpart to Delacroix, who was strongly opposed to this type of "official" art.

Jordaans, Jacob (1593 Antwerp – 1678 Antwerp) was one of Flanders' leading Baroque artists. He trained under Adam van Noort (who also taught Rubens) from 1607 to 1615. He joined the Artists' Guild in 1515 and became Dean in 1621. He frequently collaborated with Rubens on large representative commissions. Jordaans' style was similar to Caravaggio's, and also incorporated the realistic tendencies in Dutch art. Although a strict Calvinist, his works – which covered a wide range of subjects – consisted of strong, brightly colored, cheery figures.

La Tour, Georges de (1593 Vic-sur-Seille – 1652 Lunéville) was first mentioned in Lunéville in Lorraine in 1618. He worked for Duke Charles IV of Lorraine, and for French King Louis XIII; he was appointed court painter in 1646. The few remaining religious historical and genre paintings are night pieces. His compositions, which consist of a few large figures at the front and reflect a strong management of contrasting light effects, are based on the style of the Caraveggists, although the shapes are highly simplified.

La Tour, Maurice Quentin de (1704 Saint-Quentin – 1788 Saint-Quentin) was a student of Flemish artist Jean Jacques Spoëde and Claude Dupouch. After spending time in England and in his hometown, he lived in Paris from 1727 to 1784. He devoted himself entirely to watercolors, which were just coming into fashion, and produced a number of portraits in which he attempted to characterize the sitter psychologically as well as producing a clearly defined, carefully shaded likeness. An extraordinarily successful artist, he became a member of the Académie Royale in 1748 and was appointed *Peintre du Roi* in 1750.

Le Nain, Louis (1600/1610 Laon – 1648 Paris) maintained a shared studio in Paris with his brothers Antoine (1588–1648) and Mathieu (1607–1677). Le Nain was the most talented of the three brothers, although it is often difficult to differentiate between their work. He was made a member of the Académie Royale de Peinture et Sculpture in 1648. In addition to historical pictures, the Le Nains painted mainly scenes from simple farmers' lives, which provided a strong contrast to the court art of the time.

Leonardo da Vinci (1452 Vinci, Empoli – 1519 Cloux, Amboise) trained in Florence from about 1468 under Verocchio, for whom he continued to work until 1477 after joining the Guild of Artists. He served Ludovico il Moro in Milan from 1482/83 to 1499, and returned there in 1506 after traveling to Mantua, Venice, and Florence. Went to Rome in 1513, then to France in 1516 when summoned by Francis I. As a painter, sculptor, architect, engineer, art theoretician, and scientist, Leonardo was the first to embody the Renaissance ideal of the universally educated artist.

Leyden, Lucas van (1494 Leiden – 1533 Leiden), known for his extensive graphic work, several large winged altars, small portraits, and allegorical genre scenes, which were still somewhat unusual at the time. He met Albrecht Dürer in Antwerp in June 1521, a meeting which had a lasting effect on him. Jan Gossaert, the teacher of Romance languages and literature, became more of an influence, and Italian elements gradually became more evident in Lucas van Leyden's work.

Lippi, Filippo (1408 Florence – 1489 Spoleto) was a Carmelite monk in Florence, but later left the monastery and married. He worked mainly in Florence. Between 1452 and about 1484 he produced the large cathedral frescoes in Prato, although he died before completing the frescoes begun in Spoleto cathedral in 1487. Lippi's early work was linked to that of Masolino. From 1437 his work revealed a special beauty of line as well as a sculptural development of shape. Lippi's students included his son Filippino Lippi, and Sandro Botticelli among others.

Lorenzo di Credi (ca. 1458 Florence – 1537 Florence) was a student of Andrea del Verocchio, under whom Leonardo da Vinci was also studying at the same time. His religious pictures and portraits are noteworthy for their technical perfection and the sporadic Dutch influence in the coloring, although his repertoire was limited to faces and figures.

Lorrain, Claude (1600 Chamagne, Lorraine – 1682 Rome), real name Claude Gellée; also known as "Le Lorrain" – the man from Lorraine. He moved to Rome around 1613, and lived there for the rest of his life apart from the years 1625 to 1627, which he spent in France. A member of the Roman Accademia, Lorrain soon became the leading landscape artist. In contrast to Poussin's heroic interpretation of nature, he developed the lyrical, romantic style evident in his idealistic landscapes, which were bathed in golden morning or evening light.

Lotto, Lorenzo (ca. 1480 Venice – 1558 Loreto) was first mentioned in 1503. He was an important intermediary between the Venetian old masters and the later Baroque art of upper Italy. Much traveled, working in Treviso, Recanati, Bergamo, Venice, and Ancona, among other places. Initially his work leaned toward Bellini and Antonello da Messina, then to Giorgino, Titian, and Raphael. He developed a sensitive feeling for human expressions and the representation of moving figures, and had a unique understanding of how to reproduce materials and for colors.

Mantegna, Andrea (1431 Isola di Carturo, Padua – 1506 Mantua) was one of the defining artists of the Early Renaissance. Studied in Padua under Squarcione, where he worked independently from 1448, but spent most of his life as court artist to the Gonzaga family in Mantua. Mantegna's works are noteworthy for the anatomical construction of the figures, the precise attention to the details, and virtuoso construction of perspective. These innovations strongly influenced his brothers-in-law Gentile and Giovanni Bellini, and were taken north of the Alps in his copper engravings.

Martini, Simone (?1284 Siena – 1344 Avignon) was the main exponent of Gothic painting in Siena and was held in high esteem around 1315. He was in the service of his hometown of Siena and of the king, Robert d'Anjou, in Naples. By 1339 he had joined the papal court in Avignon, where he met and befriended the Italian poet and scholar Petrarch. Next to that of Giotto, his style of art, which is noted for its elegance, sensitivity, and gentle lyricism, was the most important of the 14th century, and its influence spread far beyond the borders of Italy.

Massys, Quentin (ca. 1468 Leuwen – 1530 Antwerp) joined the Antwerp Guild of St. Luke in 1491 as a free master. He was the first of the Dutch artists to represent

Francesco (?)Melzi, Portrait of Leonardo da Vinci, after 1510, Royal Library, Windsor

man as an independent individual without referring to Christian iconography. He initially followed artists such as Bouts, but later combined the Old Dutch tradition of painting with Renaissance-like elements, and was strongly inspired by Leonardo da Vinci. Quentin Massys occasionally collaborated with the landscape artist Joachim Patenir.

Meissonier, Ernest (1815 Lyon – 1891 Paris) was one of the leading Salon painters of his time. He was trained in Paris and exhibited regularly at the Salon from 1834 onward. He traveled to Italy in 1859, 1860, and 1870, and became a member of the Académie des Beaux-Arts in

1861. He and Puvis de Chavannes founded the Société Nationale des Beaux-Arts in 1890. Meissonier initially produced miniature genre paintings, and later portraits and representations of France's war history.

Meléndez, Luis (1716 Naples – 1780 Madrid) is widely regarded as one of the leading Spanish still-life artists of the 18th century. He had an Italian mother and a Spanish father. The family moved to Spain in 1717, where Meléndez later worked as a miniaturist, like his father before him. He became known for his still lifes when commissioned to produce a sequence of 44 paintings for the castle at Aranjuez, which he did between 1760 and 1773.

Memling, Hans (ca. 1435 Seligenstadt am Main – 1494 Bruges) came originally from the Middle Rhine region; there is evidence of his presence in Brussels in 1485. In Bruges from 1486. He started with the art of Weyden and Bouts, and found his own style around 1470. This is noted for its opulent colorfulness, the grace of the figures, and carefully observed details. Memling varied the details widely and combined them to create a calmly ordered unit. In his later works he included elements from the Italian Early Renaissance.

Michelangelo Buonarroti (1475 Caprese, Tuscany – 1465 Rome) was born Michelangiolo di Ludovico di Lionardo di Buonarroti Simoni, and was an imposing figure in Western art. In Florence he worked mainly for Lorenzo de' Medici, which inspired him to study Antiquity and philosophy. He was associated with the Vatican in Rome for a long time and in 1535 was appointed senior architect, sculptor, and painter. Michelangelo developed entirely new forms of expression in his art and produced independent spiritual creations of high sculptural intensity.

Monet, Claude (1840 Paris – 1928 Giverny) grew up in Le Havre, where Boudin inspired him to try plein-air painting. Studied at the Académie Suisse in Paris from 1859, where he met Pissarro, and at the Ecole des Beaux-Arts. Like that of Bazille, Renoir, and Sisley, his work was mainly of nature. In London during the war years of 1870/71, he saw Turner's work. He lived in Argenteuil

Luis Meléndez, Self-portrait with a Nude Study, 1746, Musée du Louvre

from 1872 to 1878, then in Vétheuil, Possy near Paris, and from 1883 in Giverny. Monet's oeuvre is the very embodiment of Impressionism.

Mor van Dashorst, Anthonis (1519 Utrecht – 1575 Antwerp). There is evidence that he was working as an independent artist and a citizen of Utrecht in 1548. He moved to Antwerp in 1547 after visiting Italy. In 1549 he entered into the service of Anton Perrenot de Granvella, the bishop of Arras, who introduced Mor to the courts of the Habsburgs in the Netherlands and Spain. Mor traveled widely and painted most of the rulers of his day before finally settling in Antwerp in 1568.

Murillo, Bartolomé Esteban (1618 Seville – 1682 Seville) was Spain's most famous Baroque artist. He worked mainly in Seville and was one of the founders of an academy of art there in 1660. At the start of his career he received important encouragement from Zurbarán and Ribera. Around 1650 he modeled his painting on van Dyck, Rubens, and Raphael. Murillo developed an airy style, the "estilo vaporoso," in his religious paintings and genre scenes, with gentle contours, warm, gently shaded colors, and a gold or silver sheen.

Patenir, Joachim (ca. 1475/1480 Dinant or Bouvignes – 1524 Antwerp) also known as Patenier or Patini(e)r. He joined the Antwerp Guild of St. Luke as a master in 1515. Albrecht Dürer, whom he met in 1520/21, described him as a "good painter of landscapes." In line with Hieronymus Bosch and Gerard David, he painted religious historical pictures with extensive landscapes. These scenes, which often also contained bizarre rock and cliff formations, were an important contribution to the development of landscape painting in its own right.

Perugino, Pietro (ca. 1450 Città della Pieve, Perugia – 1523 Fontignano) was born Pietro di Cristoforo Vannucci, and was the leading Umbrian artist before his student Raphael. He worked mainly in Florence, Rome, and Perugia. After starting with Verrocchio and Piero della Francesca, whose student he may have been, Perugino occupied himself with the new space and body formation of the Renaissance and the balance between picture surface and space. He produced clear, closed compositions with gentle gradations of color.

Piazzetta, Giovanni Battista (1683 Venice – 1754 Venice) trained in Venice and Bologna, where he was influenced primarily by the genre painting of Giuseppe Maria Crespis. Piazzetta settled permanently in Venice in 1711. He and Tiepolo were regarded as the most exciting church artists of the Venetian Settecento. His main patrons included Elector Clemens August of Cologne, and the Field Marshal Johann Matthias von der Schulenburg.

Piero di Cosimo (1461/62 Florence – 1521 Florence) was born Piero di Lorenzo. He studied in Florence under Cosimo Rosselli, whose first name he assumed. Collaborated with Rosselli on the frescoes in the Sistine Chapel in Rome in 1481/82, after which he worked mainly in Florence. His style, which was inspired by Filippino Lippi, Domenico Ghirlandaio, the early works of Leonardo da Vinci, and by Hugo van der Goes, combined lyrical and dramatic picture elements and was frequently fantastic and grotesque.

Pilon, Germain (1528 Paris – 1590 Paris) was considered one of the best French sculptors of the 16th century. He created a number of tombstones for the French court, his main client. He also produced statues, busts, fireplace surrounds, and fountain decorations. Pilon's style was inspired by the School of Fontainebleau, and especially by Primaticcio. The artist revealed a highly developed feeling for sculptural effects, in which Mannerist elegance and naturalist precision overlap.

Piombe, Sebastiano dei (ca. 1485 Venice – 1547 Rome) was born Sebastiano Luciani and known as Viniziano. He studied first under Bellini, then under Giorgione in Venice. He settled in Rome in 1511, where he produced large altar panels for churches and also worked as a portraitist. His style was influenced by Raphael and Michelangelo and was noted for its monumentality and strong formal language.

Pisanello (ca. 1395 Pisa – 1455 probably in Rome), real name Antonio di Pucci Pisano. Studied under Gentile da Fabriano in Venice from 1481 to 1420, and assisted him with painting the doge's palace; followed him to Rome ca. 1423. Lived in Rome after the master's death in 1427. From around 1430 Pisanello was one of the most sought after artists of his time, and worked for the courts in Mantua, Ferrara, and Milan, and for King Alphonse of Aragon in Naples. A representative of International Gothic, this artist, draftsman, and medallist combined delicacy and elegance, a love of storytelling, and a keen observation of nature.

Pisano, Nino (ca. 1315 – before 1368 Pisa) was the son of Andrea Pisano, probably the leading Italian sculptor of the Trecento. Because the style of Nino's picture works was extremely similar to his father's, which was influenced by French Gothic and unsigned (with a few exceptions), it is often impossible to ascribe them. Nino Pisano is first mentioned in 1349, when he was commissioned to design the cathedral of Orvieto, a task which had previously been entrusted to his father. He died either in or before 1368.

Pontormo (1494 Pontormo, Empoli – 1557 Florence) was born Jacopo Carrucci, and went to Florence in 1508. After his first artistic contact with Leonardo da Vinci and Piero di Cosimo, he probably studied under Fra Bartolommeo and from 1512 to 1513 under Andrea del Sarto. He studied the works of Dürer and based his own on Michelangelo. By 1520 he had achieved a new, expressive style that transcended the style of the High Renaissance. Pontormo and Rosso Fiorentino were regarded as the main exponents of the first dramatic and expressive phase of Mannerism.

Poussin, Nicolas (1594 Les Andelys – 1685 Rome) was permanently resident in Rome from 1624, apart from the period from 1640 and 1642 which he spent at the court in Paris as official painter to Louis XIII. Poussin's painting was based on the art of Antiquity and the Italian Renaissance, historical, religious, and mythological pictures, portraits, and landscapes, which were always subject to a strict, high level of perfection and principle of order. His Classical painting had a marked influence on the art and artists of the Paris Académie.

Prud'hon, Pierre Paul (1758 Cluny – 1823 Paris) trained in Dijon and Paris. In Italy between 1782 and 1788, he trained himself in the style of Leonardo da Vinci and Correggio before finally settling in Paris in 1789. Although he linked his art to the Classical art of the time of Louis XVI, it differed in the definition of its contours, the gentle transition between shades, and quite muted use of chiaroscuro.

Puget, Pierre (1620 Marseille – 1694 Fougette, Marseille) trained under a woodcarver who worked in shipbuilding, and continued his training in Rome. The artist lived far from the art center of Paris, first in Toulon and Marseille, but spent time in Rome and Genoa in the 1660s. As well as decorating ships, he produced statues, busts, reliefs, and architectural designs. Only a few of his later works were intended for the royal court, differing from his Bernini-inspired works in the dynamics of the painting and emotional intensity.

Quarton, Enguerrand (worked from 1444 to 1486), also known as Charonton, Charton, and Charretier. Worked in Provence in the mid-15th century, mainly in Avignon, where he was last mentioned in 1486. Along with Jean Fouquet he was regarded as the leading French painter of the late Gothic. His style, which was influenced by Old Dutch art, was characterized by steady, evenly expressive, ornamental lines and a division of shapes.

Quercia, Jacopo della (1374 ?Siena – 1438 Siena) was active in Siena, Bologna and Lucca, and elsewhere. In 1401 he joined in the competition to design the bronze door to the Baptistery in Florence. Committed to the Gothic style in the early stages of his career, the artist became the leading Sienese sculptor of the Early Renaissance. His powerful, highly expressive style impressed artists of the High Renaissance, and Michelangelo in particular.

Raphael (1483 Urbino – 1520 Rome) was born Raffaello Santi, and studied under Perugino in Perugia. He went to Florence in 1504 until he was called to Rome by Pope Julius II in 1508. He worked on some frescoes for the Vatican and was put in charge of the construction of St. Peter's basilica on the death of Bramante in 1514. Raphael is considered to have been the most important artist of the High Renaissance. His famous altar panels, empathic Madonnas, portraits, and complicated frescoes are marked by formal clarity and deeply perceived natural expressiveness.

Rembrandt Harmensz. van Rijn (1608 Leiden – 1689 Amsterdam) studied under Pieter Lastman in Amsterdam, where he settled after leaving Leiden in 1631. He married Saskia van Uylenburg in 1633, who died in 1642. He then lived with Hendrickje Stoffels. Although he was much in demand as a painter and etcher, he found himself increasingly in financial difficulties. Rembrandt was known for his religious and historical pictures and portraits, in which he broke from the traditional designs of his chosen subjects. In his subtle chiaroscuro painting he reproduces the spiritual condition of the individual with sensitivity and feeling.

Reynolds, Sir Joshua (1723 Plympton, Plymouth – 1792 London) worked as a portrait artist in London, and was extremely influential during his many years as the president of the Royal Academy. He was knighted in 1769. His time in Italy from 1749 to 1752, during which he studied the art of Antiquity and of the Renaissance in Rome and the works of Titian, Tintoretto, and Veronese in Venice, was extremely important for the development of his style. Reynolds was the most successful and productive English portraitist of the 18th century. He was also an extremely important expert on the theory of art and English Classicism.

Ribera, Juspo de (1591 Játiva, Valencia – 1652 Naples) left Spain as a young artist and went to Italy, where Caravaggio's Roman works had a lasting effect on him. Ribera settled in Naples in 1615 and worked for the Spanish viceroy of the Kingdom of of the Two Sicilies, the count of Osuna, and his successors. He painted mainly religious pictures, which are noted for the quick brush strokes of his painting style.

Riemenschneider, Tilman (1460 Heiligenstadt in Eichsfeld – 1531 Würzburg) was the most famous southern German woodcarver of his time, and maintained his own large workshop in Würzburg. Keenly aware of his social responsibilities, he joined the town council and was made mayor in 1520/21. Against the animated, colorful, gold-painted picture works of the late Gothic, his figures are notable for the simplification of gestures and mimicry and the new monochrome approach which matched the character of the wood and facilitated a nuanced surface treatment.

Rigaud, Hyacinthe (1659 Perpignan – 1743 Paris) was based in Paris from 1691. He became the preferred portraitist of the royal family, French nobility, and the church. He was made a member of the Académie Royale in 1700, and became its principal in 1733. The influential artist was elevated to the knighthood in 1709. Guided by the elegant likenesses of Sir Anthony van Dyck and trained in the works of Charles Le Brun, Rigaud's paintings were exemplary for the whole of European court painting in the 18th century.

Raphael, Self-portrait with a Friend, ca. 1518/19, Musée du Louvre

Rosa, Salvatore (1615 Arenella, Naples – 1673 Rome) left Naples for Rome in 1635. He served the Medicis in Florence from 1641 and again in 1649, but returned to Rome in 1649. Rosa, who was also an etcher, poet, and musician, is regarded as one of the most multitalented Italian artists of the Seicento. He painted mainly landscapes and pictures of battles, but also portraits and religious, allegorical, and historical figure pictures, which, because of their often dark pathos, were particularly highly valued in the 19th century.

Rosso, Fiorentino (1495 Florence – 1540 Fontainebleau), real name Giovanni Battista di Jacopo. Studied in Florence under Andrea del Sarto. After leading an unsettled life, he was called to the French court in 1530 and organized the interior work at the palace of Fontainebleau, where he produced his main work, the design of the Francis I gallery with frescoes and stucco work that strongly influenced the Mannerist style of Rosso's and Primaticcio's School of Fontainebleau.

Rousseau, Théodore (1812 Paris – 1867 Barbizon) studied the works of Lorrain and 17th-century Dutch landscape painters while training at the Ecole des Beaux-Arts in Paris. He exhibited at the Salon of 1831 for the first time, but was rejected repeatedly until finally receiving a medal in 1849. He lived in Barbizon from 1847 and became one of the main representatives of the Barbizon School. The woods at Fontainebleau provided the motifs for his dark, moodily executed landscape pictures.

Rubens, Peter Paul (1577 Siegen – 1640 Antwerp) trained in Antwerp, where he was accepted as a master into the Guild of St. Luke in 1598. From 1600 to 1608 he was court painter to Vincenzo Gonzaga II, the count of Mantua, Italy. In 1609 he became court painter to Archduke Albrecht and Archduchess Isabella in Brussels, but lived and maintained his large workshop in Antwerp. There were many commissions in association with diplomatic activities, which helped to spread his fame throughout Europe. Rubens was the leading Flemish artist of the Baroque, and incorporated a number of different traditions in his works.

Ruisdael, Jacob Isaacksz. van (1628/29 Haarlem – 1682? Amsterdam) was one of the leading Dutch landscape artists of his time. He was accepted as a master into the Guild of St. Luke of Haarlem in 1648. He was based in Amsterdam from about 1656/57. In 1676 he was made a doctor of medicine in Caen. His first pictures, which were influenced by his uncle Salomon van Ruysdael, are fragments of simple landscapes. His later works, by contrast, exhibit more excitement, their natural forms exaggerated dramatically.

Sansovino, Jacopo (1486 Florence – 1570 Venice), real name Jacopo Tatti. Assumed the name of his teacher, the Florentine sculptor Andrea Sansovino, and accompanied him to Rome in 1505, where he worked as a respected sculptor until 1527 (apart from the period 1511 to 1518). He fled to Venice when the troops of Charles V stormed the city in 1527. The city established its connection with the latest Roman influences in architecture and sculpture through Sansovino. However, with Titian's encouragement, he developed his style in a specific Venetian form.

Sittow, Michael (ca. 1468 Reval – 1525/26 Reval) came from the northern Hanseatic town of Reval (now Tallinn, Estonia). He moved to the Netherlands in 1482, where he was strongly inspired by Hans Memling in Bruges. In Spain in 1492 he became court painter to Isabella the Catholic of Castile. From 1502 he was in the service of various other European courts before finally returning to his hometown in 1518.

Terbrugghen, Hendrick (1588 Deventer – 1629 Utrecht) was, like Honthorst, a student of Abraham Bloemaert and a representative of the Utrecht Caravaggists. He

Rembrandt Harmensz. van Rijn, Self-portrait in Old Age, ca. 1664, Uffizi Gallery, Florence

spent the years between 1604 and 1614 mainly in Rome and Naples. It is possible that he met Caravaggio in person. Back in Utrecht, he joined its Guild of Artists in 1616. Terbrugghen, whose only known works date from the 1620s, painted numerous genre pictures and religious works, which are typified by a light, muted color palette and soft lines.

Titian (1488/1490 Pieve di Cadore – 1576 Venice), real name Tiziano Vecellio, was regarded as the leading Venetian artist of the Cinquecento. One of his teachers may have been Giovanni Bellini. While his earlier works were still influenced by Giorgione, with whom he painted the frescoes of the Fondaco dei Tedeschi in Venice in 1508/09, Titian developed his expressive style

Peter Paul Rubens, Self-portrait wearing Hat,
ca. 1623–1625, Uffizi Gallery, Florence

that combined shapes and spaces over the course of time. He had numerous important clients, including Emperor Charles V, who appointed him court painter in 1533, Pope Paul III, and Philip II of Spain.

Turner, Joseph Mallord William (1775 London – 1851 Chelsea) became a student at the Royal Academy in 1789. He was made an ordinary member in 1802, and professor of the study of perspective in 1809. His works of this time confront the art of Poussin and Lorrain. On travels through England, Scotland, Wales, France, and Switzerland, Turner produced topographic sketches of the nature he saw. His style changed after visits to Italy in 1819 and 1828, and his earlier landscape impressions, which were bathed in light, were followed by visionary picture creations.

Uccello, Paolo (1397 Pratovecchio, Arezzo – 1475 Florence) trained in Lorenzo Ghiberti's studio in Florence between 1407 and 1412, and worked as his assistant on the execution of the Baptistery towers. In 1415 Uccello was accepted as a master in the Guild of *Medici e Speciali* to which painters also belonged. He was in Venice from 1425 to 1431, then settled in Florence. Influenced by the works of Masaccio and Donatello, Uccello developed into the leading exponent of his generation of the mastery of perspective.

Velázquez, Diego Rodriguez de Silva y (1599 Seville – 1660 Madrid) is regarded as the main Spanish artist of the 17th century. He studied under Francisco Herrera the elder and Francisco Pacheco in Seville. His career flourished from 1627 at the court of Philip IV, peaking in 1652 when he was appointed seneschal. He traveled to Italy in 1629, presumably inspired by Peter Paul Rubens, whom he had met the year before in Madrid. A second journey followed between 1649 and 1651. Velázquez was influenced by Venetian art. He used loosely applied warm colors, blending them gently and softly.

Vermeer, Jan (1632 Delft – 1675 Delft), also Jan or Johannes Vermeer van Delft. He was accepted by the Guild of St. Luke of Delft as a master in 1553 while he

Diego Rodriguez Velázquez, Self-portrait, ca. 1640,
Uffizi Gallery, Florence

Tintoretto he was one of the three great Venetian painters of the Cinquecento), consists of ceiling frescoes, altar panels, mythological stories, and portraits.

Vigée-Lebrun, Elisabeth-Louise (1755 Paris – 1842 Paris) studied under her father, the watercolorist Louis Vigée, and under Gabriel Doyen and Fabriel Briard. In 1778 she married the wealthy artist and art dealer Lebrun. In 1779, at the age of 24, she was appointed court artist by Marie-Antoinette. During the years of the Revolution she traveled to Rome, and then to Vienna, Berlin, Dresden, St. Petersburg, and London. She did not return to Paris until 1809, by which time she had become a highly successful and valued portraitist to the European aristocracy.

Vouet, Simon (1590 Paris – 1649 Paris) studied under his father Laurent Vouet, and was already much in demand as a portrait painter at an early age. In 1611 he traveled to Rome via Constantinople and Venice, and lived there for many years from the end of 1613. Appointed *Peintre du Roi*, he returned to Paris on the orders of Louis XIII in 1627. This date is generally regarded as the beginning of Classicist painting in France. He produced altar panels and portraits, but from his workshop came mainly pictures of elegant Parisian residences.

continued to run his father's art dealership at the same time. His oeuvre consisted of no more than 34 paintings, usually parts of bourgeois interiors that are illuminated through side windows and in which an individual or a few figures are engrossed in some activity. Due to his fine feeling for color and light values, which Vermeer developed from Fabritius, the Delft-born artist became the most important Dutch genre painter of the 17th century.

Veronese, Paolo (1528 Verona – 1588 Venice), real name Paolo Calieri. Settled in Venice in 1553. From 1553 he worked in the Sala del Consiglio dei Dieci in the doge's palace, and around 1555–1570 on paintings in the church of San Sebastian. After a trip to Rome he produced the famous frescoes in the Villa Barbaro in Maser near Treviso ca. 1561/62. The artist's oeuvre, which belongs to the Late Renaissance (with Titian and

Watteau, Jean-Antoine (1684 Valenciennes – 1721 Nogent-sur-Marne) studied under Jacques-Albert Gérin in Valenciennes. He returned to Paris around 1702, and continued studying under Claude Gillot and Claude Audran III. These masters introduced Watteau to the motifs of the Commedia dell'Arte and the free painting style of the arabesque. In 1717 he was accepted by the Académie Royale de Peinture et Sculpture as *peintre de fêtes galantes*. In 1719 and 1720 the artist, who was much in demand, worked in London. Watteau was one of the most important French painters of the 18th century.

Weyden, Rogier van der (ca. 1399 Tournai – 1484 Brussels) was also known as Rogelet de la Pasture. He studied under Robert Campin from 1427. In 1435/36 he was city painter in Brussels. On a pilgrimage to Rome in 1450

he worked in Ferrara, and probably in Florence. Rogier's is the art of a van Eyck and master of Remalle, who was often identified with Campin, but spurned their realism in favor of an overall greater stylization of shape, as is revealed by his slim, elegant figures. His works are carefully balanced compositions of space and surface.

Wright, Joseph (1734 Derby – 1797 Derby) was known as Joseph Wright of Derby, and was a student of the London-based portraitist Thomas Hudson. He lived in his hometown of Derby, apart from a few brief sojourns in Liverpool (1768–1770), Italy (1773–1775), and Bath (1775–1778). His well-known scientific society pieces gained their effectiveness from the Caravaggist-inspired lighting. His landscapes, which were executed in shades of green and brown, hinted at the emerging style of Romanticism.

Zurbarán, Francisco de (1598 Fuente de Cantos – 1664 Madrid) studied under Pedro Diaz de Villanueva in Seville. He settled in Llerena in 1617, but received most commissions from Seville, so he moved there. His career peaked in the 1630s: he worked for Philip IV at the court of Madrid from 1634–1636, and then completed his most important picture cycles for various monasteries. From about 1645, Zurbarán was increasingly sidelined by Murillo. He moved to Madrid in 1658, hoping for more commissions.

Bibliography

Alcouffe, Daniel, Anne Dion-Tenenbaum, and Ameury Lefebure: Le Mobilier du Musée du Louvre, 2 volumes, Paris 1994

Aulanier, Christiane: Histoire du Palais et du Musée du Louvre, 10 volumes, Paris 1947–68

Berenson, Bernard: Die italienischen Maler der Renaissance, Zurich 1952

Berger, Robert W.: The Palace of the Sun. The Louvre of Louis XIV, University Park, PA 1993

Biasini, Emile: The Grand Louvre: A Museum Transfigured 1981-1993, Nichols Publishing Co. 1990

Bresc, Geneviève: Mémoires du Louvre, Paris 1993

Bresc, Geneviève: Le Louvre, histoire et architecture, Paris 1995

Bresc, Geneviève: The Louvre: An Architectural History, London 1995

Chaine, Catherine and Jean-Pierre Verdet: Le Grand Louvre. Du donjon à la pyramide, Paris 1989

Chatelain, Jean: Dominique Vivant Denon et le Louvre de Napoléon, Paris 1973

Cantarel-Besson, Yveline (ed.): La Naissance du Musée du Louvre (notes et documents), 2 volumes, Paris 1981

Coignard, Jérome: Le Grand Louvre, le palais, les collections, les nouveaux espaces, Paris 1994

D'Archimbaud, Nicholas: Louvre: Portrait of a Museum, New York 1998

Dufresne, Jean-Claude: Louvre et Tuileries, architectures de papier, Liège 1987

Durand, Jannic and Daniel Alcouffe: Decorative Arts at the Louvre, 1995

Denoyelle, Martine: Chefs-d'oeuvre de la céramique grecque, Paris 1995

Dictionnaire du Louvre, Paris 1997

Farmer, David: Oxford Dictionary of Saints, Oxford 1997

Fuchs, R. H.: Dutch Painting, London 1984

Gaborit, Jean-René: La Sculpture européenne, Paris and Florence 1984

Galard, Jean, with Anne-Laure Charrier: Visiteurs du Louvre, Paris 1993

Gowing, Lawrence: Paintings in the Louvre, London 1994 (Published in French: Les Peintures du Louvre, Paris 1998; and German: Die Gemäldesammlung des Louvre, Cologne 1994)

Hautecoeur, Louis: Le Louvre et les Tuileries, Paris 1927

Hautecoeur, Louis: Histoire du Louvre, le château, le palais, le musée des origines à nos jours, Paris 1928, re-published 1940

Hillairet, Lacques: Le Palais du Louvre. Sa Vie, ses grands souvenirs historiques, Paris 1955

Hours, Magdeleine (ed.): La Vie mystérieuse des chefs d'oeuvre. La science au service de l'art, exhibition catalogue, Paris 1980

Laclette, Michel (ed.): Le Louvre, Paris 1986

McClellan, Andrew: Inventing the Louvre: Art, Politics and the Origins of the Modern Museum in Eighteenth-Century Paris, Cambridge 1994

Saint-Fare Garnet, Pierre-Nicolas: Le Décor des Tuileries sous Louis XIV, Paris 1988

Saint-Fare Garnet, Pierre-Nicolas and Emmanuel Jacquin: Le Château des Tuileries, Paris 1988

Schick, Ingrid T. (ed.): Schätze aus dem Louvre, Munich 1996

Tuetey, Alexandre and Jean Guiffrey: La Commission de Museum et de la création du Louvre, 1792–93, Paris 1910

Wright, Christopher: The World's Master Paintings from the Early Renaissance to the Present Day, London 1992.

Ziegler, Christiane: Der Louvre. Die ägyptische Sammlung, Munich 1992

Ziegler, Christiane: Der Louvre, Munich 1993

Index

Picture and Map References

The majority of the picture material was provided by SCALA GROUP S.A. of Florence. The publishers would also like to thank the museums, collectors, archives, and photographers for approving reproduction and for their friendly support in bringing this project to fruition. The publishers endeavored, up to the time of publication, to establish the holders of other publication rights. We would ask any persons or institutes whom we were not able to contact and who hold the rights to any pictures reproduced here to contact us.

Photo: © AKG, Berlin (560/561; 573 index 1 ill. 1, 574 index 5 ill. 2) / Erich Lessing (24); photo: © Archives Nationales de France, Paris (573 index 5 ill. 2, 574 index 2 ill 2); photo: © Associated Press, Frankfurt (307); photo: © Bibliothèque Historique de la Ville de Paris / Leyris (576 index 2 ill. 3); photo: © Bibliothèque Nationale de France, Paris (50, 244, 573 index 1 ill. 3, 573 index 2 ill. 1, 575 index 5, ill. 1); photo: © Bildagentur Schuster / Hoa Qui / Yann Arthus-Bertrand, Paris (16, 257) / Explorer (576 index 5 ill. 5); photo: © Bildarchiv Preussischer Kulturbesitz, Berlin / Margarete Büsing (570); photo: © Blauel/Gnamm – Artothek Peissenberg (170); photo: © The British Museum, London (199, 588); photo: © Cameraphoto – Immagini, Venice (334); from: Champollion le Jeune: Grammaire égyptienne, Paris 1836 (118); from: Description De l'Egypte, Paris 1820, vol. 1 (116); photo: © The Hulton Getty Picture Collection, London (576 index 1 ill. 5); photo: © Laif, Cologne / Thomas Ebert (254, 255, 256) / Hartmut Krinitz (255); © Könemann Verlagsgesellschaft mbH, Cologne / photo: Achim Bednorz (573 index 5 ill. 3) / map: Peter Frese, Munich after: ADAC Verlag, Haupka Verlag, Bad Soden (original) / graphics: Rolli Arts, Essen (19, 21, 52, 152, 560, 581, 585), from: J. Jahn / W. Haubenreiter: Wörterbuch der Kunst, 12th edition 1995, 646, Alfred Kröner Verlag, Stuttgart (597), from: Michelin-Reiseführer Paris, 6th edition, 1955 (18), after: Bettina Pell / Musée du Louvre (8/9, 10/11, 12/13, 14/15, 60/61, 94/95, 106/107, 138, 146-149, 194/195, 218-220, 272-274, 344/345, 362-365, 452/453, 484/485, 542-544) / photo: Lothar Schnepf, Cologne (561, 563) / map: Studio für Landkartentechnik, Norderstedt (79, 80/81); photo: © Lexikon der christlichen Ikonographie – Bildarchiv Verlag Herder, Freiburg 1971 (593); photo: © Photothèque des Musées de la Ville de Paris / Cliché: Tomazet (574 index 5 ill. 3, 575 index 1 ill. 4); photo: © Photothèque Giraudon, Paris (33, 576 index 5 ill. 3) / Lauros (527); photo: © The National Gallery, London (565 r.); photo: © E. Revault / Louvre, Paris (37, 182, 245); photo: © Rheinisches Bildarchiv Cologne (594); photo: © E. Rioufol, Paris (494); photo: © RMN, Paris (25, 38, 74, 76, 89, 92, 99, 102, 122 left, 139, 203 bottom, 242, 308, 309, 311, 386, 416, 417, 418, 424, 532, 533, 538/539, 540, 541, 547, 548, 574 index 1 ill. 4, 576 index 1 ill. 3, 575 index 2 ill. 2, 575 index 5 ill. 2, 576 index 5 ill. 2) / D. Arnaudet (35, 174, 217, 279 left, 282, 458 left, 459, 523, 535, 546) / D. Arnaudet; J. Scho (77, 508 left, 510, 536) / M. Beck; Coppola (209, 251, 530, 531, 550, 552, 556, 609) / M. Bellot (23) / J.G. Berizzi (214, 286, 290, 464, 574 index 1 ill. 2) / P. Bernard (243) / G. Blot (47 middle right, 82, 104, 140, 226, 420, 454, 508 right, 574 index 1 ill. 3) / G. Blot; C. Jean (47 right, 166, 197, 224 right, 238 right, 252, 428, 555, 574 index 4 ill. 4) / Bulloz (230) / D. Chenon (414) / Chuzeville (51, 110, 122 right, 125, 132, 154 right, 154 middle, 171, 179, 183, 534, 537) / Coursaget; C. Jean (200, 310) / C. Jean (46 left, 48, 49, 51, 196, 202, 203 top, 207 left, 211, 213, 225, 228, 231, 234 left and right, 238 left, 253, 285, 479, 514, 569) / C. Jean; J. Schormans (292) / Ch. Larrieu (28, 31) / H. Lewandowski (46 middle left, 68, 69, 73, 87, 91 bottom, 97, 101, 103, 114, 141, 153, 154 left, 155 left, 155 right, 160, 163, 172/173, 186, 188, 207 middle and right, 210, 224 left, 227, 229, 246, 336, 373, 573 index 5 ill. 5) / R.G. Ojeda (75, 199, 201, 215, 222, 223, 232, 233, 235, 247, 337, 575 index 5 ill. 4) / R.G. Ojeda; Hubert (208) / R.G. Ojeda; Le Mage (206, 212) / Reversement MET NY (83, 84) / C. Rose (20, 158, 575 index 2 ill. 2, 576 index 2 ill. 5) J. Schormans (46 middle right, 54/55, 421, 575 index 2 ill. 4) / T. Ollivier (100) / Willi (522); photo: © The Royal Collection / © HM Queen Elizabeth II (608); photo: © Sipa Press, Paris (29, 30); photo: © SMPK – Preussischer Kulturbesitz, Nationalgalerie / photo: Jörg P. Anders, 1986 (423); photo: SMPK, Kupferstichkabinett (573 index 1 ill. 2); photo: © Thomas Struth, Cologne (267); photo: © Roger-Viollet (22, 27, 32, 36, 39, 41, 42, 43, 44, 45, 204, 302, 303, 318, 319, 320, 321, 350, 351, 371, 388, 389 top, 390, 432, 433, 434, 435, 495, 496, 520/521, 573 index 1 ill. 4, 573 index 5 ill. 1, 576 index 5 ill. 4)

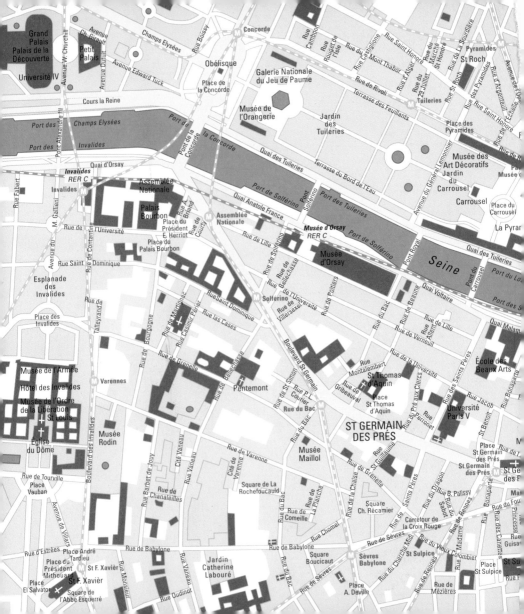